JUSTICE

ADVANCES IN GROUP PROCESSES

Series Editors: Edward J. Lawler and Shane R. Thye

Recent Volumes:

Volumes 1–17:	Edited by Edward J. Lawler
Volume 18:	Edited by Edward J. Lawler and Shane R. Thye
Volume 19:	Group Cohesion, Trust and Solidarity – Edited by Edward J. Lawler and Shane R. Thye
Volume 20:	Power and Status – Edited by Edward J. Lawler and Shane R. Thye
Volume 21:	Theory and Research on Human Emotions – Edited by Jonathan H. Turner
Volume 22:	Social Identification in Groups – Edited by Shane R. Thye and Edward J. Lawler
Volume 23:	Social Psychology of the Workplace – Edited by Shane R. Thye and Edward J. Lawler
Volume 24:	Social Psychology of Gender – Edited by Shelley Correll

ADVANCES IN GROUP PROCESSES VOLUME 25

JUSTICE

EDITED BY

KAREN A. HEGTVEDT
Department of Sociology, Emory University

JODY CLAY-WARNER
Department of Sociology, University of Georgia

Emerald
JAI

United Kingdom – North America – Japan
India – Malaysia – China

JAI Press is an imprint of Emerald Group Publishing Limited
Howard House, Wagon Lane, Bingley BD16 1WA, UK

First edition 2008

British Library Cataloguing in Publication Data
A catalogue record for this book is available from the British Library

ISBN: 978-0-7623-0898-9
ISSN: 0882-6145 (Series)

Printed and bound by MPG Books Ltd, Bodmin, Cornwall

CONTENTS

LIST OF CONTRIBUTORS

Christopher W. Bauman	Department of Management and Organization, Michael G. Foster School of Business, University of Washington, Seattle, WA, USA
Susan Clayton	Department of Psychology, College of Wooster, Wooster, OH, USA
Jessica L. Collett	Department of Sociology, University of Notre Dame, Notre Dame, IN, USA
Lisa M. Dilks	Department of Sociology, University of South Carolina, Columbia, SC, USA
Claudia Geist	Department of Sociology, Indiana University, IN, USA
Guillermina Jasso	Department of Sociology, New York University, New York, NY, USA
John T. Jost	Department of Psychology, New York University, New York, NY, USA
Sang-Wook Kim	Department of Sociology, Sungkyunkwan University, Korea
Pamela Koch	Department of Sociology, University of South Carolina, Columbia, SC, USA
Kathryn J. Lively	Department of Sociology, Dartmouth College, Hanover, NH, USA
Barry Markovsky	Department of Sociology, University of South Carolina, Columbia, SC, USA
Shannon McDonough	Department of Sociology, University of South Carolina, Columbia, SC, USA

Dahlia Moore	Department of Behavioral Science, College of Management, Tel Aviv, Israel
Charles W. Mueller	Department of Sociology, University of Iowa, Iowa City, IA, USA
Elizabeth Mullen	Graduate School of Business, Stanford University, Stanford, CA, USA
Tyler G. Okimoto	School of Psychology, Flinders University, Adelaide, South Australia
Susan Opotow	Sociology Department, College of Criminal Justice, City University of New York, New York, NY, USA
Shelley N. Osborn	Department of Sociology, University of California, Riverside, CA, USA
Brian Powell	Department of Sociology, Indiana University, IN, USA
Linda J. Skitka	Department of Psychology, University of Illinois, Chicago, IL, USA
Lala Carr Steelman	Department of Sociology, University of South Carolina, Columbia, SC, USA
Jan E. Stets	Department of Sociology, University of California, Riverside, CA, USA
Jennifer Triplett	Department of Sociology, University of South Carolina, Columbia, SC, USA
Tom R. Tyler	Department of Psychology, New York University, New York, NY, USA
Jan-Willem van Prooijen	Department of Social Psychology, VU University, Amsterdam
Leia Velasquez	Department of Sociology, University of South Carolina, Columbia, SC, USA
Cheryl J. Wakslak	Department of Psychology, New York University, New York, NY, USA
Michael Wenzel	School of Psychology, Flinders University, Adelaide, South Australia

PREFACE

To do "justice" to the theorizing and empirical work on the topic of justice would be a formidable, if not impossible, task. The study of justice spans centuries (see, for example, Solomon & Murphy, 1990) and disciplines – psychology, sociology, political science, philosophy (Cohen, 1986; Scherer, 1992). Some previously published edited volumes on justice circumscribe the content as applicable, for example, to organizations (Greenberg & Colquitt, 2005), to the affectional bond (Lerner & Mikula, 1994), or with regard to the role of emotions (De Cremer, 2007). Other volumes fall loosely under titles to the effect of "justice in social behavior" (e.g., Bierhoff, Cohen, & Greenberg, 1986; Montada & Lerner, 1996) or "research and applications" (e.g., Törnblom & Vermunt, 2007). These volumes offer a variety of theoretical and empirical analyses of justice issues, largely from the point of view of scholars trained in psychology. Indeed, in the social psychological realm, focus is often on individual perceptions of and reactions to various forms of injustice.

Yet, justice is essentially a collective process (Hegtvedt & Johnson, 2000) insofar as the meaning of distribution or procedural principles is socially constructed and upheld. Individuals are active (as well as miserly) perceivers whose interpretations – as well as subsequent actions – often depend upon the social contexts in which they are embedded. Sociologists, with their emphases on structures and groups, are poised to contribute to the discussion of justice in social relationships. Ironically, however, there is really no American sociology of justice. We sociologists who examine justice processes draw from the well-developed approaches of our colleagues in psychology and attempt to introduce sociological concerns in order to remind ourselves of the promise that justice holds not simply for an individual but for the collectivity as well.

The *Advances in Group Processes* series has a long tradition of highlighting the scholarly advances of social psychologists from a sociological viewpoint. Special volumes in the past have focused on fundamental processes such as power and status, or group cohesion, trust, and solidarity – decidedly issues of group structures and dynamics. As Jasso (this volume) argues, power, status, and justice constitute basic forces in society. Thus, while this volume cannot do "justice" to the topic of "justice," it seems that the series editors have fairly included "justice" as a special topic.

Moreover, as volume editors, we attempted to make fair choices about what might be included here. We sought diversity – in the nature of the chapters as well as in the academic disciplines and nationalities of the authors. Thus, the range of chapters covers abstract theoretical reasoning, empirical tests (using a variety of methodologies), and applications to current and historical domains. Research pertains to all types of justice – distributive, procedural, and interactional. About half of the chapters are written by psychologists and half by sociologists. And we have authors representing five regions of the world: America, Europe, Australia, Asia, and the Middle East. What all have in common is a passionate concern for revealing how justice processes operate in small groups, organizations, institutions, or society as a whole. Below we provide an overview of these multi-faceted contributions.

Although often only implicit in justice research, the first two chapters in the volume tackle the critical question of what motivates individuals in their assessments of the fairness of distributions, procedures, and interaction dynamics. Linda Skitka, Christopher Bauman, and Elizabeth Mullen extend the dichotomy between people as utility or status maximizers to include consideration of people as innately concerned about morality. They review conceptualization of and empirical support for an integrated theory of moral conviction that predicts that individuals' moral convictions decrease the likelihood of obeying immoral demands of authorities, influence the perceived fairness of decision-makers, and result in stronger emotional reactions to issues pertaining to those moral convictions. In doing so, the authors highlight how concerns beyond a person's own material or social well-being captures the essence of what justice means to a collectivity.

Jan-Willem van Prooijen poses a specific challenge to the assumption that being a valued member of a valued group is the driving motivation underlying assessments of procedural justice. While he does not fully discount this pro-social motive, he argues that egocentric motives influence procedural justice judgments as well. Using a social-cognitive framework on human perception, he theorizes about how egocentric concerns automatically and unconsciously may influence justice judgments. In addition, he provides evidence showing that people respond more negatively when they personally suffer a procedural injustice than when they observe others similarly ill-fated. Moreover, such effects are amplified by an egocentric self-focus. This chapter augments reasoning about procedural justice while also drawing attention to the importance of considering justice for the self versus justice for others.

At the core of three chapters that apply justice theories to understand issues within concrete groups is consideration of the comparisons invoked to determine what is just for one's self or one's group, and implicitly what is just for others. Susan Opotow analyzes the inclusionary gains and losses of black Americans during Reconstruction and later during the Jim Crow era. These two periods represent different justice trajectories – the former allows inclusion of Blacks and the latter promotes exclusion of them in the scope of justice as defined by Whites. Inclusion within a scope of justice ensures considerations of fairness, access to resources, and sacrifices for the well-being of the collective whereas exclusion results in derogation, lack of resources, and degrading treatment. Opotow instantiates theoretical conditions fostering the emergence and decline of exclusionary practices, thereby enhancing our understanding of this particular historical period. Moreover, her theoretical argument highlights the instability and long-term implications of inclusionary/exclusionary practices in groups regardless of historical time.

Likewise, the application of equity theory to dynamics and evaluations within the family serves to enlarge our knowledge about that fundamental group. Kathryn Lively, Brian Powell, Claudia Geist, and Lala Carr Steelman's theoretical and empirical analyses of justice processes within the family articulate the complementarity of applied family research and basic social psychological inquiry. Using survey data from domestic and international sources, they show that emotional responses vary based on the direction of the perceived inequity in household labor and in terms of the emotion considered. Moreover, analysis reveals that housework inequity is a weaker predictor of negative emotions within a relationship than inequities pertaining to paid work and spending. In addition, cross-national findings suggest that Americans are more likely to perceive disadvantageous inequity than are citizens of 25 other countries. Such findings reinforce the importance of considering the effects of the social context on justice perceptions.

Charles Mueller and Sang-Wook Kim also highlight international comparisons as well as bridge social psychological work on justice with organizations research. Focusing on the "paradox of the contented female worker," these authors examine organizational and justice-based arguments to explain why women who generally receive lower material rewards compared to men nonetheless voice equal satisfaction with their jobs. Justice arguments draw attention to differential job inputs, own-gender comparisons, differential entitlement standards, and the like. Their preliminary analysis of cross-national data reveals that the paradox exists in 27 of 30 countries and generally rules out the impact of factors identified from the nonjustice-based arguments. The authors speculate on the importance of the justice arguments and the need to examine gender differences explicitly in the justice valuation process.

While Lively et al. and Mueller and Kim examine emotional responses to injustice in applied contexts, other researchers endeavor experimental investigations of the role of emotions in justice processes. Jan Stets and Shelley Osborn use identity control theory to explore emotional responses to unjust outcomes over time. Their empirical results show that individuals are initially motivated by an enhancement motive, expressing positive emotions regarding over-reward, but that status processes and "hold-over effects" of earlier emotions predict emotions in later periods. People respond more negatively to unjust rewards provided by a high-status actor whereas previously experienced positive emotions buffer the negative emotions engendered by subsequent disadvantageous injustice. Their study reiterates the importance of understanding underlying motivations and situational conditions shaping reactions to injustice.

John Jost, Cheryl Wakslak, and Tom Tyler also examine emotional reactions to over-reward, though they do so through the lens of system justification theory. System justification theory seeks to explain how inequitable systems of distribution are maintained, which, of course, is a core issue in sociology. In this chapter, Jost and colleagues offer and test hypotheses related to the role of ideology in assuaging both negative emotions and moral outrage. In testing their predictions, they present results of two small group exchange studies in which each participant is randomly assigned to a high, medium, or low position in the power/status hierarchy. They find that those in the high-status position are significantly more likely to justify the system than those either in the medium or low-status position and that system justification is positively related to satisfaction. Their follow-up study indicates that ideology also assuages moral outrage, which in turn decreases willingness to correct the inequity in the system.

The importance of ideologies is reinforced in two other contributions, both of which make specific links between ideologies and social action. In "Towards a More Just World: What Makes People Participate in Social Action," Dahlia Moore examines how belief in a just world mediates the relationship between personal, political, and social characteristics and willingness to participate in social action. In doing so, she extends research on belief in a just world by examining both personal and group antecedents of such beliefs. She tests her hypotheses in a representative sample of Israeli citizens, which provides a unique opportunity to consider the impact of the cultural context. She finds not only that belief in a just world is negatively related to willingness to participate in social action, but that another ideology – patriotism—is positively related to social action. Thus, this chapter highlights the crucial role that ideologies play in responses to social injustices.

Susan Clayton's emphasis on ideology incorporates issues of group identity. She argues that people often adopt a particular ideology as a result of identification with a group. As a result, the activation of a group identity also activates an ideology, which then leads to particular perceptions of justice. She uses support for animal rights as an example, predicting that when people feel a sense of identification with animals they are more likely to support animal rights. In a test of these ideas among a group of college students, she finds that those who possess a strong "environmental identity" (seeing themselves as sharing an identity with nature) were more likely to agree with survey items that promoted animal justice ("justice is not only for humans; animals also deserve justice") and to posit pro-animal rights solutions when presented with animal-related issues. Together, the Clayton and Moore chapters suggest that ideologies are strongly related to group identities which, in turn, shape perceptions of justice.

Beyond perceptions of and emotional responses to injustice are actual attempts to restore justice. Two chapters address this topic. Jessica Collett examines alternative dispute resolution procedures and argues that arbitration may actually result in more positive relational outcomes than mediation, which is generally thought to be more procedurally just. She invokes theory and research in social exchange generally and affect exchange theory specifically to argue that arbitration may reduce conflict by placing the final decision in the hands of a third party, while mediation gives so much control to the disputants that it increases conflict. Her model has important implications for handling disputes between parties who have ongoing contact, such as in child custody cases or contract disputes.

Tyler Okimoto and Michael Wenzel also address justice restoration, focusing on how symbolic concerns surrounding justice affect the restoration process. In particular, they consider how transgressions can affect the balance of power and status between parties, as well as the ways in which justice transgressions can violate the sense of shared values previously held between disputants. In problematizing these symbolic concerns, Okimoto and Wenzel argue that the context of injustice, as well as the perceiver's dispositional factors, affect the relative degree to which status/power issues and concerns over shared values influence reactions to injustice. The authors then offer a framework for understanding how such concerns motivate disputants to respond to justice in either retributive or restorative ways. They argue that such a framework is necessary in order to understand when restorative responses to justice might be most effective.

Rounding out the volume are two theoretical chapters. In "Shall We Kill or Enslave Caesar," Guillermina Jasso offers a formal model of extreme responses to injustices wrought by tyrannical leaders. History indicates that populations sometimes seek death for such leaders (e.g., Caesar) while other times imprisonment (e.g., Napoleon). Jasso's formal analysis suggests that in the three types of society (justice-nonmaterialistic, status, or power-nonmaterialistic), the general gains achieved by enslavement appear to be greater than those achieved by death. But those gains may benefit the advantaged more than the disadvantaged. Only in justice societies will the death of a ruler such as Caesar uphold the desire for equality – equal gains for all societal members, regardless of rank. Jasso's analysis also identifies other societal features (e.g., group size) that affect the consequences of various ways to depose oppressive leaders.

In their modular approach to justice theory, Barry Markovsky, Lisa Dilks, Pamela Koch, Shannon McDonough, Jennifer Triplett, and Leia Velasquez would cast responses to injustice as only one building block of an integrated theory. Their chapter reviews a theoretical method that integrates two or more theories of justice. Essentially, modularlization creates the fabric of a theory by allowing units involving abstract conceptualization of phenomenon to "plug into each other." The authors illustrate their ideas by showing how a "fundamental justice process" module may be augmented by other modules, pertaining to topics such as choice of referent or choice of justice criterion for shaping perceptions of injustice, the role of uncertainty in justice judgments, and emotional responses to injustice. Their strategy may be a means to integrate what sometimes seem to be the distinct paths of justice researchers from various disciplines.

REFERENCES

Bierhoff, H. W., Cohen, R. L., & Greenberg, J. (Eds). (1986). *Justice in social relations*. New York: Plenum Press.

Cohen, R. F. (Ed.) (1986). *Justice: Views from the social sciences*. New York: Plenum Press.

De Cremer, D. (Ed.) (2007). *Advances in the psychology of justice and affect*. Charlotte, NC: Information Age Publishing.

Greenberg, J., & Colquitt, J. A. (Eds). (2005). *Handbook of organizational justice*. Mahwah, NJ: Lawrence Erlbaum Associates.

Hegtvedt, K. A., & Johnson, C. (2000). Justice beyond the individual: A future with legitimation. *Social Psychology Quarterly*, *63*, 298–311.

Lerner, M. J., & Mikula, G. (Eds). (1994). *Entitlement and the affectional bond: Justice in close relationships*. New York: Plenum Press.

Montada, L., & Lerner, M. J. (Eds). (1996). *Current societal concerns about justice*. New York: Plenum Press.

Scherer, K. R. (Ed.) (1992). *Justice: Interdisciplinary perspectives*. Cambridge: Cambridge University Press.

Solomon, R. C., & Murphy, M. C. (Eds). (1990). *What is justice: Classic and contemporary readings*. New York: Oxford University Press.

Törnblom, K., & Vermunt, R. (Eds). (2007). *Distributive and procedural justice*. London: Ashgate Publishing.

Karen A. Hegtvedt
Jody Clay-Warner
Volume Co-Editors

MORALITY AND JUSTICE: AN EXPANDED THEORETICAL PERSPECTIVE AND EMPIRICAL REVIEW

Linda J. Skitka, Christopher W. Bauman and Elizabeth Mullen

ABSTRACT

Two metaphors of human motivation have dominated justice theory and research: homo economicus *(people as rational utility maximizers) and* homo socialis *(people as status and social value maximizers). This chapter reviews theory and research inspired by a recent third perspective:* homo moralis, *that is, people as innately concerned about morality. When people have strong moral convictions at stake, their perceptions of outcome fairness and decision acceptance are shaped more by whether outcomes are consistent with perceivers' moral priorities than by whether authorities act in procedurally fair ways; moreover, whether authorities yield morally correct outcomes shapes subsequent perceptions of the legitimacy of these authorities or authority systems. Emotion plays an important role in both of these effects.*

Justice
Advances in Group Processes, Volume 25, 1–27

ISSN: 0882-6145/doi:10.1016/S0882-6145(08)25001-0

Research tends to be guided by "hard-core" assumptions, or guiding metaphors (Lakatos, 1978). For example, the metaphor of *homo economicus*, the idea that people are rationally self-interested utility maximizers, represented a hard-core assumption of classic social exchange theories, as well as early theories of distributive justice (e.g., Adams, 1965; Blau, 1964; Homans, 1961; Walster, Walster, & Berscheid, 1978). The assumption was that people are basically selfish, but rational, because they defer their immediate self-interest and engage in social cooperation to maximize their long-term self-interest. Justice theories that used economic exchange as a metaphor, not surprisingly, led to studies that focused on the fairness of outcome allocations and people's reactions to what they "got" out of a given encounter or relationship.

A shift in the metaphor that guided justice theorizing and research in social psychology occurred during the early 1980s with the introduction of the group value model of procedural fairness. The guiding metaphor of this program of research was the notion that people more often seek to satisfy relational motives, such as needs to feel valued, respected, and included in important social groups, than pursue material self-interest; that is, *homo economicus* yielded to *homo socialis*. Therefore, research began to focus more on how leaders' or authorities' behavior and decision making affected recipients' reasoning about fairness and less on outcome distributions and the factors that determined them (e.g., Lind & Tyler, 1988; Tyler & Lind, 1992). By using "need to belong" as a lens for examining what mattered in the psychology of justice, researchers broadened their understanding of how and why people make fairness judgments. For example, researchers identified the pervasive influence of procedural treatment (such as variations in opportunities for voice, being treated with dignity and respect, and freedom from bias) on perceptions of fairness. Researchers may not have discovered the importance of treatment to justice judgments had they remained solely committed to constructs consistent with a guiding metaphor of economic exchange.

Now another shift seems to be underway. Specifically, there is increasing interdisciplinary interest in the notion that a concern with morality may be an evolutionary adaptation that facilitates social cooperation, e.g., in behavioral economics (e.g., Fehr & Fischbacher, 2004), primatology (e.g., de Waal, 1996; Brosnan & de Waal, 2003), organizational behavior (e.g., Folger, 2001; Turillo, Folger, Lavelle, Umphress, & Gee, 2002), evolutionary psychology (Cosmides & Tooby, 2006), as well as social psychology (e.g., Haidt, 2001). The assumption guiding this recent line of thinking is that people are born with an innate capacity to care about morality, and they are predisposed to maintain cooperative systems by rewarding those who behave morally and punishing those who do not. The moral perspective maintains that humans have a basic predisposition to care about morality independent of their material self-interests or belongingness needs. In short, an emerging alternative guiding metaphor in justice research and closely related areas is *homo moralis*, that is, the notion that people have an intrinsic propensity for caring about and acting on conceptions of morality.

Guiding metaphors strongly influence what is to be observed and scrutinized, what questions are considered interesting and important, how these questions are to be structured, as well as how the results of scientific investigations are interpreted (Kuhn, 1962). For example, the initial focus on *homo economicus* led to research on reactions to allocations and resource exchange (e.g., wages for labor). Then, the *homo socialis* metaphor led to studies of procedures and interactional treatment. Now, a shift in guiding metaphor toward *homo moralis* directs attention to a different set of research questions. For example, to what extent are justice judgments related to concerns about basic questions of right and wrong, moral and immoral, rather than only concerns about serving self-interests or belongingness needs? Does the relative importance of different types of justice-relevant information (e.g., procedural treatment and outcome distributions) change as a function of whether people perceive their strong moral convictions to be at stake? The goal of this chapter is to begin to explore these questions by presenting (a) an updated and integrated theory of how and why people's moral convictions reflect something different from equally strong, but non-moral preferences, (b) focused discussion on how and why moral convictions shape perceptions of outcome and procedural fairness, (c) a brief review of research that has tested hypotheses generated from this theory, and (d) a delineation of directions for future research and justice theory.

AN INTEGRATED THEORY OF MORAL CONVICTION

Our integrated theory of moral conviction (ITMC[1]) posits a number of ways that attitudes held with strong moral conviction differ from equally strong but non-moral attitudes (see also Skitka, Bauman, & Sargis, 2005; Skitka & Bauman, 2008). Building on insights from theory and research on moral development, we propose that there are important distinctions between people's senses of subjective preference, normative convention, and morality

(Nucci & Turiel, 1978; Rest, Narvaez, Bebeau, & Thoma, 1999; Turiel, 2002) that have important implications for how people think about justice. Preferences are by definition subjective and in the eye of the beholder. Preferences represent instances when people favor one outcome more than another, but there is no expectation that others would or should feel the same way. Others' preferences about the same object are not seen as either right or wrong; they are simply different. For example, it is acceptable for you to prefer apples even though I prefer oranges because people are entitled to have different tastes about fruit.

People's sense of normative convention, in contrast, is based on formal or informal group rules or expectations about the way things are done. For example, someone might expect a raise after one year of employment at a company because that is the informal or formal rule in that organization. Although it would be normative to expect a raise after one year in that particular organization, people would not generalize from the norm and assume that individuals at all jobs everywhere should get a raise after one year or perceive it to be unfair if they did not. Moral convictions, in contrast, are absolute convictions about right and wrong that transcend specific contexts.[2]

There may be individual variation, however, in the degree that people view the same attitude object as a preference, convention, or a moral imperative. Although many people seem to see the abortion issue in a moral light, for example, other people have conventional attitudes about this issue. For example, someone with a conventional attitude about abortion may believe that abortion is acceptable in their state because it currently is legal there, but would think it was wrong if it was against the law; alternatively, they may support or oppose abortion because their neighbors do, but would change their mind if the opinion of the majority changed.

People's sense of morality differs psychologically from their sense of preference or normative convention in a host of ways. For example, moral sensibilities are experienced as more objectively and universally true than preferences or conventions. Moral sensibilities also are inherently more motivating and self-justifying, are more autonomous, and have different and potentially stronger ties to affect than preferences or conventions. Each of these characteristics of moral conviction is explained in more detail below.

Universality

Unlike preferences or conventions, people tend to believe that their personal moral standards ought to apply to everyone. If one has a strong moral conviction that female circumcision is wrong, for instance, then one is likely to believe that the practice is wrong not only in one's culture-of-origin, but in other cultures as well. For example, some western activists vehemently object to the practice of female circumcision in Middle Eastern and African nations where the practice is normative and culturally valued (Dorkenoo, 1994), and consumers will boycott a foreign good when they learn it is produced by child labor (Chowdhry & Beeman, 2001). People experience attitudes held with moral conviction as absolutes, or universal standards of truth that others should also share.

Objectivity

Another distinguishing feature of people's self-identified moral convictions is that people treat their moral beliefs as if they were readily observable, objective properties of situations, or facts about the world. For example, if you ask people with a strong moral conviction about female circumcision why it is wrong, they probably would be somewhat confused by the question and likely would respond by exclaiming, "Because it's wrong!" The "fact" that it is wrong is psychologically as self-evident to morally motivated perceivers as $2+2 = 4$. Consistent with this notion, research by Haidt (2001) demonstrates that when you push people to explain why incest is wrong, even in circumstances where a couple used birth control and neither person was psychologically damaged, people continue to insist that incest is "wrong" even if they cannot generate a reason for it.

Autonomy versus Heteronomy

The ITMC also predicts that moral convictions represent something different from, and independent of, people's concerns about being accepted or respected by authorities or groups. Building on insights from developmental and social theories of morality, the ITMC proposes that moral motivation is more autonomous than heteronomous (e.g., Kohlberg, 1984; Piaget, 1932/1997; Turiel, 2002, cf. Durkheim, 1925). In other words, moral motivation comes more from within, rather than from outside the person, such as from society or authorities. The authority independence hypothesis is consistent with the notion that recognition of moral wrongs may be relatively innate (e.g., de Waal, 1996) and with developmental research that indicates that even very young children (3 years of age) can distinguish morality from normative convention. For example, children say that hitting and stealing are wrong, even if a teacher says it is okay (Nucci & Turiel, 1978; Smetana, 1981, 1985). Similarly, children endorse obedience to moral requests (e.g., to stop fighting) made by any person, including other children, but they only endorse obedience to norms (e.g., seat assignments) from legitimate authorities (Laupa, 1994). Likewise, adolescents think it is appropriate to disobey immoral commands (and to lie about doing so), even when it means disobeying and lying to their parents (Perkins & Turiel, 2007). Young children's and adults' abilities to make distinctions between the moral and conventional domains replicates across a wide array of nationalities and religious groups, even when religious devotees are confronted with counterfactuals about God's authority (for reviews, see Smetana, 1993; Tisak, 1995; Nucci, 2001). Also intriguing is the finding that adult psychopaths and children who exhibit psychopathic tendencies do not make distinctions between the conventional and moral domains (Blair, 1995, 1997).

In sum, there are numerous examples from moral development research that support the basic premise that conceptions of morality develop very early and are relatively authority independent. Personal conceptions of morality often override the duty to obey authorities, even among quite young children and adolescents; moreover, a failure to distinguish between the moral and conventional domains appears to be a symptom of severe mental illness. Some use this evidence in support of the notion that psychologically healthy people, including very young children, have an objective sense that some things are right and wrong, much like they can recognize the difference between furniture and their parents (e.g., Turiel, 1983; Nucci, 2001). Others use these findings to argue for the primary function of affect and responses to recognition of harm as foundational in forming moral judgments (Nichols, 2004). These results are also consistent with the proposition that people may have an innate capacity for making moral judgments (e.g., de Waal, 1996).

Motivation and Emotion

The ITMC predicts that the intensity of emotion that people experience in conjunction with moral convictions (and perhaps especially related to threats to moral convictions) is stronger than the intensity of emotions people experience in association with threats to preferences or conventions (Haidt, 2001, 2003a; Kohlberg, 1984; Nucci, 2001; Shweder, 2002). Moral violations represent especially strong attacks on people's basic worldviews and sense of moral order (e.g., Tetlock, Kristel, Elson, Green, & Lerner, 2000), whereas violations of preferences or conventions do not cut quite so deep into people's core conceptions of the way the world works. Thus, although violated preferences or normative expectations may lead to disappointment or even anger, the magnitude of these reactions is likely to pale in comparison to the outrage associated with a violated or threatened sense of basic right and wrong. Consistent with this notion, some scholars differentiate between anger and righteous anger. Whereas anger arises when a goal incongruent event is caused by a responsible other (e.g., Lazarus, 1991), "righteous anger" arises when another's behavior represents a violation of moral standards (Tangney, Stuewig, & Mashek, 2007). In addition to righteous anger, responses to moral violations also include intense feelings of contempt and disgust – reactions that may not similarly occur in response to violated preferences or conventions (e.g., Haidt, 2003b; Skoe, Eisenberg, & Cumberland, 2002). Although more research has examined reactions to actions that subvert rather than sustain the moral order, people's affective reactions in response to validated moral convictions may similarly differ from validated preferences or conventions. For example, the emotions of "elevation" and "awe" elicited in response to particularly moral actions may not be produced by actions that reflect preferences or conventions (Haidt, 2003b).

The ITMC's emphasis on moral emotion is consistent with a growing body of literature that suggests that discrete emotions function either as a source of moral judgment or as predictors of moral judgment (Haidt, 2001). For example, Haidt's (2001) social intuitionist model argues that people make moral judgments quickly and intuitively on the basis of their gut-level reactions, and that moral reasoning only comes into play when people are asked to justify their conclusions or when their intuitions conflict and thus prompt more careful reasoning. Thus, people's intuitions and emotions are a significant driving force in their moral judgments (see also Damasio, 1994; Greene & Haidt, 2002, for related neurological research).

In sum, there are theoretical and empirical suggestions that moral judgments or reactions are affectively laden and that moral emotions differ from feelings associated with non-moral preferences or conventions. Given that moral emotions provide the motivational force for people to live up to and enforce their moral standards (Kroll & Egan, 2004), we argue that moral emotions will be an especially important psychological component of people's justice reasoning when their moral convictions are at stake.

MORAL CONVICTIONS AND JUSTICE

The ITMC leads to a number of more specific predictions and hypotheses about how people reason about fairness and legitimacy when moral convictions are at stake, including the (a) authority independence, (b) litmus test, and (c) emotion hypotheses. Although these hypotheses do not represent an exhaustive list of testable hypotheses that can be derived from the ITMC, they represent reasonable starting positions for testing the viability of the notion that people's basic concerns about morality – independent of their concerns about material self-interest or belongingness – have some explanatory and predictive power in the context of how people reason about fairness. We provide below detailed discussions of these hypotheses, as well as research in support of them.

The Authority Independence Hypothesis

The authority independence hypothesis asserts that people feel a weaker sense of duty or obligation to obey or accept orders, decisions, or outcomes when they believe them to be immoral, rather than simply counter to their preferences or normative expectations. Although there may be reasons at times to publicly accept immoral decisions (e.g., in totalitarian regimes in which dissent could come at the peril of one's freedom or life), doing so will come at a psychological cost (e.g., Bandura, 1990), and private acceptance should remain quite low. In short, the authority independence hypothesis predicts that perceived fairness in moral contexts is driven largely by internal moral judgments about right or wrong rather than by social rules, a compulsion to obey legitimate authorities, or non-moral factors such as due process or respectful treatment.

Although the authority independence hypothesis derives directly from the ITMC theoretical premise that moral judgments are more autonomous than non-moral judgments, this hypothesis is nonetheless at odds with a considerable amount of other justice theory and research. For example, various forms of legitimacy theory predict that when people perceive an authority system to be legitimate, neither "consent of the governed" nor "benefits received" are required to justify obedience or acceptance (e.g., Gelpi, 2003; Tyler, 2006). Instead, legitimacy is believed to create a duty and obligation to obey that replaces even personal moral standards as a relevant guide (Kelman & Hamilton, 1989). Although people are more likely to obey and cooperate with unpopular decisions when they perceive decision-making procedures to be fair and authorities to be legitimate (e.g., Brockner & Wiesenfeld, 1996; Gibson, Caldeira, & Spence, 2005; Hegtvedt, Clay-Warner, & Johnson, 2003), until recently, it has been relatively unclear whether obedience to authority and decision acceptance similarly are likely to be high when people perceive a decision or outcome to violate a strong moral conviction.

Research Support for the Authority Independence Hypothesis
Support for the authority independence hypothesis comes from a number of studies that have examined people's perceptions of outcome fairness and decision acceptance as a function of whether outcomes are consistent with their personal sense of moral right and wrong. For example, one recent study tested the authority independence hypothesis in the context of *Gonzales v. the State of Oregon*, a Supreme Court challenge to Oregon's Death with Dignity Act, which legalized physician-assisted suicide (PAS) under some circumstances. Skitka (2006) assessed a national random sample of non-Oregonian's moral convictions about whether PAS should be allowed, perceptions of the procedural fairness and legitimacy of the Supreme Court, and the degree to which participants' feelings about legalizing PAS were held as moral convictions before the Supreme Court heard arguments in this case. When the Court announced its decision several months later, the same sample was surveyed again to assess their post-decision reactions, such as how fair they felt the decision was and the degree to which they accepted it as the final word on the question posed. (*Note:* the Supreme Court ruled in favor of Oregon's right to decide to legalize PAS, and against the Bush Administration's claim that PAS procedures violated the Federal Controlled Substance Act.)

People's pre-decision strength of moral conviction about PAS – but not their pre-decision perceptions of the procedural fairness and legitimacy of the Supreme Court – predicted their post-decision perceptions of outcome fairness and decision acceptance. People who morally supported PAS perceived the decision to be fair and were willing to accept the Court's decision. In contrast, people who morally opposed PAS perceived the decision to be unfair and were unwilling to accept the decision as the final word on this issue. It should also be noted that the effects for moral conviction emerged even when controlling for a host of alternative explanations, including participants' general levels of religiosity, as well as the specific degree that participants' position on PAS reflected their religious convictions. Moreover, the effect of moral conviction on perceptions of outcome fairness and decision acceptance was equally strong regardless of whether people's pre-decision perceptions of the procedural fairness and legitimacy of the Court were low or high. Therefore, the results of the PAS study supported the authority independence hypothesis. People's willingness to see the decision in the *Gonzales v. Oregon* case as fair and to accept the Supreme Court's decision as the final word on the issue depended more on whether the decision was consistent with perceivers' moral convictions than it did on whether procedures were perceived as fair or rendered by a legitimate authority.

More controlled experiments also have found results consistent with the authority independence hypothesis. For example, Bauman and Skitka (2007a) enhanced the perceived legitimacy of policy decision making in the U.S. for half of the participants in a study by reminding them of their voice in democratic decision making and indicating that participants' survey responses would be shared with policy makers in Washington, DC (see Tyler, 1994, for a further discussion and evidence of how voice enhances perceptions of institutional legitimacy). Following the voice manipulation, participants evaluated a hypothetical policy decision that was either consistent or inconsistent with their position about abortion. Voice enhanced perceived fairness of the policy decision when participants' reported weak but not strong moral conviction about abortion. Results also indicated that moral support for or opposition to abortion – but not voice – predicted decision acceptance. Participants accepted policy decisions about abortion when they were consistent with their moral convictions and rejected decisions when they were inconsistent with their moral convictions.

Other studies have tested hypotheses in the context of authority relationships that may feel "closer to home" than citizens' relationships with policy makers or the Supreme Court. For example, Bauman and Skitka (2007b) examined college students' reactions to a decision rendered by university authorities. These studies manipulated information about how the university made and communicated policy decisions (e.g., decision and treatment quality) and therefore the extent that students perceived the university authorities and their decision as legitimate. What students learned was at stake in this experiment was whether a university committee decided to use student fees to fund abortions at the student health clinic.

Consistent with the authority independence hypothesis, students who morally disagreed with the decision were prepared to petition, protest, withhold tuition and fees, and "make trouble" for the university administration, even when they perceived the decision-making procedures as maximally fair. Conversely, students had no ambition to protest a decision when it was consistent with their moral beliefs, even when they had explicitly acknowledged that the procedures used to make the decision were illegitimate and unfair. In short, the results of Bauman and Skitka (2007b) demonstrated that people do not yield to authority when they perceive their personal moral beliefs to be at stake, even in contexts that are close to home and that directly involve a salient and important social identity.

In another demonstration of the authority independence hypothesis, Skitka and Houston (2001, Study 2) found that people were willing to accept the actions of extremely illegitimate authorities (vigilantes), as long as they produced the morally right outcome. Specifically, the researchers presented participants with hypothetical news reports that depicted whether a defendant in a capital murder case appeared to be truly guilty or innocent, and whether the defendant was executed by the state following a fair trial, or killed by a family member of a victim before the trial began. Results indicated that people perceived the death of a guilty defendant to be fair, regardless of whether it was the product of a full trial and meted by the state or was an act of vigilantism. Consistent with the authority independence hypothesis, what mattered most to people's perceptions of outcome fairness was whether people perceived the outcome in the case – i.e., that the defendant was punished – was morally right if he was thought to be guilty, or morally wrong if he was thought to be innocent. Other results indicated that when defendant guilt was ambiguous, however, perceptions of outcome fairness were consistent with the predictions of theories of procedural justice. Punishment of the ambiguously guilty defendant was seen as unfair if it was a consequence of improper procedures and fair if it was a consequence of due process (Skitka & Houston, 2001, Study 1b).

In summary, a growing body of research supports the authority independence hypothesis. Small children and adolescents do not blindly follow trusted authorities' dictates when they perceive that those dictates are inconsistent with basic beliefs about right and wrong. Moreover, perceived legitimacy and procedural fairness does not increase adults' willingness to accept authorities' decisions when those decisions are at odds with perceivers' personal moral convictions. Instead, perceptions of outcome fairness and decision acceptance are based on whether decisions are consistent or inconsistent with perceivers' *a priori* beliefs about the degree that an outcome is morally right or wrong.

The Litmus Test Hypothesis

Research guided by the *homo economicus* and *homo socialis* metaphors has focused on two important roles that procedural information can play. People use procedural information to evaluate the likelihood that they will receive just deserts in the long run (e.g., Thibaut & Walker, 1975) and to assess their position within the group and in the eyes of authorities (e.g., Folger & Cropanzano, 1998; Lind & Tyler, 1988). In each role, procedural information provides a way for people to make goal-relevant inferences in the absence of specific information about the appropriateness of a particular outcome. In contrast, the *homo moralis* metaphor suggests that there will be situations in which people are likely to have moral certainty about what outcome authorities and procedures should deliver. Therefore, moral convictions about outcomes may act as crucial manipulation checks on procedural fairness and authority legitimacy under these circumstances, because perceivers already know the right answer. The litmus test hypothesis posits that people use outcomes they perceive to have moral implications to check whether individuals, groups, or systems responsible for decisions are fair and legitimate. "Right" answers indicate that leaders, authorities, other group representatives, and decision-making procedures are appropriate and deserve their role. "Wrong" answers signal that the system is broken and that the perceiver and the group are being misled. In short, people use their sense of morality as a benchmark to assess whether leaders, authorities, procedures, or those who align themselves with the decision are valid or invalid.

Research Support for the Litmus Test Hypothesis

Support for the litmus test hypothesis comes from a host of studies that have evaluated people's reactions to authorities' public policy decisions. For example, particularly persuasive evidence comes from a longitudinal study of people's perceptions of the widely publicized Elián González custody battle (Skitka & Mullen, 2002). In November 1999, 5-year-old Elián González, his mother, and 12 others unsuccessfully attempted to cross from Cuba to the United States. Their boat capsized somewhere in the Straights of Florida, and Elián's mother and most of the others died. Elián was rescued off the Florida coast, and his father in Cuba petitioned the United States to return Elián to his custody. The Immigration and Naturalization Service (INS), however, put Elián in the temporary care of Miami relatives, who in turn filed a petition to grant him political asylum in the United States. Months of court decisions and appeals culminated in a ruling that

Elián would return to Cuba. After Elián's relatives and many others in the Miami community refused to comply with the court's ruling, Federal agents took Elián by force from his Miami relatives' home and eventually returned Elián to his father in Cuba.

Skitka and Mullen (2002) conducted a natural experiment by collecting data from a nationally representative sample of U.S. households to assess public reactions as the case unfolded. Judgments were collected several weeks before the Federal raid, immediately after the raid, and several weeks after Elián returned to Cuba. Results of the study were consistent with the litmus test hypothesis. For example, 83% of people with a moral mandate made at least one critical comment about the U.S. government, compared with only 12% of those without a moral mandate about how the case should be resolved. Analyses of open-ended comments about the case indicated that people who morally supported Elián's U.S. asylum criticized specific authorities (e.g., the INS, U.S. Attorney General Janet Reno) and the decision to use force to remove Elián from his relatives' home. People who thought the only moral solution was to return Elián to Cuba and his father criticized authorities for taking too long to act, even though they accepted the final decision and perceived it to be fair in the end.

Analysis of closed-ended questions about people's reactions to the case similarly supported the litmus test hypothesis. Specifically, people's perceptions that the raid and the ultimate resolution of the case were procedurally fair and legitimate were determined primarily by whether the raid and decision were consistent with pre-raid levels of moral conviction people had about how the case should be resolved, and less by pre-raid perceptions of procedural fairness and legitimacy. In sum, strong moral convictions about how the Elián case should be resolved led people to be quite critical of authorities, rather than to accept blindly or reject authorities' decision. As predicted by the litmus test hypothesis, people perceived the authorities and procedures as more legitimate when the outcome of the case was consistent and more illegitimate when the outcome was inconsistent with their *a priori* moral beliefs about whether Elián should stay in the U.S. or be returned to Cuba.

Controlled laboratory studies also supported the litmus test hypothesis. For example, moral convictions about just ends affected perceptions of just means in perceptions of jury trials and verdicts (Skitka & Houston, 2001). In addition to finding support for the authority independence hypothesis, that is, that perceptions of outcome fairness and acceptance were determined more by whether outcomes matched moral standards than by the procedures used to arrive at them, Skitka and Houston (2001) found that when trial verdicts failed to match moral standards (e.g., when the guilty were acquitted, or the innocent were convicted), people derogated the legitimacy of the police investigation of the crime and the trial. People found the exact same procedures to be perfectly legitimate, however, when they yielded a verdict consistent with their moral standards (Skitka & Houston, 2001, Study 1b; see also Mullen & Skitka, 2006b). Manipulations of whether the trials involved proper versus improper procedures only affected perceptions of the trial's procedural fairness when defendant guilt was ambiguous – in these cases, improper investigation and trial procedures were correctly perceived to be less procedurally fair than proper investigation and trial procedures.

Further support for the litmus test hypothesis comes from Skitka's (2006) PAS Supreme Court study. As discussed earlier, pre-decision perceptions of the legitimacy of the Supreme Court did not affect people's reactions to the Court's ruling in the case; instead, whether the decision matched people's morally vested outcome preferences predicted their perceptions of outcome fairness and decision acceptance. Important to the litmus test hypothesis, however, results of the PAS Supreme Court study also indicated people's perceptions of the legitimacy and procedural fairness of the Supreme Court changed as a function of whether the Court ruling was consistent or inconsistent with perceivers' a priori moral beliefs about the "correct" resolution of the case. People who morally supported PAS thought that the Supreme Court was more legitimate and procedurally fair, whereas those who morally opposed PAS thought that the Supreme Court was less legitimate and procedurally fair, after it made its ruling on *Gonzales v. Oregon* – a finding that was not qualified by how legitimate or fair they felt the Court had been pre-decision. In other words, people rejected the decision and the system that yielded it when the Supreme Court ruling was inconsistent with their moral convictions, even when they previously thought the Court was legitimate. Similarly, people accepted the decision and felt stronger faith in the Supreme Court when its decision was consistent with their moral convictions, even if they previously thought the system was broken and illegitimate.

Finally, other research has found behavioral support for the litmus test hypothesis. Specifically, when people were exposed to unjust laws, they were more likely to report intentions to flout other unrelated laws in the future (Nadler, 2005), presumably because their faith in the system had been eroded. Mullen and Nadler (2008) further tested the flouting hypothesis in an experiment that involved exposing people to legal decisions that supported, opposed, or were unrelated to participants' moral convictions.

The experimenters distributed a pen with a post-exposure questionnaire, and asked participants to return the questionnaire and pen at the end of the experimental session. Consistent with the notion that decisions, rules, and laws that violate people's moral convictions erode perceptions of the legitimacy of authority systems, participants were more likely to steal the pen after exposure to a legal decision that violated rather than supported their personal moral convictions.

Taken together, the results of several studies that used a variety of methods converge and support the litmus test hypothesis. In many situations that involve decisions about personal preferences or normative conventions, people are unsure about what would be a fair outcome. Therefore, they use fair treatment and procedures to guide their perceptions of the decision. In situations that involve their personal conceptions of right and wrong, moral and immoral, however, people *know* that one decision alternative is valid and right and other alternatives are invalid and wrong. When people have a moral investment in decision outcomes, they use whether these outcomes are achieved as an important check on the true fairness and legitimacy of leaders, authorities, and the procedures they employ.

The Emotion Hypothesis

The emotion hypothesis goes one step further than the authority independence and litmus test hypotheses and makes a prediction about at least one of the motivational underpinnings of these other effects. Specifically, the ITMC predicts that people have stronger and perhaps different emotional reactions to decisions that involve issues about which they have strong moral convictions, and that these emotions in turn influence and color perceptions of fairness, decision acceptance, and related variables.

Research Support for the Emotion Hypothesis

Considerable research supports the notion that people's fairness reasoning will be driven by different kinds, and perhaps stronger emotions overall, when their personal moral convictions are involved compared to when they are not. For example, Mullen and Skitka (2006a) assessed people's reactions to hypothetical jury decisions that either supported or opposed participants' moral beliefs about abortion. Rather than manipulating procedural fairness, each jury trial was described as containing both positive aspects of procedures as well as a few procedural flaws. Results revealed that when people had a moral conviction about abortion, they reacted with anger when the outcome of the case opposed their moral conviction, and anger in turn led them to devalue the fairness of the procedures and the outcome in the case. In contrast, when the outcome of the case supported or was unrelated to people's moral convictions, participants reported little anger and consequently rated both the procedures and outcome to be fair. Thus, participants rated identical procedures to be differentially fair as a function of whether the outcome supported or opposed their moral beliefs. Other results, however, indicated that emotional reactions to procedures did not mediate the influence of moral conviction on perceptions of procedural or outcome fairness. In short, anger in response to morally untenable *outcomes* colored people's subsequent perceptions of outcome and procedural fairness, but anger at the *procedures* did not (see also Mullen & Nadler, 2008).

One could argue that participants might have experienced less anger and been more willing to accept an outcome that was inconsistent with their moral beliefs had the experiment manipulated procedural fairness and included a condition that involved extremely fair procedures. To address this concern, Mullen and Nadler (2008) replicated the previous results using a strong manipulation of procedural fairness and including a measure of decision acceptance. In particular, Mullen and Nadler (2008) assessed participants' reactions to hypothetical jury decisions that either supported or opposed participants' moral beliefs and varied whether the trial procedures were exemplary or contained egregious procedural flaws. Results were consistent with Mullen and Skitka (2006a); participants reported more anger when outcomes were inconsistent with their moral convictions, and this outrage led them to judge the outcome to be less fair and to report an increased tendency to reject the decision, even in conditions when procedures were objectively fair. Further evidence indicated that anger at the outcome (but not anger at the procedures) colored people's subsequent perceptions of outcome fairness and decision acceptance.

In addition to evidence that anger about outcomes mediates the relationship between moral conviction and perceived fairness, research suggests that outrage (a blend of anger and disgust) caused by perceived moral transgressions increases intentions to protest decisions or sever ties with groups (Bauman, 2006). For example, Bauman (2006) found that greater moral disagreement with a university decision made students more willing to protest, withhold their tuition and fees, and "make trouble" for a university administration, and this effect was mediated by the degree of outrage students reported in response to the decision. Other results indicated that outrage varied as a function of whether outcomes were consistent or inconsistent with students' moral convictions, but not as a function of whether decision-making procedures were exemplary or egregiously unfair.

The effects of procedures and outcomes, and perhaps especially moral investments in outcomes, may influence justice reasoning through two very different processes. Research suggests that under conditions of uncertainty, people carefully attempt to evaluate whether procedures are fair (e.g., Lind & Van den Bos, 2002). Under conditions of certainty provided by moral conviction about the outcomes, however, people may use more intuitive and emotional processes to judge whether outcomes and procedures are fair or unfair (cf. Epstein, 1990). Consistent with this idea, attempts to explore alternative explanations for why people seem to pay less attention to features of procedures when they have moral convictions about outcomes found no difference in the amount of information that people paid attention to or processed as a function of whether they had a moral conviction at stake (Mullen & Skitka, 2006a). For example, people with and without strong moral convictions about the outcome of a decision were equally likely to remember details of the procedures used to make it. However, people with moral convictions at stake appeared to weight procedural information insufficiently when they made fairness judgments (Mullen & Skitka, 2006a). These results suggest that people's emotional reactions to violated or threatened moral convictions may engulf the perceptual field and lead them to judge the entire situation as fair or unfair.

Summary

In summary, a body of theory and research on justice has grown out of the *homo moralis* guiding metaphor. The assumption that people are predisposed to care about morality leads to novel hypotheses about the factors that affect perceptions of fairness. Like research in other disciplines working from the same metaphor, a willingness to explore and test the implications of *homo moralis* has led to some important and surprising findings. For example, one long-standing truism in social psychology is that obedience and cooperation with legitimate authorities generally overwhelms people's personal sense of morality. Our findings, however, suggest that there are some limitations to this general conclusion. Increasing evidence indicates that people actively resist when authorities make decisions that are at odds with their core moral beliefs. Moreover, people use whether authorities make decisions consistent with their moral beliefs as an important check on procedural fairness and authority legitimacy. Even a single immoral decision appears to have the potential to undercut perceptions of authority and institutional legitimacy.[3] Other findings indicate that affect plays an especially important social psychological function or cue when perceivers have a moral investment in decision outcomes.

BROADER THEORETICAL IMPLICATIONS

Guiding metaphors, such as *homo economicus*, *socialis*, and *moralis* are useful for theory generation. Each provides a possible frame for thinking about how and why people might care about justice, that in turn leads to testable hypotheses. That said, each metaphor in itself is limited in scope and range. Justice research may therefore be like the poet John Godfrey Saxe's blind men of Indostan, who each examined a different part of an elephant and therefore came to different conclusions about the fundamental character of "elephantness" ("it is very like a tree," "a wall," or "a snake"). The tree, wall, and snake descriptions were each accurate but limited descriptions of an elephant (its leg, body, and trunk). Similarly, justice theory and research guided by the *homo economicus*, *socialis*, and *moralis* metaphors have each found considerable evidence consistent with their respective predictions, but may provide limited views of the psychology of justice when viewed in isolation. What justice theory and research therefore needs is a more general theory that can help guide predictions about the contingencies when people's justice reasoning is shaped more by their bounded but rational self-interests, status concerns and the need to feel valued and belong, or by their core moral convictions.

Our approach has assumed that not everyone looks at a given situation with the same motivational priorities. Consider our example of a university considering whether to use student fees to fund abortions at a student health clinic. One perceiver might be concerned primarily about whether her student fees are likely to increase and how this will affect her budget. Because this perceiver is taking a more *homo economicus* perspective on this issue, the criteria she uses to decide whether using student fees to fund abortions are fair may be quite different from another student, who sees the issue more in terms of his social identity as a member of the university. This other student may be more concerned about whether he has voice in the decision-making process about whether to increase student fees, and whether authorities are respecting students' opinions. Yet another student may perceive the issue in terms of the fundamental morality of blocking or facilitating students' access to abortion services. All three students are viewing exactly the same reality, but from very different points of view. What they see as at stake in the decision – their self-interests, their status and standing, or basic questions of right or wrong – has considerable potential to influence the decision rules and heuristics they bring to bear on deciding whether the decision-making procedures and the decision outcome are fair.

A theory of justice that takes each of these possible perspectives into account and develops contingent predictions about how people think about fairness within each of these frames of reference has considerable promise to integrate research inspired by the three metaphors reviewed here. Moreover, a more contingent approach to justice theory would be able to handle the empirical reality that (a) people care more about due process considerations than they do about outcomes under some circumstances (e.g., see Lind & Tyler, 1988; Tyler & Smith, 1997, for reviews), and (b) people care more about outcomes than they do about due process under other circumstances (e.g., the research reviewed here; Van den Bos, Lind, Vermunt, & Wilke, 1997), as well as a host of other contradictory findings that are otherwise difficult to explain when taking only one metaphorical perspective into account.

Just as we have taken an ideographic rather than nomothetic approach to studying whether individual perceivers see a given situation in moral terms, one could measure other motivational priorities ideographically as well. For example, other research has found some value in measuring the strength of people's social identity motivations in specific contexts. Research that has measured the relative importance of social identity concerns finds that voice and other aspects of procedural fairness are more important to people's justice judgments when people identify with decision-relevant groups and authorities than when they do not (e.g., Huo, Smith, Tyler, & Lind, 1996). Therefore, our moral conviction research and research on identification are complementary because they both reveal factors that affect the relative impact of a particular motive on perceptions of justice rather than assert categorically which motive always is primary. Although there has been some movement toward more contingent theories of justice reasoning (e.g., Heuer, Stroessner, & Vale, 1998; Skitka, 2003), few studies have measured or manipulated more than one motivational priority within a given study to test the full implications of the notion that people's justice reasoning may be contingent on the motivational priorities of individual perceivers. Thus, exploring contingent theories of justice reasoning is an important area of inquiry for future research.

In sum, the field could benefit from more attempts to understand multiple factors that influence how people evaluate fairness. Most research has attempted to pit theories that position one motivational priority against another in horse races in an effort to determine which one is more important. Understanding *when* different motivational priorities are salient or dominant (rather than which motivational priority is presumably more universally dominant), and how different motivational priorities might lead people to differentially weight information in their judgments or apply different definitions or criteria to a judgment of fairness or unfairness, could provide novel insight into the social side of the psychology of justice. Although understanding how individuals judge whether a given situation is fair or unfair is interesting, understanding how people socially negotiate and come to some kind of group consensus about whether fairness has been achieved in a given situation seems potentially much more important to understand. Social conflicts may often be a consequence of people interpreting the same situation from very different points of view; thus understanding what might lead to these differences in points of view, and then how people work together to resolve conflicting interpretations of fairness or what should be weighed in a fairness judgment, represent neglected and fascinating questions for future research.

In addition, our review of the research supporting the ITMC could lead one to wonder whether moral convictions should be construed as a positive or negative aspect of people's fairness reasoning and judgments. On the one hand, moral conviction seems to provide people with the necessary motivational force to stand up for what they believe in and to protest against authorities that do not meet moral standards. Thus, moral convictions could contribute to pro-social behaviors and needed social change. On the other hand, people's moral convictions can also be viewed as leading people to make potentially biased evaluations of procedures. In a world where people's positions on politicized issues such as abortion and capital punishment are not uniform, moral convictions may serve to fuel social conflicts and lead people to endorse any "means" that justifies their morally motivated "ends." The value spin one places on whether morally motivated behavior that ignores means in favor of ends is likely to be colored by whether one shares the moral priorities of the actor. One person's terrorist is likely to be another's freedom fighter or hero.

Our work with the ITMC approach to understanding the psychology of fairness also draws much needed attention to the role of emotion in justice reasoning. Emotions have been surprisingly understudied in the justice literature. Of the studies that have investigated a relationship between justice and affect, most have examined affect as a consequence of an experience with injustice rather than as a cause of justice judgments (Mullen, 2007). However, there are many reasons to consider affect as a causal factor in justice reasoning and judgments. For example, there is some evidence that people's incidental affective states (i.e., their mood) can influence their fairness judgments (e.g., Van den Bos, 2003; Sinclair & Mark, 1991, 1992). In addition, research suggests that people's emotional reactions to events can occur relatively quickly and with little conscious cognitive processing (e.g., Lazarus, 1991). Thus, there may be times (perhaps particularly when moral convictions are at stake) when people's emotional reactions to events occur before their more carefully reasoned fairness judgments (Scher & Heise, 1993). If this is the case, then scholars need to consider how emotions that are elicited during the course of a justice-related encounter (i.e., integral emotional reactions) influence people's fairness reasoning and judgments.

People's emotions could influence not only their fairness judgments, but also the depth of information processing they engage in about fairness-related events (Mullen, 2007). For example, emotions associated with appraisals of certainty (e.g., anger) tend to be associated with more heuristic information processing, whereas emotions associated with appraisals of uncertainty (e.g., fear) tend to be associated with more systematic processing (Tiedens & Linton, 2001). The effects of emotion on depth of information processing may help to explain why people's judgments of fairness when their moral convictions are at stake are driven more by whether outcomes are consistent or inconsistent with their moral convictions than by procedural fairness. When feeling certain, people engage in more heuristic processing. Thus, when outcomes are consistent with moral convictions people judge both the procedures and outcome to be fair without carefully weighing the fairness of the procedures. In contrast, when people are feeling uncertain they engage in more systematic information processing that includes a consideration of whether procedures were fair or unfair and not just whether outcomes were favorable or unfavorable. Thus, people's emotions in response to morally relevant events have the potential to influence not just their fairness judgments, but also the process through which they arrive at their judgments. Future research should continue to explore these possibilities.

In addition, future research should focus on both positive and negative emotional reactions to morally relevant events. Research on positive emotions in general is sparse relative to the amount of research on negative emotions (Snyder & Lopez, 2002), and very little research has addressed the role of positive affect in moral contexts. We have demonstrated that feelings of anger and disgust in response to morally untenable outcomes predict perceptions of outcome and procedural fairness, decision acceptance, and reactions to authorities. However, we know little about the role that positive emotions such as gratitude and righteousness in response to outcomes that support moral convictions might play in people's perceptions of fairness, decision acceptance, and reactions to authorities.

CONCLUSION

Our current thinking about moral conviction has expanded considerably since our first publications and tests of the moral mandate hypothesis, beginning with Skitka and Houston (2001) and through our work on the value protection model in Skitka (2002) and Skitka and Mullen (2002). At that time, we focused most heavily on the notion that people's personal identities and need to defend their personal sense of moral authenticity were the primary explanatory mechanisms for why people's justice reasoning might be influenced by people's moral attachments to specific outcomes. Our subsequent work on the moral conviction and mandate construct more generally (e.g., Skitka et al., 2005), our discovery of the important role of affect and the apparently limited role of motivated reasoning in explaining the moral mandate effect (Mullen & Skitka, 2006a), as well as integrating predictions from a variety of interdisciplinary sources, has led us to a much more nuanced theoretical understanding of moral conviction and how and why it may matter to justice reasoning. As noted above, it is not our position that moral convictions or motivations drive *all* justice reasoning or justice-related behavior. We already know that a host of other concerns and motivations can influence how people think about fairness. Although future research exploring further implications of moral motivations and priorities on how people understand justice and fairness in social life will be both needed and important, in the grand scheme we feel that the real future of justice theory and research will be to develop more sophisticated and contingent theories that move beyond one-dimensional motivational accounts of why people care about, and therefore how they reason about, fairness.

NOTES

1. We refer to our theory as an "integrated theory" because the basic framework has been developed through an integration of various other theories of moral philosophy, development, cultural anthropology, and psychology.

2. Some may see a similarity between our conception of moral conviction and what Zelditch and Walker (1984) and Zelditch (2001) call a sense of propriety ("… a particular individual's personal belief that an act, norm, value, belief, practice or procedure is right," Zelditch, 2001, p. 6). It is not clear, however, whether propriety is a strong sense of normative convention or has the weight of moral imperative.

3. Future research is needed to examine whether making subsequent "moral" decisions can re-enhance authority legitimacy, or how many times authorities are subsequently required to "get it right" to regain perceived legitimacy after they violate perceivers' moral convictions. The converse question would also be of interest (whether making a moral decision more effectively buffers authorities from subsequent backlash from other unpopular or immoral decisions).

ACKNOWLEDGMENT

Preparation of this chapter was facilitated by grant support from the National Science Foundation (NSF-0518084, NSF-0530380).

REFERENCES

Adams, J. S. (1965). Inequity in social exchange. In: L. Berkowitz (Ed.), *Advances in experimental social psychology* (Vol. 2, pp. 267–299). New York: Academic Press.

Bandura, A. (1990). Selective activation and disengagement of moral control. *Journal of Social Issues*, *46*, 27–46.

Bauman, C. W. (2006). *Procedural and moral influences on fairness judgments and group rejection*. Unpublished doctoral dissertation, University of Illinois at Chicago.

Bauman, C. W. & Skitka, L. J. (2007a). *Moral conflict and procedural justice: Moral mandates as* constraints to *voice effects*. Manuscript under review.

Bauman, C. W. & Skitka, L. J. (2007b). Fair but wrong: Procedural and moral influences on fairness judgments and group rejection. Manuscript under review.

Blair, R. (1995). A cognitive developmental approach to morality: Investigating the psychopath. *Cognition*, *57*, 1–29.

Blair, R. (1997). Moral reasoning and the child with psychopathic tendencies. *Personality and Individual Differences*, *26*, 731–739.

Blau, P. (1964). *Exchange and power in social life*. New York: Wiley.

Brockner, J., & Wiesenfeld, B. M. (1996). An integrative framework for explaining reactions to decisions: The interactive effects of outcomes and procedures. *Psychological Bulletin*, *120*, 189–208.

Brosnan, S. F., & de Waal, F. B. M. (2003). Monkeys reject equal pay. *Nature*, *425*, 297–299.

Chowdhry, G., & Beeman, M. (2001). Challenging child labor: Transnational activism and India's carpet industry. *The Annals of the American Academy of Political and Social Science*, *575*, 158–175.

Cosmides, L., & Tooby, J. (2006). Evolutionary psychology, moral heuristics, and the law. In: G. Gigerenzer & C. Engel (Eds), *Heuristics and the law* (pp. 181–212). Cambridge, MA: MIT Press.

Damasio, A. (1994). *Descartes' error: Emotion, reason, and the human brain*. Cambridge, MA: Bradford/MIT Press.

De Waal, F. (1996). *Good natured: The origins of right and wrong in humans and other animals*. Cambridge, MA: Harvard University Press.

Dorkenoo, E. (1994). *Cutting the rose: Female genitalia mutilation: The practice and its prevention*. London: Minority Rights Publications.

Durkheim, E. (1925). *Moral education*. Glencoe, IL: The Free Press.

Epstein, S. (1990). Cognitive-experiential self-theory. In: L. Pervin (Ed.), *Handbook of personality theory and research* (pp. 165–192). New York: Guilford Press.

Fehr, E., & Fischbacher, U. (2004). Third-party punishment and social norms. *Evolution and Human Behavior*, *25*, 63–87.

Folger, R. (2001). Fairness as deonance. In: S. W. Gilliland, D. D. Steiner & D. P. Skarlicki (Eds), *Research in social issues in management* (Vol. 1, pp. 3–33). Greenwich, CT: Information Age Publishers.

Folger, R., & Cropanzano, R. (1998). *Organizational justice and human resource management*. Thousand Oaks, CA: Sage.

Gelpi, C. (2003). *The power of legitimacy: Assessing the role of norms in crisis bargaining*. Princeton, NJ: Princeton University Press.

Gibson, G. L., Caldeira, G. A., & Spence, L. K. (2005). Why do people accept public policies they oppose? Testing legitimacy theory with a survey-based experiment. *Political Research Quarterly*, *58*, 187–201.

Greene, J., & Haidt, J. (2002). How (and where) does moral judgment work? *Trends in Cognitive Sciences*, *6*, 517–523.

Haidt, J. (2001). The emotional dog and its rational tail: A social intuitionist approach to moral judgment. *Psychological Review*, *108*, 814–834.

Haidt, J. (2003a). Elevation and the positive psychology of morality. In: C. L. M. Keyes & J. Haidt (Eds), *Flourishing: Positive psychology and the life well-lived* (pp. 275–289). Washington, DC: American Psychological Association.

Haidt, J. (2003b). The moral emotions. In: R. J. Davidson, K. R. Scherer & H. H. Goldsmith (Eds), *Handbook of affective sciences* (pp. 852–870). New York: Oxford University Press.

Hegtvedt, K. A., Clay-Warner, J., & Johnson, C. (2003). The social context of responses to injustice: Considering the direct and indirect effects of group-level factors. *Social Justice Research*, *16*, 343–366.

Heuer, L., Stroessner, S., & Vale, L. W. (1998). The role of multiple motives for justice judgments: Extending the group value model. Paper presented at the annual meeting of the International Society for Justice Research, Denver, CO.

Homans, G. C. (1961). *Social behavior: Its elementary forms*. New York: Harcourt Brace.

Huo, Y. J., Smith, H. J., Tyler, T. R., & Lind, E. A. (1996). Superordinate identification, subgroup identification, and justice concerns: Is separatism the problem, is assimilation the answer. *Psychological Science*, *7*, 40–45.

Kelman, H. C., & Hamilton, V. L. (1989). *Crimes of obedience*. New Haven, CT: Yale University Press.

Kohlberg, L. (1984). *Essays on moral development: Vol. 2. The psychology of moral development*. New York: Harper.

Kroll, J., & Egan, E. (2004). Psychiatry, moral worry, and moral emotions. *Journal of Psychiatric Practice*, *10*, 352–360.

Kuhn, T. S. (1962). *The structure of scientific revolutions*. Chicago, IL: University of Chicago Press.

Lakatos, I. (1978). *The methodology of scientific research programmes: Philosophical papers volume 1*. Cambridge: Cambridge University Press.

Laupa, M. (1994). Who's in charge? Preschool children's concepts of authority. *Early Childhood Research Quarterly*, *9*, 1–17.

Lazarus, R. S. (1991). *Emotion and adaptation*. New York: Oxford University Press.

Lind, E. A., & Tyler, T. R. (1988). *The social psychology of procedural fairness*. New York: Plenum Press.

Lind, E. A., & Van den Bos, K. (2002). When fairness works: Toward a general theory of uncertainty management. In: B. M. Staw & R. M. Kramer (Eds), *Research in organizational behavior* (Vol. 24, pp. 181–224). Greenwich, CT: JAI Press.

Mullen, E. (2007). The reciprocal relationship between affect and perceptions of fairness. In: K. Tornblom & R. Vermunt (Eds), *Distributive and procedural justice: Research and social applications* (pp. 15–37). Burlington, VT: Ashgate.

Mullen, E., & Nadler, J. (2008). Moral spillovers: The effect of moral violations on deviant behavior. *Journal of Experimental Social Psychology*, doi:10.1016/j.jesp.2008.04.001.

Mullen, E., & Skitka, L. J. (2006a). Exploring the psychological underpinnings of the moral mandate effect: Motivated reasoning, identification, or affect? *Journal of Personality and Social Psychology*, *90*, 629–643.

Mullen, E., & Skitka, L. J. (2006b). When outcomes prompt criticism of procedures: An archival analysis of the Rodney King case. *Analyses of Social Issues and Public Policy*, *6*, 1–14.

Nadler, J. (2005). Flouting the law. *Texas Law Review*, *83*, 1440–1441.

Nichols, S. (2004). *Sentimental rules: On the natural foundations of moral judgment*. Oxford: Oxford University Press.

Nucci, L. (2001). *Education in the moral domain*. Cambridge: Cambridge University Press.

Nucci, L. P., & Turiel, E. (1978). Social interactions and the development of social concepts in pre-school children. *Child Development*, *49*, 400–407.

Perkins, S. A., & Turiel, E. (2007). To lie or not to lie: To whom and under what circumstances. *Child Development*, *78*, 609–621.

Piaget, J. (1932/1997). *The moral judgment of the child*. Glencoe, IL: The Free Press.

Rest, J. R., Narvaez, D., Bebeau, M. J., & Thoma, S. J. (1999). *Postconventional moral thinking. A neo-Kohlbergian approach*. Mahwah, NJ: Lawrence Erlbaum.

Scher, S. J., & Heise, D. R. (1993). Affect and the perception of injustice. *Advances in Group Processes*, *10*, 223–252.

Shweder, R. A. (2002). The nature of morality: The category of bad acts. *Medical Ethics*, *9*, 6–7.

Sinclair, R. C., & Mark, M. M. (1991). Mood and the endorsement of egalitarian macrojustice principles versus equity-based microjustice principles. *Personality and Social Psychology Bulletin*, *17*, 369–375.

Sinclair, R. C., & Mark, M. M. (1992). The influence of mood state on judgment and action: Effects on persuasion, categorization, social justice, person perception, and judgmental accuracy. In: L. L. Martin & A. Tesser (Eds), *The construction of social judgments*. Hillsdale, NJ: Lawrence Erlbaum.

Skitka, L. J. (2002). Do the means always justify the ends, or do the ends sometimes justify the means? A value protection model of justice reasoning. *Personality and Social Psychology Bulletin, 28*, 588–597.

Skitka, L. J. (2003). Of different minds: An accessible identity model of justice reasoning. *Personality and Social Psychology Review, 7*, 286–297.

Skitka, L. J. (2006). Legislating morality: How deep is the U.S. Supreme Court's reservoir of good will? Paper presented at the meeting of the International Society for Justice Research, Berlin, Germany.

Skitka, L. J., & Bauman, C. W. (2008). Moral conviction and political engagement. *Political Psychology, 29*, 29–54.

Skitka, L. J., Bauman, C. W., & Sargis, E. G. (2005). Moral conviction: Another contributor to attitude strength or something more? *Journal of Personality and Social Psychology, 88*, 895–917.

Skitka, L. J., & Houston, D. (2001). When due process is of no consequence: Moral mandates and presumed defendant guilt or innocence. *Social Justice Research, 14*, 305–326.

Skitka, L. J., & Mullen, E. (2002). Understanding judgments of fairness in a real-world political context: A test of the value protection model of justice reasoning. *Personality and Social Psychology Bulletin, 28*, 1419–1429.

Skoe, E. E., Eisenberg, N., & Cumberland, A. (2002). The role of reported emotion in real life and hypothetical moral dilemmas. *Personality and Social Psychology Bulletin, 28*, 962–973.

Smetana, J. (1993). Understanding of social rules. In: M. Bennett (Ed.), *The development of social cognition: The child as psychologist*. New York: Guilford Press.

Smetana, J. G. (1981). Preschool children's conceptions of moral and social rules. *Child Development, 52*, 1333–1336.

Smetana, J. G. (1985). Preschool children's conceptions of transgressions: Effects of varying moral and conventional domain-related attributes. *Developmental Psychology, 21*, 18–29.

Snyder, C. R., & Lopez, S. J. (2002). *Handbook of positive psychology*. New York: Oxford University Press.

Tangney, J. P., Stuewig, J., & Mashek, D. J. (2007). Moral emotions and moral behavior. *Annual Review of Psychology, 58*, 345–372.

Tetlock, P. E., Kristel, O. V., Elson, S. B., Green, M. C., & Lerner, J. S. (2000). The psychology of the unthinkable: Taboo trade-offs, forbidden base rates, and heretical counterfactuals. *Journal of Personality and Social Psychology, 78*, 853–870.

Thibaut, J., & Walker, L. (1975). *Procedural justice: A psychological analysis*. Mahway, NJ: Erlbaum.

Tiedens, L. Z., & Linton, S. (2001). Judgment under emotional certainty and uncertainty: The effects of specific emotions on information processing. *Journal of Personality and Social Psychology, 81*, 973–988.

Tisak, M. (1995). Domains of social reasoning and beyond. In: R. Vasta (Ed.), *Annals of child development* Vol. 11). London: Jessica Kingsley.

Turiel, E. (1983). *The development of social knowledge: Morality and convention*. New York: Cambridge University Press.

Turiel, E. (2002). *The culture of morality: Social development, context, and conflict*. Cambridge: Cambridge University Press.

Turillo, C. J., Folger, R., Lavelle, J. J., Umphress, E. E., & Gee, J. O. (2002). Is virtue its own reward? Self-sacrificial decisions for the sake of fairness. *Organizational Behavior and Human Decision Processes, 89*, 839–865.

Tyler, T. R. (1994). Psychological models of the justice motive. *Journal of Personality and Social Psychology*, *67*, 850–863.

Tyler, T. R. (2006). Psychological perspectives on legitimacy and legitimation. *Annual Review of Psychology*, *57*, 376–400.

Tyler, T. R., & Lind, E. A. (1992). A relational model of authority in groups. In: M. Zanna (Ed.), *Advances in experimental social psychology* (Vol. 4, pp. 595–629). Boston: McGraw-Hill.

Tyler, T. R., & Smith, H. (1997). Social justice and social movements. In: D. Gilbert, S. Fiske & G. Lindzey (Eds), *Handbook of social psychology* (pp. 595–629). New York: McGraw-Hill.

Van den Bos, K. (2003). On the subjective quality of social justice: The role of affect as information in the psychology of justice judgments. *Journal of Personality & Social Psychology*, *85*, 482–498.

Van den Bos, K., Lind, E. A., Vermunt, R., & Wilke, H. A. M. (1997). How do I judge my outcome when I do not know the outcome of others? The psychology of the fair process effect. *Journal of Personality and Social Psychology*, *72*, 1034–1046.

Walster, E., Walster, G. W., & Berscheid, E. (1978). *Equity: Theory and research*. Boston: Allyn and Bacon.

Zelditch, M. (2001). Processes of legitimation: Recent developments and new directions. *Social Psychology Quarterly*, *64*, 4–17.

Zelditch, M., & Walker, H. A. (1984). Legitimacy and the stability of authority. *Advances in Group Processes: Theory and Research*, *1*, 1–25.

EGOCENTRISM IN PROCEDURAL JUSTICE EFFECTS

Jan-Willem van Prooijen

ABSTRACT

In the current contribution I suggest that reactions to decision-making procedures often are influenced by egocentric concerns. Such egocentrism can be inferred from various theories that assume people's procedural justice judgments to be based on the implications of decision-making procedures for themselves instead of for others. The present review considers evidence for two propositions: (1) People respond more negatively to procedural injustice when it happens to themselves than when it happens to others, and (2) an egocentric self-focus amplifies people's fairness-based responses to decision-making procedures. It is concluded that egocentric motives play a central role in procedural justice effects.

Human perceptions, emotions, and behaviors are shaped substantially by social justice, that is, the extent to which people believe that social situations are fair or unfair. For instance, perceived social justice has an influence on a range of variables that people generally associate with the extent to which they consider life as worthwhile, such as positive and negative affect, self-esteem, well-being, and general life satisfaction (for overviews, see Folger & Cropanzano, 1998; Lind & Tyler, 1988; Tyler & Lind, 1992; Van den Bos &

Justice
Advances in Group Processes, Volume 25, 29–54

ISSN: 0882-6145/doi:10.1016/S0882-6145(08)25002-2

Lind, 2002). A very common distinction in conceptualizations of social justice is between distributive and procedural justice. Distributive justice refers to the extent to which people believe that the resources that are allocated to them (e.g., their salaries) are fair, either in absolute terms or in comparison to resources that are allocated to comparable others (Adams, 1965). Besides seeking fair outcomes, people also want the decision-making procedures that precede these outcomes to be fair. The perceived fairness of decision-making procedures is generally referred to as procedural justice (Thibaut & Walker, 1975; see also Brockner & Wiesenfeld, 1996; Cropanzano, Byrne, Bobocel, & Rupp, 2001; Lind & Tyler, 1988; Van den Bos & Lind, 2002). Although distributive and procedural justice judgments often are positively correlated, research indicates that people indeed make separate evaluations of the fairness of procedures and outcomes (Thibaut & Walker, 1975).

A central question in the psychology of people's justice judgments concerns the origins of people's quest for justice: Why are people influenced so strongly by whether or not they perceive social situations as fair? (e.g., Folger & Cropanzano, 1998; Tyler & Blader, 2003; Van den Bos & Lind, 2002). The current contribution is therefore focused on possible motivations that people have to evaluate social situations as fair or unfair. In particular, the present contribution seeks to illuminate the role of egocentric motives in people's justice judgments: To what extent do people have the tendency to base their justice judgments on self-serving concerns? Based on theoretical insights on egocentrism in people's perception of the social world, I propose that justice judgments are often shaped substantially by egocentric motives. In the following, I introduce this idea in more detail, and focus my line of argumentation specifically on egocentrism in procedural justice. I describe how egocentrism is implicitly assumed in various procedural justice theories and consider evidence for two core propositions that can be derived from the general theoretical notion that procedural justice judgments are shaped by egocentric concerns.

EGOCENTRISM AND PROCEDURAL JUSTICE

Research on distributive justice indicates that people often have an egocentric interpretation of what constitutes a fair outcome, particularly in the context of relatively complex resource allocation situations (Thompson & Loewenstein, 1992). In everyday life, the question of how to allocate scarce resources between litigants can often be rather complex.

To illustrate, whereas managers generally try to take subordinates' contributions to the organization into account during allocation decisions (as dictated by equity theory; Adams, 1965), it is often hard to make a meaningful comparison between various contributions given different job requirements. In complex allocation situations of this sort, people have the tendency to overestimate their own contributions and to downgrade their competitors' contributions. As a consequence, people have an egocentrically inflated perception of the resources that they believe themselves to deserve (Messick & Sentis, 1979). Such egocentric interpretations of distributive justice can have detrimental consequences in a variety of social situations. For instance, research indicates that egocentric interpretations of distributive justice can impede negotiation processes: When the negotiating parties differ fundamentally in their perceptions of what outcome would be fair, it is very hard to reach an agreement that is satisfactory to all parties involved (Babcock & Loewenstein, 1997; Thompson & Loewenstein, 1992).

Although the influence of egocentrism on distributive justice judgments is relatively well documented, not much research attention has been devoted to the possibility that procedural justice judgments are substantially shaped by egocentric motives. One possible reason why research has ignored this possibility is that instrumental motives (and, hence, material egoism concerns) have been found to influence procedural justice judgments only in a limited way (Lind, Kanfer, & Earley, 1990; Lind & Tyler, 1988; Tyler, 1989, 1994; Tyler & Blader, 2003; Tyler & Lind, 1992). In fact, it is often assumed that procedural justice judgments predominantly originate from prosocial motives, such as social norms, moral values, and principles that dictate equality and impartiality (e.g., Folger, 1998; Lerner, 2003). Several research findings might be taken as evidence to justify this assumption. For instance, fair procedures often have positive consequences for all parties involved in the decision-making process, as fair procedures often provide the best prospects to reach fair decisions (Thibaut & Walker, 1975). In addition, fair procedures promote social harmony and cohesion between group members, which is reflected in a positive influence of procedural justice on cooperation in social dilemmas (De Cremer & Tyler, 2005). These findings, however, do not automatically imply that procedural justice judgments are prosocially motivated. Although procedural justice undeniably has positive consequences for collective goals in many situations, procedural justice also has numerous beneficial consequences for individual recipients. As such, it is very well possible that people predominantly have the beneficial implications for themselves (instead of for others) in mind when evaluating how fair they believe the procedure is.

The general argument that egocentric motives influence procedural justice judgments has been raised previously (e.g., Hegtvedt, 1993, 2006; Thibaut & Walker, 1975). Building on a rational choice perspective, Hegtvedt (2006) noted that people's self-interested motivations to maximize their own outcomes might predict their desire for fair procedures. The reason for this is that fair procedures are likely to lead to positive outcomes, and these positive outcomes may either be tangible (e.g., money, services) or non-tangible (social rewards, such as status and respect) in nature (see also Cropanzano & Ambrose, 2001). This chapter seeks to extend this line of reasoning in two ways. First, this chapter advances a social-cognitive framework on human perception to determine the extent to which egocentrism shapes procedural justice judgments. It is argued that, besides stemming from rational choice considerations, people's egocentric motives often are produced automatically and influence justice reasoning outside of people's conscious awareness. Second, recent evidence is reviewed for two novel propositions that are distilled from the general idea that procedural justice judgments are shaped by egocentric motives.

The idea that fairness-based reactions to decision-making procedures substantially originate from egocentric motives was inspired by models of social-cognitive processes regarding human perception and perspective taking. According to these models, people automatically have an egocentric perception of the surrounding social world: People directly experience their own perspective, but they must make inferences to understand the perspective of someone else (e.g., Caruso, Epley, & Bazerman, 2006). As a consequence, people's own perception of the social world occurs automatically and effortlessly, but to see the world through the eyes of someone else, people need to be motivated and exert a cognitive effort. But even if people are willing to take the perspective of someone else, research suggests that people do so by serially adjusting from their own perspective (Epley, Keysar, Van Boven, & Gilovich, 2004). This line of reasoning suggests that human perception is fundamentally and inevitably egocentric in nature.

This egocentric nature of human perception has implications for people's fairness-based responses to decision-making procedures. These implications become apparent when illuminating the affective nature of procedural justice judgments. More generally, a characteristic feature of moral judgments is that people tend to base these judgments on intuitions rather than on rationalistic deliberations (Haidt, 2001). Likewise, although people often are capable of giving a rational argument why they believe procedures were fair or unfair, empirical findings suggest that procedural justice judgments are primarily based on people's intuitions (Van den Bos, 2003).

When responding to decision-making procedures, people intuitively feel good or bad about the situation, and this moral sentiment prompts them towards a judgment of procedural justice or injustice. Rationalistic arguments usually are psychological post hoc justifications that people make *after* forming procedural justice judgments (Haidt, 2001; Van den Bos, 2003). Thus, two premises are relevant for the current purposes: (1) human perception of the social world essentially is egocentric in nature, and (2) fairness-based responses to decision-making procedures are based on how good or bad one feels about the procedure. When these two premises are combined, it is plausible to reason that people's fairness-based responses to procedures are based upon their perceptions of these procedures as good or bad for themselves (see Epley & Caruso, 2004, for a comparable line of reasoning).

Such egocentrism can be observed in a variety of influential procedural justice theories. These theories are generally focused at explaining a range of typical procedural justice effects. An illustration of such a typical procedural justice effect can be found in the effects of voice: People evaluate procedures that allow them an opportunity to voice their opinions as fairer than procedures that deny them such an opportunity (Folger, 1977; cf. Brockner et al., 1998; Lind et al., 1990; Van den Bos, 2001; Van den Bos, Wilke, & Lind, 1998; Van Prooijen, Karremans, & Van Beest, 2006a). These procedural justice judgments subsequently influence a range of other responses that are frequently associated with fairness (i.e., fairness-based responses), such as positive and negative affect, relational treatment evaluations, protest intentions, and work performance (Tyler & Lind, 1992). Many theoretical perspectives have sought to explain these procedural justice effects, and a complete overview of these perspectives is beyond the purpose of this contribution (for a more complete overview, see Cropanzano et al., 2001). In the following, I therefore focus on the three categories of models that have been most influential in explaining procedural justice effects: the instrumental models, the relational models, and the social-cognitive models. I argue that, although these three classes of explanations are conceptually different, they share one common assumption: People evaluate procedures as fairer to the extent that the procedures have more positive implications for themselves. Furthermore, these positive implications for the self may follow from rational choice considerations (e.g., striving for beneficial outcomes), but also from more general self-regulatory needs that are less likely produced by rational contemplation (e.g., regulating feelings of uncertainty). After presenting these theoretical perspectives, I discuss recent empirical studies that tested more specific hypotheses regarding the role of egocentrism in procedural justice judgments.

Instrumental Models

The role of egocentrism can be most clearly observed in the classic instrumental models of procedural justice effects. These models assume a direct link between procedural justice effects and the anticipated outcomes of the decision-making process. In particular, these instrumental models are based on findings that people prefer procedures that grant them a certain amount of process control, that is, control over the way decisions are made (Thibaut & Walker, 1975). For instance, people usually want to be able to have a constructive dialogue with decision-makers. The typical instrumental explanation of procedural justice effects, then, is that a higher amount of process control offers better prospects for fair or favorable outcomes (Houlden, LaTour, Walker, & Thibaut, 1978). Fair procedures are thus functional because they may serve as a means to accomplish desirable outcomes.

Given that people have an egocentric interpretation of what outcome distributions are fair (Messick & Sentis, 1979), even strivings for fair (instead of favorable) outcomes are likely to lead people to evaluate procedures as fair to the extent that these procedures offer better prospects for self-favoring decisions. Research indeed reveals that the valence of outcomes is related to the perceived fairness of procedures (Thibaut & Walker, 1975; cf. Brockner & Wiesenfeld, 1996). It can thus be concluded that people evaluate procedures as fairer to the extent that these procedures are more likely to produce positive outcomes for the self (cf. Houlden et al., 1978; Thibaut & Walker, 1975).

Relational Models

Although strivings for fair or favorable outcomes are related to procedural justice judgments, it is widely recognized that instrumental explanations provide only limited explanations of procedural justice effects. The limited role of outcome expectancies is illuminated in an experiment by Lind et al. (1990). This experiment revealed that voice procedures positively influence perceived procedural and distributive justice even in situations where the procedures cannot possibly influence the outcomes. This illustrates that, besides instrumental motivations, people have non-instrumental motivations to evaluate procedures as fair or unfair. A very influential category of models to explain these non-instrumental aspects of procedural justice effects is formed by the relational models of procedural justice (Tyler & Lind, 1992; cf. Lind & Tyler, 1988; Tyler & Blader, 2003). A central tenet of these models is that people derive a significant part of their sense of self-worth from the groups to which they belong. In particular, people feel a strong need to be a valued and respected member of their social groups (Baumeister & Leary, 1995). A consequence of this need to belong is that people search for information about the extent to which they are valued and respected within their group. Because decision-makers often are regarded as representative for the group, people make inferences about the extent to which they are valued and respected group members from the way they are treated by group decision-makers. When a group decision-maker uses appropriate procedures to make decisions that have implications for the recipient (for instance, by giving voice opportunities), recipients feel that they are taken seriously and that they are considered as valuable and worthwhile members of the group. When a group decision-maker uses inappropriate procedure to make these kinds of decisions, however (for instance, by denying voice opportunities), the recipient does not feel taken seriously or considered as a valuable and worthwhile member of the group (e.g., De Cremer, 2002; Lind & Tyler, 1988; Tyler, 1989, 1994; Van Prooijen, Van den Bos, & Wilke, 2002, 2004, 2005).

This line of reasoning illuminates that relational models of justice focus on the connection that recipients have with their social environment to explain procedural justice effects. At first glance, the social focus of this approach might be interpreted as an indication that procedural justice effects can be explained by means of prosocial motivations. Closer inspection of the relational model's core propositions suggests, however, that this approach predominantly assumes egocentric motivations among recipients to evaluate procedures as fair or unfair. After all, this theoretical approach stipulates that people evaluate procedures as fairer to the extent that these procedures communicate that *they themselves* are respected and valued by others, because this has positive consequences for their *own* sense of self-worth (Lind, Kray, & Thompson, 1998; Lind & Tyler, 1988). It has been noted that people are concerned that fellow group members are also subjected to fair procedures, in order to have pride in one's group membership. But even such a concern for group pride has been assumed to ultimately be egocentric in nature, as group pride is functional to elevate one's *own* self-esteem (Clay-Warner, 2001; Tyler, Degoey, & Smith, 1996).

Whereas instrumental explanations take a desire for material benefits as point of departure to explain procedural justice effects, relational explanations focus on a desire for social benefits such as belongingness or status. As such, it has been noted that instrumental and relational models of procedural justice are more similar than many scholars initially believe (Cropanzano & Ambrose, 2001; Hegtvedt, 1993, 2006).

Social-Cognitive Models

Whereas instrumental and relational models seek to delineate the motivational processes that lead to procedural justice effects by focusing on the hedonic implications of procedures (Van Prooijen, Karremans, & Van Beest, 2006a), social-cognitive models seek to explain the cognitive processes of how people form procedural fairness judgments. In these models, a central role is assigned to regulation of human uncertainty (Van den Bos & Lind, 2002). In many everyday life situations that involve questions about justice, people are confronted with uncertainty. For instance, in corporate life, downsizing or mergers are very common phenomena that may create uncertainty regarding one's career opportunities within an organization. In addition, people often do not know how satisfied their superiors are with their performance, or whether decision-makers are trustworthy individuals. According to social-cognitive justice models, procedural justice is functional in uncertain situations of this sort because fair procedures help people to regulate uncertain feelings by providing structure and meaning to the situation. As such, fair procedures are assumed to calm people down in an uncertain social environment. This process of uncertainty regulation provides the basis for the main hypothesis of the 'uncertainty management model' (Van den Bos & Lind, 2002): People are particularly in need of procedural justice in situations that they experience as uncertain, and as a consequence, they display stronger procedural justice effects in uncertain as opposed to certain situations.

Accumulating evidence supports this hypothesis. For instance, research indicates that in situations where people lack social comparison information and are thus uncertain about the fairness of their own outcomes, perceived procedural justice exerts a stronger influence on distributive justice judgments as compared to situations where people are certain about the fairness of their own outcomes (Van den Bos, Lind, Vermunt, & Wilke, 1997). Likewise, procedural justice effects have been found to be stronger when recipients are uncertain whether decision-makers are trustworthy as opposed to when recipients know that the decision-maker can or cannot be trusted (Van den Bos et al., 1998). These findings were extended in more recent studies that reveal that making uncertainty salient is sufficient to amplify procedural justice effects when compared with a control condition (Van den Bos, 2001). Also, procedural justice effects are stronger among people who are uncertain about themselves than among people who are not uncertain about themselves (De Cremer & Sedikides, 2005). Taken together, these studies suggest a consistent and predictable relation between human uncertainty and procedural justice effects.

To summarize, fair procedures help people deal with the uncertainties that they must face in their life, because these procedures provide structure and meaning to social situations. Even though this process is more likely to operate outside of people's conscious awareness than strivings for positive instrumental or relational goals, it is striking that, also according to the social-cognitive models, people are responsive to the fairness of decision-making procedures because of the psychological benefits that these procedures have for themselves. In particular, these models focus on the *self*-regulatory functions of procedural justice, thereby assuming a certain degree of self-orientation in the justice judgment process. As is the case in instrumental and relational models, the social-cognitive models emphasize the consequences of decision-making procedures for the recipients self, and not for others, to explain procedural justice effects.

EMPIRICAL EVIDENCE

In the following, I discuss empirical evidence for two core propositions that I derive from the assertion that egocentric motivations have a substantial impact on procedural justice effects. The first proposition to be discussed here focuses on recipients' responses to *un*fair procedures. Such a focus is of importance, given that several authors noted that the negative effects of unfair procedures are stronger than the positive effects of fair procedures (Folger, 1984; Van den Bos & Van Prooijen, 2001; Van Prooijen, Van den Bos, Lind, & Wilke, 2006b; cf. Baumeister, Bratlavsky, Finkenauer, & Vohs, 2001). Building on the line of reasoning that people respond negatively to unfair procedures out of egocentric concerns, it can be predicted that people respond more negatively to the procedural injustices that target themselves than to the procedural injustices that are targeted towards others (Proposition 1). The second core proposition of the present contribution pertains to the direct influence of an egocentric self-focus on procedural justice effects. Based on the general idea that egocentric concerns substantially shape procedural justice effects, it can be predicted that procedural justice effects are stronger to the extent that people are more egocentrically self-focused. In other words, the second proposition is that an egocentric self-focus amplifies procedural justice effects (Proposition 2). In the following, both propositions are discussed in more detail.

Proposition 1: Self-Other Asymmetry in Responses to Procedural Injustice

The notion that procedural justice effects may be associated substantially with egocentric concerns is based on the insight that people automatically take their own (and not someone else's) perspective as point of departure when evaluating social situations (Epley et al., 2004). It can therefore be reasoned that fairness-based reasoning is more pronounced when situations are relevant to the self than when they are irrelevant to the self. For instance, the direct experience of being the target of injustice may lead people to more strongly make inferences about unfairness rather than observing someone else being the target of injustice. In a recent study by Ham and Van den Bos (2008), results indeed supported the idea that self-involvement in social situations increases spontaneous associations with fairness and unfairness. In an experiment, participants read descriptions of fair or unfair events either in the first person singular (e.g., "You and your colleague do the same work. You make 1400 Euros a month and your colleague makes 4100 Euros a month") or in the third person singular (e.g., "He and his colleague do the same work. He makes 1400 Euros a month and his colleague makes 4100 Euros a month"). The main dependent variable was a reaction time measure designed to indicate automatic and implicit justice activation among participants. The results revealed that the automatic and implicit activation of the justice construct was stronger following self-related descriptions than following other-related descriptions. As such, fairness-based reasoning indeed seems to be automatically facilitated when events are self-relevant as opposed to self-irrelevant.

A plausible consequence of such differential automatic processing of fairness-related information is that people's responses to directly experienced procedural injustice is more pronounced than their responses to similar or worse procedural injustices that one observes happening to others. Preliminary evidence for such a self-other asymmetry in responses to injustice was obtained by Lind et al. (1998), who tested the idea that people might evaluate a minor procedural injustice that happens to the self as worse than a major procedural injustice that one sees happening to someone else. In a business simulation experiment, groups of three participants received a voice or a no-voice procedure following various tasks on three separate occasions. In the *concentrated injustice condition*, it was consistently the same participant who received a no-voice procedure after each task, whereas the other two participants consistently received a voice procedure after each task. Thus, one participant received a no-voice procedure on all three occasions and the other two participants received a voice procedure on all three occasions. In the *distributed injustice condition*, it was after each task a different participant who received a no-voice procedure, whereas the remaining two participants received a voice procedure. Thus, in the end every participant received one no-voice procedure and two voice procedures. Results revealed that, both before and after a group discussion, procedurally privileged participants in the concentrated injustice condition evaluated the supervisor's behavior as fairer than participants in the distributed injustice condition. Indeed, after the group discussion the mean collective ratings were more positive in the concentrated injustice condition than in the distributed injustice condition. These results suggest that the personal experience of a relatively mild procedural injustice (as was the case in the distributed injustice condition) is considered as less fair than a major procedural injustice that one observes happening to someone else (as was the case in the concentrated injustice condition). The Lind et al. (1998) study hence provides preliminary empirical evidence for the assertion that there is a self-other asymmetry in people's evaluations of injustices that happen to self versus others.

An additional implication of the idea that people respond egocentrically to fairness-based information relating to self versus others pertains to people's perception of unfair procedural disadvantages. Based on the idea that negative social information prompts inferences of unfairness more strongly when it is targeted to the self as opposed to others, it might be reasoned that a biased decision-maker elicits judgments of unfairness more easily when the bias puts the self rather than someone else at a disadvantage. As such, the proposed self-other asymmetry in procedural justice may lead people to interpret favorable or unfavorable procedural biases in self-serving ways. This idea was investigated in an experiment by Van Prooijen et al. (2006b, Exp. 2), in which participants found out that the experimenter had either a positive or a negative attitude towards them. Furthermore, participants found out that the experimenter had either a positive or a negative attitude towards another participant (for specific operationalizations, see Van Prooijen et al., 2006b). As such, there were two conditions where the experimenter was consistent between persons: positively consistent (i.e., the experimenter had a positive attitude towards both the participant and the other) and negatively consistent (i.e., the experimenter had a negative attitude towards both the participant and the other). In addition, there were two conditions where the experimenter was inconsistent, and thus biased in favor of one of the recipients: positively inconsistent (i.e., the experimenter had a positive attitude towards the participant but a negative attitude towards the other) and negatively consistent (i.e., the experimenter had a negative attitude towards the participant but a positive attitude towards the other).

Results revealed that the experimenter's consistency between persons did not influence procedural justice judgments following a voice procedure, but it did following a no-voice procedure. In particular, being denied an opportunity to voice an opinion was considered as more unfair in the negatively inconsistent condition as compared with the two consistent conditions and the positively inconsistent condition. These results suggest that information that an authority is negatively inconsistent creates an interpretational framework for subsequent no-voice procedures: When people have reason to suspect that the authority is biased in an unfavorable way, people more easily interpret subsequent negative behaviors of that authority (i.e., denying voice opportunities) as unfair. For the present purposes, it is also noteworthy that the two consistent conditions did not differ from the positively inconsistent condition. Thus, only negative inconsistency, and not positive inconsistency, produces more extreme judgments of procedural injustice. As such, when an authority is biased by affectively favoring one out of two recipients, people associate this bias with procedural injustice only when the bias is unfavorable to them, and not when the bias happens to work in their favor. This study further corroborates the proposition that there is an asymmetry in judgments of procedural injustice when it concerns the self as opposed to when it concerns others, in ways that are consistent with the idea that egocentric motivations are of importance in procedural justice judgments.

Proposition 2: Egocentric Self-Focus Amplifies Procedural Justice Effects

One of the core assumptions of the idea that procedural justice effects are egocentrically motivated entails that people initially focus on their own concerns when evaluating the fairness of decision-making procedures. This assumption implies that the extent to which people are egocentrically focused on themselves is predictive of their fairness-based responses to decision-making procedures. In particular, it can be hypothesized that the more people are focused on themselves, the more sensitive their fairness-based judgments are to variations in decision-making procedures. This hypothesis constitutes the second proposition of the present contribution. It must be noted, though, that both situational and individual difference factors may lead people to focus on themselves. In the following, I review findings that are informative about the second proposition by investigating both situational and individual factors that lead to differences in self-focus.

Situational Factors

A very powerful way to manipulate the extent that people are focused on themselves is to make the self salient. The implications of such self-salience for procedural justice effects were first demonstrated by Miedema (2003). In various experiments, self-salience was manipulated by asking participants to write down their thoughts when they were thinking of themselves. In the control conditions, participants were asked to write down their thoughts when they were thinking of a subject that was not self-relevant (i.e., watching TV). Following a procedural justice manipulation (i.e., voice versus no-voice procedures), Miedema measured participants' negative emotions by asking questions pertaining to how angry they felt about the way they were treated by the experimenter. Results indicated that procedural justice exerted a stronger effect on negative emotions when the self was salient than when the self was not salient. These results provided preliminary support for the idea that procedural justice has a stronger impact on people to the extent that they are more strongly focused on themselves.

Although promising, a drawback of the Miedema findings is that the self was operationalized in a very broad way, ignoring various levels of self-definition. People can think of themselves at various levels, and a common distinction in level of self-definition is between the individual and the social self (Gaertner, Sedikides, Vevea, & Iuzzini, 2002). The individual self is the part of the self-concept that focuses on differentiation of the self, emphasizing characteristics that make the self unique compared to others. The social self is the part of the self-concept that focuses on integration of the self, emphasizing characteristics that make the self similar to others. These various levels of self-definition can be made more or less accessible by means of contextual influences. Based on the second proposition of the present contribution, it can be predicted that procedural justice effects are particularly strong when the individual self is accessible. After all, the individual self is egocentrically focused on one's own unique self, whereas the social self emphasizes similarity and connectedness with others.

In an experiment by Van Prooijen and Zwenk (2007, Exp. 3) these various levels of self-definition were activated by means of a priming procedure that was validated in previous research (Brewer & Gardner, 1996). All participants read a brief description of a trip to the city. In the individual self-condition, this description was written in the first person singular (i.e., "I love this city. To me, this city is a place to enjoy ..."). In the social self-condition, the description was written in the first person plural (i.e., "We love this city. To us, this city is a place to enjoy ..."). Participants' task was to count all the personal pronouns in the text. In addition, there was a control condition in which all personal pronouns were replaced by a string of letters (ABC, XYZ) or by the word "it." In this condition, participants' task was to count the occurrence of this string of letters and the word "it" in the text. Results indicated that a manipulation of voice versus no-voice procedures exerted stronger effects on participants' evaluations of how respectful and polite they were treated when the individual self was activated than when the social self was activated. These results, which are in correspondence with the second proposition of this chapter, were replicated in two comparable experiments (for details, see Van Prooijen & Zwenk, 2007).

Taken together, the evidence suggests that individual self-activation has a causal influence on procedural justice effects. Interestingly, recent research also found evidence for the reversed causal order: Being confronted with procedural justice or injustice activates the individual self (Loseman, Van den Bos, & Ham, 2005). This reversed causal order is perfectly in line with the central tenets of the current contribution, as it is assumed that people associate procedural justice or injustice with concerns that relate to the individual self. Loseman et al. (2005) tested this causal order by first confronting participants with hypothetical scenarios where they were granted or denied voice in a decision-making process in order to prime them with procedural justice and injustice. There also was a neutral control condition where no procedural justice information was made salient. After this, participants responded to a measure that was designed to measure self-construal level activation, that is, the extent to which either the individual or social self is activated (Dijksterhuis & Van Knippenberg, 2000). Results indicated that the individual self was more strongly activated following both procedural justice and injustice primes as compared to the control condition. These findings further corroborate an empirical association between the individual self and procedural justice.

The previously discussed studies all suggest that manipulating situational factors can elicit psychological processes that correspond to the proposition that procedural justice effects are associated with the extent to which people are focused on themselves. Yet, it must be noted that these findings can be alternatively interpreted following objective self-awareness theory (Duval & Wicklund, 1972). One of the tenets of this theory is that self-focused attention increases people's desire to act in correspondence with their internalized standards. Evidence suggests that this process generalizes to people's moral standards (for an overview, see Silvia & Duval, 2001). As such, it may be the case that self-salience or activation of the individual self increases people's concern for morality towards both self and others. However, empirical evidence suggests that increased self-awareness only increases prosocial behavior towards others when a clear moral norm to act altruistically is made salient. When no such a norm is salient, people have been found to predominantly benefit themselves following self-awareness in a moral dilemma (Batson, Thompson, Seuferling, Whitney, & Strongman, 1999). Nevertheless, to strengthen faith in the processes that are assumed in Proposition 2 of the present contribution, it is important to fully exclude this alternative explanation by means of research that investigated individual differences in people's structural inclinations to reason egocentrically, instead of increasing situational self-awareness.

Individual Differences

Of the most frequently studied individual difference variables, social value orientation that has been found to be predictive of egocentric behavioral tendencies in various social situations (Messick & McClintock, 1968; Van Lange, Otten, De Bruin, & Joireman, 1997). Social value orientation is a personality variable that distinguishes between three categories: prosocial, individualistic, and competitive orientations. Prosocials are defined in terms of enhancing collective outcomes and equality in outcomes between themselves and others; individualists are defined in terms of enhancing outcomes for self with no or very little regard for other's outcomes; and competitors are defined in terms of enhancing relative advantage over others (Van Lange, 1999). These individualistic and competitive orientations are often combined into a single category of proself orientation, because both seek to enhance own outcomes, either in an absolute sense (individualists) or in a relative or comparative sense (competitors) (e.g., De Cremer & Van Lange, 2001; Parks, 1994; Smeesters, Warlop, Van Avermaet, Corneille, & Yzerbyt, 2003).

Based on the second proposition of the current contribution, it stands to reason that particularly proselfs (and not prosocials) display strong procedural justice effects. To test this hypothesis, social value orientations were measured among participants in a series of experiments (Van Prooijen et al., in press). After this measurement, participants were told that they would participate in an allegedly unrelated study, in which participants were granted or denied an opportunity to voice their opinion about a resource division decision by the experimenter (cf. Miedema, 2003; Van Prooijen & Zwenk, 2007). The main dependent measures consisted of participants' procedural justice judgments. Results revealed that voice versus no-voice procedures had a strong influence on procedural justice judgments, but only for proselfs, and not for prosocials. Similar effects were found on a variety of other fairness-based responses, including positive and negative affect, relational treatment evaluations, and intentions to accept the experimenter's decisions. Given that proselfs are structurally more inclined to reason egocentrically than prosocials, these results provide further evidence for the proposition that people are more responsive to variations in procedural justice to the extent that they are more egocentrically focused on themselves.

A limitation of the empirical findings presented thus far is that they were restricted to the psychological laboratory and to the specific population of university students. Although laboratory experiments are very well-suited to investigate the causal influence of the theoretical constructs on dependent variables while assuring high internal validity, one may question whether the processes observed in the laboratory generalize to situations outside of the laboratory and to different populations. To get an indication of the generalizability of the effects of social value orientation on procedural justice effects, Van Prooijen et al. (in press; Study 4) investigated these effects in an applied situation. In a questionnaire among a random sample of the Dutch working population, both social value orientation and perceived procedural justice were assessed. The main dependent variables were participants' organizational citizenship behaviors (OCBs; Moorman & Blakely, 1995), that is, behaviors that are rarely described in employees' formal job requirements but that are essential to healthy organizational functioning. Results revealed that there was no significant relation between procedural justice and OCB among prosocials. Among proselfs, however, this relation was significant: proselfs were more inclined to display OCBs to the extent that they perceived organizational procedures as fairer. These findings supported the egocentric justice hypothesis in an applied setting.

Traditionally, research on social value orientations focused on differences between prosocials and proselfs when faced with situations that involve questions about distributive justice, that is, situations in which behavior directly shaped tangible outcomes – such as money, points, or services – for the self and others (e.g., McClintock & Liebrand, 1988; Van Lange, 1999). As such, one may wonder whether the observed relation between procedural justice and social value orientation occurs for instrumental reasons only. After all, it might be possible that proselfs are more responsive to variations in procedural justice because fair procedures offers better prospects for favorable outcomes (cf. Thibaut & Walker, 1975). This assumption is not supported by the data, however. In the applied study by Van Prooijen et al. (in press), results revealed that the interaction between procedural justice and social value orientation on OCBs still materialized after controlling for distributive justice judgments. This suggests that proselfs display stronger procedural justice effects for reasons that go beyond instrumental concerns only. Hence, it is plausible to speculate that proselfs and prosocials differ on more dimensions than materialistic self-focus. In particular, the described findings may suggest that proselfs (versus prosocials) find it more important that they are acknowledged and respected in procedures, which suggests potential differences between prosocial and proselfs in a variety of self-relevant motives such as the need for recognition, the desire to be respected, and the need to belong.

To conclude, there is solid empirical evidence for the proposition that variations in decision-making procedures exert stronger effects on people to the extent that they are more focused on themselves. Both situationally induced self-focus as well as structural egocentric behavioral tendencies amplify procedural justice effects, which is consistent with the general theoretical idea that people's fairness-based responses to decision-making procedures originate from egocentric concerns.

DISCUSSION

Both propositions that illuminate the role of egocentrism in procedural justice effects were supported in the current review. Empirical evidence indicates that people indeed respond more negatively to procedural injustice that is targeted at themselves than at others, suggesting a self-other asymmetry in procedural justice reasoning (Ham & Van den Bos, 2008; Lind et al., 1998; Van Prooijen et al., 2006b). Also, the evidence discussed reveals that an egocentric self-focus amplifies procedural justice effects when compared to relatively more other-focused situations or persons (Loseman et al., 2005; Miedema, 2003; Van Prooijen et al., in press; Van Prooijen & Zwenk, 2007). These findings are in correspondence with a common assumption of three classes of explanations for procedural justice effects, given that these explanations all assume that people's fairness-based reactions to decision-making procedures occur because of self-focused motivations. It can thus be concluded that egocentric motives are of central importance to understanding people's fairness-based reactions to decision-making procedures.

Although early instrumental explanations associated procedural justice effects to some extent with instrumental egoism (Thibaut & Walker, 1975), the present contribution extends these insights by proposing that also non-instrumental concerns that commonly are associated with procedural justice essentially are egocentric in nature. A very direct empirical indication for this assertion can be observed in the finding that the interactive effect between social value orientation and procedural justice was found even after controlling for instrumental motives (Van Prooijen et al., in press). But also other indications suggest that reflections of egocentrism in procedural justice effects are not attributable to material egoism only. Both in the Miedema (2003) and the Van Prooijen and Zwenk (2007) studies it was tested whether egocentric self-focus influenced the opinions that participants in the voice conditions expressed. Participants in the self-focused conditions did not believe themselves to be entitled to more resources than participants in the control conditions, suggesting that self-focus does not exert a substantial influence on participants' instrumental motivations. Furthermore, research by Tyler (1989, 1994) consistently reveals that instrumental motives are responsible for only a small portion of the variance in procedural justice effects. These arguments suggest that it is not plausible that material egoism is the only reflection of egocentrism in procedural justice effects.

Although the processes described in the present contribution consistently were framed in terms of people's egocentric "motivations," it is noteworthy that people do not necessarily need to be consciously aware of their motivations when determining fairness judgments. It is very well possible that people often do not realize that they are reasoning egocentrically when dealing with moral issues. For instance, it has been noted that people may engage in self-deception by honestly believing that their moral reasoning objectively considers the interests of all parties involved, but in reality their moral reasoning is biased towards egocentrism (Batson et al., 1999). Also, the previously discussed Ham and Van den Bos (2008) study suggested a certain degree of automaticity in egocentric fairness inferences by showing differences in justice activation following self-related versus other-related descriptions. It is particularly noteworthy that, in the Ham and Van den Bos study, the self-related descriptions only increased *implicit* justice activation, and that *explicit*, controlled judgments of justice or injustice were unaffected by the perspective manipulation. These results further suggest that egocentric biases in responses to moral questions initially start at the automatic and implicit level. More generally, these ideas fit into a broader theoretical framework of egocentric perceptual processes, underscoring that people's tendency to perceive the surrounding social world in an egocentric fashion is likely to be an automatic rather than a deliberative process (Epley et al., 2004).

Limitations

The distinction between self-related versus other-related descriptions (Ham & Van den Bos, 2008) points at a possible limitation in the role of egocentrism in procedural justice effects: It may be that the extent to which procedural justice judgments are egocentrically biased depends on the evaluator's perspective. The present contribution was focused on situations in which the evaluator is the direct recipient of the decision-making procedure, and the decision to be taken is of direct concern for the evaluator. This recipient perspective is most commonly studied in the psychology of procedural justice (for overviews, see Brockner & Wiesenfeld, 1996; Cropanzano et al., 2001; Folger & Cropanzano, 1998; Lind & Tyler, 1988; Tyler & Blader, 2003; Tyler & Lind, 1992; Van den Bos & Lind, 2002). In many everyday life situations, however, people are observers instead of recipients, and perceive how other people receive fair or unfair procedures. In organizational justice literature, such an observer perspective has been studied in the context of employees who respond to the layoff of their colleagues following organizational downsizing. It has been noted that, even from such an observer perspective, decision-making procedures influence a variety of important variables like identification and work motivation (e.g., Brockner, DeWitt, Grover, & Reed, 1990). It might be speculated that the influence of egocentric concerns in the justice judgments process are weaker from an observer perspective than from a recipient perspective (cf. Ham & Van den Bos, 2008). After all, from an observer perspective people have less direct personal concern in the decision-making process, decreasing the potential for egocentric biases.

As an additional limitation, the studies reviewed here all pertained to procedures that preceded decisions that had direct personal consequences for the individual recipients (individual-level decision). However, as Leung,

Tong, and Lind (2007) recently pointed out, procedural justice concerns also can be associated with collective or group-level decisions, as for instance is the case in political decision-making where the decisions that are made have consequences for a whole nation. The results from their study indicate that typical procedural justice phenomena play out differently in collective situations. For instance, contrary to typical findings in individual-level decisions, the Leung et al. (2007) results indicate that in the case of collective decisions, outcome favorability explains more variance than procedural justice in the extent to which people accept decisions. Although the specific findings of the Leung et al. (2007) study are not directly related to the question of how egocentrically biased justice judgments are, it is plausible to reason that the influence of egocentrism on justice judgments might decrease in situations that are not specifically focused on the individual. These considerations further suggest that one should be reluctant to conclude that egocentrism is the only possible motivation of people when responding to decision-making procedures. What can be concluded, however, is that egocentrism has a considerable impact on procedural justice effects among the direct individual recipients of decision-making processes pertaining to individual-level decisions.

Competing Theoretical Perspectives

In the present contribution, I sought to make the case that in many situations egocentrism is inherently connected to people's justice evaluations. This insight runs counter to previous theoretical arguments that people's desire for justice is unrelated to human egocentrism. For instance, Lerner (2003) contrasted people's desire for justice with rational self-interest and concluded that the justice motive is fully distinct from self-serving concerns. Such a conclusion is missing the point in at least two ways. First, self-interest is not necessarily "rational," as people often are unaware that their justice-based reasoning is biased towards benefiting the self (Batson et al., 1999; Ham & Van den Bos, 2008). As such, people may often honestly believe themselves to reason or act fairly, yet in reality their thoughts and behaviors can be egocentrically biased. Such implicit egocentrism in fairness-based reasoning may for instance explain why people respond negatively to overpayment in simple allocation decisions (Adams, 1965), yet display egocentrism in relatively more complex allocations, where various inputs are hard to compare (Messick & Sentis, 1979; Thompson & Loewenstein, 1992). Second, the conclusion that justice motivation is distinct from self-serving concerns ignores the fundamental subjectivity of justice judgments. Fairness is in the eye of the beholder, and hence, what people believe to be fair may very well partially depend on what people *want* to believe to be fair. Such motivated reasoning can serve a variety of goals, and it is highly plausible that these goals sometimes can be egocentric in nature.

To further illuminate this position, consider for instance the question of why people often assume that people generally get what they deserve in life (i.e., the "belief in a just world"), leading them to derogate innocent victims. According to Lerner (2003) this is a clear manifestation of the justice motive, independent from self-serving concerns. Yet, the dominant and widely accepted explanation of phenomena such as victim blaming is that upholding the belief in a just world validates people's confidence that it is useful for them to strive for long-term goals in life (Lerner, 1980). As noted by Hafer and Bègue (2005), if people would not believe in a just world there would be "little point in investing time, energy, and other resources in the hopes of obtaining the rewards one believes one deserves" (p. 130). Thus, one of the main reasons why people try to uphold the belief in a just world is to psychologically ensure themselves that their well-intended efforts in life ultimately will be rewarded. Such a concern to ensure personal rewards for one's own investments undeniably is a self-focused motivation, suggesting that just world beliefs, and related phenomena such as victim blaming, at least in part originate from egocentric concerns.

Concluding Remarks

Fair procedures often have positive consequences for many parties involved in a dispute. It has therefore been suggested that procedural justice effects are predominantly attributable to "prosocial" motives such as social norms, moral values, and general moral principles that dictate equality and impartiality. It would be premature, and probably incorrect, to fully exclude these prosocial motives as contributing factors to procedural justice effects. Nevertheless, it might be speculated that truly "objective" fairness judgments are possible only in situations where people are independent evaluators, who evaluate the situation from "behind the veil of ignorance" (Rawls, 1971). When people do have some personal concern in a complex moral dilemma, their fairness-based reasoning is likely to be influenced by egocentrism, sometimes without being very much aware of it. This chapter sought to illuminate that procedural justice phenomena indeed are shaped substantially by egocentric motives, such as instrumental motives (e.g., endorsing fair procedures to ensure satisfactory outcomes for the self), social needs that can only be provided by others (e.g., respect, admiration, belongingness), and a need for structure in an uncertain world. These considerations may suggest that, although people often publicly emphasize violations of general moral principles in response to unfair procedures, privately their responses may be substantially motivated by self-oriented motives, such as a desire to be respected and appreciated in procedures. It can thus be concluded that egocentrism is of importance to understand why decision-making procedures have such a strong impact on a wide variety of human perceptions, emotions, and behaviors.

REFERENCES

Adams, J. S. (1965). Inequity in social exchange. In: L. Berkowitz (Ed.), *Advances in experimental social psychology* (Vol. 2, pp. 267–299). New York: Academic Press.

Babcock, L., & Loewenstein, G. (1997). Explaining bargaining impasse: The role of self-serving biases. *Journal of Economic Perspectives*, *11*, 109–126.

Batson, C. D., Thompson, E. R., Seuferling, G., Whitney, H., & Strongman, J. A. (1999). Moral hypocrisy: Appearing moral to oneself without being so. *Journal of Personality and Social Psychology*, *77*, 525–537.

Baumeister, R. F., Bratlavsky, E., Finkenauer, C., & Vohs, K. D. (2001). Bad is stronger than good. *Review of General Psychology*, *5*, 323–370.

Baumeister, R. F., & Leary, M. R. (1995). The need to belong: Desire for interpersonal attachments as a fundamental human motive. *Psychological Bulletin*, *117*, 497–529.

Brewer, M. B., & Gardner, W. (1996). Who is this "we"? Levels of collective identity and self representations. *Journal of Personality and Social Psychology*, *71*, 83–93.

Brockner, J., DeWitt, R. L., Grover, S., & Reed, T. (1990). When it is especially important to explain why: Factors affecting the relationship between managers' explanation of a layoff and survivors' reactions to the layoff. *Journal of Experimental Social Psychology*, *26*, 389–407.

Brockner, J., Heuer, L., Siegel, P. A., Wiesenfeld, B., Martin, C., Grover, S., Reed, T., & Bjorgvinsson, S. (1998). The moderating effect of self-esteem in reaction to voice: Converging evidence from five studies. *Journal of Personality and Social Psychology*, *75*, 394–407.

Brockner, J., & Wiesenfeld, B. M. (1996). An integrative framework for explaining reactions to decisions: Interactive effects of outcomes and procedures. *Psychological Bulletin*, *120*, 189–208.

Caruso, E. M., Epley, N., & Bazerman, M. H. (2006). The costs and benefits of undoing egocentric responsibility assessments in groups. *Journal of Personality and Social Psychology*, *91*, 857–871.

Clay-Warner, J. (2001). Perceiving procedural injustice: The effects of group membership and status. *Social Psychology Quarterly*, *64*, 224–238.

Cropanzano, R., & Ambrose, M. L. (2001). Procedural and distributive justice are more similar than you think: A monistic perspective and research agenda. In: J. Greenberg & R. Cropanzano (Eds), *Advances in organizational justice* (pp. 119–151). Stanford, CA: Stanford University Press.

Cropanzano, R., Byrne, Z. S., Bobocel, D. R., & Rupp, D. E. (2001). Moral virtues, fairness heuristics, social entities, and other denizens of organizational justice. *Journal of Vocational Behavior*, *58*, 164–209.

De Cremer, D. (2002). Respect and cooperation in social dilemmas: The importance of feeling included. *Personality and Social Psychology Bulletin*, *28*, 1335–1341.

De Cremer, D., & Sedikides, C. (2005). Self-uncertainty and responsiveness to procedural justice. *Journal of Experimental Social Psychology*, *41*, 157–173.

De Cremer, D., & Tyler, T. R. (2005). Managing group behavior: The interplay between fairness, self, and cooperation. In: M. Zanna (Ed.), *Advances in experimental social psychology* (pp. 151–218). New York: Academic Press.

De Cremer, D., & Van Lange, P. A. M. (2001). Why prosocials exhibit greater cooperation than proselfs: The roles of social responsibility and reciprocity. *European Journal of Personality*, *15*, S5–S18.

Dijksterhuis, A., & Van Knippenberg, A. (2000). Behavioral indecision: Effects of self-focus on automatic behavior. *Social Cognition*, *18*, 55–74.

Duval, T. S., & Wicklund, R. A. (1972). *A theory of objective self-awareness*. New York: Academic Press.

Epley, N., & Caruso, E. M. (2004). Egocentric ethics. *Social Justice Research*, *17*, 171–188.

Epley, N., Keysar, B., Van Boven, L., & Gilovich, T. (2004). Perspective taking as egocentric anchoring and adjustment. *Journal of Personality and Social Psychology*, *87*, 327–339.

Folger, R. (1977). Distributive and procedural justice: Combined impact of "voice" and improvement on experienced inequity. *Journal of Personality and Social Psychology*, *35*, 108–119.

Folger, R. (1984). Emerging issues in the social psychology of justice. In: R. Folger (Ed.), *The sense of injustice: Social psychological perspectives* (pp. 3–24). New York: Plenum Press.

Folger, R. (1998). Fairness as moral virtue. In: M. Schminke (Ed.), *Managerial ethics: Moral management of people and processes* (pp. 13–34). MahWah, NJ: Erlbaum.

Folger, R., & Cropanzano, R. (1998). *Organizational justice and human resource management*. Thousand Oaks, CA: Sage.

Gaertner, L., Sedikides, C., Vevea, J. L., & Iuzzini, J. (2002). The "I," the "we," and the "when": A meta-analysis of motivational primacy in self-definition. *Journal of Personality and Social Psychology*, *83*, 574–591.

Hafer, C. L., & Bègue, L. (2005). Experimental research on just-world theory: Problems, developments, and future challenges. *Psychological Bulletin*, *131*, 128–167.

Haidt, J. (2001). The emotional dog and its rational tail: A social intuitionist approach to moral judgments. *Psychological Review*, *108*, 814–834.

Ham, J., & Van den Bos, K. (2008). Not fair for me! The influence of personal relevance on social justice inferences. *Journal of Experimental Social Psychology*, *44*, 699–705.

Hegtvedt, K. A. (1993). Approaching distributive and procedural justice: Are separate routes necessary? *Advances in Group Processes*, *10*, 195–221.

Hegtvedt, K. A. (2006). Justice frameworks. In: P. Burke (Ed.), *Contemporary social psychological theories* (pp. 46–69). Stanford, CA: Stanford University Press.

Houlden, P., LaTour, S., Walker, L., & Thibaut, J. (1978). Preference for modes of dispute resolution as a function of process and decision control. *Journal of Experimental Social Psychology*, *14*, 13–30.
Lerner, M. J. (1980). *The belief in a just world: A fundamental delusion*. New York: Plenum Press.
Lerner, M. J. (2003). The justice motive: Where social psychologists found it, how they lost it, and why they may not find it again. *Personality and Social Psychology Review*, *7*, 388–399.
Leung, K., Tong, K.-K., & Lind, E. A. (2007). Realpolitik versus fair process: Moderating effects of group identification on acceptance of political decisions. *Journal of Personality and Social Psychology*, *92*, 476–489.
Lind, E. A., Kanfer, R., & Earley, P. C. (1990). Voice, control, and procedural justice: Instrumental and noninstrumental concerns in fairness judgments. *Journal of Personality and Social Psychology*, *59*, 952–959.
Lind, E. A., Kray, L., & Thompson, L. (1998). The social construction of injustice: Fairness judgments in response to own and others' unfair treatment by authorities. *Organizational Behavior and Human Decision Processes*, *75*, 1–22.
Lind, E. A., & Tyler, T. R. (1988). *The social psychology of procedural justice*. New York: Plenum Press.
Loseman, A., Van den Bos, K., & Ham, J. (2005). The influence of justice and injustice on self-activation. Paper presented at the 14th EAESP General Meeting, Würzburg, Germany.
McClintock, C. G., & Liebrand, W. B. G. (1988). Role of interdependence structure, individual value orientation, and another's strategy in social decision making: A transformational analysis. *Journal of Personality and Social Psychology*, *55*, 396–409.
Messick, D. M., & McClintock, C. G. (1968). Motivational bases of choice in experimental games. *Journal of Experimental Social Psychology*, *4*, 1–25.
Messick, D. M., & Sentis, K. P. (1979). Fairness and preference. *Journal of Experimental Social Psychology*, *15*, 418–434.
Miedema, J. (2003). *Fairness and the self*. Academic dissertation, Leiden University.
Moorman, R. H., & Blakely, G. L. (1995). Individualism-collectivism as an individual difference predictor of organizational citizenship behavior. *Journal of Organizational Behavior*, *16*, 127–142.
Parks, C. D. (1994). The predictive ability of social values in resource dilemmas and public good games. *Personality and Social Psychology Bulletin*, *20*, 431–438.
Rawls, J. (1971). *A theory of justice*. Cambridge, MA: Harvard University Press.
Silvia, P. J., & Duval, T. S. (2001). Objective self-awareness theory: Recent progress and enduring problems. *Personality and Social Psychology Review*, *5*, 230–241.
Smeesters, D., Warlop, L., Van Avermaet, E., Corneille, O., & Yzerbyt, V. (2003). Do not prime hawks with doves: The interplay of construct activation and consistency of social value orientation on cooperative behavior. *Journal of Personality and Social Psychology*, *84*, 972–987.
Thibaut, J., & Walker, L. (1975). *Procedural justice: A psychological analysis*. Hillsdale, NJ: Erlbaum.
Thompson, L., & Loewenstein, G. (1992). Egocentric interpretations of fairness and interpersonal conflict. *Organizational Behavior and Human Decision Processes*, *51*, 176–197.
Tyler, T. R. (1989). The psychology of procedural justice: A test of the group-value model. *Journal of Personality and Social Psychology*, *57*, 830–838.

Tyler, T. R. (1994). Psychological models of the justice motive: Antecedents of distributive and procedural justice. *Journal of Personality and Social Psychology*, *5*, 850–863.

Tyler, T. R., & Blader, S. L. (2003). The group engagement model: Procedural justice, social identity, and cooperative behavior. *Personality and Social Psychology Review*, *7*, 349–361.

Tyler, T. R., Degoey, P., & Smith, H. (1996). Understanding why the justice of group procedures matters: A test of the psychological dynamics of the group-value model. *Journal of Personality and Social Psychology*, *70*, 913–930.

Tyler, T. R., & Lind, E. A. (1992). A relational model of authority in groups. In: M. Zanna (Ed.), *Advances in experimental social psychology* (Vol. 25, pp. 115–292). San Diego, CA: Academic Press.

Van den Bos, K. (2001). Uncertainty management: The influence of human uncertainty on reactions to perceived fairness. *Journal of Personality and Social Psychology*, *80*, 931–941.

Van den Bos, K. (2003). On the subjective quality of social justice: The role of affect as information in the psychology of justice judgments. *Journal of Personality and Social Psychology*, *85*, 482–498.

Van den Bos, K., & Lind, E. A. (2002). Uncertainty management by means of fairness judgments. In: M. P. Zanna (Ed.), *Advances in experimental social psychology* (Vol. 34, pp. 1–60). San Diego, CA: Academic Press.

Van den Bos, K., Lind, E. A., Vermunt, R., & Wilke, H. A. M. (1997). How do I judge my outcome when I do not know the outcome of others? The psychology of the fair process effect. *Journal of Personality and Social Psychology*, *72*, 1034–1046.

Van den Bos, K., & Van Prooijen, J.-W. (2001). Referent cognitions theory: The psychology of voice depends on closeness of reference points. *Journal of Personality and Social Psychology*, *81*, 616–626.

Van den Bos, K., Wilke, H. A. M., & Lind, E. A. (1998). When do we need procedural fairness? The role of trust in authority. *Journal of Personality and Social Psychology*, *75*, 1449–1458.

Van Lange, P. A. M. (1999). The pursuit of joint outcomes and equality in outcomes: An integrative model of social value orientation. *Journal of Personality and Social Psychology*, *77*, 337–349.

Van Lange, P. A. M., Otten, W., De Bruin, E. M. N., & Joireman, J. A. (1997). Development of prosocial, individualistic, and competitive orientations: Theory and preliminary evidence. *Journal of Personality and Social Psychology*, *73*, 733–746.

Van Prooijen, J.-W., De Cremer, D., Van Beest, I., Ståhl, T., Van Dijke, M., & Van Lange, P. A. M. (in press). The egocentric nature of procedural justice: Social value orientation as moderator of reactions to decision-making procedures. *Journal of Experimental Social Psychology*.

Van Prooijen, J.-W., Karremans, J. C., & Van Beest, I. (2006a). Procedural justice and the hedonic principle: How approach versus avoidance motivation influences the psychology of voice. *Journal of Personality and Social Psychology*, *91*, 686–697.

Van Prooijen, J.-W., Van den Bos, K., Lind, E. A., & Wilke, H. A. M. (2006b). How do people react to negative procedures? On the moderating role of authority's biased attitudes. *Journal of Experimental Social Psychology*, *42*, 632–645.

Van Prooijen, J.-W., Van den Bos, K., & Wilke, H. A. M. (2002). Procedural justice and status: Status salience as antecedent of procedural fairness effects. *Journal of Personality and Social Psychology*, *83*, 1353–1361.

Van Prooijen, J.-W., Van den Bos, K., & Wilke, H. A. M. (2004). Group belongingness and procedural justice: Social inclusion and exclusion by peers affects the psychology of voice. *Journal of Personality and Social Psychology*, *87*, 66–79.

Van Prooijen, J.-W., Van den Bos, K., & Wilke, H. A. M. (2005). Procedural justice and intragroup status: Knowing where we stand in a group enhances reactions to procedural justice. *Journal of Experimental Social Psychology*, *41*, 664–676.

Van Prooijen, J.-W., & Zwenk, F. (2007). Self-construal level and voice procedures: The individual self as psychological mechanism for procedural fairness effects. Manuscript submitted for publication.

CONFLICT AND JUSTICE AFTER THE AMERICAN CIVIL WAR: INCLUSION AND EXCLUSION IN THE RECONSTRUCTION AND JIM CROW ERAS

Susan Opotow

ABSTRACT

After war, societies can undergo change that extends justice to formerly excluded groups. Using theories of moral exclusion and moral inclusion as a lens, this chapter examines societal change in two consecutive periods after the American Civil War (1861–1865): Reconstruction and Jim Crow. Focusing on the well being of black Americans in the American South, this chapter examines Reconstruction's inclusionary gains and setbacks. It then describes challenges faced by black Americans during Jim Crow, a period of white supremacy and violence, and factors associated with Jim Crow's decline. Applying social psychological theory to these historical periods offers insight into the dynamics of inclusionary and exclusionary change.

Justice
Advances in Group Processes, Volume 25, 55–85

ISSN: 0882-6145/doi:10.1016/S0882-6145(08)25007-1

Social contexts inevitably undergo change and as they do, prevailing conceptions of fairness change too. This chapter focuses on the post-war period when societal changes can be profound, affecting laws, rules, norms, and conventions about who deserves to be treated justly. Utilizing social psychological theory as a lens and history as data, this chapter examines conflict and justice in two consecutive periods after the American Civil War (1861–1865): the Reconstruction (1863–1877) and the Jim Crow era (ca. 1877–mid-1950s).

At the end of the Civil War, abolition of chattel slavery in the American south mandated a change in long-standing political, economic, legal, and social relations between black and white southerners. Reconstruction, the period officially designated to bring about a more inclusionary society, was followed by Jim Crow, a period that institutionalized white supremacy predominantly, but not entirely, in the American south. Understanding how the scope of justice changed in these periods delineates the full and partial successes, challenges, and failures that inclusionary efforts can entail (cf., Crosby & Lubin, 1990). This understanding has relevance to contemporary post-war societies throughout the world as people struggle to effect inclusionary political, economic, legal, and social change. To understand these changes, this chapter examines two very different justice trajectories, one inclusionary and one exclusionary, to learn how they progressed and to identify contextual factors that influenced change.

The first section of this chapter describes moral inclusion and moral exclusion and the American Civil War and two periods that followed it. The second section focuses on the moral inclusion of black Americans in the Reconstruction. The third section focuses on moral exclusion in the Jim Crow period. For both periods, the chapter focuses on change in the scope of justice with an emphasis on understanding factors that extend social justice more broadly.

THEORETICAL AND HISTORICAL BACKGROUND

Moral Inclusion and Moral Exclusion

Morton Deutsch has defined the *scope of justice* as follows:

> the narrower one's conception of one's moral community, the narrower will be the scope of situations in which one's action will be governed by considerations of justice. (Deutsch, 1985, p. 37).

This definition suggests that the scope of justice can change, and this change has implications for justice (Opotow, 1990, 2006a, 2006b). Research indicates that inclusion in the scope of justice (or *moral inclusion*) means that a social unit (i.e., an individual, a group, an institution, or a nation) is willing to: (1) apply considerations of fairness to another, (2) allocate resources to another, and (3) make sacrifices to foster the well being of another social unit (Opotow, 1993, 1995). Stated negatively, *moral exclusion* occurs when one social unit views another as outside their scope of justice and therefore as undeserving of fairness, resources, or sacrifices. Those excluded are then seen as appropriate targets for exploitation, oppression, and harm.

Seeing some kinds of people as outside the scope of justice can set in motion a vicious cycle, in which those excluded are debilitated by degrading treatment and then seem unworthy (cf., Hafer, 2000; Kipnis, 1976; Lerner, 1980; Lerner & Simmons, 1966). Similarly, distributive injustice expressed as insufficient and unequal resource allocations can make some groups seem less worthy than others (Wenzel, 2002). Severe forms of moral exclusion are characteristic of intergroup conflicts in which some groups are derogated as "subhuman" or "vermin."

Moral exclusion can be mild or severe, narrowly focused or widespread, and active or passive (Opotow, 2001). Thus, moral exclusion can occur as mild, ordinary, and institutionalized inequality or as extraordinarily brutal and characterized by direct and structural violence. In either case, however, moral exclusion is a social psychological orientation in which those who are relatively advantaged view those excluded from the scope of justice as: psychologically distant, unconnected with themselves, undeserving of constructive obligations, and eligible for harms that would be unacceptable for those inside the scope of justice (Opotow, 1990, 1995).

Hegtvedt (2005) argues that justice research has emphasized how individuals perceive and react to injustice, but that injustice also has relevance for groups, particularly in conflictual interactions that delineate and redefine the scope of justice. Like individuals, groups want to see themselves as fair and morally upstanding (Brewer & Brown, 1998; LeVine & Campbell, 1972; Luhtanen & Crocker, 1992). They can therefore rationalize, justify, and ignore structural inequalities that benefit their own group at the expense of others. Because these rationalizations are shared, it can be difficult to detect exclusionary conventions, norms, and practices within a society. Moral exclusion is more evident with greater geographic or temporal distance.

A wider scope of justice is consistent with the broader applicability of procedural and distributive justice norms, human rights, wide participation in societal decision making and functioning, and an appreciation of the value of diverse perspectives. A narrower scope of justice is consistent with the narrower applicability of procedural and distributive justice norms, a press toward greater uniformity and social control, and concerns with security.

To detect inclusionary and exclusionary change in the post-war period, the empirically derived definition of moral inclusion (Opotow, 1993, 1995) directs our attention to considerations of fairness, allocation of resources, and making sacrifices to foster another's well being. These are operationalized in everyday life and can be studied as changes that occur in key societal spheres: political, legal, economic, and social (cf., Diesing, 1962).[1] In politics, inclusion can occur as participation, representation, and authority; in law, as having standing, rights, and freedom; in the economic sphere, as employment, advancement, and wealth; and in the social sphere, as education, health, and housing. In general, moral inclusion can be operationalized as the broad application of procedural and distributive justice, grounded in the extensive, significant, and ongoing participation of a society in all aspects of decision making and resource allocation.

This study focuses on the social psychological conditions associated with inclusionary and exclusionary change. In the post-war period, when societal change is anticipated and can be mandated by law, we can see shifting boundaries of the scope of justice and changes in justice-related laws, rules, norms, conventions, and practices affecting vulnerable groups and their relations with others.

The Post-War Period

In a post-war period, changes can result from forces within and outside a society (e.g., the post–World War II Marshall Plan), and these changes have implications for the extension of justice to previously disenfranchised groups. The post-war period, however, is underscrutinized by scholars. Wars are extensively studied by social science and humanities scholars, but considerably less research has examined the post-war period. Conflict resolution scholars concerned with protracted intergroup conflicts have helpfully distinguished conflict settlement from resolution and reconciliation (Kelman, 2004; Rouhana, 2004), but few have examined reconstructions lasting for decades (but see Staub's, 2004, work in Rwanda). Rouhana (2004) describes the difficulties of undoing institutionalized injustice. Kelman (2004) observes that settlement and resolution may resolve outward hostilities and maintain distinctive and oppositional between-group identities; reconciliation allows groups that were formerly in conflict to view each others' identities as less threatening to and more compatible with their own. In general, scholarly work on the extended reconstruction period has generally focused on specific geographical/political contexts and time-limited situations, such as initiatives conducted by international and non-governmental organizations concerned with development and peace (e.g., the Bretton Woods institutions[2] and the United Nations).

One indicator of disinterest in the post-war period is the *Encyclopedia Britannica*, which devotes 30 pages to the American Civil War, a 4-year period (American Civil War, 2007); one page to the Reconstruction, a 14-year period (Reconstruction, 2007); and half a page to the Jim Crow era, a 70-year period (Jim Crow Law, 2007). Perhaps this skewed emphasis is because war rivets all attention, while the post-war trajectory competes for attention with emerging contemporary events. From the perspective of bystanders, a war's end and the signing of peace treaties has a finality that ends the conflict. For people within a post-war society, however, war's end can lead to an increase of conflicts at all levels of analysis – personal, intergroup, institutional, and societal. These conflicts can be less obvious to the outside world, but can nevertheless be destructive and eventually reignite intergroup violence and war. Two scholar/practitioner/activists of post-war Latin America, one a political scientist (J. Spence, personal communication, February 26, 2007) and the other a clinical psychologist (J. Flores, personal communication, April 9, 2007), confirmed the paucity of post-war research and offered the same reason why: when intergroup hostilities end, civil violence increases. The post-war period can therefore be a dangerous and difficult time to conduct research.

Because of my interest in the dynamics in moral inclusion and the extension of justice to previously excluded groups, I situated my research in a historical post-war period, a context in which moral inclusion could occur. By first looking at the immediate post-war period and then turning to what came next, I study the dramatic changes in the well being of black Americans and white–black relations over a 90-year period in American history.

American Civil War, Reconstruction, and Jim Crow

The American Civil War (1861–1865), also called The War Between the States and, in the south, The War of Northern Aggression, was a fratricidal 4-year war between the United States government ("the Union"[3]) and

11 southern states that seceded from the Union.[4] When the Civil War began, slavery had been abolished in the North many years before (i.e., 1780s for many northern states[5]). Although abolition is often put forward as the main cause of the Civil War, the war began as a result of a failed negotiation. Southern planters sought to expand their cotton plantations into the newly opened western territories taking slavery, what they called "our peculiar institution," with them. This southern euphemism implies that slavery, an institution distinctive to the south at that time, was appropriate because it established a "proper relation between the races."[6]

After the Chinese Taiping Rebellion (1851–1864), the American Civil War has been ranked as the second deadliest in history. It resulted in 620,000 deaths (of 1 million combatants), a staggering loss of life in a society of 30 million people. As the death toll mounted, support for or opposition to slavery increasingly served as a post hoc moral justification for a war that incurred so much loss on both sides (Altschuler, 1982). How did the press for abolition – eventually the goal of the North – fare after the war? The answer, elaborated in this chapter, is that after the war, inclusionary gains during Reconstruction did bring about a somewhat more inclusionary and interracial society. These gains were ultimately eclipsed by inclusionary losses, particularly toward the end of the 19th century, when Jim Crow laws, policies, practices, norms, and customs increasingly segregated the south with a violently exclusionary ethos.

Reconstruction began midway through the Civil War with President Abraham Lincoln's 1863 Proclamation of Amnesty and Reconstruction. It concluded with the Compromise of 1877 that ended federal military occupation of the south and restored southern home rule. Reconstruction after the Civil War generally refers to efforts to solve political, social, and economic problems arising from the readmission of the 11 states that seceded from the Union. My focus is not on relations between the north and the south, but on the societal changes that included black Americans in the south.

Jim Crow describes a period of extreme racial segregation and refers to practices that were institutionalized community by community and state by state in the south, starting as the Reconstruction ended in some locales and later in others (cf., Gilmore, 1996). Jim Crow was a standard character in minstrel shows and a racial slur used by white southerners. "Jim Crow" or "Jumpin' Jim Crow" became one of many popular derogatory stereotypes (along with Sambos, Coons, etc.) representing black people as simple and inferior. By the end of the 19th century, a wide range of discriminatory practices were called *Jim Crow Laws*. Jim Crow ended gradually in the mid-1950s and early-1960s as the Civil Rights Movement gained momentum.

Social Groups Relevant to the Post-Civil War South

"The Union vs. the Confederacy" and "the North vs. the South" is how the American Civil War is often described. These binaries oversimplify the within-group heterogeneity of northerner, southerner, white, and black Americans at that time. In the north and the south, white Americans included slave owners, abolitionists, Democrats, Republicans,[7] and people supporting and opposing rights for black Americans. Black Americans included northerners and southerners, free and enslaved people, and people with a variety of political beliefs and ideologies. Attention to the way that race, class, geography, and gender interact clarifies that beliefs supporting the inclusion in and exclusion from the scope of justice after the American Civil War varied within as well as between groups.

Black Americans were among the earliest settlers of the New World. The first Europeans arrived in the colonies of Massachusetts, New Jersey, New Hampshire, New York, Connecticut, Rhode Island, Pennsylvania, and Vermont in the early 17th century, and enslaved people arrived shortly after.[8] The number of enslaved people increased over the next two centuries as a result of Atlantic slave trade.[9] The United States 1860 census reported 4 million enslaved people.[10] When the Civil War began in 1861, slavery had been part of American life for more than two centuries.

Free Black Americans

According to the 1860 United States census,[11] free black people constituted 1.5% of the American population and 10% of all black Americans in 1860, the year before the Civil War began. Free black Americans were 12% in Delaware and 18% in Maryland, and 1–4% of the population in eight states, evenly divided between the south (North Carolina, South Carolina, and Virginia, Louisiana) and the north (Ohio, Pennsylvania, New York, and Connecticut). Thus, while they were a small proportion of the population, free black Americans were a noteworthy presence in 10 states.[12]

Reconstruction historians John Hope Franklin and Eric Foner describe the large, vibrant, and successful free black community in New Orleans just before the Civil War.[13] Franklin (1995) wrote:

> More than 18,000 free blacks who were living in New Orleans when the war came owned property valued at fifteen million dollars. They had a long and distinguished record of responsible and loyal service, dating back to their military exploits under Andrew Jackson in the battle of New Orleans of 1815. Most of them could read and write, and many could be described as educated and refined. Among the thousands of quadroons and octoroons were acknowledged kinsmen of some of the "best white families" in the state. (p. 21)

Foner (1990) wrote:

> In New Orleans lived the largest free black community of the Deep South. Its wealth, social standing, education, and unique history set it apart not only from the slaves but from free persons of color elsewhere. Most were the descendants of unions between French settlers and black women or of wealthy mulatto emigrants from Haiti. Although denied suffrage, they enjoyed far more rights than free blacks in other states, including the ability to travel freely and testify in courts against whites. On the eve of the Civil War, they owned some $2 million worth of property and dominated skilled crafts like bricklaying, cigar-making, and shoe-making. This community, with a strong sense of its collective history and network of privately supported schools, orphanages, and benevolent societies, was well positioned to advance its interests under Union rule. (pp. 20–21)

What is clear from both accounts, despite the discrepancy in property values,[14] is that almost 150 years ago free black Americans were a notable presence in New Orleans, were better-off than black Americans elsewhere, and had achieved inclusion in some societal spheres while they remained excluded from others.

Between Enslavement and Freedom

The line between free and enslaved was not clearcut. Some craft- and tradespeople were free; others, still enslaved, were allowed to live on their own and remit a portion of their earnings to their owners (Magdol, 1977). Some enslaved people were purchased from slaveholders by their own family members (e.g., parent or husband) who intended to free (i.e., "manumit") them. If prevailing laws prevented manumission, however, they legally remained slaves of their family.

Gilmore (1996) reports on one such case in North Carolina in 1815, in which Edmund Pasteur, through incredible efforts, came to own his entire family, but they remained his slaves. In 1827 Pasteur unsuccessfully petitioned the court to manumit his wife Dinah and their two young children, Richard and Sarah. At that time, it was difficult for white slaveholders to emancipate slaves, but it was a task that was "nearly impossible for a black man" (Gilmore, 1996, p. 6). When her father died on 1843, Sarah, who was then 25 years of age, was sold as a slave with her two young children.

Enslaved Black Americans

The cultural and historical roots of free black Americas were in the slave community, resulting in a deep and lasting connection (Berlin, 1974; Magdol, 1977). Just as free black Americans varied in education, status, and economic well being, there was variation, too, among enslaved people. Those with brutal owners experienced relentless oppression. Some worked the hardest jobs, often in the field; others, sometimes house servants, enjoyed small comforts and privileges in their work. Some were allowed to live away from their owners, work for others, or run their own businesses.

But even enslaved people in relatively favorable circumstances were property. Their situation could change abruptly because of bankruptcy or the death of their owner. Throughout their lives they could be bought and sold, exploited at will, and had no rights. Brutalities that befell them included the lash, separation of families, prohibitions on education, no claims on the fruits of their labor, and sexual exploitation (e.g., Douglass, 1845; Jacobs, 2000/1861). Slaves, however favorable their position, were far outside the scope of justice.

But within the confines of their lives as chattel, enslaved people were resourceful, creative, and resisted oppression. Even in bleak circumstances, they sought learning, which could be punished by death, and they created a rich community life and cultural achievements in art and music that remain an American treasure. Magdol (1977) describes how enslaved black Americans took control of their lives well before the Emancipation Proclamation in 1863 by "emancipating themselves and affecting the arrangements and reconstruction of Southern society before the war was over" (p. 3). There is ample evidence that oppression did not extinguish agency in enslaved communities. Grassroots efforts to improve and control their lives began in enslaved communities well before top-down political efforts sought abolition.

White Southerners

White southerners included plantation-owning slave owners, merchants, professional people, and poor, upcountry farmers. Slave owners and upcountry farmers, the two largest groups of white southerners, were divided by class and culture, and the war strained relations between them. Draft laws of the Confederacy allowed "one able-bodied white male" (Foner, 1990, p. 7) to be exempted for 20 slaves. Owners of a significant number of enslaved people were able to avoid military service; poor white farmers, who were rarely slaveholders, could not. These poor farmers eked out a living from the land, and military service interfered with their ability to provide for their families, who suffered in their absence. Although poor farmers were the majority of Confederate soldiers, they had little to gain from the war. As a result, they were well represented among draft resisters and the 100,000 men who deserted the Confederate Army. The war produced enmity between poor white farmers and wealthy southerners, whose economic interests had ultimately devastated the south.

White southerners also include two groups of outsiders: Republicans in the south, who tended to support greater racial equality, were denounced as "scalawags." White northerners who came to south, some as teachers, social workers, and religious leaders, were denounced as "carpetbaggers" (Ayers, 2005, p. 20). Wealthy white southerners were often pro-slavery, but some were passionate advocates of abolition and equality (e.g., Blair, 1964/1889).

White Northerners

It is axiomatic that the abolition of slavery was supported in the North, but racism was common. Abolition was controversial and, later, there was "strong resistance to Negro suffrage in the Northern states" (Woodward, 1960, p. 97). For more than two centuries, the slave and cotton trade were central to New York's economy; 20% of colonial New Yorkers were enslaved Africans (http://www.slaveryinnewyork.org; Berlin & Harris, 2005). Even northern Radical Republicans – the abolitionist left wing of the Republican party – were divided about how extensive inclusion should be and whether or not they supported suffrage and ceding land to formerly enslaved people (Woodward, 1964).

This brief description of key groups in the American Civil War period has emphasized that highlighting one dimension – geography in the case of "north vs. south" – oversimplifies within-group diversity. At least three dimensions of group identity were prominent at the time of the Civil War and the period afterward: geography, race, and class. Other relevant dimensions include occupation, gender, and age. More nuanced understandings of intergroup contacts in their period will be sensitive to the way that intersectional identities (cf., Crenshaw, 1991) influence within- and between-group dynamics, tensions, and alliances. As one example, northern white people varied in their politics and social philosophy; not all were abolitionists, as "north vs. south" binaries imply. After the Civil War, not all northern abolitionists or educated black Americans were willing to extend suffrage to ex-slaves or support ex-slaves' bid for land ownership. Later, in the Jim Crow era when strict segregation in the south and "white vs. black" was a conventional binary, alliances between middle-class white and black women worked to found black schools and acquire scarce resources for the black community (Gilmore, 1996).

THE INCLUSIONARY TRAJECTORY OF THE RECONSTRUCTION

The Reconstruction began during the Civil War in 1863 with the Reconstruction Acts and continued until 1877 when the United States Congress abandoned Reconstruction and its inclusionary goals in the south. The Reconstruction is now understood as a remarkable period. It sought to achieve a more equal and democratic society and succeeded in some ways, albeit briefly. Yet, for the first half of the 20th century, prominent white northern historians[15] described the Reconstruction as a disgrace and a disaster. Their version of history, later discredited as ideologically driven and one-sided, remained in textbooks throughout the United States in the mid-20th century, including my public elementary school in New York City. In the late 1950s, as the Civil Rights movement began, revisionist historians (e.g., Woodward, 1966; Stampp, 1965) revisited largely ignored accounts of Reconstruction by black historians (cf., Du Bois, 1935) who described the period as more complex and positive.

Like contemporary post-war periods throughout the world,[16] important issues in Reconstruction concerned education, voting rights, political representation, laws fostering more equal societal arrangements, land distribution, and personal and community safety (e.g., Spence, 2004). As the next sections describe, these were contested resources during Reconstruction. Black communities were able to achieve inclusionary gains that went well beyond initial expectations. Ultimately, however, many of these gains were lost when Reconstruction ended. Although I describe social, economic, political, and legal changes in separate sections, it is important to keep in mind that these kinds of changes occurred simultaneously during the Reconstruction.

Social Inclusion

As Kenneth Stampp (1965) describes, at the end of the Civil War black Americans "emerged from bondage in complete destitution, without land, without shelter, without a legal claim even to the clothes on their backs" (p. 122). In spite of this impoverished beginning, black Americans and their allies built churches, benevolent societies, and schools – three key community institutions. Before the war, enslaved people worshipped in biracial churches led by slave owners. After the war, churches were among the first institution founded and owned by the black community. Several decades after the war, in 1880, there were 1.3 million black Baptists in the South.

During the post-war period, thousands of benevolent associations were founded throughout the south, including debate, fire, burial, equal rights, temperance clubs, drama groups, and many others. These groups sought to better individuals and the black community as a whole:

> Offering social fellowship, sickness and funeral benefits and, most of all, a chance to manage their own affairs, these voluntary associations embodied the spirit of collective improvement ... Linking blacks across lines of occupation, income, and pre-war status, the societies offered the better-off the opportunity for wholesome and respectable association, provided the poor with a modicum of economic insurance, and opened positions of community leadership to men of modest backgrounds. (Foner, 1988, p. 95)

On many plantations learning was forbidden and punished, sometimes by death. Therefore, when the Civil War ended, many (90%) former slaves were illiterate. During the 14 years of the Reconstruction, the black community spent more than $1 million on education and enrolled more than 600,000 students in black schools. Adults as well as children attended school. Eula Wellmon Dunlap, who attended the Lincoln Academy in North Carolina, described schooling as an integral part of family life:

> For a while Father, Mother, sister, and I [then a 3 year old] all went to school. ... I spent most of my time marking on paper and playing with blocks. Several married couples went to school. (Gilmore, 1996, p. 36)

In sum, by founding churches, benevolent societies, and schools, black communities fostered individual and community advancement through worship, fellowship, and education. These efforts built self-sustaining and participatory communities that are now appreciated by historians (e.g., Brown, 2000). These institutions were inclusionary in that they were designed to foster mutual acceptance within the black community and advance the community as a whole. They were, however, unable to secure the acceptance of black Americans in the larger, white society. The black church, benevolent associations, and schools remained important institutions in black communities long after Reconstruction ended. Many institutions founded then continue today.

Political Inclusion

In societies throughout the world, who deserves the vote is a contentious issue. This is an inclusionary question concerning political rights. After the Civil War, there was considerable controversy about the participation of formerly enslaved people in electoral politics. Voting rights can be arrayed on a continuum with complete disenfranchisement anchoring one end, suffrage the other, and emancipation and citizenship without suffrage in between.

After the Civil War, two prominent northern abolitionist Republicans, Horace Greeley and William Lloyd Garrison, initially opposed suffrage. Greeley sought semi-inclusion, "a permanent resting place between slavery and citizenship" in order to "limit the voting privilege to the competent and deserving." Garrison stated, "when was it ever known that liberation from bondage was accompanied by recognition of political equality?" (Foner, 1988, p. 75). Given the strong opposition to suffrage – even from abolitionists – the vote came to formerly enslaved people with surprisingly speed. It did so as the result of the Fourteenth Amendment to the Constitution (1868) that guaranteed citizenship to all persons born or naturalized in the United States (except Native Americans), granted federal civil rights, and counted black Americans as full persons, not three-fifths as before. This increased the census population of southern states, where most black Americans lived, potentially giving these states more political power. To prevent the southern states from taking over Congress and the presidency, suffrage was conferred on black Americans in 1868 in the South and 1870 throughout the country by the Fifteenth Amendment which guaranteed that the right to vote could not be denied because of race, color, or previous condition of servitude.

Given the opportunity to participate in elections, the black community forged a vibrant political culture. By the end of Reconstruction in 1877, 600 black legislators and 18 high officials served the South (Foner, 1990). Accomplishments of state legislatures with substantial black representation (e.g., South Carolina) included: free public schools for all children, free public highways, a new penal code, and separate property for married women (Du Bois, 1910). Reconstruction historian C. Vann Woodward (1960) wrote:

> In retrospect, one is more impressed with the success that a people of such meager resources and limited experience enjoyed in producing the number of sober, honest, and capable leaders and public servant they did. The appearance of some of this sort in every state is the main comfort the record provides to the democratic faith. They give the impression of people struggling conscientiously under desperate odds to live up to a test such as no other people had ever been subjected to in all the long testing of the democratic theory. (p. 102)

These accomplishments were achieved in spite of intimidation and violence directed at black voters, electoral fraud by white supremacist election officials, and persistent ridicule directed at black legislators by southern and northern newspapers. In sum, when the opportunity came for civic and political participation, the black community acted with considerable success. Many political gains achieved during Reconstruction, however, were eventually lost through procedural impediments designed to exclude black men from exercising their right to vote, such as literacy tests or property requirements.

Economic Exclusion

In addition to suffrage, another prominent issue in post-war societies is the redistribution and ownership of land (cf., Spence, 2004). The south was an agrarian society. People who had been enslaved sought land ownership to achieve autonomy and to participate in the local economy. Although land in the western territories was being given away to timber, mining, and railroad interests, programs to sell or distribute abandoned and seized land in the south to formerly enslaved black Americans were nonexistent, weak, or short lived. Many white landowners and communities would not sell to black Americans, and land sold by some state governments came encumbered with promissory titles. Later, much of this land was repossessed by the state or the original owners (Bleser, 1969).

As political change became increasingly exclusionary, state land commissions that had been led by black officials in Reconstruction were, over time, led by white "Redeemers" who opposed rights and land ownership for black Americans. When additional land became available, Redeemer officials consolidated it into large parcels that were unaffordable to low income buyers. Land-owning patterns in the south changed in some locales, but by the end of Reconstruction, they resembled what they had been before the Civil War (Bleser, 1969). Eric Foner (1990) writes that

> Land redistribution would have had a profound consequence for Southern society, weakening the land-based economic and political power of the old ruling class, offering blacks a measure of choice as to whether, when, and under what circumstances to enter the labor market. (p. 48)

The distribution of land by local, state, or federal governmental agencies to the people who had worked it without pay for generations would have had profound effect on the well being of black Americans over time. Based on his study of the family trees of successful black Americans, Gates (2007) writes:

> If there is a meaningful correlation between the success of accomplished African-Americans today and their ancestors' property ownership, we can only imagine how different black-white relations would be had "40 acres and a mule" really been official government policy in the Reconstruction South. (p. 14)

In sum, land, a source of income and influence in the south, was an important inclusionary resource that few black Americans could own. Merriom Howard, who had been born in slavery, said:

> Land enough existed for every man and woman to have as much as they could work, but they were left with no *land*, no *house*, not so much as place to lay our head... Despised by the world, hated by the country that gives us birth, denied of all our writs as a people, we were friends on the march ... brothers on the battlefield, but in the peaceful pursuits of life it seems that we are strangers. (Italics in the original; quoted in Foner, 1990, p. 74)

Social Exclusion and Violence

Since emancipation at the end of the Civil War in 1865, black men achieved the vote, public office, collective ownership of community institutions, and, for some, the ownership of homes, businesses, and land. These inclusionary advances triggered resentment in some white groups who saw inclusionary gains by black Americans as threatening their way of life (Thornbrough, 1972). Along with emancipation, there was an increase in vigilante violence against black individuals and communities as well as structural violence in locally enacted Black Codes. Both kinds of violence, direct and structural, were intended to disenfranchise black men.

Direct Violence

The White League, the Ku Klux Klan, and Knights of the White Camellia were some of the many white supremacist groups founded after the Civil War (Trelease, 1971) dedicated to forestalling inclusionary change. *Harper's Weekly* (1874) described white-on-black violence in the post-war period.

> In 1868 we have the raids on the Negro voters detailed in the Ku-Klux reports, when the White Camellias dominated in the streets of New Orleans. In 1869-1871 fear kept them in tolerable quiet. In 1872 they re-appear. In 1873 they burned or shot down sixty or seventy Negroes at Grant Parish, and attempted an insurrection in New Orleans. In 1874 they have murdered the United States officials at Coushatta and a large number of Negroes; they have risen in rebellion in New Orleans and shot thirty or forty Unionists in a deadly contest. They are still importing large quantities of arms, and are evidently preparing for further massacres whenever the eye of the law is withdrawn. (p. 901)

White vigilante groups intimidated, harassed, and murdered black Americans and their advocates and burned homes, churches, and businesses. Sometimes they targeted individuals with beatings, lynching, and sometimes mob violence led to the rapid depopulation of black communities, much like *ethnic cleansing* today.

Because education had often been forbidden to enslaved people, educated black leaders were a precious resource, performing multiples leadership roles and connecting their community with the outside world. When vigilante groups targeted black leaders, their violence was intended to terrorize, demoralize, and disable the entire community. This form of violence is what Aron and Corne (1994) label *sophiacide* in contemporary violence. Literally, it is the killing of knowledge.

Structural Violence

At the same time that the Thirteenth (1865), Fourteenth (1868), and Fifteenth (1870) Amendments to the Constitution were adopted to confer rights and foster inclusion of black Americans, the Black Codes enacted at the local level gave white southerners the legal means to replicate slavery. Justified by negative stereotypes of freed slaves as "unstable, ignorant of binding contracts, improvident, and lazy" (Richardson, 2001, p. 19), the Black Codes required black workers to enter into labor contracts that included such oppressive provisions as corporal punishment, workers' children serving compulsory apprenticeship, and insurrection in any form was punishable by death (Wilson, 1965).

As the Reconstruction progressed, calls for white rule and the election of "intelligent property holders" (Foner, 1990, p. 182) and the "best men" (Foner, 1990, p. 214) – euphemisms for white men – grew increasingly stronger while black political gains weakened. Ultimately, white-on-black violence eroded many political, economic, legal, and social inclusionary gains of black Americans. Henry Adams, a leader who had formerly been enslaved, said, "the whole South – every state in the South had got into the hands of the very men that held us as slaves" (Foner, 1990, pp. 244–245). The North, with its economic and political ambitions in the post-war South, played a role too, and

> watched complacently as lynching and violence terrified Southern blacks, as one Southern state after another disenfranchised African-Americans and instituted a rigorous system of racial segregation in the form of Jim Crow laws, and as blacks were forced into semi-slavery as sharecroppers. (Richardson, 2001, pp. ix–x)

A young Episcopal priest in Alabama described every aspect of exclusion as linked – from the vote to education, political intimidation, and political violence:

> Extremists proceeded from an indiscriminatory attack on the Negro's ballot to a like attack upon his schools, his labor, his life – from the contention that no Negro shall vote to the contention that no Negro shall learn, that no Negro shall labor, and (by implication) that no Negro shall live. (quoted in Tindall & Shi, 1999, p. 851)

The complex trajectory of inclusionary possibility during Reconstruction, from initial gains to losses, was succinctly summarized by W.E.B. Du Bois (1935) who said: "The slave went free, stood a brief moment in the sun, then moved back toward slavery" (p. 30). The inclusionary trajectory after the Civil War suggests that the extension of justice to previously disenfranchised groups after war is difficult to achieve and sustain.

Decline of the Inclusionary Ethos

The Reconstruction, characterized by some inclusionary political, economic, legal, and social change, ultimately gave way to the reinstitutionalization of exclusionary mores. The northern states lost interest in the Reconstruction as the south returned to an exclusionary ethos and home rule. External conditions contributed to shrinking the scope of justice, including a worldwide economic depression in the late 19th century, bad weather and floods that breached New Orleans's levees; and insect infestations that destroyed the cotton crop (Foner, 1990). In difficult times it is difficult to sustain inclusionary change.

The Reconstruction offers a context in which to generate hypotheses about the conditions that foster change in the scope of justice. First, it is difficult to sustain inclusionary change within a larger context with a robust exclusionary ethos. For social psychological research, this suggests that inclusion needs to be understood as nested within multiple levels of analysis. For marginalized groups seeking influence in the larger society, points of connection to it are valuable (cf., Moscovici, 1976). It is therefore important to study change in the larger context in which change can occur as well as kinds of connections between marginalized and dominant groups that can change the ethos of dominant groups in an inclusionary direction.

Second, studying social, political, economic, and legal change in the Reconstruction indicate that inclusionary change can be full or partial, and, in either case, vulnerable to erosion by direct and structural violence. It is therefore important to study the durability of inclusionary change to identify the kinds of changes that are more easily institutionalized and those that are more ephemeral and easily lost. Only studies attentive to change over time can detect the changes that are more likely to endure. What the Reconstruction also indicates is that change is capable of producing a reaction and this backlash can hasten the return to an idealized, exclusionary past. Thus, along with social psychological studies of change we also need studies of the conditions that trigger and sustain backlash.

Third, these inclusionary analyses of the Reconstruction suggests that moral inclusion can be transient or enduring, but even seemingly durable inclusionary changes, such as constitutional amendments, are vulnerable to erosion through procedural impediments and technicalities. For social psychological research, this suggests the value of studying how procedural impediments can maintain and normalize exclusionary practices and mores.

Fourth, the window for inclusionary change after war and violent conflict may be brief. Edward Ayers (2005) warns that

> Reconstructions are races between change and reaction; they cannot last long before they seem to be another form of oppression. Reconstructions must make their changes quickly or they are not likely to make them at all. (p. 21)

For social psychological research this suggests that in addition to the justice contingencies, *what, how*, and *who,* corresponding to distributive, procedural, and inclusionary justice, the justice contingency, *when,* warrants empirical attention.

Fifth, the end of war produces major social impacts (Licklider, 1993) that include productive and destructive conflict (cf., Deutsch, 1973). For social psychological research, this suggests that the time period under study is important. Rather than seeing peace accords as a logical endpoint of war, an expanded time period is needed to understand social change. The period following peace accords has been underscrutinized and is of considerable interest because of its potential to sustain peace or reignite war.

The next section describes Jim Crow, a period following the Reconstruction that was extraordinarily violent and exclusionary for black Americans.

THE EXCLUSIONARY TRAJECTORY OF JIM CROW

Jim Crow, characterized by the violence enforcement of racial segregation, did not come all at once to all parts of the south. Instead, the interracial society established after the Civil War in some locales (Woodward, 1966) gradually gave way, town by town and state by state, first to a biracial society, and ultimately, to what was later known as *apartheid* in 20th century South Africa – complete segregation of the races enforced by custom and law. As C. Vann Woodward (1966) described:

> By 1944 the Swedish writer Gunnar Myrdal observed that "segregation is now becoming so complete that the white Southerner practically never sees a Negro except as his servant and in other standardized and formalized caste situations." (p. 118)

When the Civil War ended in 1865, black southerners set off to find family members who had been dispersed in slave markets and to search for economic opportunity. Many settled in cites, where interracial contact became more frequent and even cordial (Woodward, 1966, p. 37). Toward the end of Reconstruction in 1877, black Americans in Columbia, Charleston, and Richmond, South Carolina rode with white Americans on trains and street cars and were freely admitted to theaters, exhibitions, and lectures. They were served at bars, soda water fountains, ice cream saloons, but not hotels (Woodward, 1966). As late as 1897, a Charleston newspaper editor declared that Jim Crow laws were unnecessary: "We have no more need for a Jim Crow system this year than last year, and a great deal less than we had twenty and thirty years ago" (p. 37). Black Americans continued to vote and hold office in the south after Reconstruction ended, and all but one southern legislature had a least one elected black member between 1869 and 1901. Charles Pettey,[17] a North Carolina church and community leader who had been born in slavery, noted that in 1896:

> We have colored coroners and State's attorney elected by a majority of white votes. Our representative in Congress is a colored man, George H. White, my neighbor. Throughout the State there are over 100 petty magistracies filled by colored men. (Gilmore, 1996, p. 78)

The end of the 19th century, however, was a difficult period for all people – black and white. Because of the long economic depression of the 1890s, economic, political, and social frustrations mounted. A quick fix for difficult times can be a scapegoat and, as Woodward (1966) describes

> all along the line signals were going up to indicate that the Negro was an approved object of aggression. These "permissions-to-hate" came from sources that had formerly denied such permission. They came from federal courts in numerous opinions, from Northern liberals eager to conciliate with the South, from Southern conservative who had abandoned their race policy of moderation in their struggle against Populists, from the Populists in their mood of disillusionment with their former Negro allies, and from a national temper suddenly expressed by imperialistic adventures and aggressions against colored peoples in distant lands. (pp. 81–82)

This shift from an interracial society to an increasingly segregated and exclusionary society required wide societal support – the go-ahead – for pervasive norm change. Hate, as Woodward emphasized, provided this shift in the 1890s.

Hate and Exclusionary Change

As contemporary work on hate indicates, hate and injustice can intensify each other. Hate can trigger harmful and unjust behavior out of proportion to an offence, and injustice has the capacity to intensify feelings of hate (Opotow & McClelland, 2007). Moss (2003) emphasizes that

> when we hate – racistly, homophobically, misogynistically – we do not hate as isolated individuals. Rather, we hate as part of a group, not in the first person singular, but in the first person plural. (p. xviii)

Racist hate expressed in any form – from a barber's refusal to cut the hair of an African American customer to a lynching – merges the individual victim with the hated group. Psychologically, the emotions, morals, and cognitions of hate's perpetrators interact to intensify hate:

> Although there can be initial distal and proximal causes of hate from the perspective of the hater, the very expression of hate circles back to change the context – materially and psychologically – for the hater and victim. This can further intensify affect, cognitions, morals, and behaviors, which are then replayed in a loop resulting in the build up of hate. (Opotow & McClelland, 2007, p. 85)

As hate builds, it can become extraordinarily destructive, particularly when justifications for inflicting harm on those hated are supplied by moral exclusion. Moral exclusion then acts as an accelerant, legitimizing previously unimaginable and harmful behavior directed toward specific people or groups (Opotow, 2005). Psychologically, the emergence of collectively experienced hate that gave rise to Jim Crow depended on having approved targets of hate who had been identified as outside the scope of justice and, in addition, well coordinated, collective action that advanced the segregation and imbued it with urgent, morally justified purpose.

The Rise of Segregation, White Supremacy, and Mob Violence

Increasingly restrictive segregation laws in the American south from 1900 to 1920 separated black and white people in all aspects of daily life:

> Jim Crow [railroad] cars became universal. And the new seating arrangements came to seem as normal, unchangeable, and inevitable as the old ways. And so it was with the soda fountains, bars, waiting rooms, street cars, and circuses ... The Jim Crow laws put the authority of the state or city in the voice of the street-car conductor, the railway brakeman, the bus driver, the theater usher, and also in the voice of the hoodlum of the public parks and playgrounds. (Woodward, 1966, pp. 106–107)

Influential social scientists of the time, including sociologist William Sumner (1906) and psychologist William McDougall (1908), reinforced the emerging racist *status quo* with the idea that

> there was something inevitable and rigidly inflexible about the existing patterns of segregation and race relations in the South; that these patterns had not been and could not be altered by conscious effort; and that it was, indeed, folly to attempt to meddle with them by means of legislation. (Woodward, 1966, pp. 103–104)

In the Jim Crow era, segregation was violently enforced with fear, threat, torture, and murder. Over 4,742 black Americans were lynched in this period, predominantly in the south but also in the north, with many lynchings uncounted (Stolberg, 2005). Sometime local law enforcement personnel participated in lynchings; other times they looked the other way. Decisive action by the U.S. Congress could have halted much of this violence, but on three occasions in the first half of the 20th century, the US Senate refused to save lives by enacting a federal law to criminalize lynching (Stolberg, 2005). Lynching was so commonplace and such an accepted part of southern life that post cards depicted lynchings and the many white men, women, and children that attended them were a cottage industry (cf., Allen, 2004).

John Hope Franklin describes the period after World War I, when black veterans – some still in uniform – were lynched, as "the greatest period of interracial strife that nature had ever witnessed" (quoted in Woodward, 1966, p. 114). Mobs took over cities for days of flogging, burning, and shooting black Americans. The Ku Klux Klan, which had originally been founded in 1866 after the Civil War, had a rebirth in 1915. It had explicitly racist and anti-Semitic goals, wide support, and five million members by 1920.

Gender and Jim Crow

Russell (1972) describes warlike societies as repressive in all ways. Consistent with this, the Jim Crow era not only excluded black Americans from the larger society but also undermined black women's influence within the black community. Although historical accounts of Jim Crow rarely differentiate between the experience of black men and women, scholars studying the lives of women in this period describe the gendered way that tyranny descended on the black community (Brown, 2000; Gilmore, 1996).

During Reconstruction and well before that, black women were influential members of their communities. After 1870, men could vote but women could not. But in their own communities, women were full participants and could vote in church and community matters. As Brown (2000) describes

> African American women assumed the political rights that came with being a member of the community even though they were denied the political rights they thought should come with being citizens of the state. (p. 38).

Southern black women drew power from the participatory ethos that characterized key community institutions (i.e., churches, benevolent societies, and schools):

> The participation of women and children in the external and internal political arenas was part of a larger political worldview of ex-slaves and free men and women, a worldview fundamentally shaped by an understanding that freedom, in reality, would accrue to each of them individually only when it was acquired by all of them collectively. (Brown, 2000, p. 39)

But as Jim Crow era took hold, socio-political conventions about gender equality and collective autonomy within the black community also changed. In the Reconstruction, forums for political discussions in the black community had included

> literary societies, ward meetings, mutual benefit society and fraternal society meetings, women's clubs, labor organizations, newspapers, streetcorners, kitchens, washtubs, and saloons. (Brown, 2000, p. 48)

In community meetings, many people could take the floor and freely talk back to speakers, building mass participation. The tightening of Jim Crow laws set off a narrowing of participation within the black community. Literary meetings, for example, had typically included working- and middle-class men and women. Over time, their informal, participatory atmosphere was replaced by formal rules that limited participation. Particular members, primarily male and middle class, were asked to prepare papers in advance of meetings or were designated to respond to others' papers. This narrowed participation by class and gender and reduced the informality and wider participation that had typified these meetings before.

Similarly, large, participatory community meetings were gradually moved from large church meeting spaces to smaller, more private venues, narrowing participation in church business and electoral politics. At the same time that black men were being disenfranchised in the larger community, leaders of the black community such as John Mitchell in North Carolina sought to limit women's political participation. He did so by questioning

> his opponents' right to participate even though they were all church members by pointing out their unfamiliarity with parliamentary procedure or their inelegant ways of speaking. The women, who were the targets of much of Mitchell's challenge, refused to

> accept these as criteria for their participation and even denigrated what he put forth as his formal qualifications by talking out when he got up to speak, saying derisively, "Don't he look pretty." (Brown, 2000, p. 47)

At the same time that black women were increasingly marginalized, white women's purity became the centerpiece of a campaign to exclude black men from the vote. Maligning black men as children, animals, and rapists and spreading false information about epidemics of black-on-white rape frightened politically liberal white men into voting to protect "the safety of the home" (Gilmore, 1996, p. 85). As was apparent in the 1914 film, *Birth of a Nation*, the violation of white women's purity was a political tool to arouse fear and hatred of black men and to justify lynching.

As a result of these tactics, the interracial society and inclusionary gains of the Reconstruction were first dismantled then erased (Gilmore, 1996). Consistent with scholarship on victim blaming (Lerner, 1980; Ryan, 1971), once the disenfranchisement of black men occurred, their disenfranchisement was then offered as evidence of their unfitness for political office rather than understood as the result of their expulsion from political life.

During Jim Crow black women worked to gain a toehold in the larger society, seeking out opportunities for interracial cooperation with white women, and if these efforts failed, used their societal invisibility to "get on with things surreptitiously" (Gilmore, 1996, p. 32). When they encountered segregation, violence, and exclusion, black activist women

> tried to peel away white supremacy's thousand disguises as well. Racism rolls along so smoothly because it seems to be impermeable. It is, however, a tightly wound tangle of individual strands, and black women set about unraveling them whatever they could. (Gilmore, 1996, p. 32)

The Decline of Jim Crow

Toward the end of Woodward's (1966) account of the rise and institutionalization of Jim Crow in the first half of the 20th century, he briefly discusses several social changes that were contemporaneous with the weakening of Jim Crow's exclusionary grip. He describes the New Deal, the Harlem Renaissance, the sting of conscience, sustained and increasing opposition to racial inequality, and the rise of the black middle class. These are social changes that offer insight into conditions that can support inclusionary change.

> *The New Deal:* "In spite of unyielding segregation," Woodward wrote, "a few new opportunities opened to the Negro in cultural life, housing, health improvement, and education through federal agencies of the New Deal (Woodward, 1966, p. 118)."

Describing the New Deal is beyond the scope of this chapter, but the essentials of moral inclusion are evident in its extension of key social resources – housing, health care, and education – to all Americans in the 1930s. Although segregation continued, opportunities opened to black and white Americans by the New Deal eased racial tensions and, as a result, lynching decreased.

The Harlem Renaissance: The Harlem Renaissance in the 1930s resulted in an "outpouring of Negro fiction, poetry, and song that was highly race conscious and inspired by the spirit of protest" (Woodward, 1966, p. 125). The work of black artists inspired white artists and intellectuals, creating cross-class and cross-racial relationships that influenced the larger society to reduce racism and promote interracial alliances cutting across class lines.

The sting of conscience: Jim Crow was clearly at odds with deeply held American values of equality of opportunity – values that were strong in the south and the north. Woodward (1966) describes efforts of southern liberals to "sting the conscience of the South into an intensified awareness of the inconsistency between creed and custom" (p. 126). By the 1940s these efforts had accumulated and a significant number of southern liberals were disapproving and vocal about racial inequalities. Over time they were able to achieve positions of influence in the south and in the larger American society as newspaper owners and editors, congressional representatives, judges, and presidential advisors.

Sustained and increasing opposition to racial inequality: Woodward (1966) observes that opponents to segregation "sustained a mounting crescendo of enthusiasm and pressure" (p. 127). In the period before the Civil War, petitions to Congress for abolition that "reached a crest and all but stopped the wheels of Congress in the mid-1830s had subsided to a trickle in the 1850s" (p. 127). But from 1937 to 1950, the number of bills favoring civil rights introduced in congress increased with each decade. In 1949–1950, the 81st Congress received 72 civil rights-related bills.

The rise of the black middle class: Through education, hard work, and as the result of societal change during and after World War II, black Americans again achieved a foothold in the middle class in the late 1940s, gains they had lost during Jim Crow (Gilmore, 1996). As a result of achievements in academic life, politics, and the arts, the black community again influenced society. The NAACP and Urban League, national organizations countering violence and fostering African-American well being, increased in membership and attracted support from white individuals and institutions, increasing their influence in local and national politics.

Theoretical Factors Fostering Exclusionary Decline

From a theoretical perspective, these five changes associated with exclusionary decline speak to the importance of three factors: equal distribution of resources, creativity as a stimulus for contact, and change over time.

Equal Distribution of Resources

The more equal distribution of societal resources during the New Deal increased well being across society. Research on moral exclusion indicates that contexts characterized by threat, scarcity, and conflict are associated with a narrower scope of justice (Opotow, 1995). In contrast, increases in societal resources have the potential to expand the scope of justice.

Creativity and Contact

The Harlem Renaissance, the flowering of creativity and achievement in the arts, legitimized and sustained a black influence in the larger culture. This led to between-group associations between black and white women, black and white citizens, artists and high society. This had the potential to result in interracial collaborations in political, legal, economic, and social spheres, reshaping the status quo. This has resonance with research on the reduction of bias and prejudicial attitudes and beliefs (Gaertner & Dovidio, 2005) and the importance of intergroup contact (Pettigrew & Tropp, 2006). Cross-group contact can gradually accumulate as greater tolerance for and appreciation of diversity, commitment to greater equality in society, and institutionalization of inclusionary efforts that can foster the well being of previously disenfranchised groups.

Change over Time

Over time, Leaders in the south who were committed to white supremacy were gradually replaced by younger leaders. Some broke with past tradition and supported inclusionary change. While tradition and change remain in conflict in the south today (Foster-Paley, 2007), this study suggests that inclusionary change needs to accumulate over a significant period of time. As these two post-war periods indicate, change can take decades to accomplish, and it can have positive or negative valence. It remains a challenge to study change over an extended period using experimental methods, but quasi-experimental approaches and historical studies offer the potential to study inclusionary change.

It is beyond the scope of this chapter to examine inclusionary change in other post-war contexts. However, it is well accepted that the availability of resources is crucial to rebuilding societies. The five societal changes that Woodward (1966) describes could have coincided with a period of increasing affluence, when inclusionary change may be more likely than during retrenchment. It is also possible that the emergence of a more inclusionary society depends on several advances that work in concert. This implies, for example, that more equal distribution of available societal resources (e.g., the New Deal), interracial cooperation, and the emergence of an influential artistic and political communities are each necessary but insufficient in themselves. The birth of the Civil Rights Movement in the 1950s, which sought the extension of social justice to black Americans, may have resulted from the synergy of several kinds of change working in concert. A third possibility is that some kinds of oppressive systems weaken over time. In the 50 years between the 1890s and the 1940s, the formal and informal institutions and mores that sustained racism eventually weakened. Resistance to the exclusionary status quo gradually developed enough so that various constituencies, black and white, could take advantage of its weakening and initiate inclusionary change.

Finally, the legal, political, economic, and social gains that had been achieved during Reconstruction provided significant gifts from the past that were later utilized as tools of change by the Civil Rights Movement. The Thirteenth, Fourteenth, and Fifteenth Amendments, the only enduring achievement of Radical Republicans, provided the legal basis for equal rights. Collective memories in the black community of their political achievements during Reconstruction, their unquenchable desire for education (Cross, 2003), and the socio-political importance of black churches fostered the development of the Civil Rights Movement. These resources, in concert with more equal distribution of societal resources and interracial cooperation, came together at the end of Jim Crow, an extraordinarily shameful period in American history that is scarcely studied in American schools today.

CONCLUSION

When I sought a post-war period in which to study inclusionary processes and the societal changes that could expand the scope of justice, I turned to the Reconstruction and its 14 years of legal, social, and political gains that had all but vanished as the 20th century began with the Jim Crow period and its pervasive moral exclusion, violence, and hate. And when I looked at Jim

Crow, a period of institutionalized white supremacy, to examine the dynamics of a virulently exclusionary society, I found the beginnings of the Civil Rights Movement in the mid-20th century, a period characterized by violence, but also by nonviolence and significant inclusionary gains.

Inclusionary and exclusionary changes in America were enormous in the 90 years from the end of the Civil War in 1865 to the beginning of the Civil Rights Movement in the 1950s – an interval as long as a single, long-lived life. In these two periods after the American Civil War, all social relations and all social conflicts – large and small – played out in a social, political, economic, and legal landscape shaped by prevailing inclusionary or exclusionary laws, rules, norms, conventions, and practices.

To grasp intergroup relations it is important to understand the scope of justice as it is and how it has changed over time. The scope of justice can only be understood in light of what came before to understand the conditions that brought about the present status quo. It is equally important to study conflicts about what the scope of justice should be. The willingness to consider fairness, allocate resources, and make sacrifices to support the well being of other societal groups influences how groups interact and whether that interaction occurs with the desire for more egalitarian or oppressive relations.

NOTES

1. Paul Diesing (1962) also describes the technical rationality.
2. The World Bank and the International Monetary Fund
3. The Union states were: California, Connecticut, Illinois, Indiana, Iowa, Kansas, Maine, Massachusetts, Michigan, Minnesota, Nevada, New Hampshire, New Jersey, New York, Ohio, Oregon, Pennsylvania, Rhode Island, Vermont, Wisconsin. Three states joined the Union after the outbreak of the war: Kansas, West Virginia, and Nevada. Five states were Border States that had common borders with Union states and states in the Confederacy: Delaware, Kentucky, Maryland, Missouri, West Virginia. In these states, loyalties were mixed and some had both pro-Confederate and pro-Union governments.
4. The states that seceded from the Union were: Alabama, Arkansas, Florida, Georgia, Louisiana, Mississippi, North Carolina, South Carolina, Tennessee, Texas, and Virginia.
5. Slavery was abolished in northern states as follows: Massachusetts (1783), New Jersey (1804), New Hampshire (1783), New York (1799), Connecticut (1784), Rhode Island (1784), and Pennsylvania (1780). Harper (2003) reports that slavery then continued in practice in some locales (with few people enslaved) into the 1840s as a result of local laws and norms and ended in practice as follows: Massachusetts (1783), New Jersey (1865), New Hampshire (ca. 1845), New York (1827), Connecticut (1848), Rhode Island (1842), and Pennsylvania (ca 1845).

6. See http://en.wikipedia.org/wiki/Peculiar_institution for a pithy description of this term.

7. At that time, Democrats, called Copperheads in the North, were the conservative, land-owning, slavery-supporting party and the Republicans were the liberal party of Lincoln. The Radical Republicans were supportive of equal rights.

8. Massachusetts (ca. 1629), New Jersey (ca. 1626), New Hampshire (1645), New York (1626), Connecticut (1639), Rhode Island (1652), and Pennsylvania (1639). Slaves arrived in Vermont considerably later (ca.1760). (For an overview, see www.slavenorth.com)

9. It is estimated that from the 15th to the 19th centuries, more than 10 million enslaved Africans were shipped from their homelands to Europe and the Americas in the Atlantic slave trade (http://encarta.msn.com/text_761595721___0/Atlantic_Slave_Trade.html).

10. http://firestone.princeton.edu/politics/guides/histcensus.htm.

11. See http://fisher.lib.virginia.edu/cgi-local/censusbin/census/cen.pl?year = 860) for data on demographics in 1860.

12. That is, 10 out of the 33 states in the United States in 1860, before 11 states seceded beginning 12/20/60 (Kane, Podell, & Anzovin, 1993).

13. In light of the death toll, displacement, loss of homes and businesses, and governmental neglect of black residents of New Orleans in the wake of Hurricane Katrina in 2005 (Garfield, 2007; Nossiter, 2007), accounts of the vibrant black community in New Orleans 150 years before are particularly poignant.

14. It is likely that this variation results from expressing monetary value in 1860 vs. 1996 dollars.

15. At the turn of the century, the Dunning School, an influential group of scholars associated with Columbia University, described the Reconstruction as a horrible mistake, misguided, and a "hypocritical effort to force an unnatural order on a helpless South" (Ayers, 2005, p. 20). According to them, the Reconstruction failed because of "Negro incapacity" (Foner, 1990, p. xii) and they described the Reconstruction as a shameful period marred by black and Republican incompetence and greed.

16. See Hemisphere Initiatives for reports on the post-war period in Central America (http://www.hemisphereinitiatives.org/hemsreports.htm).

17. Charles Pettey was born in slavery. Later he was free, educated, and became a respected church and community leader in Richmond, North Carolina (for details, see Gilmore, 1995).

REFERENCES

Allen, J. (2004). *Without sanctuary: Lynching photography in America.* Santa Fe, NM: Twin Palms.

Altschuler, G. C. (1982). *Race, ethnicity, and class in American social thought, 1865-1919.* Arlington Heights, IL: Harlan Davidson.

American Civil War. (2007). In: *Encyclopædia Britannica.* Retrieved on April 22, 2007, from Encyclopædia Britannica Online: http://www.britannica.com/eb/article-9006104

Aron, A., & Corne, S. (1994). Introduction. In: A. Aron & S. Corne (Eds), *Ignacio Martin-Baró: Writings for a liberation psychology.* Cambridge, MA: Harvard University Press.

Ayers, E.L. (2005, May 29). The first occupation. *The New York Times Magazine*, p. 20.

Berlin, I. (1974). *Slaves without masters: The free Negro in the antebellum South*. New York: Pantheon.

Berlin, I., & Harris, L. M. (2005). *Slavery in New York*. New York: New Press.

Blair, L. H. (1964/1889). *A Southern prophecy: The prosperity of the South dependent upon the elevation of the Negro* (First published in 1889). Boston: Little, Brown.

Bleser, C. K. R. (1969). *The promised land: The history of the South Carolina Land Commission, 1869–1890*. Columbia, SC: University of South Carolina Press.

Brewer, M. B., & Brown, R. J. (1998). Intergroup relations. In: D. Gilbert, S. Fiske & G. Lindzey (Eds), *The handbook of social psychology* (Vol. 2, pp. 554–594). Boston: McGraw-Hill.

Brown, E. B. (2000). Negotiating and transforming the public sphere: African American political life in the transition from slavery to freedom. In: J. Dailey, G. E. Gilmore & B. Simon (Eds), *Jumpin' Jim Crow: Southern politics from Civil War to Civil Rights* (pp. 28–66). Princeton, NJ: Princeton University Press.

Crenshaw, K. (1991). Mapping the margins: Intersectionality, identity politics, and violence against women of color. *Stanford Law Review*, *43*, 1241–1299.

Crosby, F. J., & Lubin, E. P. (1990). Extending the moral community: Logical and psychological dilemmas. *Journal of Social Issues*, *46*, 163–172.

Cross, W. E. (2003). Tracing the historical origins of youth delinquency and violence: Myths and realities about Black culture. *Journal of Social Issues*, *59*, 67–82.

Deutsch, M. (1973). *The resolution of conflict*. New Haven: Yale.

Deutsch, M. (1985). *Distributive justice*. New Haven: Yale.

Diesing, P. (1962). *Reason in society: Five types of decisions and their social conditions*. Urbana, IL: University of Illinois Press.

Douglass, F. (1845). *Narrative of the life of Frederick Douglass, an American slave, Written by himself*. Boston: Anti-slavery Office.

Du Bois, W. E. B. (1910). Reconstruction and its benefits. *American Historical Review*, *15*, 781–799.

Du Bois, W. E. B. (1935). *Black Reconstruction in America*. New York: Atheneum.

Foner, E. (1988). *Reconstruction: America's unfinished revolution, 1863-1877*. New York: Harper & Row.

Foner, E. (1990). *A short history of Reconstruction, 1863-1877*. New York: Harper & Row.

Foster-Paley, D. (2007). *Shadow of the caste: Exploring the culture of honor in a southern town*. Doctoral dissertation, Graduate Center of the City University of New York.

Franklin, J. H. (1995). *Reconstruction after the Civil War* (2nd revised ed.). Chicago: University of Chicago.

Gaertner, S. L., & Dovidio, J. F. (2005). Categorization, recategorization, and intergroup bias. In: J. F. Dovidio, P. Glick & L. A. Rudman (Eds), *On the nature of prejudice: Fifty years after Allport* (pp. 71–88). Malden, MA: Blackwell.

Garfield, G. (2007). Hurricane Katrina: The making of unworthy disaster victims. *Journal of African American Studies*, *10*(4), 55–74.

Gates, H.L., Jr. (2007). Forty acres and a gap in wealth. *The New York Times, The Week in Review*, p. 14.

Gilmore, G. E. (1996). *Gender and Jim Crow*. Chapel Hill, NC: University of North Carolina Press.

Hafer, C. L. (2000). Do innocent victims threaten the belief in a just world? Evidence from a modified Stroop task. *Journal of Personality and Social Psychology*, *79*, 165–173.

Harper, D. (2003). *Slavery in the North*. Retrieved on 12/14/07 from http://www.slavenorth.com/

Harper's Weekly (1874). Everything points to a Democratic victory this fall, p. 901. Retrieved on February 15, 2007 from http://app.harpweek.com.arugula.cc.columbia.edu:2048/

viewarticletext.asp?webhitsfile = hw18741031000007%2Ehtm&xpath = %2FTEI%2E2%5B1%5D%2Ftext%5B1%5D%2Fbody%5B1%5D%2Fdiv1%5B25%5D%2Fp%5B19%5D%2Ffigure%5B1%5D&xml = HW%5C1874%5C18741031%2Exml&titleid = HW&volumeid = 1874&issueid = 1031&pagerange = 0901ad%2D0901ad&restriction = Democratic+victory+this+fall&pageIDs = %7CHW%2D1874%2D10%2D31%2D0901%7C

Hegtvedt, K. A. (2005). Doing justice to the group: Examining the roles of the group in justice research. *Annual Review of Sociology*, *31*, 25–45.

Jacobs, H.A. (2000/1861). *Incidents in the life of a slave girl, written by herself, Harriet Jacobs.* Introduction and notes by N. I. Painter. New York: Penguin.

Jim Crow law. (2007). In: *Encyclopædia Britannica.* Retrieved on April 22, 2007, from Encyclopædia Britannica Online: http://www.britannica.com/eb/article-9043641

Kane, J. N., Podell, J., & Anzovin, S. (Eds). (1993). *Facts about the states* (2nd ed.). New York: H.W. Wilson.

Kelman, H. C. (2004). Reconciliation as identity change: A social-psychological perspective. In: Y. Bar-Siman-Tov (Ed.), *From conflict resolution to reconciliation* (pp. 111–124). Oxford: Oxford University.

Kipnis, D. (1976). *The powerholders.* Chicago: University of Chicago Press.

Lerner, M. J. (1980). *The belief in a just world.* New York: Plenum.

Lerner, M. J., & Simmons, C. H. (1966). Observers' reactions to the "innocent victim": Compassion or rejection? *Journal of Personality and Social Psychology*, *4*, 203–210.

LeVine, R. A., & Campbell, D. T. (1972). *Ethnocentrism: Theories of conflict, ethnic attitude, and group behavior.* New York: Wiley.

Licklider, R. (1993). What have we learned and where so we go from here? In: R. Licklider (Ed.), *Stopping the killing how civil wars end* (pp. 303–322). New York: New York University Press.

Luhtanen, R., & Crocker, J. (1992). A collective self-esteem scale: Self-evaluation of one's social identity. *Personality and Social Psychology Bulletin*, *18*, 302–318.

Magdol, E. (1977). *A right to the land: Essays on the freedmen's community.* Westport, CT: Greenwood Press.

McDougall, W. (1908). *An introduction to social psychology.* London: Methuen & Co.

Moscovici, S. (1976). *Social influence and social change.* New York: Academic Press.

Moss, D. (2003). (Ed.). Introduction: On hating in the first person plural: Thinking psychoanalytically about racism, homophobia, and misogyny. In: D. Moss (Ed.), *Hating in the first person plural: Psychoanalytic essays on racism, homophobia, misogyny, and terror* (pp. xvii–xxxiv). New York: Other Press.

Nossiter, A. (2007). Commemorations for a city that needs no reminders. *The New York Times*, p. A14.

Opotow, S. (1990). Moral exclusion and injustice: An introduction. *Journal of Social Issues*, *46*(1), 1–20.

Opotow, S. (1993). Animals and the scope of justice. *Journal of Social Issues*, *49*, 71–85.

Opotow, S. (1995). Drawing the line: Social categorization, moral exclusion, and the scope of justice. In: B. B. Bunker & J. Z. Rubin (Eds), *Conflict, cooperation, and justice* (pp. 347–369). San Francisco: Jossey-Bass.

Opotow, S. (2001). Social injustice. In: D. J. Christie, R. V. Wagner & D. D. Winter (Eds), *Peace, conflict and violence: Peace psychology for the 21st century* (pp. 102–109). New York: Prentice-Hall.

Opotow, S. (2005). Hate, conflict, and moral exclusion. In: R. J. Sternberg (Ed.), *The psychology of hate* (pp. 121–153). Washington, DC: American Psychological Association.

Opotow, S. (2006a). Seeking inclusion and pluralism: Two exploratory studies. *Peace and Conflict, 12*, 349–366.

Opotow, S. (2006b). Moral inclusion and post-war reconstruction. Paper presented at the 11th Biennial Conference of the International Society for Justice Research at Humboldt University, Berlin.

Opotow, S., & McClelland, S. I. (2007). The intensification of hating: A theory. *Social Justice Research, 20*, 68–97.

Pettigrew, T. F., & Tropp, L. R. (2006). A meta-analytic test of Intergroup Contact Theory. *Journal of Personality and Social Psychology, 90*, 751–783.

Reconstruction. (2007). In: *Encyclopædia Britannica.* Retrieved on April 22, from Encyclopædia Britannica Online: http://www.britannica.com/eb/article-9062908

Richardson, H.C. (2001). *The death of reconstruction: Race, labor, and politics in the post-civil war north, 1865–1901*. Cambridge, MA. Harvard University.

Rouhana, N. N. (2004). Group identity and power asymmetry in reconciliation processes: The Israeli-Palestinian case. *Peace and Conflict: Journal of Peace Psychology, 10*, 33–52.

Russell, E. W. (1972). Factors of human aggression: A cross cultural factor analysis of characteristics related to warfare and crime. *Behavioral Science Notes, 7*, 275–312.

Ryan, W. (1971). *Blaming the victim*. New York: Pantheon Books.

Spence, J. (2004). *War and peace in Central America: Comparing transitions toward democracy and social equality in Guatemala, El Salvador, and Nicaragua.* Brookline, MA: Hemisphere Initiatives.

Stampp, K. M. (1965). *The era of Reconstruction, 1865-1877.* New York: Random House.

Staub, E. (2004). Justice, healing, and reconciliation: How the people's court in Rwanda can promote them. *Peace and Conflict: Journal of Peace Psychology, 10*, 25–32.

Stolberg, S.G. (2005). Senate issues apology over failure on antilynching law. *The New York Times,* A15.

Sumner, W. G. (1906). *Folkways: A study of the sociological importance of usages, manners, customs, mores, and morals.* Boston: Ginn and Co.

Thornbrough, E. L. (1972). *Black Reconstructionists*. Englewood Cliffs, NJ: Prentice-Hall.

Trelease, A. W. (1971). *White terror*. New York: Harper & Row.

Wenzel, M. (2002). What is social about justice? Inclusive identity and group values as the basis of the justice motive. *Journal of Experimental Social Psychology, 38*, 205–218.

Woodward, C. V. (1960). *The burden of southern history*. Baton Rouge, LA: Louisiana State University Press.

Woodward, C. V. (1966). *The strange career of Jim Crow* (2nd ed.). New York: Oxford University.

INEQUITY AMONG INTIMATES: APPLYING EQUITY THEORY TO THE FAMILY

Kathryn J. Lively, Brian Powell, Claudia Geist and Lala Carr Steelman

ABSTRACT

Despite advocacy for greater dialogue between social psychologists and family scholars, there has been little cross-fertilization between the two. One exception is in the area of equity theory. We address how advances in equity theory and in family research each have even greater capacity to enrich the other. We do so by using the 1996 General Social Survey, 1992–1994 National Survey of Family and Households, and 2002 International Social Survey Programme to explore the relationship between emotion and perceived inequity in the family. We summarize key findings as a prelude to future scholarship in the United States and globally.

Over the last several decades, the social psychological study of group processes has produced an impressive array of knowledge on social interaction. One area of scholarly inquiry that has truly flourished is the application of equity – particularly, the implications of equity or, more accurately, perceived equity

Justice
Advances in Group Processes, Volume 25, 87–115

ISSN: 0882-6145/doi:10.1016/S0882-6145(08)25005-8

for emotional well-being (Hegtvedt, 1990; Hegtvedt & Killian, 1999; Stets, 2003). In its simplest form, equity theory posits that when individuals perceive an injustice, they concurrently experience emotional distress (Adams, 1965; Austin, 1977; Austin & Walster, 1974; Homans, [1961], 1974). While this may imply that distress is experienced only when an occurrence or situation disfavors oneself, the theory also suggests that distress occurs when an inequity favors oneself and disfavors another (Sprecher, 1986).

Over a decade ago in this series on advances in group processes, two of the coauthors of this chapter (Steelman & Powell, 1996) advocated more dialogue between group processes scholars and family sociologists, pinpointing the family as the key group for which group processes may or may not apply. They discussed how social psychological insights derived from experiments could, and should, inform the work of family scholars and, in turn, how family scholarship can broaden the scope of experiments. One area within family research that has begun to apply insights from social psychology is the study of the degree to which principles of equity (either explicitly or implicitly) operate among long-term intimates – with a particular focus on the psychosocial costs of perceived inequity in the division of household labor (Mikula, 1998). Building upon this work, in this chapter we bridge existing research on emotion within the family and equity theory (also see Clay-Warner's (2006) discussion of justice and the workplace). At the same time, we also speak to the ways in which new findings from scholarship on families (particularly that which has been culled from large scale, nationally representative datasets) have a similar ability to enhance our understanding of equity.

We accomplish this goal by identifying certain challenges in sociological scholarship on perceived inequity in the household division of labor and discussing some patterns gleaned from a number of different, yet complementary, data sources: the 1996 The General Social Survey (GSS) modules on emotion and gender, the 1992–1994 National Survey of Family and Households (NSFH), and the International Social Survey Programme's (ISSP), 2002 Family and Changing Gender Roles survey. We concentrate on the relationship between everyday emotions and perceived inequity with respect to numerous types of family inequity, including, but not limited to, the division of household labor. We also explore the degree to which perceptions of and consequences of inequity vary across nations. Our intention here is not to provide comprehensive and unequivocal resolutions to these issues. Rather, we offer a summary of some key patterns that have been emerging from our and others' work as a prelude to future scholarship not only in the United States but also globally.

EQUITY THEORY AND EMOTION

As noted above, equity theory (Adams, 1965; Austin, 1977; Austin & Walster, 1974; Hegtvedt, 1990; Hegtvedt & Markovsky, 1995; Homans, [1961], 1974; Walster, Walster, & Berscheid, 1978) posits that when individuals perceive an inequity (to themselves or to others in the interaction), they will suffer emotional distress. Understanding whether and how discontent accompanies a sense of unfairness may be valuable when predicting behavior and other feelings across a variety of relationships (Burke & Harrod, 2005; Clay-Warner, 2006; Hochschild, 1989; Lennon & Rosenfield, 1994; Robinson & Smith-Lovin, 1992; Van Yperen & Buunk, 1990). Most studies that delve into the link between equity and specific everyday emotions, however, evaluate results obtained in laboratory settings that ordinarily assess interaction between strangers, as opposed to encounters with acquaintances, friends, or loved ones (Hegtvedt & Killian, 1999; Krehbiel & Cropanzano, 2000). Although some scholars have attempted to examine general principles of equity in intimate or close relationships, even these have relied mostly on college student samples (Walster et al., 1978; Sprecher, 1986, 1992; also see Burke & Harrod, 2005; Van Yperen & Buunk, 1990).

Despite the theory's focus on emotional distress, equity theorists acknowledge the need to distinguish between various types of distress. Homans ([1961], 1974), for example, differentiates between anger and guilt (also see Hegtvedt, 1990; Krehbiel & Cropanzano, 2000; Mikula et al., 1998). Other scholars, too, emphasize the need to explore the relationship between equity and the positive side of emotions, including excitement, satisfaction, contentment, joy, and respect (Oliver, Shor, & Tidd, 2004; Sprecher, 1986; Stets, 2003; Weiss & Suckow, 1999). Equity theorists' attention to a range of emotions resonates with more general calls within sociology to explore more fully the variety of ways in which day-to-day feelings govern human behavior (Goodwin, Jasper, & Polletta, 2001; Lively & Heise, 2004; Lawler & Thye, 1999; Massey, 2002).

In his meta-analysis of the role of emotion in social interactions, Kemper (1978) concludes that *all* emotions offer clues about how individuals respond to perceived injustice (also see Sprecher, 1986). According to his social interactional theory, emotions typically arise out of perceptions of injustice that occur along two fundamental axes: power and status (Kemper, 1978). Anger, for example, and other similar emotions occur when actors perceive an injustice to themselves in the course of a social encounter that happens through no fault of their own. Such a proposition meshes nicely with the main principles guiding equity theory. Moreover, just as individuals are expected to experience anger and other angry feelings when denied anticipated power or status, they also are more fearful, particularly when an insult is delivered by a well-liked other. In terms of positive emotions, Kemper argues that individuals who receive what they perceive as their fair share of power and status in a given social interaction should concurrently feel positive emotions, such as happiness, tranquility, ease, and contentment (also see Smith-Lovin & Heise, 1988). When individuals receive too much power or status in a given interaction or relationship encounter, however, they are susceptible to self-reproach, particularly if they perceive their rewards came at the expense of an intimate, such as a spouse or domestic partner (Burke & Harrod, 2005; Hegtvedt, 1990; Homans [1961], 1974; Robinson & Smith-Lovin, 1992).

Kemper's theoretical predictions dovetail nicely with several experimentalists' predictions, as well as Sprecher's (1986) survey-based analysis of general investments in intimate relationships among college students. Sprecher reports that individuals who perceive an inequity, either in their own favor or that of the other, suffer more negative emotions (e.g., anger, depression, sadness, anxiety, guilt and, in some cases, fear) than those who gauge that their partner's and their investments are fairly distributed. She also finds that individuals who report overbenefiting have fewer feelings of excitement, satisfaction, contentment, joy, and respect than do their counterparts who see fairness in the relationship (Sprecher, 1986; also see Burke & Harrod, 2005).

Kemper's and Sprecher's observations also are consistent with various theories of identity (Heise, 1977; Burke, 1991). Identity control theory predicts that when individuals are subjected to social disconfirmation of their identity – whether it is positive or negative – they become disenchanted (Burke, 1991; Stets, 2004; also see Stets, 2003). Affect control theory implies that individuals who reap short-term rewards have positive feelings (Heise, 1977; Smith-Lovin & Heise, 1988). However, to do so routinely in an ongoing sequence of over rewards at the expense of another can actually culminate in an adverse re-identification (e.g., from sweetheart to tyrant). Undergoing a re-identification, the overbenefited actor should correspondingly experience negative emotions (e.g., anger, rage, self-reproach) consistent with a negative identity (Robinson & Smith-Lovin, 1992; also see Lively & Heise, 2004).

Group processes research on equity traditionally has relied primarily on experiments to test emotional reactions to unequal exchanges. Given that most experimental studies rely exclusively on college student samples and, as a result, interactions are with virtual if not actual strangers, we have little information on how individuals respond when they perceive an injustice from which they are advantaged or disadvantaged in an interaction with a significant other, or even with someone with whom they are expected to have an ongoing, long-term relationship. Because strangers in experiments do not necessarily know or see their partners nor have any attachments to them, they at least theoretically can be quite predatory in their behavior without feeling badly. As we shall see later, subjects may find it offensive to overbenefit from their own actions under conditions where they know – and are attached to – their partners.

The closely related field of procedural justice, which examines not only justice outcomes but also the procedures that lead to them, does tend to pay more attention to the effects of perceived injustice in situations populated by more enduring, if somewhat non-intimate, relationships – most typically, work relationships (Clay-Warner, Hegtvedt, & Roman, 2005; Hegtvedt, Clay-Warner, & Ferrigno, 2002). These studies provide valuable insight into how justice processes operate in more established settings, but they tell us little about how these operations affect those involved in more intimate relations (also see Van Yperen & Buunk, 1990).

Further, studies of procedural justice typically do not address how discrete emotions are affected by perceptions of unfairness (Clay-Warner, 2006). Indeed, most survey-based studies of procedural justice in either the workplace or the family tend to rely on *anticipated* emotional reactions (Hegtvedt et al., 2002), composite measures of affect (Tyler, 1994), satisfaction (Van Yperen & Buunk, 1990), or organizational commitment (Clay-Warner, Reynolds, & Roman, 2005). In fact, a recent review of this literature states that as of 2006 there had only been one procedural justice study published that deals with discrete emotion (Clay-Warner, 2006). But this study – much like its counterparts that examine discrete emotional reactions to equity outcomes – is based on the experiences of individuals who are not enmeshed in enduring intimate relationships, such as those found within families (Krehbiel & Cropanzano, 2000). We, therefore, are left with the question of the degree to which patterns discerned in laboratory settings or, to a lesser degree, in the workplace generalize to familial relationships or to other populations.

EXISTING RESEARCH ON EQUITY WITHIN THE FAMILY

In terms of equity theory, one of the most burgeoning lines of scholarship within the family looks at perceived inequity in the household division of labor. Several scholars have examined inequity's consequences for marital conflict, marital stability, marital satisfaction, and marital happiness

(Greenstein, 1996; Perry-Jenkins & Folk, 1994; Wilcox & Nock, 2006), but we believe that some of the most promising research has explored inequity's relationship to depression (Glass & Fujimoto, 1994; Kessler & McRae, 1982; Krause & Markides, 1985; Lennon & Rosenfield, 1994; Lennon, Wasserman, & Allen, 1991; Robinson & Spitze, 1992; Ross & Mirowsky, 1988; Ross, Mirowsky, & Huber, 1983). With few exceptions, these studies concur that individuals who experience their burden as unfair to themselves have more negative outcomes – in terms of increased depression, increased marital conflict, or decreased marital satisfaction and/or happiness (also see Van Yperen & Buunk, 1990). Smith, Gager, and Morgan (1998), however, propose a counter argument – that is, individuals who are already upset about their marriages are more likely to see their housework arrangements as unfair than those individuals who are either happy or satisfied (a point to which we return in the discussion).

Some family scholars writing on household division of labor explicitly refer to and seriously engage equity theory. Others make a seemingly obligatory reference to equity theory but go no further, while others ignore the theory altogether. Given the variations in the extent to which equity theory is explicitly engaged or elaborated, it is perhaps not surprising that several challenges remain. First, studies of inequity within the family to date have yet to delineate the differences – or similarities – in the implications of under and overbenefiting both at the hands of and at the expense of intimate others. Second, they have been slow to embrace fully the work of experimentalists, whose forceful demonstrations in lab experiments showcase the values of incorporating a broad array of outcomes, especially emotions. Third, these studies as a rule have yet to explore the relative influence of various forms of inequity that potentially operate simultaneously. Fourth, scholarship on the family has yet to address whether perceptions of and consequences of inequity documented in U.S. samples extrapolate to other countries. These challenges have implications for social psychologists and family scholars, as well as for experimentalists and survey researchers, and, in particular, may speak to the importance of an increased dialogue across these groups. Below we outline these challenges and offer evidence from our own research that illustrates these challenges.

Under and Overbenefiting: At the Hands or Expense of Significant Others

Most sociological work on equity within the family has focused on underbenefiting or has drawn attention to the person who is (or perceived to be) underbenefiting. In the case of housework, this refers to the person who is doing more than his or her "fair share" of the household labor. The consequences for someone who does not contribute his or her fair share is either neglected or given little thought. Some studies combine underbenefiting and overbenefiting together as an absolute pattern of inequity, without explicitly comparing the unique effect of each (Glass & Fujimoto, 1994; Lennon & Rosenfield, 1994).

Despite what these studies tell us about family life, their foci seem out of step with much of the aforementioned social psychological work on equity theory that uses either surveys of undergraduates or experiments to scrutinize the emotional consequences of both forms of inequity (Krehbiel & Cropanzano, 2000; Hegtvedt, 1990; Hegtvedt & Killian, 1999). The greater attention to underbenefiting has been justified in two ways. First, given their emphasis on domestic labor and the undervalued status of housework, family scholars argue that individuals more likely perceive themselves as doing more than their fair share than vice versa. This pattern, however, may be particularly strong in the United States, a point to which we return below. Second, these studies typically center exclusively or primarily on women, who – considering that they continue to do two-thirds of domestic labor regardless of competing time commitments – arguably may be more likely to view their burden as too cumbersome as opposed to too light. Although not explicitly stated, a third reason for the enduring attention to underbenefiting is simply sociologists' greater interest in the plights of the disadvantaged. Whatever the reason, we know little about how individuals respond to the experience of overbenefiting in the realm of household labor. Indeed, given the debates within the social psychological literature – particularly the opposing perspectives associated with identity (Burke, 1991) and affect control theory (Robinson & Smith-Lovin, 1992) – regarding the consequences of overbenefiting, this issue is one where family scholars would do well to entertain seriously the differing, if not competing, expectations.

As an illustration, we use the General Social Survey's, 1996 Emotions Module to examine the unique effects of under and overbenefiting in the household division of labor. The GSS has been the source of more survey-based analyses of emotion than any other dataset (Mabry & Kiecolt, 2005; Lively, forthcoming; Lively & Heise, 2004; Lively & Powell, 2006; Schieman, 2000; Simon & Lively, 2005; Simon & Nath, 2004; Sloan, 2004; Stets & Tsushima, 2001). The GSS includes self-reports on respondents' experiences of 18 different emotion states, as well as a subset of questions pertaining to the antecedents, the experience of, and the management of anger.[1] Because our interest lies in linking emotional experience to perceptions of inequity in the domestic division of labor, we restrict our analysis to individuals who reported being married or cohabiting with a romantic partner and who responded to both gender and emotion modules ($N = 699$).

To assess respondents' recent emotional reactions, individuals were instructed: "*Now I'm going to read a list of different feelings that people sometimes have. After each one, I would like you to tell me on how many days you have felt this way during the past seven days.*" The 18 emotions represent a gamut of emotion states – both positive and negative – that embody multiple dimensions (e.g., evaluation and activation) of emotion.[2]

Our key interest here is the relationship between individuals' perceptions of fairness of the division of labor and two composite scores of negative and positive emotions. Negative emotions include feelings of distress, anger, rage, fear, and self-reproach, while positive emotions include feelings of tranquility, hope, joy, and pride.

Perceptions of fairness are measured by one item that asked respondents "*How fair do you feel the division of work around the house is in your household? Would you say that it is fair to both you and your spouse or partner, unfair to you, or unfair to your spouse or partner?*" This question allows us to more broadly test the tenets of equity theory because we can assess the implications of inequity to self (i.e., underbenefiting) *and* inequity to others (i.e., overbenefiting). We recognize that this measure only captures the respondent's *perception* of fairness, but Thompson (1991) argues persuasively that individuals' assessments of what is "fair" is the crucial predictor when examining the psychosocial costs of perceived inequity in the division of household labor, even more so than more objective indicators of who does what (also see Major, 1987).

As seen in the first column of Fig. 1, both under and overbenefiting are positively related to the composite negative emotions score.[3,4] And, as has been found in experimental studies, the effect of underbenefiting is stronger than the effect of overbenefiting. A complementary pattern is also seen in the first column of Fig. 2 – that is, positive emotions are negatively related to the perception of doing more than and less than one's fair share. As in the case of negative emotions, the reaction is stronger when faced with underbenefiting. In other words, consistent with equity theory but contrary to the implicit assumption of much of the scholarship on the division of labor, both under and overbenefiting are associated with strong emotional responses, although the association between underbenefiting and negative emotion is greater than with that of overbenefiting. That said, a quick look at the rest of these two figures reveals an even more complicated story when examining discrete emotions, as we discuss below.

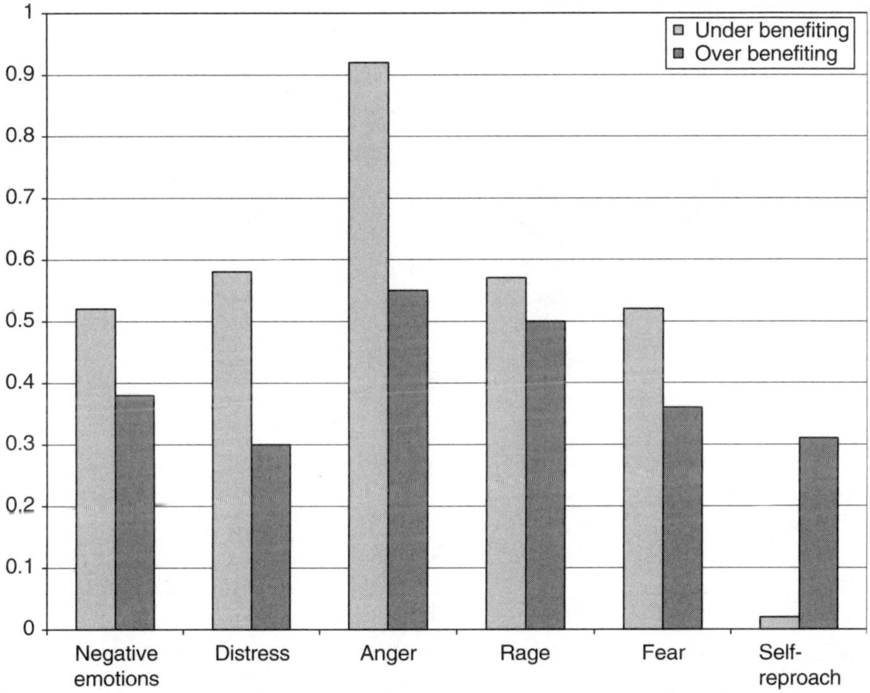

Fig. 1. Perceived Inequity in Housework: Effects of Underbenefiting and Overbenefiting on Negative Emotions. *Note:* Models also control for the reported amount of household work. *Source:* General Social Survey, $N = 699$. *Metric:* Number of days in the past week respondents felt specific emotion(s).

Emotions, Equity, and the Household Division of Labor

Sociologists who study inequity in the household typically do not portray themselves as studying emotion, but, rather, depression (Glass & Fujimoto, 1994; Lennon & Rosenfield, 1994). However, the instrument that they most typically use to tap into depression is, for all intents and purposes, a combination of emotion and affective behavior. As can be seen in Table 1, the Center for the Epidemiological Studies-Depression (CES-D) scale is, to large measure, a list of emotions that affect control theorists would refer to as simultaneously negative, weak, and inactive and may inhibit, rather than activate, human action (Lively & Heise, 2004; MacKinnon & Keating, 1989; Morgan & Heise, 1988).[5,6] Among these emotions are feeling blue, sad,

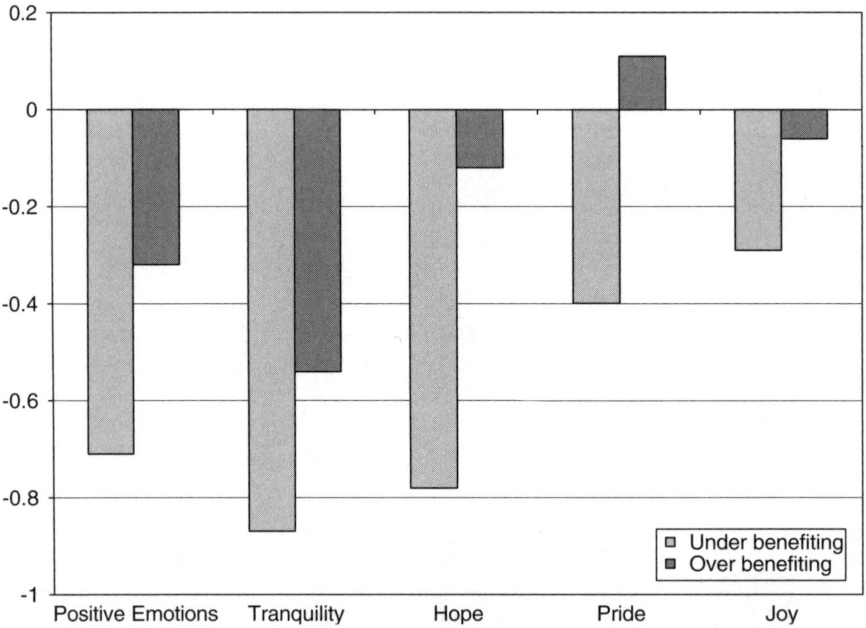

Fig. 2. Perceived Inequity in Housework: Effects of Underbenefiting and Overbenefiting on Positive Emotions. *Note:* Models also control for the reported amount of household work. *Source:* General Social Survey, $N = 699$. *Metric:* Number of days in the past week respondents felt specific emotion(s).

lonely, and fearful. Admittedly, showing how these types of emotions relate to perceived inequity in the division of household labor is instructive; however, insights from sociological scholarship on other emotions, such as affect control theory (Heise, 1977), suggest that a broader range of emotions should be scrutinized (also see Mikula, Scherer, & Athenstaedt, 1998). Perhaps the most important of these is anger (Kemper, 1978; Lively & Powell, 2006; Lovaglia & Houser, 1996; Schieman, 2000). Given anger's status as a justice emotion (Collins, 2005; Kemper, 1978), it is counter-intuitive that family scholars have virtually ignored anger as a consequence of inequity. Indeed, some have argued that anger may be a prelude to depression (Simon & Lively, 2005).

Scholars also lack a clear understanding of household inequity's effect on various positive emotions (e.g., tranquility, pride, and joy). The failure to address these emotions is particularly ironic, given that some suggest that

Table 1. Center for the Epidemiologic Studies – Depression (CESD) Scale, Shortened Version Used in the National Survey of Families and Households.

Items Included in Measure
You were bothered by things that normally do not bother you
You felt *lonely*
You felt that you could not shake off the *blues*, even with the help of friends
Your sleep was restless
You felt *depressed*
You felt that everything you did was an effort
You felt *fearful*
You had trouble keeping your mind on what you were doing
You talked less than usual
You did not feel like eating, your appetite was poor
You felt *sad*
You feel like you could not get going

positive emotions, notably pride and joy, may actually perpetuate gender inequality in families. Some scholars posit that women enjoy doing the lion's share of domestic labor because it ratifies successful enactment of traditional female activities or performances and offers immediate awareness of accomplishment (Coltrane, 2002; Sanchez, 1994; Thompson, 1991).

The above discussion suggests that scholars interested in the affective consequences of inequity must go beyond the study of depression and even beyond scales that aggregate disparate positive (or negative) emotions. As a corrective, our current work (Lively, Steelman, & Powell, 2004, 2007) uses the General Social Survey (1996) and the National Survey of Family and Households (1992–1994) to examine the correlations between perceptions of under and overbenefiting and a range of day-to-day emotions.

In our analyses, we rely primarily on the GSS, because this is the dataset with the most comprehensive set of emotion items. Its inclusion of multiple discrete emotion states enabled us to use confirmatory factor analysis to derive nine discrete emotion factors: distress, anger, rage, tranquility, hope, fear, self-reproach, pride, and joy, as suggested by Lively and Heise (2004).[7] For more information regarding reliability, see Lively and Heise (2004).

Overall, our analyses reveal that individuals' emotional reactions vary not only by the direction of the perceived inequity but also by the emotion under consideration. As represented in the last five columns of Fig. 1, we find that individuals who perceive that their burden is too heavy (that is, unfair to themselves) are likely to experience more distress, anger, rage, and fear than individuals who perceive their and their partners' contributions as fair. Individuals who view their burden as too light also experience more distress, anger, rage, and fear than those who report that they and their partners contribute equitably, although the effect of overbenefiting for these negative emotions is weaker than the effect of underbenefiting. All negative emotions do not operate similarly, though: Self-reproach is positively linked to overbenefiting but is *not* implicated with feelings of underbenefiting, a finding that is consistent with Kemper's (1978) predictions.

Patterns regarding various positive emotions, displayed in the last four columns of Fig. 2, suggest a more ambiguous relationship to perceived inequity in the division of household labor. Underbenefiting is significantly and negatively linked to tranquility and hope. For experiences of pride and joy, however, the relationship is not significant although it is in the same direction. Overbenefiting is also significantly and negatively linked to feelings of tranquility. For the other positive emotions, the relationship is weak and in the case of pride is in the opposite direction. In other words, the relationship between inequity and the composite scale of positive emotions, discussed earlier in this chapter, is not applicable across all positive emotions.

We have repeated these analyses using the National Survey of Families and Households (1992–1994). Just as the GSS emotions module receives a great deal of attention from emotions scholars, the NSFH is widely utilized by family sociologists, perhaps more so than any other recent dataset on families (Blair & Johnson, 1992; DeMaris & Longmore, 1996; Glass & Fujimoto, 1994; Greenstein, 1996; Lennon & Rosenfield, 1994; Perry-Jenkins & Folk, 1994; Sanchez & Kane, 1996; Smith et al., 1998). The NSFH includes an item on equity similar to the question in the GSS ("*How do you feel about the fairness in your relationship in each of the following areas?*"). Equity in household chores is one of the areas listed. Responses range on a 5-point scale from *very unfair to me* to *very unfair to spouse/partner*. To be consistent with GSS, these responses are transformed into three dummy variables: unfair to me, fair to both, and unfair to spouse/partner. As in the GSS, emotion items are measured by the number of days within the last week that the respondent felt, for example, fear. Unfortunately, the number of emotion items within the NSFH is comparatively small (mostly restricted to those items embedded within the CES-D), although the most recent waves notably have added a few items on anger. We limit our sample to include married or cohabitating couples only and collapse the individual emotion items into clusters (e.g., negative emotions ($\alpha = .91$), distress ($\alpha = .90$), anger ($\alpha = .85$), and fear ($N = 4{,}840$)). Our analyses of NSFH yield findings largely consistent with our analyses of GSS, although the magnitude of the relationships is somewhat smaller.[8]

Taken as a whole, this research underscores the importance of looking at a broader range of emotions, much more so than typically found in both experiments and surveys of this genre. This clearly is one area in which experimental work surely can inform and has informed survey work on family issues. And since survey researchers can test multiple emotions simultaneously, survey studies may be able to open and motivate new lines of inquiry for those who conduct their studies in more controlled settings.

Although both the GSS and NSFH show solid support for equity theory, the findings reveal some seeming discrepancies regarding gender's effect on the relationship between perceived inequity and emotion. The GSS data suggest that some patterns are more significant for men (that is, men experience significantly more anger and rage than women do when they perceive doing more than their fair share). This pattern, however, is not the case in the NSFH. Instead, these data imply that women are more emotionally reactive than men – at least, that is, when they perceive that they are doing *less* than their fair share. Differences such as this one accentuate the need for survey researchers to collect more data on emotion and its link to dimensions of inequity and for experimentalists to pay even closer attention to the effects of personal characteristics.[9]

Do All Inequities Offend Equally?

We do not dispute the potentially inequitable or emotionally laden character of domestic labor; as mentioned above, some of our own work has been on this very issue. Such an unwavering focus, however, implies that inequity in housework arrangements is more consequential than other inequities that operate within the home. Unfortunately, such an implication has been insufficiently tested.

A major strength of experimental design lies in its unparalleled ability to isolate the causal effects of an independent variable upon a corresponding dependent variable. The simple elegance associated with such designs, however, comes at a cost: Most laboratory settings also have the constraints of a limited number of items that can be manipulated. In other words, in experiments it is often the case that only one type of inequity is manipulated. But intimate group dynamics, especially among family members, tend to be messier than those captured in most experimental studies (Steelman &

Powell, 1996). One aspect of this complexity stems from the multiple forms of inequities (as well as the perceptions of inequities) that can occur. In the household, for example, there may be inequities not only in housework, but also in paid work, spending, and childcare, among others. These inequities may not go hand in hand. For example, someone who believes s/he is underbenefiting in terms of household-related tasks may perceive that s/he is overbenefiting in the realm of paid work.

Although it may be challenging to design and execute an experiment that captures the effects of multiple inequities simultaneously, this task may be simpler when using multivariate quantitative techniques applied to survey data (see Glass & Fujimoto, 1994 for one example). As an illustration, we turn once again to the NSFH. Unlike the GSS, which includes questions regarding perceived inequity in the household division of labor only, the NSFH also includes items concerning perceived inequities in paid work, spending, and childcare. In order to ascertain the relative effects of these different types of inequity on emotional reactions (i.e., a composite of all of the negative emotions, distress, anger, fear, and overall happiness), we estimate ordinarily least squares regression parameters with all four inequity measures entered into the models simultaneously. Whereas the majority of emotion items within the NSFH are measured in terms of "*the number of days in the last seven*" that the respondent experienced particular emotions, overall happiness is a global measure that ranges from extremely unhappy to extremely happy.

Fig. 3 displays the relative effects of underbenefiting and overbenefiting perceived inequity in household labor, paid work, spending, and childcare on an aggregated scale of negative emotions. As noted earlier in the chapter, when household inequity is included by itself (i.e., without other forms of inequity), the effects of underbenefiting and overbenefiting on negative emotions are strong. But, as seen in Fig. 3, when other forms of inequity in the home are controlled for, perceived inequity in household labor, along with inequity in childcare, has the *least* impact. Rather, the areas of underbenefiting and overbenefiting that appear most closely linked to negative emotions are paid work and spending.

We repeat this analysis by disaggregating negative emotions into three emotion clusters (distress, anger, and fear), as well as exploring overall happiness and a shortened version of the CES-D scale. These patterns are summarized in Table 2. For each dependent variable, each inequity is ranked in order of its relative strength (with 1 being the strongest and 4 being the weakest). For none of these variables is housework inequity the most influential. It should be quite apparent that household inequity

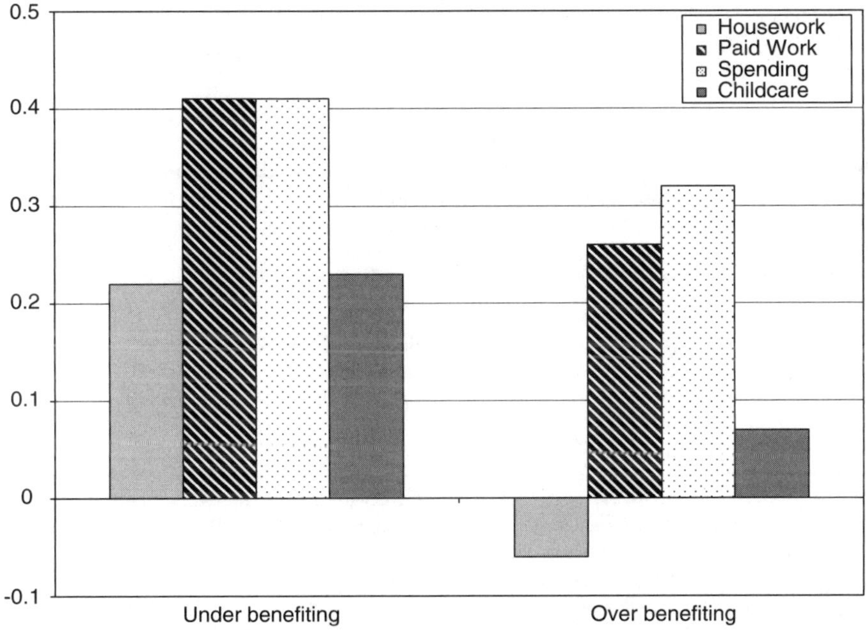

Fig. 3. Perceived Inequity in Housework, Paid Work, Spending, and Childcare: Simultaneous Effects on Negative Emotions (Aggregated Scale). *Notes:* Models included measures for perceived inequity for all domains simultaneously; models also control for gender, race, age, education, marital status (cohabiting vs. married), employment status, and reported amount of housework. *Source:* National Survey of Families and Households. *Metric:* Number of days in the past week respondents felt specific emotion(s).

typically wields the weakest or second weakest influence on the measures, with a key exception being happiness. The pattern is similar whether we look at underbenefiting or overbenefiting.

These results have clear implications and also offer challenges and opportunities for social psychologists and family sociologists. For social psychologists, especially those using experiments, they suggest that competing forms of inequity deserve study, but in a simultaneous fashion. For family sociologists, they suggest the importance of being careful not to assume the importance of any item without first explicitly comparing/contrasting its effects to the relative effects of others. These findings also speak to the importance of surveys including a broader range of familial dynamics, not just housework. Finally, and perhaps most notably, it

Table 2. Perceived Inequity in Housework, Paid Work, Spending, and Childcare: Effects on Emotions (in Order of Strength).

	Negative[a]	Distress	Anger	Fear	Depression[b]	Happiness
Underbenefiting						
Strongest effect	Paid work[c]	Spending[c]	Paid work[c]	Paid work	Spending[c]	Spending[c]
↑	Spending[c]	Paid work[c]	Spending[c]	Spending	Paid work	Housework
↓	Childcare	Childcare	Housework	Childcare	Housework	Paid work
Weakest effect	Housework	Housework	Childcare	Housework	Childcare	Childcare[c]
Overbenefiting						
Strongest effect	Paid work[c]	Paid work[c]	Spending[c]	Paid work[c]	Spending[c]	Spending
↑	Spending[c]	Spending[c]	Childcare	Spending[c]	Paid work[c]	Housework
↓	Childcare	Childcare	Paid work	Housework	Housework	Childcare
Weakest effect	Housework	Housework	Housework	Childcare	Childcare	Paid work

Notes: Models included measures for perceived inequity for all domains simultaneously; models also control for gender, race, age, education, marital status (cohabiting vs. married), employment status, and housework time.
Source: National Survey of Families and Households, $N = 4{,}840$.
[a]Negative is an aggregated score consisting of distress, anger, and fear.
[b]Depression is measured by the CESD.
[c]Significantly different from the effects of inequity in housework ($p < .05$).

implies that the emphasis on housework, although certainly important, inadvertently diverts our attention from other factors that may be even more salient. It may not be all that surprising that perceived inequities in domestic labor are less emotionally laden than other forms of inequity in the home – namely, spending and paid work. Sanchez and Kane (1996) argue that women interpret domestic labor as an opportunity to "do gender" – or, more specifically, "do femininity" – by engaging in stereotypically female tasks (DeMaris & Longmore, 1996; West & Zimmerman, 1987), whereas men may view less input as a way to "do masculinity" or to avoid tasks for which they have little preparation (Shelton & John, 1996). If so, the emotional benefits of fulfilling their feminine/masculine self-identities may counterbalance the sting of exploitation. These findings suggest that scholars' ongoing fascination with inequity in the household division of labor may have more to do with the enduring pull of Hochschild's (1989) "second shift" than with the relative effects of inequities in household labor when compared to inequities in other seemingly more volatile domains.

Cross-Cultural Variations in Perceptions and Consequences of Equity

Equity theory and its applications are rooted not in objective measures of equity, but rather in perceptions. When examining the relationship between inequity and emotions, researchers, therefore, must first take into account people's perceptions of the situation. Perceptions of inequity between strangers in brief exchanges may differ from those experienced within long-term or repeated interactions among intimates. Given cultural scripts about the nature of family and individuals' personal histories with particular family members, what people define as equitable in an experiment may not translate readily within a family.

Just as perceptions of equity may vary across the contexts of a survey or experiments, they may also vary cross-culturally. People's perceptions of equity are not created in a vacuum but are enmeshed in cultural norms regarding fairness, gender, and family. Cross-national social psychologists have championed research that takes such factors into account (Miller-Loessi, 1995). We believe that the study of equity is one realm where both experimental social psychologists and family scholars can augment our understanding of how particular cultures and their embedded norms have the ability to affect individual perceptions.

As an example, we analyzed the ISSP: 2002 Changing Family and Gender Roles. The ISSP is an ongoing program of cross-national collaboration on surveys covering topics important for social science research; this particular module, as indicated in the title, focuses exclusively on issues pertaining to family and gender issues. Our analysis of these data first examines variations in perceived inequity in the household division of labor ("*Which of the following best describes the sharing of household work between you and your spouse/partner?*"). These items are assessed using a 5-point scale ranging from "*I do much less than my fair share*" to "*I do much more than my fair share*." As in the other examples discussed earlier, these analyses are restricted to individuals who are either married or in a domestic relationship ($N = 29{,}377$).

For aggregated perceptions of equity to be accurate, a necessary (but not sufficient) condition requires a balance between those who say that they were doing more than their fair share and those who say they are doing less than their fair share. But the ISSP data show that this condition is not met in the United States: 40.4% of respondents report doing more than their fair share and only 17.9% report doing less than their fair share.

Although one could speculate that such a self-enhancing tendency is expected (Headley, 1986; Smith & Powell, 1990; Taylor & Brown, 1988), this imbalance is greater in the United States than in most other countries surveyed in the ISSP. In Hungary, for example, 20.1% say they are providing more than their fair share of housework and a comparable 19.6% say they are providing less than their fair share. In Japan, slightly more respondents (29.2%) say they do less than their fair share than those who say they do more (26.0%). Fig. 4 summarizes the result of a multinomial logistic regression comparing the odds of saying that one is doing more than one's fair share. This figure clearly demonstrates that the tendency to overestimate underbenefiting relative to overbenefiting is significantly higher in the United States than in 25 other countries.

As applied to principles of equity, these findings suggest that the United States tilts towards the extreme. In the bulk of studies on equity, either in laboratory settings or in the home, sociologists have focused routinely on the United States. But in the case of housework, Americans are more likely to perceive inequity – particularly when that inequity is disadvantageous to self. There are several plausible explanations for this pattern. As linked to the concept of self-enhancement (Headley, 1986; Smith & Powell, 1990; Taylor & Brown, 1988), individuals' tendency to self-enhance in the realm of domestic labor may be a function, in part, of the considerable discourse on household labor that occurs within the U.S. media and the academic presses. Another possibility may be tied to the American propensity towards "rugged individualism." Individuals who are more focused on their own individual contributions to household labor may be more likely to be less attuned to the contributions of others.

In the few empirical studies of equity in advanced industrial countries other than the United States, individuals appear to see the basic question of justice through a different prism and treat it with more consideration of the welfare of others in both small groups and large organizations. Indeed, the very definition of what constitutes equity in European discourse, for example, sounds more like parity or at the very least an assured equality of opportunity, regardless of individuals' real or relative contributions. These studies show that equity – including how people interpret what it is and react to it – cannot be disentangled from the cultural context in which it is embedded (Schmitt & Maes, 1998; Syroit & Poppe, 2000). They, along with the findings presented here also suggest that the scope of equity research focusing on the United States primarily may be unfortunately limited, if not skewed.

The cross-national fluctuations in perceptions of equity – and the location of the United States at one of the extremes – also prompted us to look at gender differences in perception across countries. In her ongoing work on

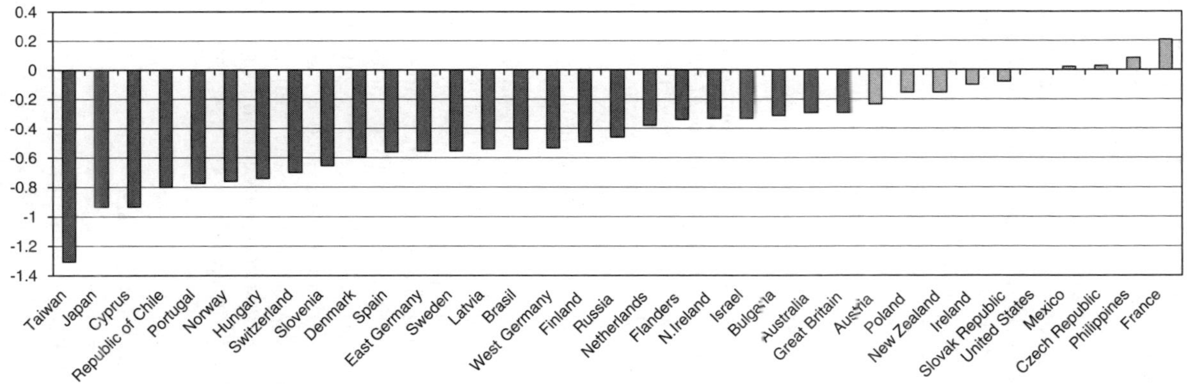

Fig. 4. Perceptions of Underbenefiting vs. Overbenefiting (Log Odds). *Notes:* Dark gray bars indicate a significant difference compare to the United States (reference category, model also controls for gender. Derived from multinomial logistic regression (categories: "more than fair share" (underbenefiting) "less than fair share" (overbenefiting), and "fair share"). Results for other comparisons (e.g., "more than fair share" vs. "fair share") are available upon request. *Source:* International Social Science Programme, $N = 29,377$.

women's and men's assessments of their contribution to the division of household labor, Claudia Geist, one of the coauthors of this chapter, finds significant gender differences not only in the reported number of hours of household labor performed, but also in perceptions of equity (or fairness). More importantly, these patterns vary considerably by country (Geist, forthcoming). As seen in Fig. 5, in only nine of the countries surveyed in the ISSP (Japan, Taiwan, Portugal, Hungary, Chile, Cyprus, Switzerland, Norway, and Slovenia) are women *more* likely than men to report that their contributions to the household labor are fair; in the majority of countries, however, men are more likely to report the same. Once again, the United States is towards the end of the spectrum – ranking among the countries with the greatest gender variation in perceptions of equity.

In addition to our interest in the effects of nationality on attributions of fairness, and gender differences therein, we have begun to examine how cross-national perceptions of equity relate to emotion. Unfortunately, ISSP includes only one item of interest on emotion: happiness ("*If you were to consider your life in general, how happy or unhappy would you say you are, as a whole?*"). Our preliminary analysis of this item reveals some intriguing cross-national variation. For example, although we see a fairly strong effect of underbenefiting occurs across countries, the effect of overbenefiting appears to be strongest in the cluster of post-communist countries (e.g., Poland and Bulgaria).

In sum, just as people's perceptions (and gender differences in perceptions) of their own contributions to household labor vary by country, so do their emotional reactions to perceived inequity. This calls into question the universality of equity principles gleaned predominantly from U.S. samples – not in terms of their existence (Mikula et al., 1998; Van Yperen & Buunk, 1990), but in terms of their relative effect on everyday emotions. Indeed, these types of variations underscore the need for equity researchers to look beyond the boundaries of the United States and to explore more comprehensively the types of political and/or welfare regimes where equity (or inequity) wields its greatest or weakest influence.[10]

CONCLUSION

Over a decade ago, we (Steelman & Powell, 1996) drew attention to the importance of applying social psychological theory to occurrences in naturalistic settings – in particular, the family. Since then, others also have advocated the need for more multi-methodological approaches to the study

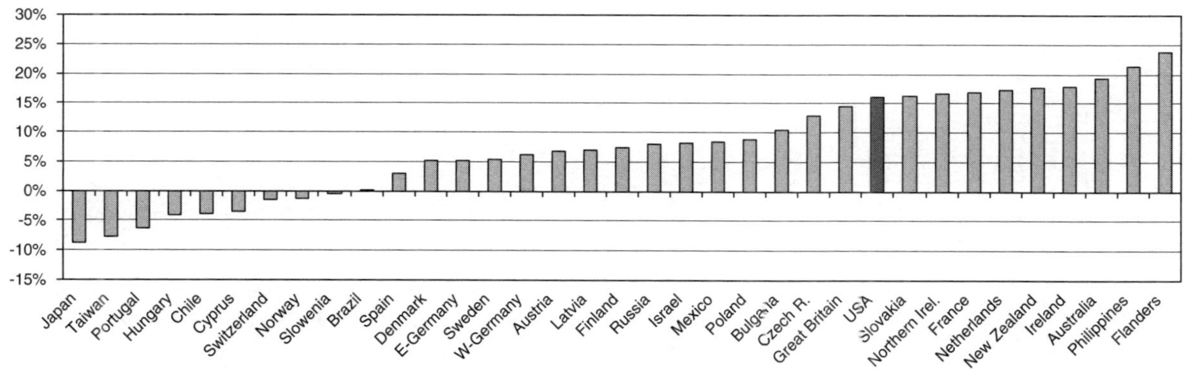

Fig. 5. Perceptions of Equity in Housework: Differences (in Percentages) between Men and Women Who Think They Do a "Fair Share" of Housework. *Note:* Positive scores indicate that men are more like than women to believe that they are doing a "fair share." *Source:* International Social Science Programme, $N = 29,377$.

of an array of topics (Lively, 2008; Morgan, 1998; Pearce, 2002). In fact, some social psychologists have already been successful in this type of merger (Blader & Tyler, 2003; Correll, Benard, & Paik, 2007; De Cremer & Tyler, 2007; Mikula, Petri, & Tanzer, 1990; Simpson & McGrimmon, 2005). We believe that equity theory is particularly ripe not only for study in naturalistic settings, but also for the development of a more synergistic relationship between survey research and experimental design.

Critics of experimental work often emphasize the utility of conducting analyses in "real-world settings"; however, to do so may undercut the ability of researchers to tease out causality and to ensure internal validity. That said, where some experimentalists could easily benefit from attending to the findings of family scholars is by broadening the scope of the emotions that they regularly study, as well as by more aggressively exploring the scope conditions by assessing whether the abstract relationships found under particular experimental conditions generalize to more complex situations and beyond the United States.

Similarly, family scholars, especially those relying on survey methodology, would do well to pay closer attention to the issue of causality in their research on the relationship between equity and emotion. When studies rely solely on survey data (particularly cross-sectional data), scholars relinquish an elegant feature of experimental design, namely random assignment of subjects to varying household labor regimens. The inability to manipulate the labor demands unfortunately raises the possibility of selection biases and challenges the causal ordering of variables.

Despite the theoretical appeal of equity theory and corroborating evidence from qualitative studies (Hochschild, 1989), most family scholars cannot unequivocally conclude that perceived inequity in the household division of labor causes emotional distress (also see Van Yperen & Buunk, 1990). Extrapolating from some tenets of affect control theory, Scher and Heise (1993), for instance, suggest that individuals may look to their environment, their own social roles, and the social roles of others in order to make sense of their feelings. Such an interpretation views emotions not as the end result of cognitive assessment of equity or justice, as do the majority of those studying perceived inequity in the family (Hochschild, 1989; Lennon & Rosenfield, 1994; Ross et al., 1983), but rather as a precursor of equity judgments. As one example, Scher and Heise contend that cultural scripts regarding feelings of anger and shame lead individuals to assess their situations as either fair or unfair. Psychological studies of mood and affect also show that individuals who are in bad moods are more likely than those who are in good moods to view their situations as inequitable (Gallagher &

Clore, 1985; Melton & Scher, 1992; O'Malley & Davis, 1984; Sinclair & Mark, 1992). If emotions do, in fact, drive equity judgments, our findings underscore the need to incorporate a wider spectrum of emotions that may facilitate such judgments not only within the context of long-term interpersonal relationships, but also in computer simulations and/or experimental settings.

The aforementioned research offers a formidable challenge to survey researchers who unwaveringly place equity as the independent variable and emotion as the dependent variable. Indeed, our reading of the literature suggests that both perspectives certainly have merits (also see Smith et al., 1998; Van Yperen & Buunk, 1990). There are, however, some statistical techniques that can be applied to cross-sectional survey data that may also shed some insight into the issue of causality. These non-recursive models enable researchers to compare the relative effects of both sides of the causal chain. In our own work, for example, we have used a series of two-stage least squares models that estimated the effects of perceived inequity and emotionality simultaneously. These auxiliary analyses suggest that the relative effect of perceived equity on emotions is greater than the effect of emotions on perceived equity (Lively et al., 2007; also see Van Yperen & Buunk, 1990). Even with advances in statistics techniques, however, these approaches remain, at best, inconclusive.

In reading through the literature on family, however, it becomes clear that the dichotomy that exists between research on equity and research on the family is not merely a methodological one, but more a split between social psychologists and family scholars. Although some family scholars use equity theory as a starting point, more often than not the theory is relegated to a minor role or is all but ignored. Even those scholars who use equity theory as part of their theoretical frame too often ignore basic insights – for example, that overbenefiting also matters to emotional well-being. This oversight ultimately disadvantages family scholars' analytic goals, which presumably include a desire to better understand how social processes (of which inequity is but one) operate within family life. By the same token, that family scholars do not rely on social psychological principles to the degree that we would prefer speaks not only to their seeming inattention to the work of social psychologists, but also to social psychologists' failure to build bridges beyond what may be perceived by others as an increasingly insular community.

These issues are not new. Over a decade has passed since we pointed to "an invisible wall" that separates social psychological research from research on the family (Steelman & Powell, 1996). Since then, some cracks have appeared, particularly as family scholars interested in the division of household labor have paid increasing attention to social psychological principles of equity. These studies, granted, have focused only on the more rudimentary principles of equity theory; nonetheless they add to earlier cross-fertilizations, including inquiries into dating, mate selection, and marriage that have drawn heavily from social psychological-based studies of exchange. Despite these advances the potential for more discussion – and collaboration – between the two fields abounds.

NOTES

1. We realize that the question of self-report data is an important one. See Simon and Nath (2004) for a detailed discussion of self-report data and social desirability within the GSS emotions module.

2. Although the module actually includes 19 emotion items, one of these – restless – is not included in our analysis because it is more appropriately classified as a cognitive-behavioral state than as an emotional one (Clore, Ortony, & Foss, 1987; Ortony, Clore, & Collins, 1988).

3. The models on which Figs. 1 and 2 are based also control for the amount of housework performed by both self and spouse (or cohabitating partner), as reported by the respondent. These items are measured by a 5-point scale ranging from 1 = very little to 5 = all. Consistent with other empirical examinations of household inequity, "actual" (i.e., reported amount) contributions wield less influence than perceived fairness of contributions. Models controlling for sex, race, age, education, income, employment status, marital status (married or cohabitating), and the presence of children in the home resulted in very similar patterns.

4. All results presented in the text are significant ($p < .05$), unless otherwise specified.

5. Inclusion of both anxious and depressive symptoms in CES-D and other depression scales also may mask the degree to which clusters of emotions are differentially affected by particular social arrangements (also see Hegtvedt & Killian, 1999). The CES-D also confounds emotion and behavior associated with generalized distress (e.g., the inability to sleep, eat, or concentrate).

6. Affect control theorists classify emotion by three culturally shared dimensions of affective meaning: evaluation (good or bad), potency (powerful or powerless), and activation (active or inactive) (Heise, 1977; Smith-Lovin & Heise, 1988). Studies indicate that positive, active, and powerful emotions correlate with positive, active, and powerful social statuses and behaviors, just as negative, inactive, and weak social statuses correlate with negative, inactive, and behaviors (Lively & Heise, 2004; Tsoudis & Smith-Lovin, 1998).

7. An appendix containing the descriptions, metrics, means, and alphas of these factors is available from the first author.

8. Although the equity items in both datasets are similar, the measurement of housework performed is not. Unlike the GSS (see footnote 3), the NSFH asks

respondents to report the number of hours they and their spouse/partner spend doing a variety of household items. These items are summed to create composite measures for both parties in the household.

9. The main effect of gender on emotions also functions differently in NSFH than in GSS. As noted in their comprehensive analysis of gender differences in emotion using the GSS emotions module, Simon and Nath (2004) report that the effects of gender on emotions are less significant than many sociological treatments on emotion might have expected. In its more limited set of emotions, the NSFH reveal much stronger main effects for gender.

10. Research regarding organizational commitment has reached similar conclusions to the ones we suggest regarding emotions. For example, Brockner et al. (2001) find considerable international variation in the effect of power distance on reactions to voice – that is, the extent to which people provide input into the decision process. See Morris and Leung (1999) for a comprehensive review of cross-national research regarding the psychology of distributive and procedural justice.

ACKNOWLEDGMENTS

The authors would like to thank Carl Ek, Christina Ek, R.D. Fulk, and Michael Yacavone for their insightful comments and support. This project was funded in part by the Nelson Rockefeller Center for Public Policy at Dartmouth College.

REFERENCES

Adams, S. J. (1965). Inequity in social exchange. *Advances in Experimental Social Psychology*, *2*, 267–299.

Austin, W. (1977). Equity theory and social comparison processes. In: J. M. Suls & R. L. Miller (Eds), *Social comparison theory* (pp. 279–305). Washington, DC: Hemisphere.

Austin, W., & Walster, E. (1974). Reactions to confirmation and disconfirmation of equity and inequity. *Journal of Personality and Social Psychology*, *30*, 208–216.

Blader, S. L., & Tyler, T. R. (2003). A four-component model of procedural justice: Defining the meaning of a "fair" process. *Personality and Social Psychology Bulletin*, *29*, 747–758.

Blair, S. L., & Johnson, M. P. (1992). Wives' perceptions of fairness and the division of household labor. *Journal of Marriage and the Family*, *54*, 570–581.

Brockner, J., Ackerman, G., Greenberg, J., Gelfand, M., Francesco, A. M., Chen, Z. X., Leung, K., Bierbrauer, G., Gomez, C., Kirkman, B., & Shapiro, D. (2001). Culture and procedural justice: The influence of power distance on reactions to voice. *Journal of Experimental Social Psychology*, *37*, 300–315.

Burke, P. (1991). Identity processes and social stress. *American Sociological Review*, *56*, 836–849.

Burke, P. J., & Harrod, M. M. (2005). Too much of a good thing. *Social Psychology Quarterly*, *68*, 359–374.

Clay-Warner, J. (2006). Procedural justice and legitimacy: Predicting negative emotional reactions to work place injustice. *Advances in Group Processes*, *23*, 207–227.

Clay-Warner, J., Hegtvedt, K., & Roman, P. (2005). Procedural justice, distributive justice: How experiences with downsizing condition their impact on organizational commitment. *Social Psychology Quarterly*, *68*, 89–102.

Clay-Warner, J., Reynolds, J., & Roman, P. (2005). Organizational justice and job satisfaction: A test of three competing models. *Social Justice Research*, *18*, 391–409.

Clore, G. L., Ortony, A., & Foss, M. A. (1987). The psychological foundations of the affective lexicon. *Journal of Personality and Social Psychology*, *53*, 751–766.

Collins, R. (2005). *Ritual interaction chains*. Princeton, NJ: Princeton University Press.

Coltrane, S. (2002). Research on household labor: Modeling and measuring the social embeddedness of routine family work. *Journal of Marriage and the Family*, *62*, 1208–1233.

Correll, S. J., Benard, S., & Paik, I. (2007). Getting a job: Is there a motherhood penalty? *American Journal of Sociology*, *112*, 1297–1338.

De Cremer, D., & Tyler, T. R. (2007). The effects of trust in authority and procedural fairness on cooperation. *Journal of Applied Psychology*, *92*, 639–649.

DeMaris, A., & Longmore, M. A. (1996). Ideology, power, and equity: Testing competing explanations for the perception of fairness in household labor. *Social Forces*, *74*, 1043–1071.

Gallagher, D., & Clore, G. L. (1985). Effects of fear and anger on judgments of risk and evaluations of blame. Paper presented at the annual meeting of the Midwestern Psychological Association, Chicago.

Geist, C. (forthcoming). Gendered views of domestic labor: Cross-national variation in men's and women's reports of housework. In: J. Treas, & S. Drobnic, (Eds), *Men, women, and household work in cross-national perspective*.

Glass, J., & Fujimoto, T. (1994). Housework, paid work, and depression among husbands and wives. *Journal of Health and Social Behavior*, *35*, 179–191.

Greenstein, T. N. (1996). Gender ideology and perceptions of the fairness of the division of household labor: Effects on marital quality. *Social Forces*, *74*, 1029–1042.

Goodwin, J., Jasper, J. M., & Polletta, F. (2001). *Passionate politics: Emotions and social movements*. Chicago: University of Chicago Press.

Headley, R. A. (1986). Everybody but me: Self-other referents in social research. *Sociological Quarterly*, *56*, 245–258.

Hegtvedt, K. A. (1990). The effects of relationship structure on emotional responses to inequity. *Social Psychology Quarterly*, *53*, 214–228.

Hegtvedt, K. A., Clay-Warner, J., & Ferrigno, E. (2002). Reactions to injustice: Factors affecting workers' resentment toward family friendly policies. *Social Psychology Quarterly*, *65*, 386–400.

Hegtvedt, K. A., & Killian, C. (1999). Fairness and emotions: Reactions to the process and outcomes of negotiations. *Social Forces*, *78*, 269–302.

Hegtvedt, K. A., & Markovsky, B. (1995). Justice and injustice. In: K. S. Cook, G. A. Fine & J. S. House (Eds), *Sociological perspectives on social psychology* (pp. 257–280). Boston: Allyn and Bacon.

Heise, D. R. (1977). Social action as the control of affect. *Behavioral Sciences*, *22*, 163–177.

Hochschild, A. R. (1989). *The second shift*. New York: Avon Books.

Homans, G. ([1961], 1974). *Social behavior: Its elementary forms*. New York: Harcourt-Brace.

Kemper, T. D. (1978). *A social interactional theory of emotion*. New York: Wiley.
Kessler, R. C., & McRae, J. A. (1982). The effects of wives' employment on the mental health of married men and women. *American Sociological Review*, *47*, 216–227.
Krause, N., & Markides, K. S. (1985). Employment and psychological well-being in Mexican American women. *Journal of Health and Social Behavior*, *26*, 15–26.
Krehbiel, P. J., & Cropanzano, R. (2000). Procedural justice, outcome favorability and emotion. *Social Justice Research*, *13*, 339–360.
Lawler, E. J., & Thye, S. R. (1999). Bringing emotions into social exchange theory. *Annual Review of Sociology*, *25*, 217–244.
Lennon, M. C., & Rosenfield, S. (1994). Relative fairness and division of housework: The importance of options. *American Journal of Sociology*, *100*, 506–531.
Lennon, M. C., Wasserman, G. A., & Allen, R. (1991). Infant care and wives' depressive symptoms. *Women and Health*, *17*, 1–23.
Lively, K. J. (2008). Emotional expression: The influence of "others" in hierarchical work settings. In: J. Clay-Warner, & D. Robinson, (Eds), *Social structure and emotion*. New York: Elsevier.
Lively, K. J. (Forthcoming). Emotional segueing and the management of emotion, by women and men. *Social Forces*
Lively, K. J., & Heise, D. R. (2004). Sociological realms of emotional experience. *American Journal of Sociology*, *109*, 1109–1136.
Lively, K. J., & Powell, B. (2006). Emotional expression at work and at home: Domain, status, or individual characteristics? *Social Psychology Quarterly*, *69*, 17–38.
Lively, K. J., Steelman, L. C., & Powell, B. (2004). Emotional responses of men and women to perceived fairness of the household division of labor. Paper presented at the annual meeting of the American Sociological Association, San Francisco.
Lively, K. J., Steelman, L. C., & Powell, B. (2007). *Equity, emotion, and household division of labor*. Unpublished manuscript.
Lovaglia, M. J., & Houser, J. (1996). Emotional reactions and status in groups. *American Sociological Review*, *61*, 867–883.
Mabry, J. B., & Kiecolt, K. J. (2005). Anger in black and white: Race, alienation, and anger. *Journal of Health and Social Behavior*, *46*, 85–101.
MacKinnon, N., & Keating, L. (1989). The structure of emotion: A review of the problem and a cross-cultural analysis. *Social Psychology Quarterly*, *52*, 70–83.
Massey, D. (2002). Emotion and the history of human society: The origin and role of emotion in social life. *American Sociological Review*, *67*, 1–29.
Melton, R. J., & Scher, S. J. (1992). The role of emotion in judgments and transgressors. Paper presented at the annual meeting of the Midwestern Psychological Association, Chicago.
Miller-Loessi, K. (1995). Comparative social psychology: Cross-cultural and cross-national. In: K. S. Cook, G. A. Fine & J. S. House (Eds), *Sociological perspectives on social psychology* (pp. 396–420). Boston: Allyn and Bacon.
Mikula, G. (1998). Division of household labor and perceived justice: A growing field of research. *Social Justice Research*, *11*, 215–241.
Mikula, G., Petri, B., & Tanzer, N. (1990). What people regard as unjust: Types and structures of everyday experiences of injustice. *European Journal of Social Psychology*, *20*, 133–149.
Mikula, G., Scherer, K. R., & Athenstaedt, U. (1998). The role of injustice in the elicitation of differential emotional reactions. *Personality and Social Psychology Bulletin*, *24*, 769–783.

Morgan, D. L. (1998). Practical strategies for combining qualitative and quantitative methods: Applications to health research. *Qualitative Health Research*, *8*, 362–376.
Morgan, R., & Heise, D. R. (1988). Structure of emotions. *Social Psychology Quarterly*, *51*, 19–31.
Morris, M. W., & Leung, K. (1999). Justice for all? Progress in research on cultural variation in the psychology of distributive and procedural justice. *Applied Psychology: An International Review*, *49*, 100–132.
Oliver, R. L., Shor, M., & Tidd, S. T. (2004). Inducing over-benefiting and under-benefiting on the web: Inequity effects on feelings and motivations with implications for consumption behavior. *Motivation and Emotion*, *28*, 85–106.
O'Malley, M. N., & Davis, D. K. (1984). Equity and affect: The effects of relative performance and reward allocation. *Basic and Applied Social Psychology*, *59*, 411–425.
Ortony, A., Clore, G. L., & Collins, A. (1988). *The cognitive structure of emotions*. New York: Cambridge University Press.
Pearce, L. D. (2002). Integrating survey and ethnographic methods for systematic anomalous case analysis. *Sociological Methodology*, *32*, 103–113.
Perry-Jenkins, M., & Folk, K. (1994). Class, couples, and conflict: Effects of the division of labor on assessments of marriage in dual-earner families. *Journal of Marriage and the Family*, *56*, 165–180.
Robinson, D., & Smith-Lovin, L. (1992). Selective interaction as a strategy for identity maintenance: An affect control model. *Social Psychology Quarterly*, *55*, 12–28.
Robinson, J., & Spitze, G. (1992). Whistle while you work? The effect of household task performance on women's and men's well-being. *Social Science Quarterly*, *73*, 844–861.
Ross, C. E., & Mirowsky, J. (1988). Child care and emotional adjustment to wives' employment. *Journal of Health and Social Behavior*, *29*, 127–138.
Ross, C. E., Mirowsky, J., & Huber, J. (1983). Work, sharing work, and in-between: Marriage patterns and depression. *American Sociological Review*, *48*, 809–823.
Sanchez, L. (1994). Gender, labor allocations, and the psychology of entitlement within the home. *Social Forces*, *73*, 533–553.
Sanchez, L., & Kane, E. W. (1996). Women's and men's constructions of perceptions of housework fairness. *Journal of Family Issues*, *17*, 358–387.
Scher, S. J., & Heise, D. (1993). Affect and the perception of injustice. *Advances in Group Processes*, *10*, 223–252.
Schieman, S. (2000). Education and the activation, course, and management of anger. *Journal of Health and Social Behavior*, *41*, 20–39.
Schmitt, M., & Maes, J. (1998). Perceived injustice in unified Germany and mental health. *Social Justice Research*, *11*, 59–78.
Shelton, B. A., & John, D. (1996). The division of household labor. *Annual Review of Sociology*, *22*, 299–322.
Simon, R., & Lively, K. J. (2005). Gender differences in dimensions of anger and their implications for distressing emotions. Paper presented at the meetings of the American Sociological Association, Philadelphia.
Simon, R., & Nath, L. (2004). Gender and emotion in the United States: Do men and women differ in self-reports of feelings and expressive behavior? *American Journal of Sociology*, *109*, 1137–1176.
Simpson, B., & McGrimmon, T. (2005). Trust and embedded exchange: A multi-method investigation. Paper presented at the annual meeting of the American Sociological Association, Philadelphia.

Sinclair, R. C., & Mark, M. M. (1992). The influence of mood state on judgment and action: Effects on persuasion, categorization, social justice, person perception and judgment accuracy. In: L. Martin & A. Tesser (Eds), *The construction of social judgments* (pp. 165–193). Hillsdale, NJ: Erlbaum.
Sloan, M. (2004). The effects of occupational characteristics on the experience of and expression of anger in the workplace. *Work and Occupations*, *31*, 38–72.
Smith, H. L., Gager, C. T., & Morgan, S. P. (1998). Identifying underlying dimensions in spouses' evaluations of fairness in the division of household labor. *Social Science Research*, *27*, 305–327.
Smith, H. L., & Powell, B. (1990). Great expectations: Variations in income expectations among college seniors. *Sociology of Education*, *63*, 194–207.
Smith-Lovin, L., & Heise, D. R. (1988). *Analyzing social interaction: Advances in affect control theory*. New York: Gordon and Breach.
Sprecher, S. (1986). The relation between inequity and emotions in close relationships. *Social Psychology Quarterly*, *49*, 309–321.
Sprecher, S. (1992). How men and women expect to feel and behave in response to inequity in close relationships. *Social Psychology Quarterly*, *55*, 57–69.
Steelman, L. C., & Powell, B. (1996). The family devalued: The treatment of the family in small groups literature. *Advances in Group Processes*, *13*, 213–238.
Stets, J. (2003). Justice, emotion and identity theory. In: P. Burke, T. Owens, R. Serpe & P. Thoits (Eds), *Advances in identity theory and research* (pp. 104–122). New York: Plenum Press.
Stets, J. (2004). Emotions in identity theory: The effect of status. *Advances in Group Processes*, *21*, 51–76.
Stets, J., & Tsushima, T. M. (2001). Negative emotion and coping responses within identity control. *Social Psychology Quarterly*, *64*, 283–295.
Syroit, J., & Poppe, M. (2000). Equity of input and outcome orientation on taking, hiving and dividing money. *Social Justice Research*, *14*, 41–53.
Taylor, S., & Brown, J. (1988). Illusion and well-being: A social psychological perspective on mental health. *Psychological Bulletin*, *103*, 193–210.
Thompson, L. (1991). Family work: Women's sense of fairness. *Journal of Family Issues*, *12*, 181–196.
Tsoudis, O., & Smith-Lovin, L. (1998). How bad was it? The effects of victim and perpetrator emotion on responses to criminal court vignettes. *Social Forces*, *77*, 695–722.
Tyler, T. R. (1994). Psychological models of the justice motive: antecedents of distributive and procedural justice. *Journal and Personality and Social Psychology*, *67*, 850–863.
Van Yperen, N. W., & Buunk, B. P. (1990). A longitudinal study of equity and satisfaction in intimate relationships. *European Journal of Social Psychology*, *20*(4), 287–309.
Walster, E. G., Walster, W., & Berscheid, E. (1978). *Equity: Theory and research*. Boston: Allyn and Bacon.
Weiss, H. M., & Suckow, K. (1999). Effects of justice conditions on discrete emotions. *Journal of Applied Psychology*, *84*, 786–794.
West, C., & Zimmerman, D. H. (1987). Doing gender. *Gender & Society*, *1*, 125–151.
Wilcox, W. B., & Nock, S. L. (2006). What's love got to do with it? Equality, equity, commitment and women's marital quality. *Social Forces*, *84*, 1321–1345.

THE CONTENTED FEMALE WORKER: STILL A PARADOX?

Charles W. Mueller and Sang-Wook Kim

ABSTRACT

The paradox of the contented female worker refers to the fact that women are generally disadvantaged (fewer material rewards) in the workplace relative to men, but are just as satisfied with their jobs as men. We review various arguments offered to explain the paradox with special attention given to justice-based explanations. Data collected from 30 countries as part of the 2005 ISSP are examined and show that the paradox is essentially a universal, worldwide phenomenon.

The phrase "the paradox of the contented female worker" (called "the paradox" in the rest of the chapter) was coined by Crosby (1982) to refer to the finding that women, although usually disadvantaged in the workplace (with lower pay, less autonomy, fewer promotions) relative to their male counterparts, do not express lower job satisfaction than their male co-workers. The large body of data consistent with this observation was not generated by concerns with explaining the paradox. Within an organizational behavior and sociology of work tradition gender has routinely been viewed as a demographic control variable and never considered important in theories of job satisfaction. Only after the paradoxical evidence became so daunting did researchers in this tradition (see Hodson, 1989; Hakim, 1991;

Justice
Advances in Group Processes, Volume 25, 117–149

ISSN: 0882-6145/doi:10.1016/S0882-6145(08)25006-X

Curtice, 1993; Phelan, 1994; Mueller & Wallace, 1996; Clark, 1997; Buchanan, 2005) begin to look seriously for theories to account for it. In contrast, those interested in microexchange justice theories (see Hegtvedt & Markovsky, 1995, for a review) have relied on equity principles outlined by Homans (1961), Blau (1964), and Adams (1965) and have often reported, and interpreted, gender differences. In fact, those from this tradition are unlikely to refer to the "contented female" as paradoxical because their arguments are formulated to explain precisely why women evaluate an apparent injustice as just.

Researchers from these two traditions have operated largely independently of each other. This is unfortunate but understandable. At the risk of over-generalizing, those specifying the paradox as their focus typically have been trained in organizational behavior and sociology of work traditions, study-dependent variables like job satisfaction, organizational commitment and absenteeism, and rely on survey data and regression models in which there are multiple independent variables with justice perceptions only sometimes being included. Those focusing on justice typically have been trained as social psychologists, emphasize justice-related processes, see job satisfaction as only one of many possible reactions to injustice, and rely more on laboratory experiments where a small number of effects (independent variables) are investigated.

What we can accomplish in this chapter is limited and we need to make our intentions clear. We come at this task from an organizational behavior/sociology of work tradition and we want to understand variation in job satisfaction and, in particular, we want to know why women are as satisfied as men when they do not receive the same rewards as men. We *will* review the arguments that have appeared in the paradox literature and sort them according to whether they are justice based or not, and we also will try to show how faithful these claims are to justice arguments as presented in the justice literature. We *will not* attempt an extensive review of the justice literature in search of *the* justice explanation for the paradox. We lack the expertise in the justice field to undertake this. In addition, our examination of this literature suggests that there is no consensus among justice scholars as to why the paradox exists.

More concretely, we have three objectives. The first is to provide some background on the study of job satisfaction. Doing this will place the study of the paradox in the broader context of this immense body of literature. The second objective is to review the arguments offered to explain the paradox. Here we differentiate between arguments that are justice based and those that are not. The third objective is to provide some preliminary, but relevant, data on the existence of the paradox in an international context. Using data on 30 countries from the 2005 ISSP survey, we are able to determine if the paradox is universal, that is, whether it exists across nations differentiated by political/economic development and by geographical location (e.g., East vs. West). This presentation of data is not meant to provide tests for any of the arguments, but instead, is to document that the paradox is still an important phenomenon deserving theoretical and empirical attention.

JOB SATISFACTION

Definition and Correlates

Job satisfaction is the degree to which people like their jobs (Spector, 1997). It is an employee's affective response to work. Job satisfaction is studied as both a dependent variable and an independent variable. Although the emergence of restructured, efficient, "lean and mean" organizations in response to globalization over the past several decades seems to have turned scholarly research away from concerns with employee satisfaction, historically, satisfaction with one's job remains as the most studied variable in the fields of organizational behavior and the sociology of work because it has important consequences for employees and the organizations that hire them.

Job satisfaction is routinely measured by self-reports in questionnaires. Measures have been shown to be both reliable and valid (see Spector, 1997, for six often used scales). Global job satisfaction refers to the employee's general feelings about a job and is typically measured by questions referencing "the job," whereas facet-specific job satisfaction measures ask about particular aspects of one's job, for example, pay, security, co-workers, and promotion opportunities. The correlations among these facet-specific job satisfaction measures vary in magnitude, but are all positive (Spector, 1997). The bulk of the research on job satisfaction involves the study of global satisfaction, which also is true in the research on the paradox.

Employee job satisfaction is important to organizations because satisfied workers are more loyal, are less likely to be absent, are more productive (Spector, 1997), and are less likely to leave (thus saving the company search, hiring, and orientation expenses). As a consequence many organizations still routinely assess the job satisfaction of their employees.

Job satisfaction is also consequential for employees. One may hear stories about people who "seem to enjoy being unhappy," but these clearly are exceptions and there is little doubt that satisfaction with one's work is rewarding and desirable. Job satisfaction is positively correlated with general life satisfaction and with family satisfaction. Meta-analyses (e.g., Iaffaldano & Muchinsky, 1985; Carsten & Spector, 1987; Fried, 1991) have identified numerous variables that are related to job satisfaction. These correlates can be cataloged as potential causes and effects of job satisfaction. On the one hand, work conditions like autonomy, opportunities for advancement, pay, and work group cohesion are positively related to job satisfaction and are logically argued to causally affect it. On the other hand, commitment (loyalty) to the organization, absenteeism, job search, and turnover are all viewed as consequences of an employee's degree of job satisfaction. Meta-analysis (Faragher, Cass, & Cooper, 2003) has even shown job satisfaction to be consistently related to one's health. The overall correlation combined across all health measures was $r = 0.312$ (0.370 after Schmidt-Hunter adjustment). Job satisfaction was most strongly associated with mental/psychological problems (e.g., –.478 for burnout and .429 for self-esteem) and was more modestly correlated with subjective physical illness ($r = -0.287$).

Theories of Job Satisfaction

Given that job satisfaction has received so much attention, it is not surprising that there are numerous theories offered to explain it. Although these theories were never developed to explain the paradox, we will indicate what each argument leads us to hypothesize about gender differences in job satisfaction.

As reviewed by Spector (1997) (see also Kalleberg, 1977, for a somewhat different review) there are two general arguments about what produces job satisfaction. The first claims that one's environment (work setting) is the key factor. This is also referred to as the *situational* (or structural) argument. The job characteristics theory (Hackman & Oldham, 1976, 1980) is the most influential theory of this type. They argue that work conditions that allow for skill variety, task identity, and task significance induce the psychological state of meaningfulness of work; autonomy in decision-making results in feelings of responsibility; and feedback increases one's knowledge of the products of work. When these three psychological states are elevated, work motivation and job satisfaction will be higher. Various extensions and modifications of this logic have led to the addition of a number of work/job conditions (e.g., organizational constraints like information needed for the job and time available to complete the job), role-theory derived factors like role ambiguity and role conflict, work-family conflict, and job stress. All of these work condition factors are viewed as producing psychological states that in turn affect work motivation and job satisfaction.

Implied hypothesis about gender differences in job satisfaction: Women will be less satisfied than men (because in reality their work situations are less rewarding). Obviously, this lower job satisfaction for women has not been found, and encourages use of the label "the gender paradox in job satisfaction."

In the mid-1980s personality (*disposition*) arguments (e.g., Arvey, Bouchard, Segal, & Abraham, 1989) re-emerged to claim that some individuals are genetically predisposed to be positive or negative and these personality-based predispositions are significant determinants of job satisfaction. In addition, there exists the general cultural belief that women report emotions more frequently than men (Simon & Nath, 2004). These dispositional arguments received a considerable boost from longitudinal research (Staw, Bell, & Clausen, 1986) showing that affective disposition in adolescence is significantly correlated with job satisfaction measured up to 50 years later.

Implied hypothesis about gender differences in job satisfaction: If women have more positive dispositions, they will be more satisfied with their jobs than men. If supported, the paradox is explained because positive dispositions of women will override the negative impact of their less rewarding work conditions.

A third category of theories attempts to account for the fact that employees in the same job have different levels of job satisfaction. Spector (1997) (see also Edwards, 1991; Mortimer & Lorence, 1979) calls these the *person-job fit* arguments, whereas Kalleberg refers to them with the phrase "the match between situational rewards and worker values." The basic claim is that if one's rewards match one's values (interests or expectations), then job satisfaction will be enhanced. Although not initially developed to explain the paradox, a form of this argument has been adopted to account for the paradox (see "differential values" and "met expectations" arguments below in the section on paradox explanations).

Implied hypothesis about gender differences in job satisfaction: Women have different values (motivations for working) than men, and if women's values are reinforced by workplace rewards, they will be as satisfied as their male counterparts.

EXPLANATIONS FOR THE PARADOX

Phelan (1994) spells out five plausible hypotheses for why women are not less satisfied with their jobs than males: (1) "differential job inputs" hypothesis, (2) "own-gender referents" hypothesis, (3) "differential entitlement standards" hypothesis, (4) "differential job values" hypothesis, and (5) "subjective rewards" hypothesis. The first three hypotheses are based on applying arguments from distributive justice theories: women accept, and are satisfied with, their lower rewards (less pay, less autonomy, fewer promotions) because they conclude that what they receive is fair and just. We elaborate on these three and then consider two additional justice-based arguments. Our review, however, begins with the explanations that are not justice based.

Explanations that are Not Justice Based

Drawing from the person-job fit approach, the "*differential job values*" hypothesis has received the most attention in explaining the paradox (see Hodson, 1989; Spector, 1997; Medgyesi & Róbert, 2002). The argument states that women's low pay and limited access to promotions will not reduce their job satisfaction because they do not value these extrinsic (material) rewards as highly as do men. In addition, it is argued that a woman's job satisfaction will be increased when nonmaterial, social rewards like co-worker and supervisor support are present because women are said to value these rewards more than men. Although this argument could be interpreted within a justice framework (what women expect (value) is what they believe is just, so if they expect less, then getting less will be considered just and job satisfaction will not be lowered), the differential values argument for the paradox simply is not presented in justice terms.

Although often "the default" explanation, little empirical support has appeared for this popular explanation for the paradox. The argument has been assessed by directly comparing men and women on the importance they give to various workplace rewards (e.g., Mueller & Wynn, 2000) or, more often, by comparing the effects (regression coefficients) of various workplace rewards on job satisfaction (Hodson, 1989; Phelan, 1994; Rowe & Snizek, 1995; Mueller & Wallace, 1996), where it is argued that gender differences in these coefficients mean that women and men differentially value these rewards. As an example, if one's pay has a positive effect on job satisfaction for men, but has no (or only a small) effect for women, then this is interpreted to mean that women do not value pay highly. The interaction tests necessary to assess this possibility, however, have consistently shown no gender differences.

The "*subjective rewards*" hypothesis is derived from the well-recognized fact that "objective" features of work like pay and promotions are not very important in explaining job satisfaction for either women or men. Instead, worker perceptions (subjective) of work features like variety, co-worker and supervisor support, job security, and workload are more important determinants of job satisfaction. The "subjective rewards" hypothesis states that because perceptions of these subjective factors (rewards) do not differ for women and men, their satisfaction levels will be the same. Phelan (1994) claims support for this argument, but Mueller and Wallace (1996) find that women do perceive lower levels of rewards for many of these more subjective workplace conditions. Empirical analysis of this type is seldom carried out by those interested in the paradox, however.

The *disposition* argument of job satisfaction as applied to the paradox does not rely on a justice-based logic, but it can be examined as an explanation for gender differences in job satisfaction. Based on a 1996 U.S. national survey, Simon and Nath (2004) find gender differences in affectivity, but their results are opposite of those needed to support the implied hypothesis about the paradox. They find that women more often report negative feelings and men more often report positive feelings. However, this claim of gender differences is not supported by the more convincing evidence from Watson's (2000) extensive review and meta-analysis of the research (cross-sectional and longitudinal studies of adults and college students) on gender differences in positive and negative affectivity. He finds that the "general Negative and Positive Affect scales are essentially unrelated to gender" (2000, p. 208). Consistent with this, a meta-analysis (Else-Quest, Hyde, Goldsmith, & Van Hulle, 2006) of research on children aged 3 months to 13 years shows "negligible gender differences" in negative affectivity (positive affectivity was not part of the analysis). We conclude that gender differences in job satisfaction are not due to gender differences in affectivity.

Finally, the "*selectivity*" hypothesis for the paradox has also been proposed. In studying gender differences in organizational commitment, where the paradox is also found, Marsden, Kalleberg, and Cook (1993) argue that traditionally women have had more choice than men in whether or not to be employed. Women who do decide to enter the labor force are thus disposed to be more committed (more satisfied) than men, who generally do not have this decision to make. This predisposition to be satisfied overrides the less rewarding work conditions women actually experience. We know of no tests of this hypothesis.

Justice-based Explanations

There are many justice theories (see Jasso, 1978, 1980; Hegtvedt & Markovsky, 1995) but what all have in common is the idea that, at the level of the individual, what is considered just (fair) is in the "eye of the beholder." Distributive justice evaluations are subjective and are based on some set of rules or norms. Justice allocation norms include the need norm (greatest rewards are distributed to those with the greatest need), the equality norm (rewards are distributed equally), and the equity norm (rewards are distributed according to one's contributions). The justice-based attempts to explain the paradox have consistently considered equity-driven perceptions of distributive justice and the following discussion assumes this unless stated otherwise.

Subjective justice evaluations are studied as an end (dependent variable) and as a means to other ends (an independent variable) (Törnblom, 1992). Whereas these two strands of justice research are often undertaken independently of each other (Hegtvedt & Markovsky, 1995), justice-based explanations for the paradox view justice evaluations as the critical mediating (intervening) variable; something triggers a justice evaluation and this justice evaluation leads to one's satisfaction level. This means both the "justice as an end" and "justice as a means" questions must be addressed by those interested in the paradox. We consider the "justice evaluations affect job satisfaction" link first. It is by far the less controversial of the two linkages.

Following Younts and Mueller (2000), we differentiate between the justice evaluation and the justice perception. The evaluation refers to the mental calculus used by the individual and is what differentiates the justice-based arguments we review below. The justice perception is the person's conclusion about justice (I'm justly rewarded, under-rewarded, or over-rewarded) and flows directly from that person's justice evaluation. We should point out, once again, differences in organizational behavior/sociology of work and social psychological approaches to justice. The former typically is concerned with the justice perception, while the latter is more interested in the justice evaluation process.

The Link between Justice Perceptions and Job Satisfaction

For justice accounts to be plausible for the paradox there must exist a positive relationship between justice perceptions and job satisfaction. In addition to the laboratory evidence (Walster, Walster, & Berscheid, 1978) that people are less satisfied with, and more likely to want change with inequitable than with equitable conditions, there is clear nonexperimental evidence of a link between justice perceptions and job satisfaction.

Mainly working within the situational approach, job satisfaction researchers often measure employee perceptions of distributive justice by obtaining Likert-type responses to items like "promotions or unscheduled pay increases here depend on how well a person performs his or her job." Witt and Nye (1992), in their meta-analysis of the justice-satisfaction relationship, found the correlation between perceived promotion fairness and job satisfaction to be .43 and perceived pay fairness and job satisfaction to be .28. So, clearly, perceptions of fairness in a work setting do positively affect job satisfaction. The more problematic question is the "justice as an end" question, that is, what determines the justice perceptions and how is this different for men and women?

Five Justice-Based Accounts of What Produces Justice Perceptions

This section is not meant to examine all explanations for justice perceptions. Such a task is well beyond the goals of this chapter. We refer to arguments about justice that have appeared in, or are closely linked to, the paradox literature.

The "*differential job inputs*" hypothesis draws from Adams (1965) and states that women perceive justice (and thus higher job satisfaction) because they believe their lower rewards are the consequence of their lower inputs (e.g., education, job tenure, effort). The comparisons implied in this argument are never directly assessed in the paradox research, however. Instead, mean gender differences in job satisfaction are examined after inputs are statistically controlled (Phelan, 1994; Mueller & Wallace, 1996). These researchers claim no support for this hypothesis.

The "*own-gender referents*" hypothesis states that women compare themselves with other women, rather than men, in evaluating whether they are treated justly. Because other working women generally are rewarded at lower levels than men, women accept this as the norm and express higher job satisfaction because they are treated just like other women (their reference group). Data consistent with this argument come from laboratory research (Major & Forcey, 1985) showing that both women and men do not compare themselves with some more general average of the rewards others receive, but instead with the rewards of others of the same gender in the same job.

Drawing from status value theory and arguments about relative deprivation, Moore (1991) utilizes survey data to address her hypothesis that

> "…at every stage of the entitlement process, women will choose different options than men (different comparison others, different wage gaps, different evaluations and reward preferences, different levels of deprivation); as a result women will report lower levels of entitlement than men, especially when they work in female-type occupations. (Moore, 1991, p. 213)"

Moore finds considerable support for the hypothesized gender differences. However, this kind of detailed nonexperimental analysis of how women and men differ in forming beliefs about entitlement is rare in the study of the paradox.

Interest in gender workplace composition as related to job satisfaction has been prominent in research in the organizational demography tradition (see Wharton, Rotolo, & Bird, 2000) that draws from arguments by Kanter (1977). It has been suggested (Major, 1989; Blysma & Major, 1992) that in female-dominant work settings women will more often compare themselves to other women not only because it is convenient to do so, but also because it helps avoid discomfort associated with gender inequity usually found in the workplace. Inferences about justice processes in this organizational demography tradition have only been indirect, however. Neither a person's comparison group nor his/her justice evaluations is actually measured.

The "*differential entitlement standards*" hypothesis is also justice-theory based and also states that women expect less than what men receive, but the emphasis is on their learning and internalizing this fact rather than their directly comparing themselves to other women. Women learn to expect less either through early socialization and/or through various workplace experiences that embed and reinforce such beliefs. Women simply become resigned to the inequality and express higher satisfaction because what they get from work is what they perceive they deserve. Laboratory research (Kahn, 1972; Major, McFarlin, & Gagnon, 1984) has produced results consistent with this hypothesis – not only do women pay themselves less than males for the same amount of work but underpayment for a designated task was assessed more favorably by women than men.

We believe that labeling this the "entitlement" argument is unfortunate and prefer to call it the "differential socialization" argument. Researchers (e.g., Moore, 1991) define entitlement as the amount of reward a person believes she/he should receive. This is the same as the "just reward" in Jasso's (1978, 1980) theory and could be based on any number of comparisons or evaluations. Specifying that the just reward comes from what one has been socialized to accept indicates where these entitlement beliefs come from. Also important to note is that the socialization argument may be subsumed more generally under the status value theory (Berger, Zelditch, Anderson, & Cohen, 1972; Hegtvedt & Markovsky, 1995). Gender is a diffuse status characteristic. Women are culturally assigned a lower status; they are expected to perform (and be rewarded) at a lower level; they are treated this way, often accept their treatment as being what they are entitled to, adjust their behavior accordingly, and are just as satisfied as their male counterparts. Although status value arguments are, in general, well-supported empirically, their application to unraveling the paradox has been limited (but see Moore, 1991).

Another approach to explaining justice perceptions seems to fit in with the differential socialization argument. Mueller, Iverson, and Jo (1999) compare U.S. and South Korean data on teachers to test the hypothesis that the more one believes his/her expectations about job related rewards have been met, the greater is the evaluation that one's own rewards are fair. The comparison of one's rewards, then, is not with the rewards for some other person or category of persons, but with one's expectations when taking the job. Met expectations are found to be strongly positively related to justice perceptions as hypothesized in both societies, while any societal differences are explained in terms of differences in the dominant societal values. Gender is only a control variable in the analysis and gender comparisons in what produces the justice perceptions are not undertaken. Also, although this research documents the connection between met reward expectations and justice perceptions, it does not tell us anything about the source of these expectations nor does it inform us as to the evaluation process the individual undertakes to determine if the expectations were met. There is potential, however, for application of this argument to understanding the paradox in terms of socialization differences.

There are two additional justice-based arguments claiming to account for the paradox. As presented in the research by Brockner and Adsit (1986), we call the first of these the "*differential norms*" hypothesis. They begin by reviewing the finding that men are more likely to use an equity norm in allocating rewards, whereas women are more likely to use an equality norm (Leventhal & Lane (1970); Lane & Messe, 1971; Kahn, 1972). From this conclusion about allocation they make the "jump" to justice as a means and claim that men's job satisfaction will be influenced more by inequity than will the job satisfaction of women. They predict that when women and men assess their rewards using an Adams type of equity evaluation, the evaluation will matter less for the job satisfaction of women. Their small-sample study confirms this when they find a considerably stronger positive relationship between equity perceptions and job satisfaction for men. Stated with respect to the paradox, women are just as satisfied as men because their satisfaction is not strongly determined by their evaluation of equity in the workplace. We note that this is not the same argument as the differential inputs explanation, which has both women and men relying on the equity norm in making justice evaluations.

This conclusion has been challenged by Witt and Nye (1992), who conducted a meta-analysis for gender differences in the relationship between distributive justice perceptions and job satisfaction. Counter to the Brockner and Adsit (1986) conclusion, they find that the positive relationship between perceptions of equity and job satisfaction is the same for women and men. So, women may use equity norms less in the allocation of rewards, but reward distributions based on an equity norm are just as critical as they are for men in determining their job satisfaction. Additional research is consistent with this conclusion. Across ten studies that measured workplace values (how important is feature X to you?), Mueller and Wynn (2000) find that "the importance of being treated fairly for the work you do" did not differ significantly between women and men in four of the studies; in the other six studies, the significant difference indicated that women actually value distributive justice more than men. Clearly, then, and using Markovsky's (1985) term, women are not more "indifferent" than men to equity-based reward distributions. We may importantly conclude that women's paradoxically high job satisfaction is not because they care less about equitable workplace treatment.

The Witt and Nye (1992) meta-analysis produces one additional finding of importance in understanding the paradox. They find no mean gender difference in justice perceptions (the degree to which they perceive they are rewarded fairly). Also important and consistent with these results, (Jasso & Wegener, 1999, Figure 1A) report very small gender differences in perceived (expressed) pay justice (under-reward) for 11 of 13 countries in the early 1990s. However, when considering Jasso's justice evaluation (ln [actual reward/just reward]), under-rewarded women generally experience less injustice than under-rewarded men (Jasso & Wegener, 1999, Figure 1B). Assuming women are, indeed, usually under-rewarded relative to men, women's evaluations of less injustice could explain why their job satisfaction is not lower.

To sum up this section on differential norms, women, although receiving fewer workplace rewards (in nonexperimental settings), *perceive* the same level of equity-based treatment as men and this perception of justice has the same effect on job satisfaction as it does for men. This is precisely what the justice-based arguments predict, and it amplifies our conclusion that the critical unanswered question is what produces the perceptions of justice and not whether justice perceptions affect job satisfaction.

The final justice-based argument, although usually directed only at earnings as a reward and not claimed to explain the paradox, is offered by Jasso and Webster (1997, 1999) and Jasso and Wegener (1999). The strategy draws from Jasso's (1978, 1980) earlier work and involves what is called the *multiple standards framework*: "… *observers* judge the *just rewards* of *rewardees*; and characteristics of both observers and rewardees may affect judgements" (Jasso & Webster, 1999, p. 368). An individual's justice evaluation involves the comparison of that individual's (or another's) actual reward and just reward (what individuals regard as just for themselves or for others). As referred to above, this is represented mathematically as the natural log of the ratio of actual reward to just reward. The justice evaluation is zero if justice is perceived, negative if under-reward injustice is perceived, and positive if over-reward injustice is perceived. Gender differences are examined with respect to gender gaps in both just and actual earnings and in the functions that predict these. Specifically, in her research with Webster (1997, 1999) using a quasi-experimental design and in cross-national research (Jasso & Wegener, 1999) the gender gap in actual and just earnings is examined.

Although not directed at explaining the paradox, this line of research has yielded important data on gender differences in justice evaluations. Perhaps more importantly, the multiple standards framework actually subsumes the "differential inputs," differential norms," and "same-gender referent" arguments under a general theoretical framework. Comparing results (U.S. data) with an earlier study (Jasso & Rossi, 1977), the authors report historical changes in the gender gap in actual and perceived just earnings. The actual earnings gap (female/male ratio) has been reduced with time; in the 1970s it was in the .60s, whereas in 1998 it was .76. And although the earlier data are less reliable and pose comparison problems, the just gap appears to have been reduced also; the just gap was .85 among a sample of white Baltimore adults in 1974 and was 1.06 for college students in 1995. Also, in 1974 women were somewhat less favorable (than men) toward other women, while in 1995 men were more favorable (than women) toward women. We learn that female and male college students believe women should receive more than men.

The most valuable conclusions come from the second part of this approach to justice, which is an analysis of whether similar principles of justice are used to arrive at just earnings by women and men. The authors find that there are significant gender differences in just base wage and in just returns to schooling and experience. For both women and men, women are assigned a higher just base wage and a higher just rate of return to education than men, while men are assigned a higher rate of return to experience. They also observe consistent differences in how women and men arrive at just earnings; women are more attentive to gender differences in returns to education and experience than men, and it appears that men are essentially blind to gender in assessing just returns to human capital investments.

Assuming this last finding can be replicated, it gives us potential insight into the paradox. For the own-gender referent argument to be valid, women must recognize that what produces just earnings for women and men is different before they can then reference other women in deciding if their own rewards are just. Although Jasso and Webster (1997, 1999) limit the number of standards (gender of observer and rewardee and experience [age] and education), this approach has the potential for other standards to be used. It must be remembered, however, that these two studies do not examine how the observer arrives at his/her own just reward, but assesses just rewards for fictitious others in a vignette format. The Jasso and Wegener (1999) study does, however, estimate just and actual functions for one's own actual earnings and carries out a very similar analysis separately for 13 countries. This strategy is consistent with what Phelan has called the differential inputs argument – individuals evaluate what a just reward is based on what they "input" to the work setting.

We are optimistic about application of the Jasso and Webster arguments and their research design in better understanding the paradox. The multiple factors argument, in fact, suggests that there are numerous other factors (e.g., family situation, employment of the mother, the gender composition of the workplace, the gender composition of their occupation, sexual harassment in the workplace) that could affect perceptions of justice and in turn job satisfaction. Although there is considerable potential in the application of this strategy to the study of the paradox, we must mention some concerns.

We want to remind the reader again that Jasso's justice evaluation is not the same as the justice perception (how an individual directly responds to questions about being fairly rewarded given one's inputs) measured in the paradox literature. Younts and Mueller (2001) recognize this in their paper that utilizes the Jasso justice evaluation of pay to predict perceptions of pay fairness and in turn pay satisfaction. Relative to other independent variables the pay justice evaluation has the strongest net effect on pay justice perceptions, but the zero-order correlation between the Jasso justice evaluation and perceived pay justice is only .44. Although this is but one study, the magnitude of this relationship suggests considerable slippage between the Jasso justice evaluation measure and what individuals say they perceive about justice in the workplace. Jasso clearly is aware of this distinction and argues for her measurement strategy as producing the "true" just score, whereas the more direct measures like those in the paradox studies yield a "disclosed" or "expressed" just score that is "contaminated by rhetoric, socialization, and other elements" (Jasso & Webster, 1999). Given, however, that it is differences in job satisfaction that we want to explain, it is important to point out that, in the Younts and Mueller (2001) study, pay satisfaction (global satisfaction was not included) is correlated .65 with the "disclosed" pay justice perception, .83 with the "disclosed" global justice perception, but only .39 with the Jasso "true" justice evaluation. This only goes to show what was learned some time ago in the organizational behavior/sociology of work literature: employee subjective perceptions of their work conditions, rather than more objective measures of these conditions, are consistently more important in explaining outcomes like job satisfaction and work commitment. Simply put, people respond based on their perceptions.

We want to close this section with a comment on the importance of justice perceptions in explaining job satisfaction relative to "self-interest" claims. Younts and Mueller (2001) find that pay is correlated .25 with pay satisfaction (see also Randall & Mueller, 1995), whereas perceived justice in the pay distribution is correlated .65 with pay satisfaction. This supports our conclusion that justice-based accounts are critical in explaining the paradox.

DATA AND METHODS

The data come from the 2005 ISSP (International Social Survey Programme). The ISSP is an international collaborative research network of academic social surveys covering major topics of social scientific interest. Established in 1984, the ISSP embodies two basic missions of generating quality survey data and disseminating it all over the world, just like what the GSS has been doing in the U.S. since 1972. Those missions are accomplished by developing a common survey module each year concerning a specific topic and implementing it simultaneously in the member countries. As of 2007, 43 countries are participating in these cross-national surveys. With a stringent adherence to basic guidelines in designing major aspects of the social survey, such as sampling, questionnaires, and fieldwork, the ISSP is renowned for its quality data. Work Orientations III, the 2005 ISSP module, provides the data we use in the chapter. The module is the third replication following the 1st (1989) and 2nd (1997) modules directed at Work Orientations. A total of 30 member countries have fielded the module survey, and we analyze data from all of these countries.

The data we present are not meant, in any way, to provide a critical test of the various hypotheses. The purpose is to provide recent descriptive data on the 30 countries. We want to determine if the paradox exists worldwide. To do this we report gender differences in job satisfaction (and organizational commitment) for each country and we report gender differences in logged earnings and access to a supervisory position. We also present data on the degree to which women and men value eight workplace rewards. This provides information on whether there are gender differences in workplace values. Also, as relevant to the "subjective rewards" hypothesis, we present data on the degree to which women and men differ in their perceptions of various workplace rewards they receive. Finally, in considering the differential socialization argument, we present data on gender differences in job satisfaction by age.

We display results separately for each country but have also grouped countries following Medgyesi and Róbert (2002). Western developed countries are France, Germany, Great Britain, Switzerland, Australia, Canada, United States, Ireland, Israel, New Zealand, and Flanders. Asian developed countries are Japan, South Korea, and Taiwan. Nordic countries are Denmark, Norway, Sweden, and Finland. The EU periphery countries are Portugal, Spain, and Cyprus. Developed countries that have transitioned from socialist economic/political systems are Czech Republic, Hungary, and Slovenia, while two transition countries that are less developed are Russia and Latvia. Two Latin American countries are Mexico and Dominican Republic. Finally, in the "other" category are the Philippines and South Africa.

Our goals did not include developing a theoretical framework for hypothesizing cultural differences in the existence of the paradox. For this reason, we are reluctant to attempt interpretations of cross-cultural differences we observe. This certainly deserves attention, but is beyond the scope of this chapter.

Finally, unless stated otherwise, the results we report in tables are for individuals who are working, are not self-employed, and report nonzero earnings for the previous year. However, because women are more likely to be part-time employees for whom pay and access to a position of authority are lower, we also report, when appropriate, results for only full-time employees.

RESULTS

Gender Differences in Job Satisfaction

Job satisfaction was measured with the question "How satisfied are you with your job?" and is coded as (1) completely dissatisfied, (2) very dissatisfied, (3) fairly dissatisfied, (4) neither satisfied nor dissatisfied, (5) fairly satisfied, (6) very satisfied, and (7) completely satisfied. There is no significant difference in the job satisfaction of women and men in 27 of the 30 countries (Table 1). In Australia and the Philippines women are significantly more satisfied than men, while in Taiwan men are more satisfied. When only full-time employees are analyzed (data not shown), there are four changes in these results. There is no gender difference in job satisfaction in Australia, women are more satisfied than men in Hungary and South Africa, and men are more satisfied than women in Latvia. We also observe between-country variation in the reported levels of job satisfaction, but this is not relevant for understanding the paradox and likely is due to differences in between-country work conditions and perhaps to cultural differences in how individuals respond to Likert-type items.

Although we had not stated the paradox in terms of organizational commitment, we report data (Table 1) on gender differences in commitment (loyalty) to the organizations for which individuals work. In 26 of the 30 countries there are no significant gender differences. This too is paradoxical because we would predict lower commitment for women if they are disadvantaged with respect to workplace rewards, and if they are more often part-time, as is true in all 30 countries.

These data clearly are consistent with what has been reported previously about the gender paradox – with only a few exceptions, women and men do not differ in their level of job satisfaction or organizational commitment.

Gender Differences in Extrinsic Rewards to Work

For the job satisfaction (and commitment) results to be labeled a paradox, women must receive lower material rewards in the workplace. Earnings is the natural log of yearly earnings transformed to U.S. dollars. Supervisory position is a dichotomy based on the answer to the question "Do you supervise the work any other people do?" Table 2 displays gender differences in pay and access to a position of authority (whether they supervise others). Women earn less than men in 25 countries. There is no significant difference

Table 1. Gender Differences in Job Satisfaction and Organizational Commitment by Country.

Country	Job Satisfaction		Organizational Commitment	
	Female	Male	Female	Male
Western developed	5.25	5.26	3.30	3.35
France	4.92	4.93	2.71	2.81
Germany	5.43	5.39	3.36	3.40
Great Britain	5.35	5.16	3.45*	3.29
Switzerland	5.56	5.69	3.58*	3.72
Australia	5.19*	5.03	3.34	3.26
Canada	5.17	5.26	3.37	3.44
U.S.	5.31	5.40	3.59	3.55
Ireland	5.57	5.53	3.48	3.60
Israel	5.42	5.37	3.44	3.33
New Zealand	5.17	5.13	3.43	3.33
Flanders	4.95	4.97	3.26	3.28
Asian developed	4.87	4.93	3.31**	3.44
Japan	4.93	4.76	3.43	3.56
Korea	4.75	4.83	3.26	3.40
Taiwan	4.91*	5.06	3.30**	3.42
Nordic	5.32	5.28	3.17*	3.23
Denmark	5.46	5.52	3.28*	3.40
Norway	5.29	5.25	3.35	3.30
Sweden	5.19	5.05	2.99	3.03
Finland	5.32	5.22	3.01	3.11
EU Periphery	5.21	5.26	3.33	3.29
Portugal	5.21	5.24	3.50	3.47
Spain	5.13	5.16	2.90	2.94
Cyprus	5.29	5.38	3.30	3.35
Developed transition	5.02	4.96	3.08	3.11
Czech Republic	4.94	4.94	3.08	3.10
Hungary	5.28	4.89	3.01	2.91
Slovenia	4.89	5.05	3.15	3.33
Less developed trans.	4.82	4.95	2.84	2.82
Russia	4.91	4.89	2.87	2.84
Latvia	4.70	5.04	2.80	2.81
Latin America	5.35	5.23	3.56	3.60
Mexico	5.98	5.83	3.62	3.65
Dominican Republic	5.00	4.84	3.53	3.58
Other	–	–	–	–
Philippines	6.00**	5.47	3.76	3.70
South Africa	5.07	4.89	3.37	3.44

$^{*}p < .05$; $^{**}p < .01$; $^{***}p < .001$ (two-tailed)

Table 2. Gender Differences in Extrinsic Rewards (Logged Earnings and Supervisory Position) by Country.

Country	ln Earnings		Holds Supervisory Position	
	Female	Male	Female	Male
Western developed	9.934***	10.347	.36***	.50
France	9.767***	10.152	.32***	.50
Germany	9.583***	10.008	.38***	.50
Great Britain	10.032***	10.611	.44	.52
Switzerland	10.214***	10.848	.34***	.57
Australia	10.131***	10.495	.39***	.52
Canada	10.246***	10.703	.44*	.54
U.S.	10.098***	10.423	.29**	.41
Ireland	10.109***	10.548	.30**	.45
Israel	9.230***	9.553	.35*	.47
New Zealand	9.943***	10.380	.40**	.53
Flanders	9.751***	10.071	.20***	.32
Asian developed	9.465***	10.007	.14***	.34
Japan	9.896***	10.886	.00***	.18
Korea	9.574***	10.207	.16***	.49
Taiwan	9.278***	9.586	.18***	.29
Nordic	10.474***	10.782	.21***	.39
Denmark	10.679***	10.950	.25***	.45
Norway	10.662***	10.989	.24***	.42
Sweden	10.255***	10.522	.23***	.37
Finland	10.087*	10.290	.11***	.27
EU Periphery	9.308***	9.611	.13***	.22
Portugal	9.021***	9.239	.13**	.23
Spain	9.412***	9.651	.15	.22
Cyprus	9.712***	10.021	.12*	.19
Developed transition	8.921***	9.189	.18*	.24
Czech Republic	8.686***	9.055	.18	.22
Hungary	8.471	8.576	.08	.08
Slovenia	9.892	9.948	.30*	.42
Less developed trans.	7.739***	8.158	.20	.21
Russia	7.539***	8.035	.19	.22
Latvia	7.974***	8.370	.22	.20
Latin America	8.240*	8.341	.32**	.43
Mexico	8.453*	8.631	.53	.54
Dominican Republic	8.119	8.144	.20*	.36
Other	–	–	–	–
Philippines	6.812	7.039	.12	.12
South Africa	7.886	7.990	.21	.24

*$p < .05$; **$p < .01$; ***$p < .001$ (two-tailed)

in the post-socialist countries of Hungary and Slovenia, the developing Latin American country of the Dominican Republic, the Philippines, and South Africa. These results are replicated when full time only employees are analyzed. Overall, these data are consistent with the existence of a paradox.

In 21 of the countries women are less likely to be in positions of supervisory authority. There are no significant differences in Great Britain, Spain, the Czech Republic, Hungary, Russia, Latvia, Mexico, the Philippines, and South Africa. When only full-time employees are selected, five additional countries (Germany, Canada, Israel, Cyprus, and Slovenia) exhibit no significant difference in access to a position of authority. It must be said, however, that women uniformly across all of the countries are less often in authority positions, but in 14 instances these differences do not reach statistical significance. Although not as strong as the data for earnings, these data also are consistent with the claim of a paradox.

Gender Differences in Workplace Values

According to the differential values argument, men value extrinsic (material) rewards more than women, while women value nonmaterial, intrinsic rewards more than men. This remains as the most often cited explanation for the paradox. In the ISSP data, respondents were asked to indicate the degree to which a given workplace reward (condition) is important to them. Table 3 displays gender differences for the eight workplace rewards identified in the survey. Individuals responded to each work condition using a five-point scale: (1) "not important at all," (2) "not important," (3) "neither important nor unimportant," (4) "important," and (5) "very important."

We consider first the degree to which women and men value extrinsic workplace rewards: job security, high pay, and advancement opportunities (Table 3). For job security, in only six countries (France, Australia and the four Nordic countries: Denmark, Norway, Sweden, and Finland) were there significant gender differences, with women valuing security more than men in all six.

Similarly, the degree to which high pay is valued does not differ much between women and men. There is a significant difference in only three countries – Ireland, Flanders, and Cyprus – where women value it less than men. For the importance of advancement opportunities, there are no significant gender differences for 23 of the countries. Men value such opportunities more in France, Germany, Ireland, Flanders, and Japan, whereas women value advancement opportunities more in Korea and Portugal.

Table 3. Gender Differences in Workplace Values (Importance of the Workplace Condition to the Respondent) by Country.

Country	Job Security		High Pay	
	Female	Male	Female	Male
Western developed	4.56**	4.50	3.93*	3.99
France	4.56**	4.43	4.04	4.08
Germany	4.70	4.70	3.96	4.04
Great Britain	4.41	4.53	3.80	3.93
Switzerland	4.60	4.49	3.52	3.62
Australia	4.55*	4.47	3.80	3.82
Canada	4.49	4.47	4.02	4.02
U.S.	4.57	4.48	3.96	4.00
Ireland	4.45	4.47	3.85*	3.97
Israel	4.76	4.80	4.57	4.61
New Zealand	4.37	4.28	3.81	3.90
Flanders	4.45	4.47	3.85*	3.97
Asian developed	4.49	4.49	4.11	4.07
Japan	4.15	4.13	3.92	4.02
Korea	4.66	4.65	4.40	4.31
Taiwan	4.52	4.50	4.03	3.92
Nordic	4.43***	4.22	3.78	3.80
Denmark	4.12***	3.89	3.55	3.61
Norway	4.51***	4.35	3.77	3.79
Sweden	4.63***	4.39	3.93	3.90
Finland	4.54*	4.41	3.95	4.00
EU Periphery	4.58	4.56	4.41	4.47
Portugal	4.67	4.59	4.40	4.42
Spain	4.62	4.69	4.62	4.57
Cyprus	4.45	4.44	4.34**	4.48
Developed transition	4.62*	4.54	4.24	4.26
Czech Republic	4.59	4.52	4.15	4.14
Hungary	4.77	4.67	4.38	4.43
Slovenia	4.53	4.46	4.27	4.27
Less developed trans.	4.54	4.46	4.61	4.67
Russia	4.48	4.42	4.62	4.68
Latvia	4.61	4.53	4.60	4.65
Latin America	4.40	4.39	4.49	4.50
Mexico	4.68	4.75	4.51	4.53
Dominican Republic	4.24	4.14	4.48	4.47
Other	–	–	–	–
Philippines	4.66	4.59	4.52	4.60
South Africa	4.70	4.71	4.46	4.50

Table 3. *(Continued)*

Country	Advancement Opportunities		Interesting Job	
	Female	Male	Female	Male
Western Developed	3.98**	4.05	4.58*	4.54
France	3.84**	4.01	4.68	4.65
Germany	3.72*	3.87	4.40	4.48
Great Britain	3.90	3.94	4.47	4.40
Switzerland	3.54	3.57	4.63	4.64
Australia	4.01	4.00	4.51	4.42
Canada	4.02	4.08	4.65*	4.54
U.S.	4.17	4.27	4.52	4.48
Ireland	3.78*	3.92	4.37	4.34
Israel	4.60	4.58	4.82**	4.65
New Zealand	4.08	4.03	4.58	4.54
Flanders	3.78*	3.92	4.38	4.34
Asian developed	3.84	3.93	4.33	4.26
Japan	2.61**	2.95	4.05	3.92
Korea	4.54*	4.42	4.58*	4.46
Taiwan	3.86	3.92	4.28*	4.25
Nordic	3.28	3.27	4.54***	4.46
Denmark	3.11	3.18	4.54	4.55
Norway	3.40	3.36	4.54**	4.40
Sweden	3.42	3.36	4.41***	3.42
Finland	3.22	3.18	4.50	4.42
EU Periphery	4.12	4.06	4.23*	4.12
Portugal	4.43*	4.32	4.50*	4.40
Spain	4.36	4.34	4.49	4.43
Cyprus	3.52	3.53	4.03	3.94
Developed transition	3.57	3.69	4.19	4.17
Czech Republic	3.43	3.49	4.18	4.12
Hungary	3.68	3.76	4.00	4.06
Slovenia	3.74	3.94	4.44	4.36
Less developed trans.	3.76	3.74	4.31	4.30
Russia	3.66	3.75	4.28	4.28
Latvia	4.33	4.35	3.78	3.78
Latin America	4.54	4.53	4.35	4.35
Mexico	4.62	4.68	4.50	4.50
Dominican Republic	4.49	4.43	4.26	4.25
Other	–	–	–	–
Philippines	4.39	4.44	4.15	4.33
South Africa	4.44	4.47	4.44	4.34

Table 3. (*Continued*)

Country	Work Independently		Job that Helps Others	
	Female	Male	Female	Male
Western developed	4.08	4.09	4.14***	3.93
France	3.68	3.64	3.79***	3.46
Germany	4.25	4.30	4.02**	3.79
Great Britain	3.84	3.97	3.99*	3.77
Switzerland	4.30	4.38	4.12**	3.90
Australia	4.10	3.98	4.17**	3.90
Canada	4.22	4.12	4.17*	4.03
U.S.	4.12	4.09	4.40**	4.23
Ireland	3.73***	4.00	3.76	3.65
Israel	4.27	4.42	4.44	4.37
New Zealand	4.16	4.07	4.16***	3.86
Flanders	4.00	4.01	3.97***	3.73
Asian developed	3.59	3.59	4.02	3.95
Japan	2.91	3.16	3.75	3.68
Korea	4.00	3.93	4.20*	4.06
Taiwan	3.59	3.51	4.02	3.97
Nordic	4.18	4.14	3.97***	3.60
Denmark	4.40	4.39	4.08***	3.73
Norway	4.06	4.00	3.83***	3.52
Sweden	4.18	4.09	4.05***	3.56
Finland	4.03	3.93	3.86***	3.51
EU Periphery	4.04	4.04	4.19***	4.03
Portugal	4.16	4.13	4.35	4.25
Spain	4.24	4.24	4.27	4.20
Cyprus	3.75	3.81	3.92**	3.72
Developed transition	3.87	3.96	3.96**	3.81
Czech Republic	3.70	3.72	3.81	3.57
Hungary	3.94	4.01	4.05	3.91
Slovenia	4.16	4.29	4.18	4.09
Less developed trans.	3.65	3.75	3.87**	3.70
Russia	3.55*	3.73	3.84	3.76
Latvia	3.78	3.78	3.91***	3.60
Latin America	4.18	4.18	4.34	4.30
Mexico	4.17	4.28	4.31	4.41
Dominican Republic	4.18	4.11	4.36	4.22
Other	–	–	–	–
Philippines	4.09	4.18	4.08	4.25
South Africa	4.12	4.07	4.31	4.30

Table 3. *(Continued)*

	Job Useful to Society		Flexible Work Schedule	
Country	Female	Male	Female	Male
Western developed	4.10***	3.97	3.70***	3.53
France	3.83***	3.68	3.82***	3.46
Germany	3.94*	3.78	3.35	3.38
Great Britain	3.89	3.75	3.56	3.40
Switzerland	3.98	3.90	3.82	3.73
Australia	4.10**	3.94	3.81***	3.43
Canada	4.19*	4.02	3.67	3.63
U.S.	4.42	4.30	3.46	3.48
Ireland	3.79*	3.60	3.79*	3.60
Israel	4.38	4.28	3.78	3.89
New Zealand	4.08***	3.84	3.78**	3.54
Flanders	3.76	3.65	3.79	3.60
Asian developed	4.08	4.03	3.84***	3.63
Japan	3.86	3.75	3.42	2.29
Korea	4.24	4.14	3.93**	3.71
Taiwan	4.07	4.02	3.92***	3.68
Nordic	3.78***	3.48	3.83**	3.72
Denmark	3.83**	3.65	3.68	3.65
Norway	3.87***	3.47	3.76*	3.60
Sweden	3.79***	3.38	3.98**	3.82
Finland	3.60***	3.32	3.94	3.86
EU Periphery	4.19**	4.06	3.74	3.80
Portugal	4.40	4.30	3.79	3.88
Spain	4.27	4.22	4.17	4.10
Cyprus	3.87*	3.71	3.42	3.47
Developed transition	4.01***	3.78	3.55	3.62
Czech Republic	3.93***	3.56	3.49	3.47
Hungary	4.12	4.01	3.33	3.46
Slovenia	4.06	3.91	3.94	4.02
Less developed trans.	3.95*	3.82	3.64	3.60
Russia	4.03	3.95	3.48	3.42
Latvia	3.86**	3.61	3.82	3.91
Latin America	4.27	4.30	3.96	3.99
Mexico	4.33	4.66	4.01	4.03
Dominican Republic	4.23	4.20	3.93	3.96
Other	–	–	–	–
Philippines	4.10	4.24	3.86	3.82
South Africa	4.20	4.27	3.72	3.70

*$p < .0.5$; **$p < .01$; ***$p < .001$ (two-tailed)

Overall, then, with only a few exceptions, women and men equally value extrinsic workplace rewards. This is not what is argued in the differential values explanation for the paradox.

Five intrinsic reward values also are examined, with the results for three values being inconsistent and two being consistent with the differential values argument. There are significant gender differences in the importance of "having an interesting job" in only seven of the 30 countries. Women consistently value, more than men, having interesting work in Canada, Israel, Korea, Taiwan, Norway, Sweden, and Portugal. The importance of having "independence in one's job" (autonomy) is different for women and men in only two countries; men value autonomy more in Ireland and Russia. The importance of having "flexible work arrangements" is significantly different in eight of the 30 countries (France, Australia, Ireland, New Zealand, Korea, Taiwan, Norway, and Sweden) where women value this more than men.

There are two workplace rewards for which there are gender differences that are more consistent with the differential values argument. Having a job that "allows for helping others" is significantly different by gender in 16 of the 30 countries (France, Germany, Great Britain, Switzerland, Australia, Canada, U.S., New Zealand, Flanders, Korea, Denmark, Norway, Sweden, Finland, Cyprus, and Latvia). In all 16 countries women value helping others more than their male counterparts.

A similar pattern is found for the value of a "job that is useful to society." In the 13 countries where there is a significant difference between women and men, women consistently value this more than men (France, Germany, Australia, Canada, Ireland, New Zealand, Denmark, Norway, Sweden, Finland, Cyprus, Czech Republic, and Latvia).

In sum, women do generally value more the two intrinsic rewards of helping others and being useful to society, but even here in almost one-half of the countries there is no gender difference. Given this rather weak support for intrinsic reward differences and the strong rejection of gender differences in the importance of extrinsic rewards, we conclude that there is only limited support for this argument.

With regard to societal differences in gender value differences we should note that the Nordic countries stand out as distinct. Although true in differing degrees from one Nordic society to another, gender equality is an espoused goal and labor issues are, by law, addressed jointly by management organizations, labor organizations and the government. As has been found for union members having low job satisfaction, it is likely that greater awareness of equity issues accentuates values differences between women and men.

Gender Differences in Workplace Perceptions (Subjective Rewards)

This argument suggests that women and men have similar levels of job satisfaction because it is employee perceptions of workplace conditions, rather than objective material conditions that produce job satisfaction. And, as the argument continues, because women and men do not differ in how they perceive work conditions, their levels of job satisfaction will be the same. To shed some light on this argument, we compare male and female perceptions of eight workplace conditions: (1) my job is secure, (2) my income is high, (3) my job provides good opportunities for advancement, (4) my job is interesting, (5) I can work independently, (6) my job allows me to help other people, (7) my job is useful to society, and (8) my job allows me to improve my skills. Individuals were asked to respond to each of these work conditions using a five-point Likert scale: (1) "strongly disagree," (2) "disagree," (3) neither agree nor disagree," (4) "agree," and (5) "strongly agree."

We tested (data not shown) for gender differences in these eight work condition perceptions and found in only three countries (Portugal, Spain, and South Africa) are there no gender differences in all eight work conditions. In the other 27 countries women and men do not consistently have the same perceptions of their work conditions. These results do not support the "subjective rewards" argument predicting no gender satisfaction difference because of no gender differences in these perceptions.

Differential Socialization (Entitlement)

The differential socialization argument claims that women are socialized to expect less, so when they receive less, they accept it, and are satisfied. As discussed above, this argument is certainly consistent with various justice-based arguments (and status value theory). We do not question that differential socialization is operating, but tests of this claim in understanding the paradox have been only indirect. Our data are no different.

We argue that women's movements worldwide, and especially in Western developed countries, should have produced changes in gender differences in values and expectations and these changes would be reflected in age differences in gender job satisfaction "gaps." Specifically, a greater awareness of inequalities can be expected for younger women and this should be reflected in lower job satisfaction, relative to men, than is found among older women. To assess this, we disaggregated by age into those younger than age 40 and those 40 and older and compared gender

Table 4. Gender Differences in Job Satisfaction by Age.

Country	Less Than Age 40		Age 40 and Older	
	Female	Male	Female	Male
Western developed	4.83	4.87	4.91	5.00
France	4.95	4.96	4.88	4.91
Germany	5.44	5.45	5.42	5.35
Great Britain	5.14	5.16	5.55*	5.15
Switzerland	5.31*	5.61	5.74	5.76
Australia	5.08	4.93	5.28*	5.09
Canada	5.17	5.09	5.19	5.32
U.S.	5.16	5.29	5.42	5.50
Ireland	5.51	5.35	5.64	5.78
Israel	5.41	5.36	5.46	5.39
New Zealand	4.96	5.00	5.36	5.23
Flanders	5.02	4.94	4.87	4.99
Asian developed	4.83	4.87	4.91	5.00
Japan	4.94	4.53	4.92	4.87
Korea	4.72	4.78	4.80	4.88
Taiwan	4.87	5.00	4.98	5.14
Nordic	5.28	5.17	5.35	5.35
Denmark	5.43	5.49	5.47	5.53
Norway	5.34*	5.10	5.27	5.34
Sweden	5.07	4.98	5.26	5.10
Finland	5.26	5.06	5.35	5.34
EU Periphery	5.15	5.26	5.29	5.31
Portugal	5.12	5.20	5.28	5.27
Spain	4.99	5.08	5.32	5.26
Cyprus	5.26	5.29	5.34	5.48
Developed transition	5.02	5.01	5.04	4.90
Czech Republic	5.12	4.96	4.84	4.90
Hungary	5.06	4.91	5.46*	4.88
Slovenia	4.78	5.19	5.00	4.92
Less developed trans.	4.76	4.92	4.86	4.98
Russia	4.85	4.87	4.96	4.91
Latvia	4.63*	5.00	4.74*	5.09
Latin America	5.38	5.36	5.24	4.98
Mexico	5.80	5.79	6.50*	5.97
Dominican Republic	5.17	5.06	4.36	4.50
Other				
Philippines	5.94	5.46	6.05	5.49
South Africa	5.01*	4.64	5.16	5.20

*$p < .05$; **$p < .01$; ***$p < .001$ (two-tailed)

differences in job satisfaction for these two age categories (Table 4). As can be seen these data reveal no such pattern. In only four countries are there significant gender differences in job satisfaction in the younger age category, while this is true in five countries for the older age category. We must be cautious here, however. Not only is this a very weak test of the socialization differences, but any inferences are confounded because those in the younger age cohort would have experienced greater access to educational institutions and occupations in the labor force because of worldwide legal and social changes regarding gender equality.

CONCLUSIONS

Two conclusions need to be highlighted. First, the paradox of the contented female worker exists worldwide and continues to be a phenomenon worthy of study – women receive fewer material rewards, but they are just as satisfied with their jobs as men. Second, our review of the arguments and research directed at explaining the paradox, as well as our analysis of recent data from 30 nations, lead us to conclude that justice-based arguments offer the greatest potential for understanding the paradox. We want to briefly summarize our assessments of the various paradox arguments and offer some comments regarding what needs to be done next. As was our strategy throughout the chapter, we separate the arguments according to whether they rely on a justice-based logic.

The arguments that are not justice based have been prominent in the organizational behavior/sociology of work tradition. The "different dispositions" argument, although seldom examined empirically in paradox research, offers little potential for explaining the paradox because gender differences in dispositions (positive and negative affectivity) are very small and, therefore, cannot alone explain the paradox. The "selectivity" hypothesis, however, keeps this argument in play. If women who decide to work are different in dispositions (greater positive affectivity than those in the total female population), then this heightened emotion could be operating to elevate their job satisfaction. This possibility deserves further attention because we know that job satisfaction is higher when positive affectivity is higher.

Although most empirical assessments of gender differences in workplace values ("differential values" argument) have shown no differences, this argument remains as the most often referred to explanation for the paradox. The cross-national data we examined showed in about one-half of the countries distinct gender differences in the degree to which "helpful" and "useful" work is valued (women value these more than men). Possible gender differences in nonmaterial workplace values should not be totally dismissed when trying to account for the paradox. However, overall, gender differences in workplace values are small or nonexistent across societies with varying political and economic systems, and we do not believe the explanation for the paradox will be found in gender differences in values.

The "subjective rewards" argument claims that it is employee perceptions of workplace rewards that influence job satisfaction, and argues that because women and men have similar perceptions of various material and, especially, nonmaterial rewards, their levels of job satisfaction will be the same. Women and men, however, do not consistently perceive that their work conditions are the same. As a consequence, we do not see much utility in this explanation for the paradox.

We now turn to the explanations that rely on justice-based arguments. From previous research we know the following: (1) the positive relationship between distributive justice perceptions and job satisfaction is well established; (2) the magnitude of this positive relationship is the same for women and men; (3) there is no gender difference (same mean level) in perceived workplace distributive justice. We can link these findings as follows: job satisfaction is the same for women and men because, even though women are disadvantaged with regard to material rewards, they perceive distributive justice at the same level as men and the justice they perceive is translated into the same degree of job satisfaction as men. From this linkage we infer that the critical question to be answered is: why do women in disadvantaged work settings perceive distributive justice at the same level as their advantaged male co-workers? Answering this question requires an understanding of gender differences in the justice evaluation processes that lead to the same mean justice perceptions for women and men. This is precisely what the various justice-based accounts of the paradox have attempted to provide.

The best that can be said about the bulk of the justice-based research on the paradox in the organizational behavior/sociology of work tradition is that it is suggestive. One of the problems is that most of this research is based on small, occupation- or company-specific samples. There are also measurement problems. The variables and mechanisms hypothesized to be important are typically not observed or measured. At the top of this list is justice perceptions, which is measured in only a few of the large-scale studies claiming to have investigated the paradox. And even in the studies that rely on justice perception measures, there is no standardization in the measures used, and most of the measures do not allow for capturing both under- and over-reward. Since so few perceive over-reward this latter problem is not so critical, but it is not trivial either. Probably the biggest problem with the nonexperimental research that measures justice perceptions is that the justice evaluation process is not examined; there is no information on the referent (comparison group or norm) that is being used in forming this perception. Attempts to test the "differential inputs," "differential socialization," and "same-gender referent" hypotheses have generally been crude and inadequate. A notable exception to this conclusion is the work of Moore (1991). It carefully examines the gender composition of the work setting and the gender of the referent in assessing perceptions of entitlement.

Experimental and quasi-experimental research has been valuable in specifying gender differences in allocation of rewards and in how justice evaluations occur. Because it is the question of "how justice evaluations occur" that is the critical issue in understanding justice-based claims about the paradox, such research can continue to contribute to this understanding. The work of Jasso and her colleagues is potentially very valuable in this enterprise. The multiple standards framework allows for examining differential inputs, differential norms, and differential referents within the same general theoretical framework. We believe that, in combination with the type of natural setting research conducted by Moore (1991), experimental studies and the quasi-experimental studies in the tradition of Jasso and her colleagues will enhance our understanding of how justice perceptions are formed for women and men. Understanding gender differences in justice evaluation processes is what is required if the paradox of the contented female worker is to be explained.

ACKNOWLEDGMENT

The Korea Research Foundation supported the work reported here through its grant, KRF-2005-078-BM0005, titled "The 3rd, 4th, 5th Korean General Social Surveys and the Exemplary Studies."

REFERENCES

Adams, J. S. (1965). Inequality in social exchange. In: L. Berkowitz (Ed.), *Advances in experimental social psychology* (pp. 267–299). New York: Academic Press.

Arvey, R. D., Bouchard, T. J., Segal, N. L., & Abraham, L. M. (1989). Job satisfaction: Environmental and genetic components. *Journal of Applied Psychology*, *74*, 187–192.

Berger, J., Zelditch, M., Anderson, B., & Cohen, B. P. (1972). Structural aspects of distributive justice: A status value formulation. In: J. Berger, M. Zelditch & B. Anderson (Eds), *Sociological theories in progress* (Vol. 2, pp. 119–146). Boston: Houghton Mifflin.

Blau, P. (1964). *Exchange and power in social life*. New York: Wiley.

Blysma, W. H., & Major, B. (1992). Two routes to eliminating gender differences in personal entitlement: Social comparisons and performance evaluation. *Psychology of Women Quarterly*, *16*, 193–300.

Brockner, J., & Adsit, L. (1986). The moderating effect of sex on the equity-satisfaction selationship. *Journal of Applied Psychology*, *71*, 585–590.

Buchanan, T. (2005). The paradox of the contented female worker in a traditionally female industry. *Sociological Spectrum*, *25*, 177–213.

Carsten, J. M., & Spector, P. W. (1987). Unemployment, job satisfaction, and employee turnover: A meta-analytic test of the muchinsky model. *Journal of Applied Psychology*, *72*, 374–381.

Clark, A. E. (1997). Job satisfaction and gender: Why are women so happy at work? *Labor Economics*, *14*, 21–40.

Crosby, F. J. (1982). *Relative deprivation and working women*. New York: Oxford University Press.

Curtice, J. (1993). Satisfying work – if you can get it. In: R. Jowell, L. Brook & L. Dowds (Eds), *International social attitudes: The 10th BSA report*. London: SCPR.

Edwards, J. R. (1991). Person-job fit: A conceptual integration, literature review, and methodological critique. In: C. L. Cooper & I. T. Robertson (Eds), *International review of industrial and organizational psychology* (pp. 283–357). Chichester, UK: Wiley.

Else-Quest, N. M., Hyde, J. S., Goldsmith, H. H., & Van Hulle, C. A. (2006). Gender differences in temperament: A meta-analysis. *Psychological Bulletin*, *132*, 33–72.

Faragher, E. B., Cass, M., & Cooper, C. L. (2003). The relationship between job satisfaction and health: A meta analysis. *Occupational and Environmental Medicine*, *62*, 105–112.

Fried, Y. (1991). Meta-analytic comparison of the job diagnostic survey and job characteristics inventory as correlates of work satisfaction and performance. *Journal of Applied Psychology*, *76*, 690–697.

Hackman, J. R., & Oldham, G. R. (1976). Motivation through the design of work: Test of a theory. *Organizational Behavior and Human Performance*, *16*, 250–279.

Hackman, J. R., & Oldham, G. R. (1980). *Work redesign*. Reading, MA: Addison-Wesley.

Hakim, C. (1991). Grateful slaves and self-made women: Fact and fantasy in women's work orientation. *European Sociological Review*, *7*, 30–45.

Hegtvedt, K., & Markovsky, B. (1995). Justice and injustice. In: K. Cook, G. Fine & J. House (Eds), *Sociological perspectives on social psychology* (pp. 257–280). Boston: Allyn & Bacon.

Hodson, R. (1989). Gender differences in job satisfaction: Why aren't women more dissatisfied? *Sociological Quarterly*, *30*, 385–399.

Homans, G. C. (1961). *Social behavior: Its elementary forms*. New York: Harcourt, Brace & World.

Iaffaldano, M. T., & Muchinsky, P. M. (1985). Job satisfaction and job performance: A meta-analysis. *Psychological Bulletin*, *97*, 251–273.

Jasso, G. (1978). On the justice of earnings: A new specification of the justice evaluation function. *American Journal of Sociology*, *83*, 1398–1419.

Jasso, G. (1980). A new theory of distributive justice. *American Sociological Review*, *45*, 3–32.

Jasso, G., & Rossi, P. H. (1977). Distributive justice and earned income. *American Sociological Review*, *42*, 639–651.

Jasso, G., & Webster, M. (1997). Double standards in just earnings for male and female workers. *Social Psychology Quarterly*, *60*, 66–78.

Jasso, G., & Webster, M. (1999). Assessing the gender gap in just earnings and its underlying mechanisms. *Social Psychology Quarterly*, *62*, 367–380.

Jasso, G., & Wegener, B. (1999). Gender and country differences in the sense of justice. *International Journal of Comparative Sociology*, *40*, 94–116.

Kahn, A. (1972). Reactions to the generosity or stinginess and the gender wage gap: A test of equity theory in a direct exchange relationship. *Journal of Personality and Social Psychology*, *21*, 116–123.

Kalleberg, A. L. (1977). Work values and work rewards: A theory of job satisfaction. *American Sociological Review*, *42*, 124–143.

Kanter, R. (1977). *Men and women of the corporation*. New York: Basic Books.

Lane, I. M., & Messe, L. A. (1971). Equity and the distribution of rewards. *Journal of Personality and Social Psychology*, *20*, 1–17.

Leventhal, G. S., & Lane, D. (1970). Sex, age, and equity behavior. *Journal of Personality and Social Psychology*, *15*, 312–316.

Major, B. (1989). Gender differences in comparisons and entitlement: Implications for comparable worth. *Journal of Social Issues*, *45*, 99–115.

Major, B., & Forcey, B. (1985). Social comparisons and pay evaluations: Preferences for same sex and same job wage comparisons. *Journal of Experimental Social Psychology*, *21*, 393–405.

Major, B., McFarlin, D. B., & Gagnon, D. (1984). Overworked and underpaid: On the nature of gender differences in personal entitlement. *Journal of Personality and Social Psychology*, *47*, 1399–1412.

Markovsky, B. (1985). Toward a multilevel distributive justice theory. *American Sociological Review*, *50*, 822–839.

Marsden, P. V., Kalleberg, A. L., & Cook, C. (1993). Gender differences in organizational commitment. *Work and Occupations*, *20*, 368–390.

Medgyesi, M., & Róbert, P. (2002). Satisfaction with work in a European perspective: Center and periphery, "Old" and "new" market economies compared. Revised version of paper presented at the World Congress of Sociology, Brisbane, Australia, July 7–13.

Moore, D. (1991). Entitlement and justice evaluations: Who should get more and why. *Social Psychology Quarterly*, *54*, 208–223.

Mortimer, J., & Lorence, J. (1979). Work experience and occupational value socialization: A longitudinal survey. *American Journal of Sociology*, *84*, 1361–1385.

Mueller, C. W., Iverson, R., & Jo, D. G. (1999). Distributive justice evaluations in two cultural contexts: A comparison of U.S. and South Korean teachers. *Human Relations*, *52*, 869–893.

Mueller, C. W., & Wallace, J. E. (1996). Justice and the paradox of the contented female worker. *Social Psychology Quarterly*, *59*, 338–349.

Mueller, C. W., & Wynn, T. (2000). The degree to which justice is valued in the workplace. *Social Justice Research*, *13*, 1–24.

Phelan, J. (1994). The paradox of the contented female worker: An assessment of alternative explanations. *Social Psychology Quarterly*, *57*, 95–107.

Randall, C. S., & Mueller, C. W. (1995). Extensions of justice theory: Justice evaluations and employee reactions in a natural setting. *Social Psychology Quarterly*, *58*, 178–194.

Rowe, R., & Snizek, W. E. (1995). Gender differences in work values. *Work and Occupations*, *22*, 215–229.

Simon, R., & Nath, L. (2004). Gender and emotion in the United States: Do men and women differ in self-reports of feelings and expressive behavior? *American Journal of Sociology*, *109*, 1137–1176.

Spector, P. A. (1997). *Job Satisfaction*. Thousand Oaks, CA: Sage.

Staw, B. M., Bell, N. E., & Clausen, J. A. (1986). The dispositional approach to job attitudes: A lifetime longitudinal test. *Administrative Science Quarterly*, *31*, 56–77.

Törnblom, K. Y. (1992). The social psychology of distributive justice. In: K. Scherer (Ed.), *Justice: Interdisciplinary perspectives* (pp. 177–236). Cambridge, UK: Cambridge University Press.

Walster, E. H., Walster, G. W., & Berscheid, E. (1978). *Equity theory and research*. Boston: Allyn & Bacon.

Watson, D. (2000). *Mood and temperament*. New York: Guilford Press.

Wharton, A. S., Rotolo, T., & Bird, S. R. (2000). Social context at work: A multilevel analysis of job satisfaction. *Sociological Forum*, *15*, 65–90.

Witt, L. A., & Nye, L. G. (1992). Gender and the relationship between perceived fairness of pay or promotion and job satisfaction. *Journal of Applied Psychology*, *77*, 910–917.

Younts, C. W., & Mueller, C. W. (2001). Justice processes: Specifying the mediating role of perceptions of distributive justice. *American Sociological Review*, *66*, 125–145.

INJUSTICE AND EMOTIONS USING IDENTITY THEORY

Jan E. Stets and Shelley N. Osborn

ABSTRACT

Recent developments in identity theory are used to understand emotions in distributive justice theory. Three issues are examined: the consistency vs. enhancement dynamic, the status dynamic, and the resource dynamic. Results reveal individuals initially react positively to over-rewards; later they react more negatively. We suggest that the enhancement *process occurs initially; the* consistency *process occurs later. Regarding* status, *persons respond negatively to unjust outcomes when they come from higher status persons. Finally, positive emotions are a* resource *for individuals initially and across encounters, buffering the effect of repeated unjust outcomes. Overall, this study helps develop emotions in distributive justice theory.*

In this research, we examine how people feel when they experience injustice in a situation. From distributive justice theory, it is clear what we would expect to find. People will feel good when they receive expected outcomes, and they will feel bad when they receive unexpected outcomes. The evaluation of just outcomes involves comparing one's own ratio of rewards to investments with a standard. This standard may be based on (1) one's past outcomes, (2) another's ratio of rewards to investments, (3) a referential

Justice
Advances in Group Processes, Volume 25, 151–179

ISSN: 0882-6145/doi:10.1016/S0882-6145(08)25010-1

structure (expectations regarding what people are believed to receive given the social structure and the status value attached to their investments and rewards), or (4) a group (a within-group comparison or between-group comparison can be made) (Hegtvedt, 2006). Since Homans' (1974) early and direct connection between justice and emotions, important sociological and psychological work has been accumulating in this area (Cook & Hegtvedt, 1983; DeCremer, 2007; Hegtvedt, 1990; Hegtvedt & Killian, 1999; Jasso, 1980, 2006).

In this study, we attempt to develop our theoretical understanding of the relationship between distributive justice and emotions. While people's feelings in a situation involve the cognitive process of comparing expected outcomes with actual outcomes, we think we can expand our understanding of people's emotional reactions by considering other theoretical processes operating in the situation. We discuss three processes, and we use identity theory to frame this research (Burke, 2004; Stryker & Burke, 2000). We rely on identity theory because it has an affinity with distributive justice theory but has broader applicability. How the identity process operates is similar to how the distributive justice process operates (Stets, 2003, 2005). Theorists in both research traditions share the idea that in situations, people have a *standard* that guides perceptions and behavior, they engage in a *comparison process* to assess whether actual outcomes match expected outcomes, and they feel positive or negative *emotions* given the evaluation of consistency or inconsistency between actual and expected outcomes. Given the affinities in these two theoretical traditions, we rely on recent developments in identity theory to advance our understanding of emotional reactions to injustice.

THE THEORETICAL ISSUES

Both identity theory and distributive justice theory assume that emotions emerge from the cognitive consistency principle (Stets & Asencio, 2008). People feel good when they get what they expect, and they feel bad when they get what they do not expect. However, in simulating repeated, unexpected outcomes in the laboratory, Stets (2003, 2005) found that people engage in an immediate *enhancement* process (rather than a *consistency* process) where they welcome outcomes that exceed their expectations but reject outcomes that fall short of their expectations. This is inconsistent with identity theorizing, and Stets suggests that identity theorists may need to re-evaluate how individuals respond to disconfirming outcomes. We examine this issue in this study by investigating people's emotional reactions to obtaining unjust outcomes over a series of trials.

A second theoretical issue involves the impact others in the situation have on emotional reactions to injustice. Both identity theorists and justice researchers are beginning to acknowledge that people's emotions in a situation are not simply the result of an internal process of comparing expected and actual outcomes. People's emotional state is also the result of the external process of others influence in the situation. Individuals' feelings and their evaluations of outcomes are influenced by what others are feeling in the situation (DeCremer, van Kleef, & Wubben, 2007). Further, people's feelings are influenced by the status and power of others, particularly when those others are responsible for their unjust outcomes (Stets, 2004; Stets & Burke, 2005). Following from recent work in identity theory, we examine the *status* of the person providing repeated unjust outcomes. We investigate persons' emotional reactions when high-status compared to low-status others provide unjust outcomes. We also investigate the effects of status regarding the recipient of unjust outcomes.

Our third theoretical issue pertains to whether emotions continue to exert an influence in situations beyond the initial encounter. We raise this issue because we are examining injustice across several trials or situations in this study. We do not think that people create their affective state anew in each situation. Rather, we think that there is a "carryover" effect from previous encounters, and we think that positive emotions are particularly relevant in this regard. To examine this issue, we turn to recent work in identity theory on *resources*. Resources are anything that function to sustain the self and the interaction in which a person finds himself (Freese & Burke, 1994). Like high self-esteem (Cast & Burke, 2002), we see positive emotions as a resource for individuals (Trope, Ferguson, & Raghunathan, 2001). Feeling good when one enters an unjust situation serves to buffer the negative feelings that would otherwise emerge. In this sense, positive feelings protect the self as the person moves into and out of difficult situations such as repeated unjust encounters. We examine this in this study.

To investigate people's emotions across unjust situations, and guided by the above theoretical considerations, we simulate a work situation in the laboratory where participants complete three tasks on a computer. After each task, the workers receive feedback from a manager on their work. The manager either over-rewards them or under-rewards them for their performance. We analyze participants' emotional reactions to their unjust outcome initially (after the first task) and then over time (after a second and third task) to examine the enhancement vs. consistency dynamic. We also examine the worker's emotional reactions to an unjust outcome given the manager's status (male or female) and the worker's status (male or female). Finally, we investigate the effect of earlier emotions on later emotions and examine whether positive emotions help buffer the effects of persistent unjust outcomes.

THEORY

Consistency vs. Enhancement Dynamic

In identity theory (Burke, 1991; Stryker, 2004) as well as various theories and empirical programs in distributive justice research (Hegtvedt & Markovsky, 1995), emotions emerge from the cognitive consistency principle (Stets & Asencio, 2008). According to this principle, people feel good when there is congruence among cognitions (whether those cognitions are about one's identity or one's sense of justice), and they feel bad when there is incongruence (Hegtvedt, 2006; Jasso, 2006; Stets, 2006). Feeling good or bad given congruence or incongruence assumes several pre-existing conditions that both identity theory and distributive justice theories acknowledge (Burke, 1991; Hegtvedt & Markovsky, 1995; Markovsky, 1985; Stryker, 2004).

First, there is a *standard* or a set of expectations that guides perceptions in a situation. In identity theory, this is an identity standard. The standard stores self-meanings of particular identities and guides how one behaves in situations. In the distributive justice process, the justice standard guides the perceived fairness of the allocation of one's outcome. Second, there is a *comparison process* in which persons evaluate the feedback or outcomes they receive with what they expect to receive given their standard. If a discrepancy emerges between the two, people feel negative emotions. A lack of discrepancy between expected outcomes and actual outcomes leads to positive emotions. Finally, there is *behavior* that exists to either maintain congruence between expected and actual outcomes or change the incongruence to congruence.

Early in distributive justice research, Homans (1974) indicated that when people receive a reward that is less than what they expect, they will feel anger. When they obtain a reward that is more than what they expect, they will feel guilt. When they get what they expect, they will be satisfied.[1] Similarly, in identity theory, Burke (1991) argued that when individuals experience identity non-verification in a positive or negative direction, they will experience negative emotions.[2] Identity verification produces positive emotions. While research supports the idea that an under-reward or identity non-verification in a negative direction influences negative feelings (Hegtvedt, 1990; Sprecher, 1992; Stets, 2003, 2004, 2005; Stets & Asencio, 2008), the findings for an over-reward or identity non-verification in a positive direction are not conclusive. Some research finds that an over-reward or identity non-verification that exceeds one's expectations does not produce negative feelings (Hegtvedt, 1990; Stets, 2003, 2004, 2005; Stets & Asencio, 2008).[3]

An over-reward or identity non-verification in a positive direction can lead to positive emotions (Stets, 2003, 2004, 2005; Stets & Asencio, 2008). Stets has argued that the theoretical process of enhancement that is at odds with the consistency process may explain why positive feelings emerge from inconsistent expectations. This process emphasizes people's desire to obtain positive information rather than consistent information (Sedikides, 1993; Sedikides, Gaertner, & Toguchi, 2003; Swann, 1990). The enhancement process affirms feeling good about oneself and one's world. Alternatively, the consistency process affirms a congruent view of oneself and the predictability of one's environment.

The enhancement process involves a simple sorting of information into good/positive and bad/negative (Swann, 1990). Individuals appear to welcome information that is good (such as an over-reward), and avoid information that is negative (such as an under-reward). The consistency process entails additional mental work. Individuals not only have to categorize the information as good or bad, but they also must retrieve from memory their expectations along the dimension of the outcome, and then compare that expectation with the outcome they receive. This entails additional "steps" (retrieval and comparison) not found in the enhancement process. If the consistency process entails additional "work," then the enhancement process may be more likely to emerge initially in a situation, particularly when cognitive processing is limited. The consistency process should follow the enhancement process if there is time and motivation for further processing. Thus, the enhancement response is subject to an "automatic process" and the consistency response is subject to a "deliberative process."

Given the above discussion, we anticipate that when individuals provide their immediate emotional reactions to an injustice:

Hypothesis 1. An over-reward compared to an under-reward will be more likely to produce positive emotion.

Status Dynamic

We have been discussing emotions as resulting from an intrapersonal process in which people compare their actual outcomes with their expected outcomes. However, emotions may also result from an interpersonal process in which others in the situation influence one's feelings. Recently, DeCremer et al. (2007) discuss how people can infer fairness judgments on the basis of how others are feeling in the situation. Others' emotions can serve as an important guide as to whether a situation is unjust, and whether one should feel good or bad. For example, if others show anger rather than happiness in a situation, it would be more likely to prompt an evaluation of injustice rather than justice in us, and in turn, trigger feelings of anger rather than happiness. Further, DeCremer and his colleagues indicate that others in the situation not only communicate their emotions, but they also signal how much power they have over others. Those with greater power over others will be more likely to influence others in terms of fairness judgments and their emotional state.

In this study, rather than examining how other actors are "feeling" in the situation, we examine what other actors are "doing." Recently, identity theorists have argued that we need to examine the "source" of one's unexpected outcomes in a situation (Stets, 2004; Stets & Burke, 2005). The idea is to investigate the status or position of the "source," and how this influences an individual's emotional reactions. One's status carries expectations for behavior. We anticipate certain behaviors of high-status actors and other behaviors of low-status actors. In this study, we examine status in terms of the gender of the manager (men as high status and women as low status) who allocates an unjust reward to workers.

Identity theory has borrowed from expectation states theory to understand the role of status in situations. According to expectation states theory, when people enter an interaction, they bring with them status characteristics or individual properties around which evaluations and beliefs about them are organized (Berger & Webster, 2006). These individual properties are rank-ordered in terms of value (e.g., high vs. low in a relative sense) and corresponding to this rank ordering is a set of performance expectations. Applying this idea to gender, gender is rank-ordered with males having a higher value than females in the social structure (Ridgeway, 1993). Correspondingly, we have higher performance expectations for men compared to women because of the cultural belief that men are more competent than women (Ridgeway, 1993; Ridgeway & Smith-Lovin, 1999). For example, we expect men more than women to generate ideas in a situation, assume a leadership role, and influence decisions. Essentially, men are seen as more legitimate occupants of high-status positions than equivalent women (Ridgeway, Johnson, & Diekema, 1994). While women can work at modifying gender expectations in order to achieve more influence, the standard by which they can prove their competence is much stricter than it is for men; they must work harder than men to show that they are capable (Foddy & Smithson, 1989; Foschi, 1989).

Identity theorists have argued that one's status provides additional meanings in the situation to which individuals respond (Stets & Burke, 2005). We consider these additional meanings. In this study, we anticipate that individuals will be more likely to react positively to an injustice when it is from higher status persons compared to lower status persons. People judge higher status actors as competent. They have more influence in situations. Thus, the actions of higher status (male) managers will influence positive emotions for workers, even if the managers are acting unexpectedly (by providing over-rewards or under-rewards). Workers may assume that there is some good reason for the unjust outcomes. Alternatively, the actions of lower status (female) managers will produce negative feelings for workers when they experience injustice. The outcome is unexpected *and* it comes from a source that workers do not hold in high regard. Therefore, we hypothesize the following:

Hypothesis 2a. An over-reward will be more likely to produce positive emotion when the source of the unexpected outcome is a male manager compared to a female manager.

Hypothesis 2b. An under-reward will be more likely to produce positive emotion when the source of the unexpected outcome is a male manager compared to a female manager.

In keeping with identity research that also has examined status in terms of the "recipient" of unexpected outcomes in situations (Stets, 2004; Stets & Burke, 2005), we examine whether the gender of the worker influences the emotions they report. In identity research, we find that higher status individuals are more likely than lower status persons to experience identity verification (Stets & Harrod, 2004). Similarly, we anticipate that higher status persons will be more likely to experience just outcomes compared to unjust outcomes, and when unjust outcomes emerge, they may be more likely to experience negative emotions (Stets, 2004). Higher status actors such as men may feel that just outcomes are a "right" that is owed them. They may feel a sense of entitlement. This entitlement may even extend to receiving an over-reward. They may reason that they are a valued and rewarded group in society and thus deserve more. Alternatively, women will be less likely to respond negatively to unjust outcomes because they come to expect less (Major, 1987; Steil, 1994). However, when they obtain more than they expect, they may feel particularly positive. Consequently, our next hypotheses are:

Hypothesis 3a. An over-reward will be more likely to produce positive emotion for female workers compared to male workers.

Hypothesis 3b. An under-reward will be more likely to produce positive emotion for female workers compared to male workers.

Resource Dynamic

Finally, while an injustice may initially arouse an emotion in a situation, we investigate whether emotions exert an influence on individuals beyond the initial encounter. This idea suggests that emotions can be antecedent to the justice evaluation process and not simply a consequence of it. For some time, there has been the recognition that a person's affective state can influence the judgment process (Forgas, 1995). For example, how persons currently feel can influence how they interpret an unexpected outcome. Affect-congruent details of an outcome can receive more attention than affect-incongruent details. Alternatively, in evaluating an unexpected outcome, persons might incorrectly attribute how they are feeling to the unexpected outcome, rather than correctly attributing their feeling to a pre-existing emotional state.

Very little research has examined the role of emotions in forming justice judgments. There are some exceptions. For example, one study finds that those in an elated mood are more likely than those in a depressed mood to endorse egalitarian compared to equity justice principles (Sinclair & Mark, 1991). Another study finds that when individuals are uncertain about how to judge a justice outcome or the procedure used in arriving at the outcome, those in a previous and unrelated positive state are more likely than those in a previous and unrelated negative state to evaluate the outcome and procedure as just (Van den Bos, 2003). Further, research finds that when people are in a positive mood, they are more likely to expose themselves to threatening and negative feedback (Trope et al., 2001; Trope & Neter, 1994; Trope & Pomerantz, 1998). Trope and his colleague argue that positive emotions serve as a resource, buffering the affective costs associated with receiving negative information.

The above findings are consistent with our idea that we can conceptualize positive emotions as a *resource* that individuals carry with them across situations. In identity theory, resources are broadly conceptualized as anything which sustains the self or system of interaction within which the self resides (Freese & Burke, 1994). Resources vary from typical objects like pens, eyeglasses, and chairs – with which to write, see, and sit, respectively – to clothes needed to cover the body, education to obtain a job, and approval from another in a relationship. To count something as a resource, it must function to sustain persons and the social interaction process. Recently, identity researchers have examined how personal, interpersonal, and structural resources are used in interaction to facilitate actors' goal of self-verification (Stets & Cast, 2007).

We conceptualize positive emotions as a personal resource for the self and interaction. When individuals feel good, it enhances their ability to withstand problematic situations such as injustice. Negative emotions act in the opposite way, draining individuals and leaving them vulnerable to "stressors." The conceptualization of positive emotions as a resource is similar to the idea that high self-esteem is a resource for persons, operating as a buffer during stressful times (Cast & Burke, 2002). It is also similar to Collins's (1990) idea of high emotional energy in which people feel good when they are full of emotional energy, and this energy motivates them to act in situations – to dominate and to lead. Similar to how high self-esteem serves as a resource to support individuals during difficult periods, and high emotional energy provides confidence and enthusiasm in an interaction, positive emotions should help individuals withstand persistent situations of injustice. Just as self-esteem or emotional energy can be "built up" through good experiences and depleted through bad experiences, the same can be said of emotions. How is this possible?

On the one hand, an interaction can serve as the stimulus for an initial emotional response such as feeling good, and as the interaction continues, these interactions can provide additional stimuli that feed back on the initial emotion of feeling good and amplify it (Hallett, 2003; Lewis, 1971; Scheff, 1990). On the other hand, people's affective state are not created anew in every situation but rather can be carried over from one situation to the next. Indeed, Collins (1990) maintains that the results of previous interactions (in terms of emotions) become inputs for subsequent interactions. Thus, for Collins, emotional energy tends to cumulate either positively or negatively over time. We suggest that positive emotion becomes particularly resourceful for individuals, enabling them to better tolerate injustice. In this way, positive emotions should temper the negative impact of under-rewards. Following from this, our final hypothesis is:

Hypothesis 4. Compared to initial negative emotions, initial positive emotions are more likely to persist across unjust situations.

In general, we extend distributive justice theory in several ways. First, departing from assumptions in distributive justice theory, we predict that when individuals receive outcomes that are unjust but beneficial to them, and they are to respond immediately, they will feel good rather than bad. At least initially, not all unjust situations are evaluated negatively. Second, individuals not only react to unfair outcomes, but they also react to the behavior of the "sender" of the outcomes. In examining the status of the senders of unjust outcomes in terms of their gender, we anticipate that individuals will feel better about their unjust outcomes when they come from a high-status other (male) compared to a low-status other (female). Correspondingly, when persons are the recipients of unfair outcomes, we expect males to react more negatively than females given their greater sense of entitlement. Finally, emotions not only influence one's outcomes in an interaction, but they also influence people's affective state in subsequent interactions. We expect positive emotions to be particularly resourceful to individuals, tempering the effects of unjust outcomes across encounters.

METHOD

Subjects and Design

Participants in this study were male and female students recruited from undergraduate classes at a large northwestern university. The setting simulated a work situation in which participants completed three tasks on a computer. After their performance on each task, the participants received feedback from the manager for their work. Regardless of how long it took workers to complete each task, the manager always told the workers that they did "average work." During training for the three tasks, respondents learned that if they did average work, they would receive 100 points. However, following the manager's feedback of "average work," the manager over-rewarded the workers (assigning 200 points) or under-rewarded the workers (assigning 50 points).[4] The workers reported their emotional reactions to their points after each task.

Table 1. Reward Structure Over Time.

Reward Structure[a]	T_1	T_2	T_3
1. UR UR OR	50	50	200
2. UR OR UR	50	200	50
3. OR UR UR	200	50	50
4. OR OR UR	200	200	50
5. OR UR OR	200	50	200
6. UR OR OR	50	200	200

[a]UR = Under-reward; OR = Over-reward.

Previous research has examined situations in which workers repeatedly get what they expect or repeatedly receive an under-reward or over-reward (Stets, 2003, 2004, 2005; Stets & Asencio, 2008). However, exposure to the same reward over time is only one type of experience. Individuals also may experience situations in which their reward fluctuates over time. We are interested in situations in which people repeatedly experience unjust rewards rather than just rewards. Moreover, we examine injustice in which a person's reward oscillates from an over-reward to under-reward (or vice versa). Such situations are common in daily life. A friend may criticize us at one moment and then later tell us how much he admires us. Our employer may provide a large raise one year but then not offer a raise the following year. Individuals do not always get what they expect either initially or repeatedly. We examine such unjust situations in this study. We randomly assigned the workers to one of six different reward schedules depicted in Table 1.[5] Of the eight possible combinations of under-reward and over-reward across three tasks, all but two are included. We did not include constant over-rewards or constant under-rewards.

Additionally, we randomly assigned the workers to a (computer-simulated) manager who was male (John) or female (Mary). We collected data on 176 participants. There were more women participants (68%) than men participants (32%).

Procedure

Upon arriving at the laboratory, participants went to a workstation. They were told that a computer virus had corrupted the database of an ad agency (fictitiously labeled *Impact*). The database contained mailing addresses for households targeted to receive promotional information about a new car that was soon to be out on the market. The workers were to recover the missing information on the families in the database so that the promotional information could be sent out. For some families, the computer virus had deleted the city in which they resided. For other families, the virus had deleted the zip code that was associated with their address. For still other families, the virus had removed both the city and state that accompanied their address.

The workers were to help in the reconstruction of the database by using the Internet website, *Mapquest*, to obtain the missing information, and then insert the missing information into an Excel spreadsheet on the computer. The spreadsheet had the appearance of looking like the actual database. Participants were told that the time they needed to reconstruct their portion of the database would give *Impact* a sense of how much time and money would be needed to clean the data file and get the ad campaign underway. Participants also were informed that a manager, working to help the ad agency *Impact*, would periodically provide feedback regarding how much they completed on each task given what the average person had completed. The manager would award the participants points based on their performance in the same way that *Impact* workers would eventually earn monetary rewards for their performance once they started to clean up the database. Workers were told that the manager was a male (John) or female (Mary).

In Task 1, workers were to find the missing cities for 12 family addresses. When they typed a family's address, state, and zip code on *Mapquest* and located the city, they wrote it down on a pad of paper next to the computer to keep track of the cities that were associated with the addresses. They continued through the address list of missing cities. Once all cities were located, they opened the computer Excel spreadsheet and entered the cities that accompanied the addresses they had written down on the pad of paper. After they completed this task, they returned to the main program on the computer and "interacted" with a manager.

The workers were informed that the manager was connected to the computer network and was keeping track of how long it took them to complete the 12 records in Task 1. Based on the experimental condition, workers actually received either an over-reward (200 points) or under-reward (50 points) for their "average work." Following the assignment of points, the workers were asked how they felt about the points they received. They were told that *Impact* would be interested in how their workers reacted to the pay they received. They then moved to the next task.

The procedure for carrying out Tasks 2 and 3 was the same as Task 1 except that in Task 2, the workers were to find the missing zip code for a different set of 12 family addresses, and in Task 3, they were to locate the city and state of still another 12 family addresses. Again, *Mapquest* was made available to them as well as a computer spreadsheet to enter their results upon completion of each set of 12 records. Following completion of each task, they "interacted" with the manager who awarded them fewer points than they expected or more points than they anticipated. The workers then reported their emotional reactions to the points they received.

Manipulation Checks

After workers received feedback on their performance after each task, they were asked, "Given John (or Mary's) evaluation of your performance, how many points do you expect John (or Mary) to give you?" Since the manager always told the workers they did average work prior to assigning an over-reward or under-reward to them, and since we set the standard of average work to be 100 points, all of the workers reported expecting 100 points for their work. Thus, they adopted the just standard of 100 points = average work. To ensure that the workers assigned responsibility for their reward to the manager, after each task and prior to moving on to the next task, the workers were asked, "Who determined how many points you got for this task?" All of the workers reported that the managers were responsible for the reward they received for each task.

Measures

After the workers received the manager's over-reward or under-reward for each task, they reported how they felt about the points they received. On a scale from 0 ("Not at all") to 10 ("Intensely"), the workers reported how sad, resentful, angry, disgusted, satisfied, grateful, and deserving they felt after receiving their points. Conceptually, we see individuals as experiencing emotions ranging from the positive to the negative. We do not see people as experiencing positive *or* negative emotions. Our factor analyses support our conceptualization of a single dimension of emotions. Table 2 contains the principle components factor analyses of the emotions for the three tasks. Respondents do not make a distinction between positive emotions and negative emotions. All of the emotion items load well on a single factor. The

Table 2. Principal Components Analyses of Emotions Over Time ($N = 176$).

Items	T_1	T_2	T_3
Satisfied	.89	.81	.83
Sad	–.61	–.71	–.66
Grateful	.79	.69	.74
Resentful	–.77	–.80	–.80
Deserving	.76	.69	.72
Angry	–.87	–.87	–.82
Disgust	–.74	–.82	–.72
Eigenvalue	4.29	4.18	4.05
α	.89	.88	.87

Table 3. Means for Emotions Over Time by Reward Structure.

Reward Structure[a]	T_1	T_2	T_3
1. UR UR OR	–.80	–.85	.67
2. UR OR UR	–.80	.57	–.78
3. OR UR UR	.81	–.49	–.66
4. OR OR UR	.81	.80	–.52
5. OR UR OR	.76	–.54	.79
6. UR OR OR	–.90	.67	.56

[a]UR = Under-reward; OR = Over-reward

alpha reliabilities for each factor are high as indicated in the bottom row of Table 2. Therefore, for each task, the items were standardized (mean = 0; variance = 1) and then summed, with a high score representing positive emotions and a low score representing negative emotions. Table 3 shows the means for the emotions scale across the three tasks by the reward condition.

Reward was coded 0 for an under-reward (50 points) and 1 for an over-reward (200 points). The worker's gender and the manager's gender were each coded 0 for female and 1 for male.

Analysis

Since we are examining individuals' emotional reactions to rewards across three tasks, the unmeasured factors that influence individuals' emotional reactions in the first task (T_1) are likely to influence individuals' emotional reactions in the section task (T_2), and the third task (T_3). Therefore, we use seemingly unrelated three-stage least squares regression (SUR), which takes into account the correlated errors among multiple observations for a particiant. The equations for all of the dependent variables are estimated simultaneously, and the least squares estimators are interpreted in the same way as ordinary least square estimators (Felmlee & Hargens, 1988).

For exploratory purposes, we examine all higher-ordered interactions in all of the analyses. This includes all four-way, three-way, and two-way interactions. If the four-way interactions are non-significant, they are dropped from the analyses and the equations are re-estimated. If the three-way interactions are non significant, they are dropped and the equations are re-estimated and so forth.

RESULTS

Table 4 presents the SUR results across the three tasks. We retain all two-way interactions. All three-way and four-way interactions were non-significant, thus we eliminated them from the final analyses.[6] Across all three tasks, the reward workers receive following their task activity significantly influences their feelings following the task. Hypothesis 1 states that an over-reward will be more likely than an under-reward to lead to positive emotion. This is what we find. When workers receive more points from the manager than what is owed for average work, and they are asked their emotional reaction to this over-reward, they report a significantly more positive response than when they receive an under-reward ($\beta = .86$, $p < .05$ in T_1; $\beta = .55$, $p < .05$ in T_2; $\beta = .46$, $p < .05$ in T_3).

The positive response to an over-reward diminishes from T_1 to T_2 ($X^2 = 4.97$, $p < .05$) and from T_1 to T_3 ($X^2 = 9.71$, $p < .05$).[7] When exposed to an over-reward that is too positive (from Task 1 to Task 2 or from Task 1 to Task 3), a worker might begin to think about the meaning of the over-reward. Time gives individuals the opportunity to engage in additional cognitive processing, allowing them to reflect on their expectations and compare those expectations with their current outcomes. The comparison process will result in greater recognition of incongruence between expected and actual outcomes (as opposed to the rewarding aspects of the outcome), thereby reducing their positive reaction to their outcomes.

In addition to the above, the size of the effect of the reward on emotions in T_1 ($\beta = .86$, $p < .05$) indicates that workers' initial feelings are influenced

Table 4. SUR of Emotional Reactions Over Time ($N = 176$).

	Emotions		
	T_1	T_2	T_3
	B	B	β
Worker gender	.01	–.21	–.06
Manager gender	–.12	.01	–.21
Reward	.86*	.55*	.46*
Worker gender * manager gender	.08	.01	–.16*
Reward * worker gender	–.15*	.04	.01
Reward * manager gender	.03	.01	.23*
$Reward_{t-1}$[a]	–	–.35*	–.41*
$Emotion_{t-1}$[b]	–	.60*	.79*
Reward * $reward_{t-1}$	–	.20	.16
Reward * $emotion_{t-1}$	–	–.27*	–.37*
$Reward_{t-1}$ * $emotion_{t-1}$	–	.06	–.01
$Reward_{t-1}$ * worker gender	–	.20	–.07
$Reward_{t-1}$ * manager gender	–	–.02	.10
$Emotion_{t-1}$ * worker gender	–	–.25*	–.06
$Emotion_{t-1}$ * manager gender	–	–.01	–.16
R^2	.66*	.56*	.58*

*$p < .05$.
[a]$Reward_{t-1}$ = Reward in prior task.
[b]$Emotion_{t-1}$ = Emotion in prior task.

primarily by the injustice they receive. When we turn to T_2 and T_3, we will find that other factors begin to take on significance in influencing workers' feelings. For example, workers' previous feelings will influence their current feelings, and this relates to Hypothesis 4 on the persistence of positive emotions across unjust situations. Further, in T_3, we will see the relevance of workers' evaluations of the manager, which relates to Hypothesis 2 and the reactions that workers have to unexpected outcomes from a male or female manager. The influence of the manager's behavior in T_3 suggests that workers do not initially react to the manager's behavior. Instead, it takes them some time to process the behavior associated with the source of their injustice. For now, let us return to the results in T_1.

In T_1, the reward influences workers' emotional reactions. Additionally, their gender interacts with the reward to exert an influence on their emotional responses. For ease of understanding this interaction effect, Table 5 presents the comparison of means for female and male workers'

Table 5. Mean Emotions in T_1 by Worker Gender and Reward.

Worker Gender	Reward	
	Under-reward	Over-reward
Female	–.87	.87
Male	–.76	.60

emotions for an under-reward and an over-reward. Female workers respond more strongly than male workers do. They are more positive to an over-reward and more negative to an under-reward. However, women's initial emotional responsiveness does not persist into T_2 or T_3 because the interaction effect is not significant.

Column two in Table 4 reveals workers' emotional reactions in T_2. We have included workers' reward (an over-reward or under-reward) from their prior task, their previous feelings (positive or negative), and all the two-way interactions related to their prior reward and feelings. First, while workers feel relatively good when they receive an over-reward compared to an under-reward ($\beta = .55$, $p < .05$), previously receiving an over-reward makes them feel worse than if they had not previously received the over-reward ($\beta = -.35$, $p < .05$). A similar pattern occurs in T_3 ($\beta = -.41$, $p < .05$). These effects in T_2 and T_3 are primarily an artifact of the design of the study and are substantively and theoretically not interesting.[8]

The findings for T_2 and T_3 also reveal that, over time, emotions from a prior period positively influence workers' current feelings. Specifically, looking at columns two and three, we find that more positive feelings in T_1 significantly result in workers' more positive feelings in T_2 ($\beta = .60$, $p < .05$). Similar results hold moving from T_2 to T_3 ($\beta = .79$, $p < .05$). Thus, emotions do carry over from one situation to the next. We also find that across time, the interaction of workers' current reward and their earlier feelings influence their current feelings. For ease of presentation, we graphically present these interactions in Figs. 1 and 2. On the x-axis, positive emotions are to the right of zero and negative emotions are to the left of zero. On the y-axis, positive emotions are above zero and negative emotions are below zero. Emotions at an earlier point are on the x-axis and emotions at a later point are on the y-axis. Upper, solid lines represent the condition of an over-reward, and lower, dashed lines represent the condition of an under-reward.

In Fig. 1, we see that the negative emotions that workers report in T_1 are likely to carryover to T_2 when workers are under-rewarded in T_2 compared to when they receive an over-reward in T_2. For example, on the left-hand

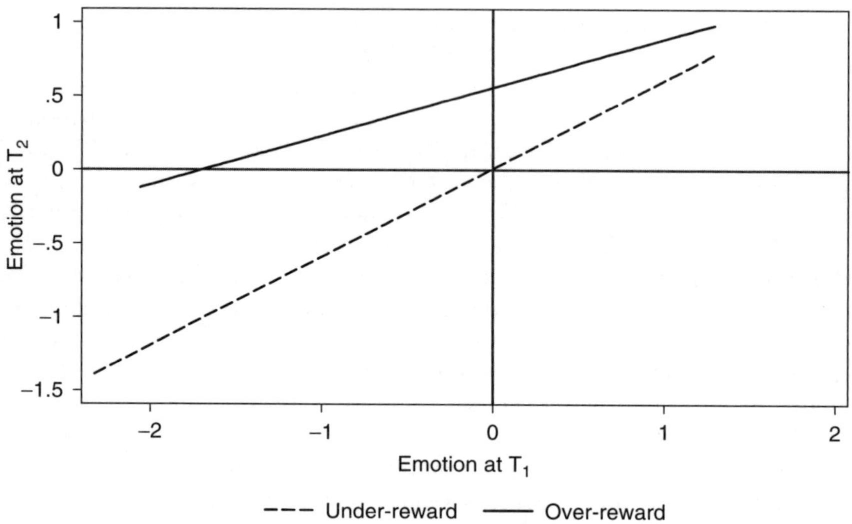

Fig. 1. Emotions at T_2 by Reward and Emotions at T_1.

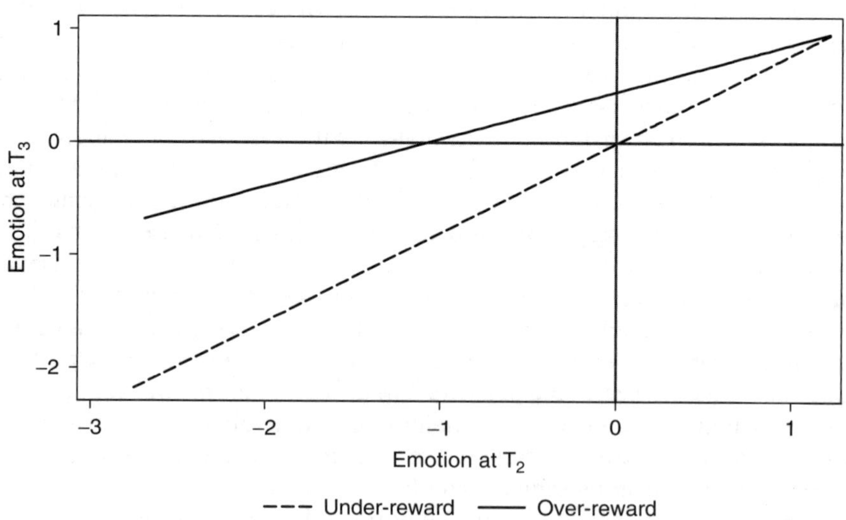

Fig. 2. Emotions at T_3 by Reward and Emotions at T_2.

side of the graph, when workers are under-rewarded in T_1 and then again under-rewarded in T_2 (bottom dashed line), they continue to report negative emotions (about −2.25 in T_1 and about −1.4 in T_2). The carryover of negative emotions is likely due to workers receiving yet another under-reward in T_2. Indeed, when they receive an over-rewarded in T_2 (top solid line), they become less negative. Their emotions change from negative (about −2) to more positive (almost zero). This difference in workers' reports when they initially receive an under-reward and continue to get an under-reward or then receive an over-reward (difference between the lines on the left-hand side of the graph) is large. It is larger than the difference in workers' reports when they initially receive an over-reward and continue to get an over reward or then receive an under-reward (difference between the lines on the right-hand side of the graph).

On the right-hand side of the graph, an over-reward followed by an under-reward (bottom dashed line) is a change in positive emotions from about 1.3 to .7. An over-reward followed by another over-reward (top solid line) is a change in positive emotions from about 1.3 to about .9. In general and consistent with Hypothesis 4, workers generally maintain positive feelings in T_2 that they had from T_1, irrespective of whether they are under-rewarded or over-rewarded in T_2.

In Fig. 2, we find similar results to those in Fig. 1. Once again, negative emotions from an earlier point in time are less likely to persist over time compared to positive emotions. What helps move workers out of a negative feeling state is receiving an over-reward in T_2. However, if workers continue to receive less than what they expect for their work, they will feel bad about it. In contrast, if one earlier felt good, and then obtained less than expected outcomes, the prior good feelings help offset or buffer the impact that an under-reward might ordinarily produce. Again, this supports Hypothesis 4.

The results in Table 4 also reveal that in T_2, previous feelings interact with one's gender to influence emotions ($\beta = -.25$, $p < .05$). We graph these findings in Fig. 3. The results reveal that women's emotions are more likely to carry over from T_1 to T_2 than men's emotions. If women feel bad in T_1 they also report feeling bad in T_2. Similarly, if they feel good in T_1 they also report feeling good in T_2. Unlike women's feelings, men's feelings tend to regress toward the mean rather than persist over time. However, looking at column three in Table 4, we find that the interaction of previous feelings and one's gender is not significant in T_3. Thus, this effect appears short-lived.

There are two other significant interaction effects in T_3. These effects highlight the influence of the status of the worker and the status of the manager in influencing one's emotional reactions. Thus, our focus is on

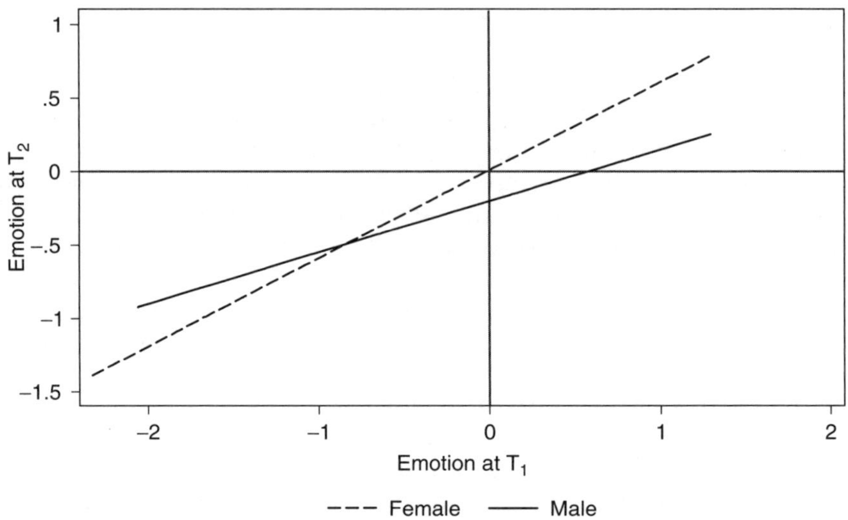

Fig. 3. Emotions at T_2 by Worker Gender and Emotions at T_1.

Table 6. Mean Emotions in T_3 by Worker Gender and Manager Gender.

Worker Gender	Manager Gender	
	Female	Male
Female	.10	–.01
Male	.06	–.35

Hypotheses 2a, 2b, 3a, and 3b. In the first effect, the worker's gender significantly interacts with the manager's gender to influence workers' emotional responses in T_3 ($\beta = -.16$, $p < .05$). In Table 6, we present the mean emotions for female and male workers given either an under-reward or over-reward from a male or female manager. The findings show that while female and male workers respond somewhat positively to an unjust reward from a female manager, male workers are more likely than female workers to report negative feelings when their unjust reward comes from a male manager (mean = $-.35$). This interaction effect is unexpected. While we anticipated that female workers would respond more positively to an under-reward than male workers (Hypothesis 3b), we did not expect males to respond more negatively when the under-reward came from a male manager. Instead, we expected male *and* female workers to respond more positively to an under-reward when it came from a male manager compared to a female manager (Hypothesis 2b).

The other significant interaction effect in T_3 is workers' emotional reactions when they receive an under-reward from the manager ($\beta = .23$, $p < .05$). We present these means in Table 7. Both male and female workers report negative feelings when they receive an under-reward compared to an over-reward from the manager. However, their emotional responses are much stronger when the unjust reward comes from a male manager compared to a female manager: they are more negative for an under-reward (mean $= -.93$) and more positive for an over-reward (mean $= .73$). Again, this interaction effect is unexpected. We anticipated a less negative reaction rather than a more negative reaction when a male manager gave an under-reward (Hypothesis 2b). Further, if there was a negative reaction to an under-reward, we expected it to come more from male workers than female workers (Hypothesis 3b) and not from both male and female workers as these results show.

Overall, the findings from this study reveal some interesting patterns. Without knowing individuals' prior affective states, people's initial emotional response to an injustice, as revealed in Task 1, is the result of *what* they are getting and not *who* they are getting it from. Persons respond positively to an over-reward and negatively to an under-reward. This is the enhancement dynamic. It supports Hypothesis 1. As we follow individuals across encounters, the consistency dynamic appears to take over. The positive feelings associated with an over-reward significantly diminish, and individuals get distressed with what they may see as unfair practices of high-status actors. As individuals are given adequate time to process information in the situation, they will begin to feel bad because their expectations are not being met. Perhaps most interesting is the carryover effect of one's feeling

Table 7. Mean Emotions in T_3 by Manager Gender and Reward.

Manager Gender	Reward	
	Under-reward	Over-reward
Female	–.41	.63
Male	–.93	.73

state across encounters. People's feelings persist beyond the point they are initially aroused. Positive emotions prove to be particularly resourceful for individuals in coping with persistent unjust situations. This supports Hypothesis 4.

DISCUSSION

In distributive justice theory, emotions are understood as an outcome of the evaluation of justice in a situation. If people do not receive what they expect, and they obtain either more or less than what they expect, they will feel bad. The findings of our research support this expectation, but only partially. In this study, when individuals obtained less than what they expected to get, they reported feeling bad, but when they obtained more than what they expected to get, they intially felt good. This is consistent with other research in the justice area (Stets, 2003) and with research in identity theory (Stets, 2004, 2005). These findings from the distributive justice and identity literatures suggest that we need to consider the fact that positive feedback, though it is incongruent with expected outcomes, may, without further cognitive processing, make individuals feel good (Stets & Asencio, 2008). This is the enhancement dynamic.

Currently, the cognitive consistency dynamic prevades most theories on emotions (Stets & Asencio, 2008). However, the consistency dynamic assumes that individuals will have enough time to cognitively process the outcomes they have received in a situation and compare those with what they expected to receive. As in this study, not all situations provide sufficient time for individuals to engage in the comparison process. When persons are asked to respond immediately to their outcomes, they may not have time to access their views about their expectations. Instead, they may simply categorize the outcome as good or bad, embrace the good, and reject the bad (Swann, 1990). This would explain the positive feelings workers reported for an over-reward and the negative feelings workers reported for an under-reward.[9] However, we do find that the reactions to an over-reward become more negative over time. Thus, the enhancement response can begin to diminish over time as cognitive resources become available (for example, sufficient time) to access one's expectations and compare them with situational outcomes. Only then may a response that fits the consistency motive emerge.

An alternative argument to the above has to do with whether individuals actually *perceive* over-rewards or under-rewards *as* unjust. If individuals do not perceive an over-reward as unfair, they may feel good about the outcome. They may feel that they deserve it. We investigated this alternative argument. In this study, after each task, workers were asked to identify on a scale from 0 ("Not at all Fair") to 10 ("Extremely Fair") how much they thought their outcome was fair. We re-analyzed the results that are presented in Table 4. While the evaluation of fairness significantly and positively influenced workers emotional reactions to their over-rewards on each task, all of the results in Table 4 remained.[10] Most importantly, the positive emotional reactions to an over-reward continued to diminish across tasks even controlling for the evaluation of fairness. Thus, while workers' evaluations of fairness contribute to their positive reaction to an over-reward, it does not help us understand why negative feelings increase across the three tasks.

As we earlier argued, individuals' emotional reactions in a situation are not simply a result of intrapersonal processes, that is, the relationship between their expected and actual outcomes, but they are also a function of interpersonal processes, namely one's relationship to others in the situation and their corresponding status in the social structure. This is the status dynamic. We expected workers to be more accepting of their unjust outcomes when they came from a male manager compared to a female manager. A male manager carries a higher status than a female manager, and higher status individuals are judged as more competent, held in higher esteem, and are more influential in persuading others that what they receive is what they deserve.

Unexpectedly, we found that male workers compared to female workers reported more negative feelings toward a male manager than toward a female manager. Additionally, both male and female workers reacted more strongly to an unjust reward when it came from a male manager than when it came from a female manager. Together, these findings reveal that workers were less inclined to accept unjust outcomes when they came from higher status managers. These results are consistent with other research that reveals that when individuals are exposed to unfair procedures, they are more likely to report negative emotions when the decision maker is seen as legitimate (Hegtvedt, Johnson, & Ganem, 2008). The researchers argue that individuals negatively respond to those whose authority is endorsed and who act unfairly because it is unexpected and perceived as inappropriate.

It is possible that having accorded higher status to the male managers, the workers were reacting to what they perceived to be the male manager's inappropriate behavior. The manager's behavior was inconsistent with the workers' expectations that they be treated justly. The workers likely expected the male managers to behave more competently than the female managers as in providing just outcomes when the workers were owed it. When they did not, this may have upset the workers. More generally, receiving an unjust outcome *and* witnessing a violation of performance expectations on the part of higher status managers may have been doubly distressful to the workers.

These findings are similar to earlier research in which workers reported more negative emotions when the managers did not verify their worker identity *and* when male managers acted friendly rather than distant in the work setting (Stets, 2004). Stets argued that we expect relations with high-status persons to be non-intimate and remote, but we expect intimate and close relations with low-status persons. When workers were exposed to the opposite behavior of male and female managers, they responded negatively. Thus, Stets reasoned that workers' negative emotions appear to have multiple bases: their worker identity was not being verified and higher status actors were behaving in an unexpected manner.

The reactions to the male manager do not emerge initially, during Task 1, but only later, during Task 3. Just as workers' emotional reactions to an over-reward become less positive over time, workers become more negative over time to what they judge to be the manager's incompetent behavior. Time is needed to access one's expectations along whatever dimension is relevant: their actual outcomes in the situation or the performance expectations of the manager. Either comparison, when given a chance to emerge, means that cognitive consistency principles of "met expectations" replace enhancement principles of "feeling good."

While intrapersonal and interpersonal factors do arouse emotions in a situation, these emotions influence subsequent interactions. Feelings are not created anew in each situation. Part of one's current feelings are the result of previous experiences and feelings from yesterday, last week, or even months ago. Further, one's current feelings will be carried into future interactions and influence later emotional reactions. The carryover effects of emotions means that we need to conceptualize emotions not only as an outcome of the justice evaluation process, but also as antecedent to the justice evaluation process. Borrowing from identity theory, positive emotions are a resource for subsequent interactions and can be precursors to the justice process. This is the resource dynamic.

As resources, positive emotions can function to sustain or enhance the self within and across situations while negative emotions threaten this function. Positive emotions that build up over time can serve as an "energy reservoir" for the self, serving as a buffer when difficult situations emerge.

Alternatively, negative emotions that build up over time can deplete the self, leaving individuals vulnerable to the "slings" and "arrows" of life. The results of this study reveal that positive emotions serve to help workers tolerate injustice across their tasks. Workers are generally able to maintain their positive feelings from one task to another, and this maintenance of positive feelings acts as a buffer, serving to soften the blow of unfair outcomes.

In general, the findings of this research reveal that emotions do more than just signal incongruency between expected and actual outcomes in a situation. Emotions generated by the justice process influence interactions beyond the initial encounter. Thus, baseline levels of emotions going into the justice process may be just as important as the emotions following from the justice process. In addition, one's feelings in situations may be due not only to the discrepancy between what one gets and what one expects to get, but also how others behave and how they are expected to behave. Finally, when theorizing about individuals' emotional reactions to injustice, we need to consider the enhancement process as well as the consistency process. The above suggests that more theoretical and empirical work lie ahead in the development of emotions not only in distributive justice theory, but other theories as well.

NOTES

1. Jasso (2006) argues that just rewards generate neutral emotion such as perfect tranquility rather than positive emotions.

2. While Burke maintained that negative emotions emerge even when identity non-verification is in a positive direction, Stryker (2004) does not discuss this idea. Stryker simply states that role performances that do not meet the expectations of others produce negative feelings. We do not know if role performances that exceed others' expectations produce negative emotions.

3. In the distributive justice studies, when participants "get more" of an outcome, it is usually not at the expense of other participants in the same situation "getting less" (Hegtvedt, 1990; Stets, 2003). Hegtvedt (1990) argues that Homans' emphasis on guilt may be overstated because the negative feeling may be contingent upon the perception that giving more to some means that others will receive less. In other words, one's outcomes are at another's expense.

4. Consistent with Jasso (1980), it takes more of an over-reward to generate injustice of an equal magnitude to that of an under-reward. This is the log (under-reward/just reward) = −log (over-reward/just reward). Therefore, in this study, the ratio of 200/100 = inverse of 50/100.

5. Across all tables, T_1, T_2, and T_3 = Task 1, Task 2, and Task 3 in the experiment.

6. These results are available upon request.

7. We investigated this finding further by examining whether workers were becoming less positive or more negative to the unjust rewards over time. A less positive response over time would mean that the workers are acclimating to the over-reward. A more negative response over time would mean that they are feeling worse with repeated unexpected rewards. To identify what was occurring, we re-ran the same analyses as shown in Table 4, but instead of using the full range of emotions (from negative to positive) as the outcome, we separated out positive emotions from negative emotions. We found that while the positive emotions remained stable over time, workers' negative emotions became increasingly negative over time. Therefore, workers are feeling more negative rather than less positive. These results are available upon request.

8. In T_2, those who were under-rewarded were more likely to have been over-rewarded than under-rewarded in T_1 (see Table 1: Conditions 1, 3, and 5). Further, those who were over-rewarded in T_2 were more likely to have been under-rewarded than over-rewarded in T_1 (see Table 1: Conditions 2, 4, and 6). The same pattern holds for T_3. This contrast in rewards across time will lead workers to report feeling bad compared to feeling good given their under-reward.

9. In addition, there was nothing in the design of this study that led individuals to think that getting more points for their work meant that others would be getting less for their work. This might have further facilitated a positive response to an over-reward.

10. These results are available upon request.

ACKNOWLEDGMENTS

This research was supported by a National Science Foundation Grant (SES-9904215) to the first author. The authors would like to thank Peter Burke, Karen Hegtvedt, and Jody Clay-Warner for their helpful feedback on an earlier draft of this chapter.

REFERENCES

Berger, J., & Webster, M. J. (2006). Expectations, status, and behavior. In: P. J. Burke (Ed.), *Contemporary social psychological theories* (pp. 268–300). Stanford: Stanford University Press.

Burke, P. J. (1991). Identity processes and social stress. *American Sociological Review*, *56*, 836–849.

Burke, P. J. (2004). Identities and social structure: The 2003 Cooley-Mead award address. *Social Psychology Quarterly*, *67*, 5–15.

Cast, A. D., & Burke, P. J. (2002). A theory of self-esteem. *Social Forces*, *80*, 1041–1068.

Collins, R. (1990). Stratification, emotional energy, and the transient emotions. In: T. D. Kemper (Ed.), *Research agendas in the sociology of emotions* (pp. 27–57). New York: State University of New York Press.

Cook, K. S., & Hegtvedt, K. A. (1983). Distributive justice, equity, and equality. *Annual Review of Sociology*, *9*, 217–241.
DeCremer, D. (Ed.) (2007). *Advances in the psychology of justice and affect*. Charlotte, NC: Information Age Publishing.
DeCremer, D., van Kleef, G. A., & Wubben, M. J. J. (2007). Do the emotions of others shape justice effects? In: D. DeCremer (Ed.), *Advances in the psychology of justice and affect* (pp. 37–59). Charlotte, NC: Information Age Publishing.
Felmlee, D. H., & Hargens, L. L. (1988). Estimation and hypothesis testing for seemingly unrelated regressions: A sociological application. *Social Science Research*, *17*, 384–399.
Foddy, M., & Smithson, M. (1989). Fuzzy sets and double standards: Modeling the process of ability inference. In: J. Berger, M. Zelditch & B. Anderson (Eds), *Sociological theories in progress: New formulations* (pp. 73–99). Newbury Park: Sage.
Forgas, J. P. (1995). Mood and judgment: The affect infusion model (AIM). *Psychological Bulletin*, *117*, 39–66.
Foschi, M. (1989). Status characteristics, standards, and attributions. In: J. Berger, M. Zelditch & B. Anderson (Eds), *Sociological theories in progress: New formulations* (pp. 58–72). Newbury Park, CA: Sage.
Freese, L., & Burke, P. J. (1994). Persons, identities, and social interaction. *Advances in Group Processes*, *11*, 1–24.
Hallett, T. (2003). Emotional feedback and amplification in social interaction. *The Sociological Quarterly*, *44*, 705–726.
Hegtvedt, K. A. (1990). The effects of relationship structure on emotional responses to inequity. *Social Psychology Quarterly*, *53*, 214–228.
Hegtvedt, K. A. (2006). Justice frameworks. In: P. J. Burke (Ed.), *Contemporary social psychological theories* (pp. 46–69). Stanford: Stanford University Press.
Hegtvedt, K. A., Johnson, C., & Ganem, N. M. (2008). It's not just what you feel: Expressing emotional responses to the injustice of others. In: J. Clay-Warner & D. T. Robinson (Eds), *Social structure and Emotion*. San Diego: Elsevier.
Hegtvedt, K. A., & Killian, C. (1999). Fairness and emotions: Reactions to the process and outcomes of negotiations. *Social Forces*, *78*, 269–303.
Hegtvedt, K. A., & Markovsky, B. (1995). Justice and injustice. In: K. S. Cook, G. A. Fine & J. S. House (Eds), *Sociological perspectives on social psychology* (pp. 257–280). Boston: Allyn and Bacon.
Homans, G. C. (1974). *Social behavior: Its elementary forms* (2nd ed.). New York: Harcourt Brace and World Inc.
Jasso, G. (1980). A new theory of distributive justice. *American Sociological Review*, *45*, 3–32.
Jasso, G. (2006). Emotion in justice processes. In: J. E. Stets & J. H. Turner (Eds), *Handbook of the sociology of emotions* (pp. 321–346). New York: Springer.
Lewis, H. (1971). *Shame and guilt in neurosis*. New York: International Universities Press.
Major, B. (1987). Gender, justice, and the psychology of entitlement. In: P. Shaver & C. Hendrick (Eds), *Sex and gender* (pp. 124–148). Newbury Park: Sage.
Markovsky, B. (1985). Toward a multilevel distributive justice theory. *American Sociological Review*, *50*, 822–839.
Ridgeway, C. L. (1993). Gender, status, and the social psychology of expectations. In: P. England (Ed.), *Theory on gender/feminism on theory* (pp. 175–198). New York: Aldine.
Ridgeway, C. L., Johnson, C., & Diekema, D. (1994). External status, legitimacy, and compliance in male and female groups. *Social Forces*, *72*, 1051–1077.

Ridgeway, C. L., & Smith-Lovin, L. (1999). Gender and interaction. In: J. S. Chafetz (Ed.), *Handbook of the sociology of gender* (pp. 247–274). New York: Kluwer Academic/Plenum.

Scheff, T. J. (1990). *Microsociology: Discourse, emotion, and social structure*. Chicago: University of Chicago Press.

Sedikides, C. (1993). Assessment, enhancement, and verification determinants of the self-evaluation process. *Journal of Personality and Social Psychology*, *65*, 317–338.

Sedikides, C., Gaertner, L., & Toguchi, Y. (2003). Pancultural self-enhancement. *Journal of Personality and Social Psychology*, *84*, 60–79.

Sinclair, R. C., & Mark, M. M. (1991). Mood and the endorsement of egalitarian macrojustice versus equity-based microjustice principles. *Personality and Social Psychology Bulletin*, *17*, 369–375.

Sprecher, S. (1992). How men and women expect to feel and behave in response to inequity in close relationships. *Social Psychology Quarterly*, *55*, 57–69.

Steil, J. M. (1994). Equality and entitlement in marriage: Benefits and barriers. In: M. J. Lerner & G. Mikula (Eds), *Entitlement and the affectional bond* (pp. 229–258). New York: Plenum Press.

Stets, J. E. (2003). Justice, emotion, and identity theory. In: P. J. Burke, T. J. Owens, R. T. Serpe & P. A. Thoits (Eds), *Advances in identity theory and research* (pp. 105–122). New York: Kluwer Academic/Plenum.

Stets, J. E. (2004). Emotions in identity theory: The effects of status. *Advances in Group Processes*, *21*, 51–76.

Stets, J. E. (2005). Examining emotions in identity theory. *Social Psychology Quarterly*, *68*, 39–56.

Stets, J. E. (2006). Identity theory and emotions. In: J. E. Stets & J. H. Turner (Eds), *Handbook of the sociology of emotions* (pp. 203–223). New York: Springer.

Stets, J. E., & Asencio, E. K. (2008). Consistency and enhancement processes in understanding emotions. *Social Forces*, *86*, 1055–1078.

Stets, J. E., & Burke, P. J. (2005). New directions in identity control theory. *Advances in Group Processes*, *22*, 43–64.

Stets, J. E., & Cast, A. D. (2007). Resources and identity verification from an identity theory perspective. *Sociological Perspectives*, *50*, 517–543.

Stets, J. E., & Harrod, M. M. (2004). Verification across multiple identities: The role of status. *Social Psychology Quarterly*, *67*, 155–171.

Stryker, S. (2004). Integrating emotion into identity theory. *Advances in Group Processes*, *21*, 1–23.

Stryker, S., & Burke, P. J. (2000). The past, present, and future of an identity theory. *Social Psychology Quarterly*, *63*, 284–297.

Swann, W. B., Jr. (1990). To be adored or to be known?: The interplay of self-enhancement and self-verification. In: E. T. Higgins & R. M. Sorrentino (Eds), *Handbook of motivation and cognition* (pp. 408–450). New York: Guilford.

Trope, Y., Ferguson, M., & Raghunathan, R. (2001). Mood as a resource in processing self-relevant information. In: J. P. Forgas (Ed.), *The Handbook of affect and social cognition* (pp. 256–274). Mahwah, NJ: Lawrence Erlbaum.

Trope, Y., & Neter, E. (1994). Reconciling competing motives in self-evaluation: The role of self-control in feedback seeking. *Journal of Personality and Social Psychology*, *66*, 646–657.

Trope, Y., & Pomerantz, E. M. (1998). Resolving conflicts among self-evaluative motives: Positive experiences as a resource for overcoming defensiveness. *Motivation and Emotion*, *22*, 53–72.

Van den Bos, K. (2003). On the subjective quality of social justice: The role of affect as information in the psychology of justice judgments. *Journal of Personality and Social Psychology*, *85*, 482–498.

SYSTEM JUSTIFICATION THEORY AND THE ALLEVIATION OF EMOTIONAL DISTRESS: PALLIATIVE EFFECTS OF IDEOLOGY IN AN ARBITRARY SOCIAL HIERARCHY AND IN SOCIETY

John T. Jost, Cheryl J. Wakslak and Tom R. Tyler

ABSTRACT

In addition to serving a hegemonic function, system-justifying ideologies serve the palliative function of enabling people to feel better about inequality. We summarize three studies supporting this proposition. In the first study, an arbitrary hierarchy was created using the "Star Power" simulation. Results reveal that system justification is associated with increased positive affect, satisfaction, and decreased negative affect, guilt, and frustration. Two additional studies demonstrate that the dampening effect of system justification on support for the redistribution of resources is mediated by reduced moral outrage but not guilt or negative affect. Implications for social change and social justice are discussed.

Justice
Advances in Group Processes, Volume 25, 181–211

ISSN: 0882-6145/doi:10.1016/S0882-6145(08)25012-5

> Life, as we find it, is too hard for us; it brings us too many pains, disappointments and impossible tasks. In order to bear it, we cannot dispense with palliative measures. (Sigmund Freud, 1930/1961, p. 22)

Despite the fact that Americans – as de Tocqueville pointed out long ago – profess a strong commitment to the principle of egalitarianism, it is clearly the case that many of our most cherished institutions, including the institution of capitalism, are in fact highly inegalitarian. A few quick economic facts serve to make the point. For instance, the richest 1% in the U.S. possesses approximately half of the total national wealth, and the top 20% possesses over 90% (Wolff, 1996). Furthermore, economic outcomes have grown increasingly unequal over the past 25 years or so (Marshall, 2000; Milanovic, 2002; Piketty & Saez, 2003, 2006). When Ronald Reagan took office in 1981, CEOs earned approximately 40 times the salary of the average worker; the ratio is now approximately 500 to 1 (Stiglitz, 2004). Nevertheless, Americans' confidence in the fairness and legitimacy of the economic system has remained high (see Jost, Blount, Pfeffer, & Hunyady, 2003a). The 1998 Gallup Poll of "Haves" and "Have Nots" (Ludwig, 1999), for example, revealed that 68% of respondents overall believed that "the economic situation in the United States is basically fair," and 52% of those in the lowest income bracket concurred (see also Jost, Pelham, Sheldon, & Sullivan, 2003b).

Understanding relatively puzzling phenomena such as this one is a top priority for system justification theory (Jost, Banaji, & Nosek, 2004; Jost & Hunyady, 2005). The key question is *why* people would imbue the status quo with legitimacy and justification, especially when it seems to fall short of satisfying justice criteria associated with equity, equality, and need principles and conflicts with both personal and collective interests and esteem. Several approaches in social psychology have suggested that support for the status quo can be explained by adherence to "dominant ideologies," including the Protestant Work Ethic, meritocratic ideology, and various other hierarchy-enhancing "legitimizing myths" (Jackman, 1994; Jost & Banaji, 1994; Katz & Hass, 1988; Kluegel & Smith, 1986; Major, 1994; Pratto, Sidanius, Stallworth, & Malle, 1994). Although it is useful to understand and appreciate the role of ideology in perpetuating the status quo, such a theoretical move only defers the crucial question. We need to ask *why* system-justifying ideologies are attractive to people in the first place (see Jost & Hunyady, 2005).

In the remainder of this chapter we first distinguish between the hegemonic and palliative functions of system-justifying ideologies, seeking to integrate theoretical insights concerning each. Next we describe a quasi-experimental study investigating the emotional and other social and psychological consequences of system justification in an arbitrarily created social hierarchy. Afterwards, we review the results of two additional studies that shed light on mediating mechanisms and help us to better understand how and why system-justifying ideologies undermine support for social change. In conclusion, we discuss the general relationships among ideology, justice beliefs, and emotions and note that a reciprocal relationship exists between individual (or psychological) needs for justification and institutional (or sociological) needs for legitimation (see also Jost & Major, 2001).

THE HEGEMONIC FUNCTION OF IDEOLOGY

Many sociological and social psychological attempts to understand the development and transmission of ideology have stressed the hegemonic function that ideology serves (e.g., Foucault, 1980; Habermas, 1975; Jackman, 1994; Sidanius & Pratto, 1999). The basic argument is that members of dominant groups, who generally control access to financial and informational resources, devise and spread ideologies that justify the system in order to preserve their own power and privileges. From this perspective, system-justifying ideologies originate with dominant group members, who then manipulate subordinates into believing that unequal social positions are deserved and the system is fair and legitimate.

Indeed, research tends to support the notion that the powerful legitimize their own positions in the social hierarchy, both directly and indirectly (e.g., Kipnis, 1976; Ridgeway, 2001; Sidanius & Pratto, 1999). Experimental and field studies of intergroup relations, for instance, demonstrate that members of dominant groups hold self-serving perceptions of the social system, asserting that the status quo has more legitimacy than other observers are willing to grant (e.g., Sachdev & Bourhis, 1987, 1991). With regard to stereotyping, members of powerful groups use group beliefs to constrain the social mobility of others, stereotyping subordinates by "default" and "design" (Goodwin, Operario, & Fiske, 1998). In addition, members of dominant groups show stronger ingroup bias on measures of stereotyping, evaluation, and resource allocation than do members of subordinate groups (e.g., Jost & Banaji, 1994; Sachdev & Bourhis, 1987, 1991; Sidanius & Pratto, 1999).

While compelling, this view of the powerful as relentlessly strategic and hegemonic in their use of ideology is at odds with research suggesting that people genuinely care about fairness and justice (e.g., Lerner, 1977, 2003; Tyler, Boeckmann, Smith, & Huo, 1997; Tyler & Smith, 1998). One of the core assumptions of theories of social justice is that virtually everyone is troubled by the possibility that inequality is unfair, whether they are themselves advantaged or disadvantaged by the inequality (e.g., Loewenstein, Thompson, & Bazerman, 1989). Walster, Berscheid, and Walster (1973) were among the first to suggest that those who are overbenefitted by inequity as well as those who are underbenefitted experience emotional distress. People who receive less than equitable treatment tend to report anger and frustration, while those who receive more than is equitable feel guilt and dissonance (Hassebrauck, 1986; Hegtvedt, 1990; Homans, 1974).

Similarly, case studies reveal that most powerholders are not entirely comfortable acting on their own selfish desires, but rather must cope with the psychological consequences of asserting social control (e.g., Darley, 2004; Milgram, 1974). For example, soldiers who participated in atrocities such as the My Lai massacre in Vietnam struggled to minimize guilt and distress through mechanisms such as authorization, routinization, and dehumanization (Kelman & Hamilton, 1989). Concerning the more passive ways in which people benefit from inequality, Nagata (1990) explored the attitudes of European Americans concerning Japanese American internment during World War II. She found that although supporters of the internment acknowledged the trauma to internees caused by evacuation and detention, they asserted that it was for "their own good" (p. 135). At the time, there can be little doubt that most Americans considered the internment to be fair and even "morally justified by a need for self-protection" (p. 136). These and related justifications allowed people to live with themselves while benefiting from a system that resulted in harm being done to others.

More broadly, work by Chen and Tyler (2001) suggests that being advantaged in a world that is perceived as unjust leads to a nagging worry that one's privileges may be undeserved, as well as to feelings of guilt and dissonance. Research confirms that many members of dominant groups suffer from guilt in connection with their group's past and present transgressions (e.g., Devine, Montieth, Zuwerink, & Elliot, 1991; Doosje, Branscombe, Spears, & Manstead, 1998; Swim & Miller, 1999). It seems, therefore, that the view of the powerful as deliberately wielding ideology as a hegemonic tool for social control is incomplete. While exercising social control generates obvious benefits for the advantaged, it also creates emotional distress that must be managed, especially if one's advantages are seen as linked to the disadvantages of others (e.g., Homans, 1974; Stets & Osborne, this volume).

The hegemonic assumption also conflicts with another observation, namely that the disadvantaged are not simply manipulated by others, but genuinely desire to see the system as justified and actively imbue it with legitimacy (see Jost, Pietrzak, Liviatan, Mandisodza, & Napier, 2007). Theoretical perspectives that emphasize the psychological benefits of ideological endorsement help to complete the picture. Lerner and Miller (1978), for example, suggested that the "belief in a just world" enables people to confront their social and physical worlds as if they were stable and orderly (even when they are not). Evidence indicates that people who embrace this belief are more trusting of others (Furnham, 1995; Zuckerman & Gerbasi, 1977), more likely to invest in the future (Hafer, 2000; Zuckerman, 1975), and less likely to experience negative emotion in the face of adversity (e.g., Dalbert, 1998; Hafer & Olson, 1989; Bulman & Wortman, 1977; Lipkus & Bissonnette, 1996; Tomaka & Blascovich, 1994). The "illusion of control" appears to operate similarly. Kluegel and Smith (1986), for instance, found that poor people who saw themselves as responsible for their own poverty reported feeling more positive emotion, less guilt, and greater satisfaction, compared to poor people who made external attributions for their situation. Jost et al. (2003b) also found that the endorsement of meritocratic ideology was positively associated with satisfaction concerning one's own economic situation, regardless of whether that situation was advantageous or disadvantageous.

THE PALLIATIVE FUNCTION OF IDEOLOGY

The research summarized above suggests that in addition to serving a hegemonic function, system-justifying ideologies fulfill a palliative function by allowing people to feel better about the status quo, regardless of their own position in society (Jost & Hunyady, 2002). It is conceivable that the alleviation of distress through system justification is not merely a passive benefit accruing to ideological adherents but also a motivating factor that encourages support for these ideologies in the first place (Chen & Tyler, 2001; Jost et al., 2003a, 2003b). Our general approach is consistent with certain tenets of equity theory, namely that unjustified forms of inequality lead to the experience of aversive emotions, which then motivate the individual to resolve inequity through cognitive or behavioral strategies such as compensating victims or, alternatively, justifying the system as fair (e.g., Lerner, 1980). The justification (or rationalization) route may be preferred because it is typically less costly, less effortful, and more easily accomplished than compensation (Walster et al., 1973).

It is important to point out that, for the advantaged, the hegemonic and palliative functions of ideology work together. While those with power may turn to system-justifying ideologies as a way of making themselves feel less guilty about inequality, endorsement of these ideologies strengthens the perceived legitimacy and stability of the system of inequality. As the Czech playwright, social critic, and politician Vaclav Havel (1991) observed, ideology facilitates power "by serving as a psychological excuse," and that "from the moment that excuse is accepted, it constitutes power inwardly, becoming an active component of that power" (p. 137). To the extent that powerful people feel that their outcomes are legitimate, justified, and deserved, they should act with even more confidence in preserving and protecting the system that gives them their privileges (French & Raven, 1959; Jackman, 1994; Keltner, Gruenfeld, & Anderson, 2004; Kipnis, 1976; Smith, Jost, & Vijay, in press). They should also be correspondingly less likely to help those who are less fortunate (Lerner, 1980; Walster et al., 1973).

OVERVIEW OF THE CURRENT RESEARCH PROGRAM

In the current research program, we investigate the structure of relations among social status (or position), ideological justification of the system, emotional distress, and support for redistributive social policies. Ideology, according to our theoretical account, is not merely a tool for social control, but also a means by which people reduce the emotional distress elicited by inequality (see also Jost & Hunyady, 2002; Wakslak, Jost, Tyler, & Chen, 2007). Those who benefit disproportionately from social arrangements are hypothesized to feel emotional distress (including guilt and dissonance) arising from contradictions between their situation of privilege and what (on some level) they recognize as being appropriate according to justice principles. To cope with this distress, they should strive to excuse themselves (and others) by finding justifications for the status quo. Similarly, those who are disadvantaged are hypothesized to experience distress (including anger and frustration) because of the inequality to which they are subjected. Thus, the endorsement of system-justifying ideologies should be associated with (a) reduced emotional distress (especially moral outrage) on the part of the advantaged and the disadvantaged, as well as (b) a withdrawal of support for social change in general and the redistribution of resources in particular (see Fig. 1 for an illustration of the overall theoretical model).

These hypotheses were investigated in a series of studies using a combination of experimental, quasi-experimental, and structural equation

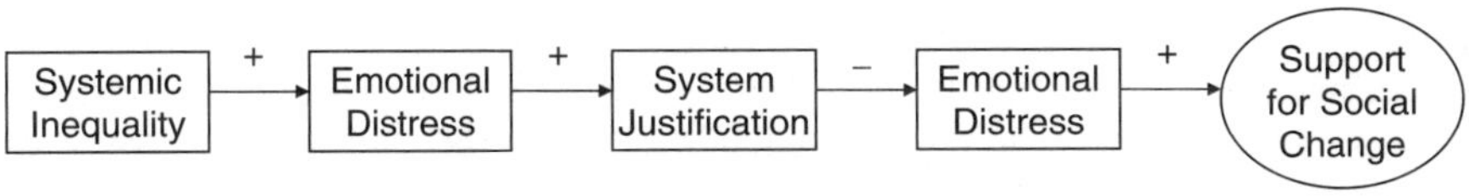

Fig. 1. An Illustration of the Overall Theoretical Model, in which the Palliative Function of System Justification is Hypothesized to Undermine Support for Social Change through its Effect on Emotional Distress (i.e., Moral Outrage).

methods. The first study made use of a quasi-experimental design in which a hierarchical system involving three groups that differed in status and power was created arbitrarily; both system justification and emotional experience were measured. The fact that in this study we introduced a new hierarchical social system allowed us to capture spontaneous forms of system justification rather than pre-existing rationalizations for well-known inequalities in society. This study, therefore, speaks to the active, goal-directed nature of system justification, and it suggests that members of both advantaged and disadvantaged groups are quick to rationalize social systems in which they find themselves, in part because seeing the situation as unjust and exploitative is emotionally costly.

We will also describe two related studies, which were reported earlier by Wakslak et al. (2007), examining the palliative effects of system justification for individuals' willingness to help and support those who are disadvantaged. The first study links the endorsement of system justification and its emotional consequences to the degree of support for social change and the redistribution of resources. The second examines the palliative hypothesis experimentally by inducing a system justification mindset and examining its effects on self-reported emotional distress and support for community service programs focused on aiding the disadvantaged. Taken in conjunction, these studies suggest that system justification alleviates emotional distress both in general and with respect to potential injustices, thereby undermining support for social change and redistributive social policies.

THE "STAR POWER" SIMULATION: JUSTIFICATION IN AN ARBITRARILY CREATED SOCIAL HIERARCHY

An engaging classroom simulation known as "Star Power" was used to create a hierarchical social system involving groups that differed in status, power, and privilege. According to an educational website that advertises materials used in the simulation (http://www.stsintl.com/schools-charities/star_power.html), the goal is to teach people about the use and abuse of power and to subtly communicate the lesson that, "To change behavior, it may be necessary to change the system in which that behavior occurs." The simulation, which is extremely engaging for most participants, mimics real-world inequalities associated with income, social class, and occupational stratification. As in society at large, there is considerable ambiguity during the "Star Power" simulation concerning the causes of inequality and therefore whether or not disparities of outcome are fair, legitimate, and deserved.

We anticipated that creating a system of relatively arbitrary inequality among peers would lead participants to experience some level of emotional distress and that this distress would lead many to spontaneously develop justifications or rationalizations for the inequality. Based on previous research, the advantaged were expected to feel dissonance and guilt, whereas the disadvantaged were expected to experience emotions such as anger and frustration (Hassebrauck, 1986; Walster et al., 1973). We hypothesized, furthermore, that these and other forms of emotional distress would be attenuated by the endorsement of system-justifying ideologies, including reassurances that the system is fair, legitimate, and meritocratic (Jost & Hunyady, 2002). Meritocratic belief systems involve the conviction that ability and hard work lead to success and, conversely, that if people fail, it is because they have not worked hard enough or they do not have the necessary abilities (e.g., Major, 1994; Martin, 1982). A belief in meritocracy, therefore, is one type of system-justifying ideology, and it seems to be especially effective at reassuring people in free market systems that inequality in society is fair, legitimate, and deserved (e.g., Ledgerwood, Jost, Mandisodza, & Pohl, 2008; McCoy & Major, 2007).

Methods

Participants

One hundred and seventy nine first-year MBA students at a top American business school participated in the context of a classroom exercise on intergroup dynamics. Participants possessed a minimum of three years' professional work experience. Sixty-seven percent were male. Data were pooled from 10 different classroom sessions.

Procedure

A modified version of the "Star Power" exercise was used to create three groups that differed in power, status, and privilege (called "triangles," "circles," and "squares" from highest to lowest, respectively). Under the pretense of a bargaining simulation, participants randomly drew and traded poker chips of different values with the goal of accumulating the greatest number of individual points across several trading rounds. The duration of the simulation was approximately 60–75 min. Although we made some relatively minor procedural changes, details pertaining to the rules of the game and the point values of chips may be found on the "Star Power" website.

The game is structured so that there is ambiguity concerning the causes of success and failure. Unequal starting points were randomly assigned, with participants drawing five chips from the bag before they knew either the rules of the game or the scoring system. Following the initial drawing, participants were allowed to bargain with one another in a series of 5–10 min trading rounds, under a set of specific rules. Point totals were cumulative throughout rounds, although new chips were drawn at the beginning of each round. The trading rounds provided a limited opportunity for participants to improve their position by negotiating with others, effectively creating attributional ambiguity concerning whether one's outcomes were earned and deserved or whether they were due to luck and chance.

On the basis of the individual point values resulting from the random allocation of resources combined with individual bargaining efforts, participants were stratified into high-, medium-, and low-status groups or classes and instructed to wear badges advertising their group memberships to others. Unbeknownst to participants, early advantages were perpetuated and magnified as a result of the experimenter's activities. For the second and third rounds, the dominant group was secretly allowed to draw their chips from a bag that was enriched with valuable chips, much as privileged groups in society enjoy better access to educational, professional, and financial opportunities. Some individual mobility – both upward and downward – was allowed to occur in the system. In general, however, the most powerful group members ("triangles") maintained a strong hegemony throughout the course of the experiment, and near the end of the session they were allowed to introduce their own rules of play.

Measures

Immediately following the conclusion of the "Star Power" exercise, members of all three groups completed questionnaires containing (in different orders) measures of system-justifying ideology as well as positive and negative emotions.

System justification. Three items were used to measure the degree to which participants experienced the hierarchical social system to be fair, legitimate, and meritocratic. Participants were asked to indicate how strongly they agreed or disagreed with each of the following statements: (a) "If you work hard in this game, it is possible to succeed"; (b) "The rules of the game as explained by the instructor were basically fair"; and (c) "The new rules introduced by the triangles were legitimate, because they earned their position." Responses were made on 9-point scales ranging from "strongly disagree" (1) to "strongly agree" (9). A system justification scale was constructed by averaging responses to the three items ($\alpha = .54$).

Positive and negative emotions. Research participants were asked to indicate how "generally positive" and how "generally negative" they felt during the "Star Power" exercise, as well as the degree to which a number of specific emotions characterized their feelings. These included four emotions related to satisfaction (pleased, proud, satisfied, happy, $\alpha = .85$), three related to guilt (guilty, ashamed, and conflicted, $\alpha = .73$), and two related to frustration (frustrated, angry, $\alpha = .64$). All responses were given on scales ranging from 1 ("not at all") to 9 ("extremely").

Questionnaire order and counter-balancing. For purposes of counter-balancing and to examine hypotheses related to question order, some participants completed the system justification items before the emotion items, while others completed them in the opposite order. The different versions of the questionnaire were distributed evenly across all 10 classroom sections, as were power differences among the three groups.

Debriefing. After all of the questionnaires were collected, the instructor led an in-depth debriefing and discussion of the "Star Power" exercise, focusing on the role of *post hoc* justification processes following abuses of power and other ethical transgressions.

Results and Discussion

To investigate relations among social position, system justification, and emotional distress, both analyses of variance and regression analyses were conducted. We begin by examining the impact of social position on system justification and emotion, and then move on to consider relations between system justification and emotion, including both correlational and experimental effects.

Effects of social position on system justification. Analysis of variance indicated that social position significantly affected endorsement of system-justifying ideology, $F(2, 176) = 4.77$, $p = .01$. Least significant difference tests revealed that members of the high-power group were more likely to engage in system justification ($M = 5.16$, SD $= 1.51$) than were members of the medium ($M = 4.58$, SD $= 1.78$) or low-power ($M = 4.32$, SD $= 1.53$) groups, who did not differ from one another. Consistent with self-interest, the strongest supporters of the system were those who benefited the most from it, although the mean differences were not as great as one might have expected on the basis of hegemonic theories alone.

Effects of social position on affect. Separate ANOVAs conducted for each emotion type indicated that social position significantly affected both satisfaction, $F(2, 165) = 4.05$, $p < .05$, and guilt, $F(2, 164) = 4.82$, $p < .01$ (Table 1). We conducted planned contrasts to compare the high-power group with the low-power group. These revealed that the most powerful group reported significantly more satisfaction, $t(165) = 2.83$, $p < .01$, and more guilt, $t(164) = 2.75$, $p < .01$, than did the low-power group. In addition, members of the low-power group were marginally more frustrated than were members of the high-power group, $t(167) = -1.66$, $p < .1$. There were no significant differences among the groups on general measures of positive or negative affect (all ps $> .2$).

Effects of system justification endorsement on affect. According to the palliative hypothesis we expected that the endorsement of system

Table 1. Affect Ratings as a Function of Social Position in the "Star Power" Study.

Type of Affect	Low Power ($n = 56$)	Medium Power ($n = 49$)	High Power ($n = 74$)
Satisfaction			
Mean	4.37^{a}	$4.82^{a,b}$	5.32^{b}
Standard deviation	1.87	1.74	1.89
Guilt			
Mean	2.21^{a}	2.27^{a}	3.08^{b}
Standard deviation	1.57	1.26	2.07
Frustration			
Mean	3.23^{a}	3.14^{a}	2.68^{a}
Standard deviation	2.10	1.97	1.74

Notes: Higher means indicate more self-reported satisfaction, guilt, and frustration. Horizontal means with different superscripts differ from one another at $p < .05$, according to Fisher LSD post hoc tests of multiple comparisons.

justification (or perhaps the related "failure" to perceive injustice in the system) would be associated with increased positive affect and decreased negative affect (Chen & Tyler, 2001; Jost & Hunyady, 2002). To investigate this possibility, we conducted a separate regression analysis for each respondent group in which we used participants' responses to the system justification items to predict the three types of affect ratings, as well as ratings of general positive and negative affect (Table 2). Results indicated that system justification was associated with (a) increased satisfaction for members of all three groups, (b) decreased frustration for members of the medium and low-power groups, and (c) decreased guilt for members of the most powerful group. In addition, system justification was associated with

Table 2. Regression Analyses Predicting Affect from System Justification Scores in the "Star Power" Study.

Type of Affect	Low Power ($n = 56$)	Medium Power ($n = 49$)	High Power ($n = 74$)
Satisfaction			
β	.38**	.27[a]	.35**
Adjusted R^2 (%)	12.6	4.8	10.9
R^2 (%)	14.3	7.0	12.1
Guilt			
β	−.06	.03	−.24**
Adjusted R^2 (%)	−1.6	−2.3	4.4
R^2 (%)	0.4	0.1	5.8
Frustration			
β	−.26[a]	−.37*	−.17
Adjusted R^2 (%)	5.0	11.7	1.4
R^2 (%)	6.8	13.7	2.9
General positive affect			
β	.26[a]	.25	.34*
Adjusted R^2 (%)	4.7	3.5	9.9
R (%)^2	7.0	6.1	11.5
General negative affect			
β	−.25	−.17	−.50***
Adjusted R^2 (%)	3.5	−0.1	23.1
R^2 (%)	6.1	2.8	24.7

Note: Regression coefficients are standardized.
*$p < .05$;
**$p < .01$; and
***$p < .001$ (two-tailed).
[a]$p < .10$.

decreased negative affect in general for the powerful group and increased positive affect for members of the most powerful and powerless groups. Although these results are correlational in nature, they are consistent with the hypothesis that system-justifying ideologies serve a palliative function, enabling individuals to cope with various types of emotional distress elicited by a system of inequality among peers.

Effects of opportunity to endorse system justification on affect. Another way of investigating palliative effects of system justification is to consider effects of questionnaire order. Some participants completed affect ratings before rating the legitimacy of the system, whereas others completed them in the reverse order. We hypothesized that simply providing people with the opportunity to engage in system justification would make them feel better. Multivariate analyses of variance of the three affect subscales, conducted separately for each of the three groups, examined this hypothesis. The opportunity to system justify did predict subsequent affective ratings for members of the high-power group, $F(3, 66) = 2.84$, $p < .05$, but not for the medium, $F(3, 40) = .22$, $p = .88$, or low-power groups, $F(3, 48) = .80$, $p = .50$. Univariate follow-up analyses indicated that members of the most powerful group reported less frustration after completing the system justification items ($M = 2.04$, SD $= 1.55$, $n = 25$) than before ($M = 2.96$, SD $= 1.74$, $n = 45$), $F(1, 68) = 4.86$, $p < .05$. Similarly, they tended to report less guilt after the system justification opportunity ($M = 2.55$, SD $= 1.94$) than before ($M = 3.38$, SD $= 2.10$), but this trend did not attain significance, $F(1, 68) = 2.66$, $p = .11$. Taken as a whole, the findings from this quasi-experimental study support our general contention that system justification serves a palliative function, especially for those who are most advantaged by the status quo.

Our first study, which made use of the "Star Power" simulation of social hierarchy, demonstrates that the creation of a social system fostering inequality among peers arouses emotional distress and that system justification serves a palliative function for the members of that system (Chen & Tyler, 2001; Jost & Hunyady, 2002). Specifically, the degree of ideological endorsement predicted increased satisfaction for members of all three groups, decreased frustration for the two relatively disadvantaged groups, and decreased guilt for members of the most advantaged group. In addition, we found that merely having the opportunity to engage in system justification tended to lower frustration and, to a lesser extent, guilt on the part of the advantaged.

What are the implications of these findings for our understanding of social change? It is noteworthy that in research on social justice, certain kinds of emotional distress are viewed positively, insofar as distress motivates action to correct injustice (Montada & Schneider, 1989). From this perspective, the findings of the Star Power Study concerning the alleviation of distress through system justification inspire some degree of pessimism with regard to prospects for social change. In the next two studies (adapted from Wakslak et al., 2007), we examine this issue more directly, investigating relations among social position, ideology, emotional distress, and willingness to help those who are disadvantaged by the system.

SYSTEM JUSTIFICATION, MORAL OUTRAGE, AND SUPPORT FOR THE REDISTRIBUTION OF RESOURCES

Given that most people do little to alter existing inequalities, what is it that motivates people to press for the redistribution of income and other valued resources? One possibility that comes from the research literature on social justice is that the emotional distress a person experiences in response to inequality will influence the likelihood that he or she will support redistributive measures. If someone feels guilt or outrage over inequality, we would expect him or her to be more likely to take steps to eliminate the source of that distress, i.e. to directly address the inequality. This idea is in line with the work of Montada and colleagues (Montada, Schmitt & Dalbert, 1986; Montada & Schneider, 1989), who argued that the emotional reactions individuals have when confronted with the suffering of the disadvantaged are a strong predictor of whether or not they will commit to helping them. Thus, ideology and the dampening effect it has on emotional distress may affect people's willingness to help others. While system-justifying ideologies may be appealing because they reduce negative emotions, this reduction may in fact weaken people's support for policies that are aimed at rectifying inequality.

To examine this issue, we conducted a study in which we measured socioeconomic status, ideological endorsement, emotional distress, and support for policies that benefit those disadvantaged by the system (Wakslak et al., 2007, Study 1). In keeping with the work of Montada et al. (1986) we investigated the construct of "moral outrage," which taps the negative emotions one feels in response to injustice, as one measure of emotional distress. We also examined feelings of existential guilt (Hoffman, 1976), defined here as the guilt one has over having privileges (see Chen & Tyler, 2001). Consistent with the self-interest findings described earlier, we expected socioeconomic status to be associated with the endorsement of system-justifying ideologies such as opposition to equality, and we expected that the endorsement of system justification would be associated with reduced emotional distress. In addition, we hypothesized that emotional distress would be positively associated with support for policies that seek to redress social inequality.

Methods

Participants

One hundred and eight undergraduates (82 women and 26 men) who were enrolled in introductory psychology at a large private university participated in return for partial course credit. Participants ranged in age from 17 to 31 ($M = 19.4$, SD = 1.8). The sample included 54 European Americans, 26 Asian Americans, 11 Latinos, 10 African Americans, and 7 participants from other racial/ethnic backgrounds.

Procedure

In group sessions lasting 1 hour and containing no more than 10 people, participants completed questionnaires on topics of (a) ideology, (b) emotional distress, (c) support for policies aimed at redesigning either job-hiring or college admissions practices to help the disadvantaged, and (d) demographics and other background information.

Measures

Income. Socioeconomic status was measured in terms of self-reported annual family income, with 12 response categories ranging from "under $20,000" to "over $220,000."

Endorsement of system-justifying ideology. We gauged participants' endorsement of a system-justifying ideology with the 8-item Opposition to Equality subscale of Pratto et al.'s (1994) social dominance orientation scale (see Jost & Thompson, 2000). Although social dominance orientation is often viewed as a personality variable reflecting preferences for inequality among social groups (e.g., Altemeyer, 1998), its endorsement can also be conceptualized in ideological terms as a belief system that provides justification and support for the status quo (e.g., Jost & Burgess, 2000).

Emotional distress. We employed two measures of emotional distress. The first, inspired by Montada et al.'s (1986) construct of "moral outrage," included 10 items tapping feelings of distress over injustice and inequality: (1) "I feel really angry when I learn about people who are suffering from injustice"; (2) "I believe that we should all work together to help those who are disadvantaged"; (3) "I feel morally outraged by social injustice"; (4) "I resent the fact that people have to suffer unjustly the consequences of unemployment"; (5) "I think it's shameful that people allow injustice to occur"; (6) "I am horrified when I hear about the filthy living conditions which some people must live in because they are poor"; (7) "I don't worry very much about the problems in this world" (reverse-scored); (8) "I rarely feel burdened by the unfairness of this world" (reverse-scored); (9) "Issues of social justice rarely cross my mind" (reverse-scored); and (10) "I tend to tune out when people talk about problems in our society" (reverse-scored).

The second measure, which was created to measure existential guilt (Hoffman, 1976), included 12 items tapping feelings of guilt concerning privilege (e.g., "I often feel guilty when I receive a privilege I don't really deserve").

Support for redistribution of resources. We assessed support for policies of redistribution by asking participants how much they favored introducing changes designed to help members of underrepresented groups gain jobs or university admission (e.g., "The federal government should set up training programs to help the unemployed make the transition to the working world"). Questions addressed governmental employment and non-governmental employment opportunities as well as public and private university educational opportunities.

Results and Discussion

Structural equation modeling was used to examine the relationships among socioeconomic status, system justification, emotional distress, and willingness to help the disadvantaged through support for redistributive social policies. The model is illustrated in Fig. 2, which also shows the standardized path coefficients from the analysis. Similarly, willingness to help the disadvantaged was conceived of as a latent construct measured in four ways, support for redistribution in government and non-government jobs and private and public university education (see Wakslak et al., 2007 for descriptive statistics and other details of the statistical model).

To assess the hypotheses described above, our model specified paths from family income to ideology, emotional distress, and support for redistribution, paths from ideology to emotional distress and support for

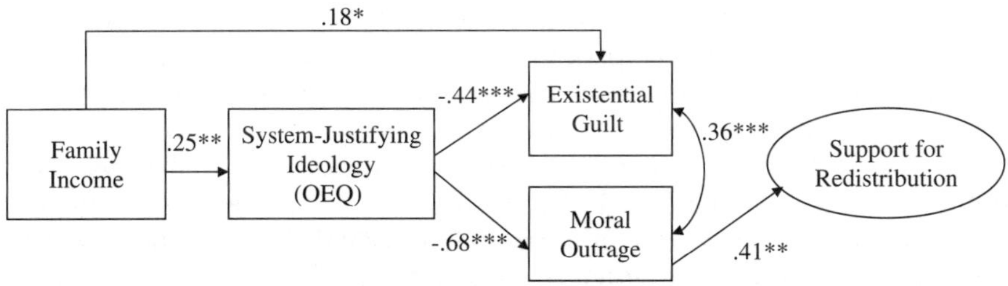

Fig. 2. Effects of Family Income and System Justification on Guilt, Moral Outrage, and Support for the Redistribution of Resources. *Notes:* All direct effects were included in the model, but only those with significant effects are illustrated (see also Wakslak et al., 2007). Latent variables were created by setting the indicator with the highest loading to have a weight of 1. Path coefficients are standardized. $^{*}p \leq .05$; $^{**}p < .01$; and $^{***}p < .001$.

redistribution, and the paths from emotional distress to support for redistribution. By all conventional criteria, our model provided an excellent fit to the data. Examination of the structural paths revealed that, consistent with self-interest, higher income predicted increased endorsement of system-justifying ideology ($\beta = .25$, $p < .01$) and increased feelings of existential guilt ($\beta = .18$, $p = .05$). As hypothesized, endorsement of system justification was strongly associated with a dampening of moral outrage ($\beta = -.68$, $p < .001$) and existential guilt ($\beta = -.44$, $p < .001$). Moral outrage was positively associated with support for redistribution ($\beta = .41$, $p < .001$), whereas existential guilt was not.

Finally, we found that the effect of system justification on support for redistribution was mediated by moral outrage (Sobel test statistic = –3.15, $p < .01$). When moral outrage was omitted from the model, system justification was associated with a significant reduction in support for redistributive social policies ($\beta = -.40$, $p < .001$). After adjusting for moral outrage, however, the effect of system justification on support for redistribution became non-significant ($\beta = -.19$, $p = .11$).

In addition to replicating the pattern of relations among social position, ideology, and emotional distress observed in the Star Power simulation, results from this study indicated that system justification was strongly related to willingness to help the disadvantaged in society through support for redistributive public policies and that this impact was mediated by feelings of moral outrage. Our findings are thus consistent with work by Montada and his colleagues suggesting that moral outrage is a key predictor of helping and other prosocial behaviors (e.g., Montada & Schneider, 1989). We expand on this previous work by situating the effects of moral outrage in a broader context in which social position, ideology, emotional distress, and support for redistributive social policies are linked to one another.

Nevertheless, the predominantly correlational nature of findings from both this study and the Star Power study described earlier constrains our ability to draw causal inferences about the diminishing effects of system justification on emotional distress and support for redistributive social policies. In our next study, we used a mindset priming approach to randomly assign members of an advantaged group to high vs. low system justification conditions and observed subsequent effects on guilt, distress, and other negative emotions, as well as on policy support. We were also able to include within the design of a single study the two different forms of emotional distress considered in the previous studies, namely general negative affect and moral outrage, respectively.

PRIMING A SYSTEM JUSTIFICATION MINDSET UNDERMINES WILLINGNESS TO HELP THE DISADVANTAGED

Our third study in this program of research, which was initially reported by Wakslak et al. (2007, Study 2), continued our investigation of the hypothesis that ideology serves a palliative function by lessening the emotional distress resulting from advantage or disadvantage. One of the primary goals of this research was to understand the palliative function as distinct from the hegemonic function that has often been assumed to motivate members of dominant groups, and because the findings of our first two studies were strongest and clearest for members of advantaged groups (but see Jost et al., 2003b for the opposite pattern). Therefore, we focused in our third and final study on a sample of highly privileged individuals. In addition, rather than measuring system justification we addressed the palliative function of ideology by experimentally priming system justification and examining the impact of this manipulation on emotional distress. We also investigated the effects of different forms of emotional distress on support for programs aimed at helping the disadvantaged.

To manipulate the strength of system justification we used a mindset priming approach. Drawing in part on the work of Ho, Sanbonmatsu, and Akimoto (2002), which demonstrated that exposure to "rags-to-riches,"

Horatio Alger-type stories serves to increase system-justifying stereotypes and beliefs, we exposed participants to essays that either contained "rags-to-riches" stories of heroic individual achievement (high system justification condition) or stories about innocent victims (low system justification condition). Afterward, participants completed a series of questionnaires, including measures of affect, moral outrage, and attitudes concerning their degree of support for various community service programs.

We hypothesized that participants who were primed with a strong system justification mindset would report less emotional distress, both in terms of affect and moral outrage, compared to those primed with low system justification. We were also interested in the manner in which emotional distress was related to support for policies that were directed at helping the disadvantaged. However, we know from previous research that emotional experience can take various forms and have vastly different consequences depending on attributional and other factors such as its mode, direction, focus of attention, and implications for action (e.g., Scherer & Wallbott, 1994; Smith & Ellsworth, 1985). Research on helping behavior, for example, suggests that negative emotions that are tied specifically to those who are in need of assistance increase the likelihood of engaging in prosocial action, whereas general mood states do not (e.g., Carlson & Miller, 1987).

Although the first two studies provided evidence of a relationship between system justification and distress, they employed measures of emotional distress that were quite different from one another. In the Star Power study, participants were given a checklist and asked to indicate the extent to which they were feeling particular emotions. In the second study, by contrast, we measured two emotion constructs that have emerged specifically from the justice literature, namely moral outrage (Montada & Schneider, 1989) and existential guilt (Hoffman, 1976). For each of these constructs, attributions about the *causes* of distress are central. Moral outrage refers to anger and distress arising from the presence of unjust forms of inequality, and existential guilt captures feelings of guilt concerning unearned privileges. While our findings from the first two studies indicate that system-justifying ideologies exert similar effects on generalized negative affect and more specific forms of distress pertaining to inequality, other research suggests that these different types of emotional experiences would be associated with divergent outcomes. Building on the results of our second study, we would expect moral outrage to lead to increased support for prosocial helping activities. With regard to generalized negative affect, however, one might well expect the opposite based on mood congruency effects. That is, negative affect could result in a reduction in prosocial activity and depressed support for programs designed to help the disadvantaged (e.g., see Moore, Underwood, & Rosenhan, 1973). In the third study, we therefore examined the relations between each of these forms of emotional distress and support for programs that help the disadvantaged.

Methods

Participants

At the beginning of the semester, a battery of questionnaires was administered to 458 undergraduate students registered for a class in introductory psychology. One item asked students to report their family's approximate annual income. For the 393 students who responded to this question, the median income category was "$80,000–$100,000" and the modal income category was "$40,000–$60,000." Those students ($n = 185$) who reported family incomes of $100,000 or higher were preselected for participation in this study. Of these, 120 (79 women and 41 men) were successfully recruited and completed the experiment in return for partial course credit. The final sample included 84 European Americans, 21 Asian Americans, and 13 people who reported having other ethnic backgrounds.

Procedure

Upon arrival at the lab, participants were informed that they would be completing materials for two separate studies: (a) a study concerning undergraduate admissions decisions and (b) a study about community service attitudes. Participants were told that the purpose of the first study was to determine whether undergraduates would make admissions decisions that were similar to those made by administrative personnel and also to examine whether participants' mood would influence their admissions decisions. Participants completed an initial affect questionnaire and were then asked to read three personal statements that had seemingly been written by college applicants. Participants were asked to summarize and to list strengths and weaknesses of each essay as well as to render an admissions decision. Afterward, participants completed the affect questionnaire again. To lend credibility to the cover story, participants were asked to indicate whether or not they believed their mood had influenced their decisions.

Participants were told that the goal of the "second study" was to measure student attitudes toward community service. Embedded in the packet were measures of moral outrage and support for a variety of community service programs. After completing these materials, participants underwent a "funnel debriefing" procedure to assess whether participants perceived a connection between the two different tasks. They did not.

Experimental Manipulation of System Justification Condition

Participants assigned to the high system justification condition read three personal statements that described instances of extraordinary personal achievement in which hard work led to the attainment of success. One essay was allegedly written by someone who had worked very hard to win a concerto competition, another who had become editor of a high school newspaper against difficult odds, and yet another who had become a successful business entrepreneur. In one way or another, all of the essays described a "rags-to-riches" story designed to prime a high system justification mindset (Ho et al., 2002).

In contrast, participants assigned to the low system justification condition read personal statements about those who are less fortunate. For example, one applicant described organizing a bone marrow drive for a friend with cancer, another described assisting doctors on a medical trip to a South American shantytown, and a third volunteering at a homeless shelter after having almost experienced homelessness. Thus, whereas the high system justification condition underscored the belief that our society possesses a meritocratic reward structure in which success is a function of effort and ability, the low system justification condition reminded participants that many people are unfairly disadvantaged and that being disadvantaged is not necessarily an indication that one lacks merit or otherwise deserves his or her suffering.

Independent Check on the Manipulation of System Justification

To check on the manipulation of system justification without arousing suspicion or biasing experimental participants' responses, we asked an independent sample of 44 students to read either the high system justification essays or the low system justification essays. Afterward, they indicated the extent to which they felt the essays supported the notion that hard work and effort are rewarded by success (versus the notion that success is sometimes a result of receiving help from others and that bad things can happen to people through no fault of their own). As expected, those who read the high system justification essays scored higher on the manipulation check than did those who read the low system justification essays.

Measures

Affect. We assessed participants' affect before and after the manipulation of system justification with the use of 24 items adapted from Elliot and Devine's (1994) measure. An exploratory factor analysis of these ratings yielded four factors with eigenvalues greater than 1, accounting for 71.8% of the total variance. The first factor was comprised of six items (angry at self, disgusted with self, annoyed at self, disappointed with self, self-critical, regretful) that Elliot and Devine (1994) labeled "NegSelf." The second factor contained six items (content, friendly, optimistic, happy, energetic, good) that captured feelings of "Satisfaction." The third factor included the items guilty, uncomfortable, shame, uneasy, and embarrassed and was labeled "Guilt." The fourth and final factor was comprised of seven items (negative, concerned, bothered, frustrated, tense, anxious, distressed) tapping "Anxiety."

Moral outrage. We administered the same 10-item moral outrage scale used in the previous study on two separate occasions. An initial baseline measure was taken during the preselection phase, several weeks before the actual experiment. The items were administered again on the first page of the "community service questionnaire" and coded so that high scores reflected a greater amount of moral outrage.

Support for social programs helping the disadvantaged. The degree of support for six different community service programs was assessed. These included an after-school tutoring program for disadvantaged children, a soup kitchen, a job training program, a crisis hotline, an adopt-a-grandparent program, and a big brother/sister program. Participants were asked the extent to which they would: support the creation of such a program; volunteer for it; vote for government funding of that program; and donate money to it. Responses were given on scales ranging from 1 ("strongly agree") to 6 ("strongly disagree") and were reverse-coded and averaged to form an overall index of support for community service programs aimed at helping the disadvantaged.

Results and Discussion

Structural equation modeling was used to examine relations among experimentally manipulated system justification (low vs. high, coded as 0 and 1, respectively), general and specific forms of emotional distress (measured both before and during the experimental session), and willingness to support community service programs (see Wakslak et al., 2007, for descriptive statistics and details of the statistical analysis). A measurement model was first assessed in which the two latent affect variables, the two moral outrage variables, the experimental dummy variable, and the willingness to support community service programs variable were allowed to covary. This model fit the data well. Next, a hybrid model was assessed in which system justification condition and the baseline measures of emotional distress (negative affect and moral outrage) were allowed to predict emotional distress at time 2, which was then used to predict willingness to help the disadvantaged. Fig. 3 shows the standardized path coefficients from this analysis. Overall fit indices for the model indicated that the model fit the data very well. A χ^2 difference test between the hybrid and measurement models revealed that the more parsimonious hybrid model fit the data as well as the measurement model, $\Delta\chi^2 = 2.695$ on seven degrees of freedom, ns. Similarly, incorporating additional structural paths, i.e., allowing initial measures of emotional distress and the system justification condition variable to predict all subsequent variables in the model, did not improve model fit ($\Delta\chi^2 = .276$ with df $= 2$, ns), nor were any of these additional paths significantly different from zero. Thus, the model illustrated in Fig. 3 summarizes the pattern of results very well.

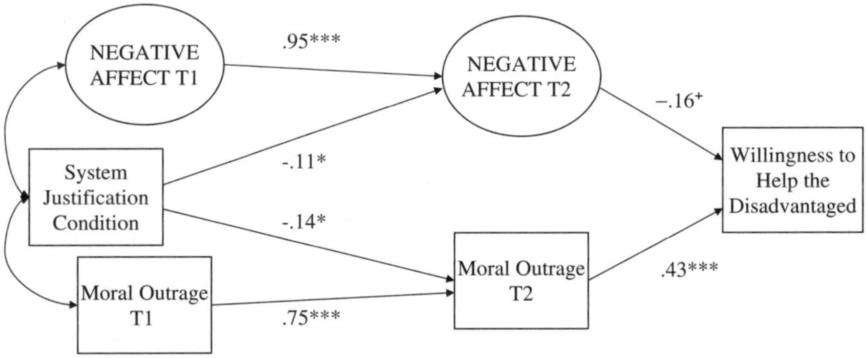

Fig. 3. Dampening Effects of System Justification on Negative Affect, Moral Outrage, and Willingness to Help the Disadvantaged. *Notes:* A higher score on the experimental variable reflects assignment to the high (vs. low) system justification condition. Higher scores on affect variables indicate higher self-reported levels of each affect type, including moral outrage (see also Wakslak et al., 2007). Latent affect variables were created by setting the indicator with the highest loading (self-critical) to have a weight of 1. Path coefficients are standardized. $^{+}p<.10$; $^{*}p<.05$; and $^{***}p<.001$.

Examination of the model's path coefficients supports our predictions. The experimental manipulation of system justification did significantly decrease both negative affect ($\beta = -.11$, $p < .05$) and moral outrage ($\beta = -.14$, $p < .05$), adjusting for baseline levels of these variables. Thus, participants assigned to the high system justification condition reported less emotional distress relative to those assigned to the low system justification condition. However, the two types of emotional distress exerted opposite effects on support for redistribution. As in the previous study, moral outrage was positively associated with support for programs to help the disadvantaged ($\beta = .43$, $p < .001$). By contrast, negative affect in general was marginally but negatively associated with helping behavior ($\beta = -.16$, $p < .10$). These results suggest that although system justification alleviates both forms of emotional distress (which may help to explain its appeal), its diminishing impact on support for policies of redistribution seems to come primarily through its effect on moral outrage, at least for those who are highly advantaged.

Sobel tests indicated that the indirect path from system justification to helping through moral outrage was negative and significantly different from zero (Sobel test statistic = −2.07, $p < .05$). The indirect path from system justification to helping through affect was positive but not significant (Sobel test statistic = 1.50). These results suggest that system justification is associated with decreased support for policies of redistribution because of its diminishing effect on moral outrage.

Results from this third study strengthen earlier findings indicating that system justification is associated with reduced feelings of emotional distress in the form of both negative affect and moral outrage, especially among members of powerful or advantaged groups. Our findings concur with evidence in the emotions literature that different types of emotional distress have different consequences for prosocial action. Although both negative affect and moral outrage were assuaged following exposure to system-justifying narratives, the two types of emotion were differentially related to expressed intentions to help the disadvantaged. As has been suggested in the helping literature (Carlson & Miller, 1987), when negative emotions were specifically focused on the person or group in need of aid (as in the case of moral outrage) distress was associated with an increase in support for helping activities. By contrast, when negative emotions were generalized and not focused on specific aid recipients, there was a tendency for these emotions to be associated with decreased support for helping activities.

GENERAL DISCUSSION

Sigmund Freud (1930/1961) probably did not have inequality in mind when he penned the quotation with which we began this chapter. His predecessor, Karl Marx, no doubt, was thinking about social and economic disparities when he and Engels drew a famous connection between the palliative functions of ideology and the drug of opium. By developing an integrated analysis of both hegemonic and palliative functions of ideology, we seek to unify prominent sociological and psychological ideas. Sociologists after Marx have long maintained that "the institutional world requires legitimation, that is, ways by which it can be 'explained' and 'justified'" (Berger & Luckmann, 1966, p. 79). The synchronous accumulation of wealth and poverty has posed the biggest challenge to the legitimacy of capitalist institutions (e.g., Habermas, 1975), and yet most people find ways of justifying the economic system (see Jost et al., 2003a, 2003b). A key to understanding how and why people tolerate inequality in both its interpersonal and institutional forms comes from the work of psychologists after Freud who have demonstrated repeatedly that people seek "post-factum cognitive justifications for [their] own behavior *and for things as they are*" (McGuire, 1999, p. 107, emphasis added).

In this chapter we have proposed that, in addition to its hegemonic function, ideology serves the palliative function of making people feel better about social systems that foster inequality (see also Jost & Hunyady, 2002). Findings from three studies supported this general proposition. Study 1 demonstrated that inequality among peers led to differences in affective experiences, with those who were most advantaged experiencing the most satisfaction and also the most guilt. The disadvantaged tended to experience more frustration. The endorsement of system-justifying ideological beliefs was, as hypothesized, associated with a reduction in all of these forms of emotional distress. Furthermore, for those who occupied a highly privileged position within this arbitrarily created social hierarchy, merely having the opportunity to endorse system justification items led to a reduction in frustration and, to a lesser extent, guilt.

Our second study augmented these findings by linking ideology and emotional distress to attitudinal support for redistributive social policies in society, including affirmative action. Once again, endorsement of a system-justifying ideology was associated with a reduction in emotional distress. In an extension of Montada et al.'s (1986) ideas, we found that moral outrage (a specific type of emotional distress) predicted support for education and employment policies aimed at helping members of underprivileged groups. Thus, by decreasing moral outrage, system justification served to weaken support for helping the disadvantaged and therefore for creating social change (Wakslak et al., 2007).

In our third and final study in this program of research, we further examined the effects of ideology and emotional distress – using measures of both general negative affect and moral outrage – on advantaged group members' support for the redistribution of resources. Using a mindset priming approach, we manipulated justification of the system by presenting half of the participants with "rags-to-riches" stories of the Horatio Alger variety. Results indicated that, adjusting for baseline levels of emotion, participants exposed to high system justification essays reported less negative affect and less moral outrage than did participants exposed to essays that were relatively low in system justification themes. Furthermore, we found that whereas decreased moral outrage was associated with less willingness to help the disadvantaged, decreased negative affect in general did not have this effect. Thus, the dampening effects of system justification on support for redistribution occurred through the waning of moral outrage.

Taken as a whole, these results demonstrate both the existence and societal consequences of palliative effects of ideology, as theorized by Chen and Tyler (2001) and Jost and Hunyady (2002). We assume that people care about justice at least to some degree and are bothered by departures from what is fair and deserved. In order to maintain their perceptions of the world as just, however, people do not necessarily strive to make changes that will increase the overall amount of fairness and equality in the system. Rather, they often engage in rationalizations or cognitive adjustments that preserve a distorted image of reality in which the world is a fair and just place – a "delusion," as Lerner (1980) dubbed it. It seems that in this context, ideology – as has so often been claimed – is a bountiful source of both rationalization and reassurance. It rises to meet needs that are social psychological in nature, and it provides relief. In this sense, we regard ideology as a coping response to the kinds of stresses that frequently arise in situations of inequality and injustice (see also Dalbert, 2002; Jost & Hunyady, 2002; Major, Quinton, & McCoy, 2002).

We conclude by noting that the legitimation needs of the system tend to become the justification needs of the individual, and the justification tendencies of the individual affect the manner in which the system is legitimized. To put the same point a different way, we propose that people learn to justify social arrangements at least in part because our societal institutions require legitimacy – and this requirement obliges us to provide justifications for, among other things, social and economic inequality. At the same time, societal arrangements stand in need of legitimation because of the fact that people feel the need to explain and justify their own actions and the actions of others. A social psychological level of analysis, therefore, is exactly what is needed if we want to understand the ways in which – as Havel (1991, p. 135) put it – ideology creates "a bridge of excuses between the system and the individual," allowing people to feel better about inequality and the myriad consequences it brings.

ACKNOWLEDGMENTS

Portions of this research were presented at the University of Michigan, University of Massachusetts, Stanford, Princeton, Yale, and New York University, as well as the Society for Experimental Social Psychology (SESP) meeting in Fort Worth, TX, the International Society for Self and Identity (ISSI) preconference in San Diego, CA, and the International Society for Justice Research (ISJR) meeting in Regina, Saskatchewan. We would like to thank Richard Bourhis, Jody Clay-Warner, Faye Crosby, Gerald Davis, Jane Dutton, Susan Fiske, Adam Galinsky, Peter Glick, Deborah Gruenfeld, Elizabeth Haines, Karen Hegtvedt, Orsolya Hunyady, Allen McConnell, Jennifer Overbeck, Jeffrey Pfeffer, Oliver Sheldon, and Larissa Tiedens for helpful discussions concerning this research program and, in some cases, its exposition here. The writing of this chapter was supported in part by NSF Award # BCS-0617558 to John T. Jost and by the June Frier Esserman Dissertation Fellowship awarded by New York University to Cheryl J. Wakslak.

REFERENCES

Altemeyer, B. (1998). The other "authoritarian personality". In: M. P. Zanna (Ed.), *Advances in experimental social psychology* (Vol. 30, pp. 47–92). San Diego, CA: Academic Press.

Berger, P. L., & Luckmann, T. (1966). *The social construction of reality: A treatise in the sociology of knowledge*. Middlesex, England: Penguin Books.

Bulman, R. J., & Wortman, C. B. (1977). Attributions of blame and coping in the "real world": Severe accident victims react to their lot. *Journal of Personality and Social Psychology*, *35*, 351–363.

Carlson, M., & Miller, N. (1987). Explanation of the relation between negative mood and helping. *Psychological Bulletin*, *102*, 91–108.

Chen, E. S., & Tyler, T. R. (2001). Cloaking power: Legitimizing myths and the psychology of the advantaged. In: A. Y. Lee-Chai & J. Bargh (Eds), *The use and abuse of power: Multiple perspectives on the causes of corruption* (pp. 241–261). Philadelphia, PA: Psychology Press.

Dalbert, C. (1998). Belief in a just world, well-being, and coping with an unjust fate. In: L. Montada & M. J. Lerner (Eds), *Responses to victimizations and belief in a just world. Critical issues in social justice* (pp. 87–105). New York: Plenum Press.

Dalbert, C. (2002). Beliefs in a just world as a buffer against anger. *Social Justice Research, 15*, 123–145.

Darley, J. M. (2004). Social production for the organization of evil. In: J. T. Jost & J. Sidanius (Eds), *Political psychology: Key readings* (pp. 383–410). New York: Psychology Press. (Originally published 1992).

Devine, P. G., Montieth, M. J., Zuwerink, J. R., & Elliot, A. J. (1991). Prejudice with and without compunction. *Journal of Personality and Social Psychology*, *60*, 817–830.

Doosje, B., Branscombe, N. R., Spears, R., & Manstead, A. S. R. (1998). Guilty by association: When one's group has a negative history. *Journal of Personality and Social Psychology*, *75*, 872–886.

Elliot, A. J., & Devine, P. G. (1994). On the motivational nature of cognitive dissonance: Dissonance as psychological discomfort. *Journal of Personality and Social Psychology*, *67*, 382–394.

Foucault, M. (1980). *Power/knowledge*. New York: Pantheon.

French, J. R. P., Jr., & Raven, B. H. (1959). The bases of social power. In: D. Cartwright (Ed.), *Studies in social power* (pp. 150–167). Ann Arbor, MI: Institute for Social Research.

Freud, S. (1930/1961). *Civilization and its discontents*. New York: W.W. Norton & Co.

Furnham, A. (1995). The just world, charitable giving and attitudes to disability. *Personality and Individual Differences*, *19*, 577–583.

Goodwin, S. A., Operario, D., & Fiske, S. T. (1998). Situational power and interpersonal dominance facilitate bias and inequality. *Journal of Social Issues*, *54*, 677–698.

Habermas, J. (1975). *Legitimation crisis*. Boston: Beacon Press.

Hafer, C. L. (2000). Investment in long-term goals and commitment to just means drive the need to believe in a just world. *Personality and Social Psychology Bulletin*, *26*, 1059–1073.

Hafer, C. L., & Olson, J. M. (1989). Beliefs in a just world and reactions to personal deprivation. *Journal of Personality*, *57*, 799–823.

Hassebrauck, M. (1986). Ratings of distress as a function of degree and kind of inequity. *Journal of Social Psychology*, *126*, 269–270.

Havel, V. (1991). The power of the powerless. In: V. Havel (Ed.), *Open letters* (pp. 125–214). London: Faber & Faber.

Hegtvedt, K. A. (1990). The effects of relationship structure on emotional responses to inequity. *Social Psychology Quarterly*, *53*, 214–228.

Ho, E. A., Sanbonmatsu, D. M., & Akimoto, S. A. (2002). The effects of comparative status on social stereotypes: How the perceived success of some persons affects the stereotypes of others. *Social Cognition*, *20*, 36–57.

Hoffman, M. L. (1976). Empathy, role-taking, guilt, and development of altruistic motives. In: T. Lickona (Ed.), *Moral development: Current theory and research* (pp. 124–143). New York: Holt, Rinehart, &Winston.

Homans, G. C. (1974). *Social behavior: Its elementary forms* (Revised ed.). Oxford: Harcourt Brace Jovanovich.

Jackman, M. R. (1994). *The velvet glove: Paternalism and conflict in gender, class, and race relations*. Berkeley, CA: University of California Press.

Jost, J. T., & Banaji, M. R. (1994). The role of stereotyping in system-justification and the production of false consciousness. *British Journal of Social Psychology*, *33*, 1–27.

Jost, J. T., Banaji, M. R., & Nosek, B. A. (2004). A decade of system justification theory: Accumulated evidence of conscious and unconscious bolstering of the status quo. *Political Psychology*, *25*, 881–919.

Jost, J. T., Blount, S., Pfeffer, J., & Hunyady, Gy. (2003a). Fair market ideology: Its cognitive-motivational underpinnings. *Research in Organizational Behavior*, *25*, 53–91.

Jost, J. T., & Burgess, D. (2000). Attitudinal ambivalence and the conflict between group and system justification motives in low status groups. *Personality and Social Psychology Bulletin*, *26*, 293–305.

Jost, J. T., & Hunyady, O. (2002). The psychology of system justification and the palliative function of ideology. *European Review of Social Psychology*, *13*, 111–153.

Jost, J. T., & Hunyady, O. (2005). Antecedents and consequences of system-justifying ideologies. *Current Directions in Psychological Science*, *14*, 260–265.

Jost, J. T., & Major, B. (Eds). (2001). *The psychology of legitimacy: Emerging perspectives on ideology, justice, and intergroup relations*. New York: Cambridge University Press.

Jost, J. T., Pelham, B. W., Sheldon, O., & Sullivan, B. (2003b). Social inequality and the reduction of ideological dissonance on behalf of the system: Evidence of enhanced system justification among the disadvantaged. *European Journal of Social Psychology*, *33*, 13–36.

Jost, J. T., Pietrzak, J., Liviatan, I., Mandisodza, A., & Napier, J. (2007). System justification as conscious and nonconscious goal pursuit. In: J. Shah & W. Gardner (Eds), *Handbook of motivation science*. New York: Guilford.

Jost, J. T., & Thompson, E. P. (2000). Group-based dominance and opposition to equality as independent predictors of self-esteem, ethnocentrism, and social policy attitudes among African Americans and European Americans. *Journal of Experimental Social Psychology*, *36*, 209–232.

Katz, I., & Hass, R. G. (1988). Racial ambivalence and American value conflict: Correlational and priming studies of dual cognitive structures. *Journal of Personality and Social Psychology*, *55*, 893–905.

Kelman, H. C., & Hamilton, V. L. (1989). *Crimes of obedience: Toward a social psychology of authority and responsibility*. New Haven, CT: Yale University Press.

Keltner, D., Gruenfeld, D., & Anderson, C. (2004). Power, approach, and inhibition. *Psychological Review*, *110*, 265–284.

Kipnis, D. (1976). *The powerholders*. Chicago: University of Chicago Press.

Kluegel, J. R., & Smith, E. R. (1986). *Beliefs about inequality: Americans' view of what is and what ought to be*. Hawthorne, NJ: Aldine de Gruyter.

Ledgerwood, A., Jost, J. T., Mandisodza, A., & Pohl, M. (2008). *Working for the system: Motivated defense of the American Dream*. Manuscript in preparation.

Lerner, M. J. (1977). The justice motive: Some hypotheses as to its origins and forms. *Journal of Personality*, *45*, 1–52.

Lerner, M. J. (1980). *The belief in a just world: A fundamental delusion*. New York: Plenum Press.

Lerner, M. J. (2003). The justice motive: Where social psychologists found it, how they lost it, and why they may not find it again. *Personality and Social Psychology Review*, *7*, 388–399.

Lerner, M. J., & Miller, D. T. (1978). Just world research and the attribution process: Looking back and ahead. *Psychological Bulletin*, *85*, 1030–1051.

Lipkus, I. M., & Bissonnette, V. L. (1996). Relationships among belief in a just world, willingness to accommodate, and marital well-being. *Personality and Social Psychology Bulletin*, *22*, 1043–1056.

Loewenstein, G. F., Thompson, L., & Bazerman, M. H. (1989). Social utility and decision making in interpersonal contexts. *Journal of Personality and Social Psychology*, *57*, 426–441.

Ludwig, J. (1999). Economic status: Americans assess opportunity, fairness, and responsibility. Retrieved on 5/1/2003 from www.globalpolicy.org/socecon/inequal/poll-usa.htm

Major, B. (1994). From social inequality to personal entitlement: The role of social comparisons, legitimacy appraisals, and group memberships. *Advances in Experimental Social Psychology*, *26*, 293–355.

Major, B., Quinton, W., & McCoy, S. K. (2002). Antecedents and consequences of attributions to discrimination: Theoretical and empirical advances. *Advances in Experimental Social Psychology*, *34*, 251–330.

Marshall, R. (Ed.) (2000). *Back to shared prosperity: The growing inequality of wealth and income in America*. London: M. E. Sharpe.

Martin, J. (1982). The fairness of earning differentials: An experimental study of the perceptions of blue-collar workers. *Human Resources*, *17*, 110–122.

McCoy, S. K., & Major, B. (2007). Priming meritocracy and the psychological justification of inequality. *Journal of Experimental Social Psychology*, *43*, 341–351.

McGuire, W. J. (1999). *Constructing social psychology: Creative and critical processes*. New York: Cambridge University Press.

Milanovic, B. (2002). True world income distribution: 1988 and 1993: First calculations based on household surveys alone. *Economic Journal*, *112*, 51–92.

Milgram, S. (1974). *Obedience to authority*. New York: Harper & Row.

Montada, L., Schmitt, M., & Dalbert, C. (1986). Thinking about justice and dealing with one's own privileges: A study of existential guilt. In: H. W. Bierhoff, R. L. Cohen & J. Greenberg (Eds), *Justice in social relations* (pp. 125–143). New York: Plenum Press.

Montada, L., & Schneider, A. (1989). Justice and emotional reactions to the disadvantaged. *Social Justice Research*, *3*, 313–344.

Moore, B. S., Underwood, B., & Rosenhan, D. L. (1973). Affect and altruism. *Developmental Psychology*, *8*, 99–104.

Nagata, D. K. (1990). The Japanese American internment: Exploring the transgenerational consequences of traumatic stress. *Journal of Traumatic Stress*, *3*, 47–69.

Piketty, T., & Saez, E. (2003). Income inequality in the United States, 1913–1998. *Quarterly Journal of Economics*, *118*(February), 1–35.

Piketty, T., & Saez, E. (2006). The evolution of top incomes: A historical and international perspective. *American Economic Review*, *96*, 200–205.

Pratto, F., Sidanius, J., Stallworth, L. M., & Malle, B. F. (1994). Social dominance orientation: A personality variable predicting social and political attitudes. *Journal of Personality and Social Psychology*, *67*, 741–763.

Ridgeway, C. L. (2001). The emergence of status beliefs: From structural inequality to legitimizing ideology. In: J. T. Jost & B. Major (Eds), *The psychology of legitimacy: Emerging perspectives on ideology, justice, and intergroup relations* (pp. 257–277). New York: Cambridge University Press.

Sachdev, I., & Bourhis, R. Y. (1987). Status differentials and intergroup behavior. *European Journal of Social Psychology*, *17*, 277–293.
Sachdev, I., & Bourhis, R. Y. (1991). Power and status differentials in minority and majority group relations. *European Journal of Social Psychology*, *21*, 1–24.
Scherer, K. R., & Wallbott, H. G. (1994). Evidence for universality and cultural variation of differential emotion response patterning. *Journal of Personality and Social Psychology*, *66*, 310–328.
Sidanius, J., & Pratto, F. (1999). *Social dominance: An intergroup theory of social hierarchy and oppression*. New York: Cambridge University Press.
Smith, C. A., & Ellsworth, P. C. (1985). Patterns of cognitive appraisal in emotion. *Journal of Personality and Social Psychology*, *48*, 813–838.
Smith, P. K., Jost, J. T., & Vijay, R. (in press). Legitimacy crisis? Behavioral approach and inhibition when power differences are left unexplained. *Social Justice Research* (expected publication date 2008).
Stiglitz, J. E. (2004). *The roaring nineties*. New York: W.W. Norton.
Swim, J. K., & Miller, D. L. (1999). White guilt: Its antecedents and consequences for attitudes toward affirmative action. *Personality and Social Psychology Bulletin*, *25*, 500–514.
Tomaka, J., & Blascovich, J. (1994). Effects of justice beliefs on cognitive appraisal of and subjective physiological, and behavioral responses to potential stress. *Journal of Personality and Social Psychology*, *67*, 732–740.
Tyler, T. R., Boeckmann, R. J., Smith, H. J., & Huo, Y. J. (1997). *Social justice in a diverse society*. Boulder, CO: Westview Press.
Tyler, T. R., & Smith, H. J. (1998). Social justice and social movements. In: D. T. Gilbert, S. T. Fiske & G. Lindzey (Eds), *The handbook of social psychology* (4th ed., Vol. 2, pp. 595–629). New York: McGraw-Hill.
Wakslak, C., Jost, J. T., Tyler, T. R., & Chen, E. (2007). Moral outrage mediates the dampening effect of system justification on support for redistributive social policies. *Psychological Science*, *18*, 267–274.
Walster, E., Berscheid, E., & Walster, G. W. (1973). New directions in equity research. *Journal of Personality and Social Psychology*, *25*, 151–176.
Wolff, E. N. (1996). *Top heavy: The increasing inequality of wealth in America and what can be done about it*. New York: The New Press.
Zuckerman, M. (1975). Belief in a just world and altruistic behavior. *Journal of Personality and Social Psychology*, *31*, 972–976.
Zuckerman, M., & Gerbasi, K. C. (1977). Belief in a just world and trust. *Journal of Research in Personality*, *11*, 306–317.

TOWARD A MORE JUST WORLD: WHAT MAKES PEOPLE PARTICIPATE IN SOCIAL ACTION?

Dahlia Moore

ABSTRACT

Citizen willingness to participate in social action depends, in part, on certain beliefs about the world and one's power to initiate change. This study examines how belief in a just world (BJW) affects willingness to participate in social action. The model also incorporates antecedents to BJW, including personality factors (authoritarianism, self-esteem, powerlessness); political orientation (national identity, patriotism); social characteristics (religiosity, ethnicity, education, income); and the relationships among these factors. Data are from a representative sample of the Jewish Israeli population. Findings indicate that as BJW decreases, so to does the willingness to act, and that personality, political, and social characteristics influence both BJW and willingness to participate in social action.

In recent years, people in many western societies have realized that their governments are unable to address *all* the needs of the citizens (Cass, 1994). This realization increased the awareness that citizens should participate in

Justice
Advances in Group Processes, Volume 25, 213–239

ISSN: 0882-6145/doi:10.1016/S0882-6145(08)25013-7

social action and take on some of the responsibilities that governments are unable or unwilling to assume (Nicolaides, 1997).

The term social action refers to all solidarity-based, voluntary actions taken by individuals to improve their society (France, 1998), and in this study it indicates willingness to contribute time, money, and/or effort to attain this goal. This definition derives from Bell's (1998) view of modern society as one in which people are active and purposeful beings whose behavior helps create not only their own future, but also the social order itself. In most societies today, citizens' involvement is sanctioned, even taken for granted (Rossi, 2001; Warren, 2002),[1] and social action is seen as having the potential to strengthen the sense of community (O'Neill, Duffy, Enman, Blackmer, & Campbell, 1988), decrease tension among groups, and increase cooperation and social justice (Bierhoff, 2002). The sphere in which citizens' involvement is legitimated in each society varies, and individuals who are members of diverse groups may be willing to assume responsibility in different spheres.

However, not all individuals are willing to act for their society. People are more willing to become involved and act when their interests are threatened, but even among those who are equally threatened, different levels of involvement are found. Moreover, people get involved in issues that do not affect them directly (O'Neill et al., 1988). Hence, direct threat to one's interests cannot explain the whole issue of participation in social action.

A comprehensive model of willingness to participate in social action should include several levels of analysis, from the social structure to the individual citizen. Most studies, however, focus either on social structure or on personality. The former emphasizes the social order and the location of the individuals' ethnic, racial, class, and/or religious group in the social structure as conditioning participation (i.e., although the poor, the weak and/or the disadvantaged may have more to gain by social change, members of these groups are less able or willing to contribute time or effort to create this change than members of the rich and advantaged groups) (Arneson, 2002; Hegtvedt, 2005; Jasso, 2005). The latter emphasizes attitudes and personality as the main factors influencing willingness to act, (e.g., individuals with weaker internal control, lower self-esteem and self-efficacy, and stronger authoritarianism are less willing and able to participate than their counterparts) (Cass, 1994).

This study is based on the notion that both the structural and personal levels are necessary to explain willingness to act, as the "social structure *and* personality" approach indicates that individuals' positions (i.e., memberships in social groups) shape their personal characteristics and attitudes which, in turn, affect their willingness to participate in social action. However, not all individuals who belong to the same social categories and have similar personality traits are equally willing to act. This study assumes that the relationship between willingness to act and social structure and personality factors is mediated by the beliefs of citizens that social action is necessary (i.e., justified), ideologically-legitimized, and within peoples'capabilities (Gecas, 2000). Here, justification takes the form of belief in a just world (BJW) (Lerner, 1980); legitimation is represented by political orientation (i.e., identification with the nation, patriotism, and voting for conservative (religious or right-wing) parties; and capabilities refer to individuals' characteristics (both social and personality). The primary goals of this study are, therefore, to examine (1) how BJW affects willingness to participate in social action and (2) how personality factors, political orientation, and social characteristics influence BJW and willingness to participate in social action.

Fig. 1 presents the theoretical model of expected relationships. The model indicates that the social context influences both personality factors and political orientation, which influence individuals' BJW, which, in turn, influences willingness to participate in social action. Direct influences of personality factors and political orientation on willingness to participate in social action are also expected.[2] Data to test the model come from a survey of Israeli citizens. As a consequence, the study highlights social factors important to that nation.

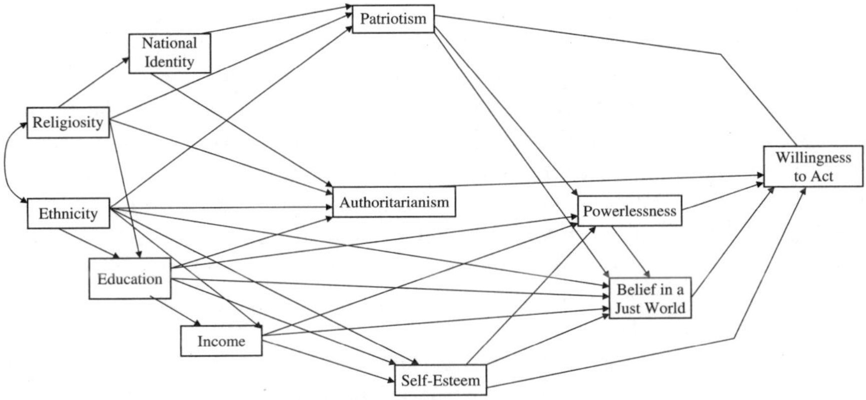

Fig. 1. Theoretical Model.

THEORETICAL BACKGROUND

Belief in a Just World and Willingness to Participate in Social Action

The belief that people get what they deserve and deserve what they get was first addressed by Melvin Lerner (1980). The belief develops in early childhood from socialization processes that create in some children the belief that their actions lead to predictable outcomes or consequences: good deeds are rewarded and evil ones are punished; those who are more talented and/or try harder should attain more than others. Moreover, people high in BJW tend to be confident that their investments will be fairly rewarded (Dalbert, 1999). Implied in these notions is a belief that the world is stable and orderly, and, therefore, predictable (Bell, 1998). However, recent studies show that when considering justice in social situations, people tend to differentiate between a belief in justice for the self (BJW-S) and justice for others (BJW-O), and that the two are often not correlated. This study focuses on BJW-O only, as it is directly related to social action (e.g., Sutton & Douglas, 2005).

According to the just world hypothesis, the intensity of BJW varies (Rubin & Peplau, 1975) so that the stronger the BJW, the stronger the need to maintain congruence between belief and the reality the individual perceives. People with a strong BJW are highly motivated to defend their belief, especially when they encounter situations of misfortune (e.g., victims of crimes (Libow & Doty, 1979), victims of accidents (Bulman & Wortman, 1977), unjust job loss (Lerner & Somers, 1992), inability to escape poverty (Appelbaum, Lennon, & Aber, 2003)).

To protect their BJW when it is threatened in a specific situation, people tend to adjust their evaluation of the situation to their belief (Lerner, 1980; Mikula, 1990). According to Crosby and Ropp (2002), three types of adjustments (or re-evaluations) can take place: re-evaluation of the victim, of the cause, or of the outcome. Re-evaluation of the victim means seeing something in the victim's character as leading to the negative consequences (i.e., the victim chose to be in the situation, Lerner & Simmons, 1966). Re-evaluation of the cause means seeing the victimization as – at least partially – the victim's fault (Karuza & Carey, 1984). Re-evaluation of the outcome means playing down the severity of the consequences (Hafer, 2002; Montada, Schmitt, & Dalbert, 1986).

Studies of BJW are usually based on laboratory experiments and focus on the evaluation of outcomes for specific individuals (including the self). Fewer studies examine how BJW affects perceptions of social situations (like group inequality), or the behavioral tendencies that follow such perceptions. Among these exceptions are studies like those of Rubin and Peplau (1975) and Furnham (1991), which examine the characteristics of people with strong beliefs in a just world. They found that people who have a strong tendency to believe in a just world also tend to be richer, more religious, more authoritarian, more conservative, more self-reliant, and more likely to have negative attitudes toward underprivileged groups.

Moreover, most of the studies of BJW derive from the individualistic approach, which focuses on individuals as independent people, who are free to choose how to act (i.e., individual freedom and life opportunities are not constrained by background characteristics, such as gender, ethnicity, or race of individuals). Consequently, if inequality exists, it should be considered just, as it is the result of differences in individual abilities and efforts. People with strong BJW also tend to see policies to reduce racial or economic inequality as a contradiction of individual efforts (Cole, Clay, & Hill, 1990), and are less likely to support programs that increase social equality (Lipkus & Siegler, 1993). These suggestions may have significant social implications, as strong BJW may undermine peoples' willingness to act to increase social justice: it is easier to assume that forces beyond their control are responsible for injustice (but see Baron & Miller, 2000). When that occurs, people may find it easier to evade personal or social responsibility. However, the relationship between BJW and willingness to act was not examined directly in previous studies.

The present study assumes that when people see circumstances rather than individual actions as causing unjust inequality, they will be more willing to act in order to decrease inequality. This willingness to act may be in the social sphere (like voluntary work with weak or disadvantaged groups), in the economic sphere (like contributing funds), and/or in the political sphere (e.g., political activism, participation in demonstrations). Factors that may influence BJW directly and willingness to act indirectly include focus on social structural and personality characteristics.

The Influence of Personality Factors, Political Orientation, and Social Characteristics on BJW and Willingness to Act

Because individuals' social positions shape their personal characteristics and political attitudes that, in turn, affect their beliefs and their willingness to participate in social action, the comprehensive model examined in this study includes personal, political, and social characteristics.

Personality Factors

Previous studies have examined the influence of diverse personality factors on BJW or on willingness to act, not on both. This study focuses on three seemingly distinct dimensions of personality that relate not only to BJW but also to willingness to act: powerlessness, self-esteem, and authoritarianism. These measures address diverse aspects of individuals' perceived capability to influence their society.

Powerlessness. Powerlessness is created when individuals believe they lack control over their life situations and that outcomes of situations are determined by forces outside the individual, which the individual cannot control (Paulhus, 1983). At the other end of the continuum, perceived control is the "belief in individual agency, synonymous with mastery, efficacy, and internal locus of control" (Mirowsky, Ross, & van Willigen, 1996, p. 322). Thus, powerlessness, like perceived control, refers to assumed internal states that explain why certain people actively and willingly try to deal with difficult circumstances, while others do not (Lewis, Ross, & Mirowsky, 1999).

Individuals who depend on the effort to produce outcomes are more apt to exert themselves when engaged in diverse tasks and are more willing to see such action as effective (Geis & Ross, 1998). In contrast, powerless individuals tend to see others (e.g., the state, fate, luck, or God) as responsible for life occurrences. Individuals who do not see outcomes as dependent on their actions are more apt to consider efforts to influence situations as futile, and will make fewer attempts to gain control (Lefcourt, 1981; Rotter, Chance, & Phare, 1972).

There are varied definitions and measures of powerlessness (Antonucci, 2001), but they greatly overlap (Prenda & Lachman, 2001). This study focuses on the social implications of powerlessness and sense of control (Rotter, Chance, & Phares, 1972; Paulhus, 1983). According to this approach, because powerless individuals do not believe in their ability to change social situations, they will be less willing to act than those who believe they have control.

Self-Esteem. Definitions of self-esteem vary but all agree that high self-esteem reflects self-approval, self-worth, self-efficacy, self-respect, and/or self-acceptance (Battle, 1990; Dalbert, 1999), and that it is correlated with social status (Faunce, 1989). More specifically, it means having a positive attitude toward life, highly valuing ones accomplishments, believing in one's abilities, and seeing oneself as competent and in control of his or her life (Blascovich & Tomaka, 1991).

Most approaches agree that the term self-esteem includes cognitive, affective, and behavioral aspects (Blank, 2003; Walker, 1999). The cognitive aspect refers to the evaluation of oneself and the perception of discrepancy between ones ideal self and the realistic appraisal of how one perceives oneself. The affective aspect refers to the feelings or emotions that one has when considering self-worth. The behavioral aspects of self-esteem are manifested in behaviors such as resilience, assertiveness, decisiveness, and social activism (Steffenhagen & Burns, 1987). Green (2003), for example, suggests that self-esteem contributes significantly to the development of tolerance and respect for culturally different groups, and Myers (2000) shows that both self-esteem and social responsibility are rising in the United States.

Sutton and Douglas (2005), show that while the belief that the world is fair to others (BJW-O) is associated with more critical and negative social attitudes, which may, in turn lead to lower willingness to act for others, BJW-S is positively associated with measures of psychological health (like self-esteem) (see also Begue, 2005; Dalbert, 2002). However, these studies consider the impact of BJW on self-esteem, not the influence of self-esteem on BJW, and they do not consider the association between self-esteem and BJW-O. Dalbert (2002), for example, shows that those who are high in BJW-S suffer no decrease in self-esteem compared to those who are low in BJW in anger provoking situations. Also, Begue (2005) shows that high BJW-S even contributes to the preservation of self-esteem in threatening social situations (however, when BJW was low, self-esteem was not affected). In the present study the effect of self-esteem is examined on both the BJW for others (BJW-O) and willingness to participate in social action.[3]

Authoritarianism. Authoritarianism is one of the main factors that explains how societies perpetuate acceptance of social orders and existing hierarchies (Mummendey, Kessler, Klink, & Mielke, 1999).[4] According to all approaches, authoritarianism reflects conformity and conservatism, and acceptance of the existing social order and the social hierarchy that it defines (Feather, 1993; Jost & Sidanius, 2004).

This study follows Altemeyer's (1981, 1996) approach in which authoritarianism is associated with submission to authority, so that authoritarians tend to expect those in legitimate power positions to assume responsibility (Peterson, 2003; Reynolds, Turner, Haslam, & Ryan, 2001). This learning-through-experience approach indicates that individuals who belong to different groups have diverse opportunities to experience situations that are more (or less) conducive to the formation of authoritarian attitudes (Pentony et al., 2000; Sutton & Carlson, 1977).

This claim is supported by the many studies that have shown the positive effect of authoritarian attitudes on nationalism, religiosity, and conservative political attitudes in diverse societies, including Israel (e.g., Altemeyer & Hunsberger, 2005; Levi, 2005). Thus, authoritarian individuals tend to be more religious, more patriotic and nationalistic, and more supportive of the existing social and political order (Feather, 1993; Feldman & Stenner, 1997). As such, they will be less willing to support attempts to change the existing order, and will be less willing to participate in social action that may lead to such changes (Rubinstein, 1995).[5]

Not many studies examined the relationship between authoritarianism and BJW, and they do not show conclusively whether BJW influences authoritarianism or vice versa. In most of them, both BJW and authoritarianism influence a behavioral tendency (e.g., Cohn & Modecki, 2007) or perceptions (like the perception of risk, e.g., Lambert, Burroughs, & Nguyen, 1999). The findings in these studies are inconclusive. In some (e.g., Cohn & Modecki, 2007; Lambert, Burroughs, & Chasteen, 1998), authoritarianism and BJW are positively correlated, indicating that authoritarians use their BJW to construct their reactions to social situations (Lambert, Burroughs, & Chasteen, 1998). In other studies (e.g., Mudrack, 2005), authoritarianism is only linked to the negative consequences of BJW (i.e., the more authoritarian believe that people suffer because they are bad, but higher authoritarianism was not associated with a belief that people prosper because they are good).

Political Orientation

Perception of the socio-political context as providing (or withholding) ideological legitimization influences willingness to participate in social action, in addition to the personality factors (powerlessness, self-esteem, and authoritarianism). Two distinct, though related factors capture the diverse aspects of how the socio-political context influences willingness to act: Identification with the national collective, and patriotism.[6]

Identification with the national collective indicates acceptance of the existing social order (Abrams & Emler, 1992; Kimmerling & Moore, 1997) and reflects feelings of belonging to a community, its symbols, beliefs, and attitudes and values (Hogg, 2003; Kalkhoff & Barnum, 2000). Those who strongly identify with the national collective, have the will to act to ensure their political destiny, and maintain the existing social order (Hinkle, Fox Cardamone, Haseleu, Brown, & Irwin, 1996; Tajfel & Turner, 1986). As several hierarchies can exist concurrently in any society, and each hierarchy reflects a different social order, identities become codes for given social orders (Moore, 2000a; Stryker & Serpe, 1994). Identification is also related to perceptions of justice (Clayton & Opotow, 2003; Moore, 2000b). Wenzel

(2001), for example, shows that social identity is the link between perception of inputs and the justice motive (see also Hegtvedt, 2004; Tyler & Blader, 2003).

Identification with the national collective tends to be more salient in societies that are in the process of building a nation, where people are often required to relinquish personal freedom (Ferge, 1997). Such societies tend to encourage "dedication to one's nation by surrendering one's personal comforts in service to the country" (Realo & Allik, 1999, p. 134), they will also tend to see collective participation in socio-political activity as legitimate-even expected-behavior (Ellemers & Bos, 1998). This dedication to one's nation is the basis for patriotism (Bar-Tal & Ben-Amos, 2004). Although there are many definitions of patriotism, most of them see patriots as individuals who are ready to sacrifice themselves to defend their nation against enemies (Realo & Allik, 1999). Patriotism is noticeable in many societies that are in the process of building a nation state, where people are required to relinquish not only material goods but also, quite often, personal freedom (Kimmerling & Moore, 1997).

Patriotism is discussed mostly in the context of nation-states, in which the civic duties of individuals are considered an important part of individuals' loyalties and obligations (Staub, 1997). In this respect, patriotism is related to national identities so that the stronger the identification with the collective, the stronger the feelings of patriotism. This study also assumes that patriotism is related to willingness to act so that more patriotic individuals will be more willing to participate in social action than those who are less patriotic.

These issues were not examined in Israel and this study examines whether Israelis whose national identity is salient are more patriotic, have stronger BJW and tend to be more willing to participate in social action than those whose national identity is less salient.

Characteristics of the Social Context

The social context is essential to the understanding of social action as it defines the viewpoints of members of diverse social groups and categories. Location in the social structure influences the willingness of members of social groups to act to improve society (France, 1998), what they see as an improvement (Bell, 1998), and whether they perceive legitimation for such action (Rossi, 2001). In each society, the social context is determined by different factors and issues such as race, ethnicity, nationality, culture, religion, SES, urbanity and/or gender. Thus, social characteristics define the major dimensions of social context.

The Israeli social context is defined by a high degree of politicization and by several, somewhat overlapping bi-polar divisions that include religion, ethnic origin, and socio-economic divisions (Horowitz & Lissak, 1989).[7] These divisions operate in tandem when socio-political issues are at stake, making the demographic categories very clear, and forming the bases for social identities, attitudes, beliefs, and social behaviors (McDonough, Barnes, & Pina, 1988). For example, Israeli Jews are "split" regarding the peace negotiations in the Middle-East (Moore & Aweiss, 2004, 2007): Religious Jews, of Eastern origin, with lower education and SES tend to be right-wingers and oppose territorial concessions, while secular Jews, of Western origin, with higher education and SES tend to be left-wingers, supporters of territorial concessions (Kimmerling & Moore, 1997; Unger & Safir, 1994).

Previous studies of willingness to participate in social action examine diverse combinations of these social categorizations (e.g., Fabick, 2004; Flanagan, Gallay, Gill, Gallay, & Nti, 2005; Linney, 2004; (Oliner & Krause, 2001), and indicate that disadvantaged racial or ethnic groups tend to be less willing to participate in social action than advantaged groups (Oliner & Krause, 2001), while religious individuals tend to be more willing than others (Keyes, 2002; Linney, 2004). Similarly, the more highly educated individuals tend to be more willing to assume responsibility than those with lower education (Markus, Ryff, Conner, Pudberry, & Barnett, 2001). Other studies demonstrate that religious individuals tend to have stronger BJW (Begue, 2002; Lipkus & Siegler, 1993; Dzuka & Dalbert, 2002), and that whites tend to have stronger BJW than Blacks or Latinos (Hunt, 2000). Differences were also found by SES, with greatest support for BJW found among persons of low SES (Hunt, 2000). No studies link these social characteristics with both willingness to act and BJW while controlling for personality characteristics and political orientation.

HYPOTHESIS AND THE MODEL OF OTHER INFLUENCES

The theoretical model presented in Fig. 1 guides my analysis. Based on the above review, I expect:

Hypothesis 1. The stronger the BJW, the weaker the willingness to participate in social action.

In addition, the review suggests inter-relationships between social context, personality factors, political orientation, and both BJW and willingness to participate in social action. Here I explore how social context influences personality factors and political orientation, which in turn affect individuals' BJW, and subsequently willingness to participate in social action. Direct influences of personality factors and political orientation on willingness to participate in social action are also expected.[8]

METHODS

Participants and Procedure

The representative sample ($N = 510$) was drawn from the Jewish Israeli population in December, 2005–January, 2006. Sampling was done in two stages. In the first stage, a representative stratified cluster sample of cities, towns, and rural areas was performed, maintaining the proportions of residents in each city in the sample. In the second stage, in each city, a random sampling of residents was performed. Data were collected by telephone interviews (only home phones were sampled, not cell phones). Interviews were conducted within 2 months in order to limit possible biases caused by national and political changes that might have sensitized respondents to the analyzed issues. Incomplete questionnaires (3%) and refusals to respond (6%) were excluded from further analysis and replaced by data from others. These percentages are similar to most phone surveys in Israel.

The respondents' ages ranged from 20 to 70 years. The sample includes 319 women and 188 men, 37% of them religious or tradition-oriented and the rest secular (63%). About 40% of the sample defined themselves as having above-average income, another 40% as having about average income, the rest as below-average income. The average education is 13.5 years of schooling. No considerable differences in religiosity, ethnicity, age, income, or education were found between the sample and the population, and the proportions of age categories, ethnic origin, and geographic location categories in the sample correspond to those of the entire population in 2004, as reported by the Israeli Bureau of Statistics (2005). The questionnaire had many other questions that pertain to political attitudes and opinions that were not analyzed in the present study and are therefore not discussed here.

Variables, Measures and their Descriptive Statistics

Dependent Variables

Willingness to participate in social action. Three questions were combined: (1) Have you ever (or do you still) volunteer for some social activity without financial reward (e.g., neighborhood watch, activity in a non-profit social association)? (1 = never volunteered, 2 = volunteered in one area of activity, 3 = volunteered in more than one area of activity). (2) Are you willing to contribute regularly from your earnings to improve the situation of weak groups (e.g., the elderly, physically impaired)? (1 = not willing to contribute at all, 2 = willing to contribute a little, and not regularly, 3 = willing to contribute regularly). (3) Did you participate in demonstrations for or against the political actions of the government? (1 = I did not participate, 2 = I participated once, 3 = I participated more than once). A principal component analysis revealed a single factor in which the higher the value, the more willing to act, Cronbach $\alpha = .73$.

BJW. Three items drawn from Dalbert (1999) constituted the BJW measure. For each item, respondents indicated on a 1–6 point scale if the statement was "totally incorrect" (1) or "very correct" (6). The statements were: (1) The good things people do often go unnoticed and unrewarded; (2) People like me do not always receive the rewards we deserve; (3) There is no justice in our world and often people are not punished for their bad actions. A principal component analysis revealed a single factor in which the higher the value the stronger the BJW ($\alpha = .66$).

Personality Factors

Socio-political Powerlessness Scale. Respondents were asked how true each of the five items was in their view. The scale ranged from (1) totally untrue to (6) very true. Items drawn from Paulhus (1983) included: (1) Things have become so complicated nowadays, that I don't really understand what's happening; (2) Things change so quickly nowadays, that I don't know what will remain the same tomorrow; (3) People like me cannot influence government policy; (4) The world is run by a few strong people and people like me cannot do anything against that; (5) People like me are powerless to change what's happening in the country. A principal component analysis revealed a single factor in which the higher the value the stronger the powerlessness ($\alpha = .79$).

Self-Esteem Scale. Based on Rosenberg's (1965) measure of self-esteem, respondents indicated how accurate (1 = totally inaccurate, 6 = very accurate) each of the following represented their perception of themselves: (1) There are a lot of things about myself I'd change if I could; (2) I often wish I were someone else; (3) I often feel worthless; (4) I'm pretty satisfied with my myself. Items 1–3 were reverse coded, and a principal component analysis revealed a single factor in which the higher the value the stronger the self-esteem ($\alpha = .68$).

Authoritarianism. Altemeyer's (1981) right-wing authoritarianism (RWA) scale was used, as it is the measure best suited for inter-cultural analyses.[9] Respondents answered: How important for you is each of the following? (Range: 1 = totally disagree to 6 = totally agree). Four of the eight RWA items relating to *Authoritarian submission* were retained on the basis of item-to-scale-correlations. The items include: (1) It is good to have a strong authoritarian leader; (2) Obedience and respect for authority are the most important virtues children should learn; (3) For their own good, children should comply with the ideas and values of their parents. (4) We should be grateful to our leaders who can tell us what to do. A principal component analysis revealed a single factor in which the higher the value the stronger the authoritarianism ($\alpha = .68$).

Political Orientation

Patriotism. The measure draws from Blank (2003) and consists of responses to: How strongly do you agree or disagree with each of the following seven items? The scale ranged from (1) totally disagree to (6) totally agree. Statements included: (1) For me Israel is the best country in the world; (2) The morality of Israelis should serve as a model for other countries; (3) The world will be a better place if all countries will be like Israel; (4) People need to support their country even when it is wrong; (5) Jews should decide most things in the country; (6) I want Israel to be a Jewish state, first and foremost; (7) I would like there to be as few non-Jews as possible in Israel. Principal component analysis revealed a single factor in which the higher the value the stronger the patriotism ($\alpha = .77$).

National Identity. Respondents were asked to rank nine components of social identities: occupation, family, nationality, civic, local, ethnic, gender, political attitudes, and religiosity. Respondents were asked to rank order all the identities they consider relevant. Only the rankings of national (Jewish/Palestinian) and civic (Israeli) identities are analyzed in the present context: 1 = most salient identity (ranked in first place); 0 = less salient identity (ranked in second place or lower) (Mean = .29; s.d. = .465).

Social Context

Religiosity. A dummy coded variable represented the respondent's religiosity: -orthodox, religious, and traditional = 1; secular = 0.

Ethnicity. The coding for ethnicity were: Asian or African origin = 1, Western origin and Israeli born = 0.

Income. The income measure stated, "The average income in Israel today is about 7,000 NIS. In comparison, do you earn more than average, less than average or about the average?" Responses were recoded so that 1 = above average and much more than the average; 0 = average or below.

Education. Measured as a continuous variable, respondents indicated the number of years of formal education that they had.

Method of Analysis

First, to analyze the basic relationships among the models' components, the Pearson correlations were examined. Then, to address the theoretical model, the study analyzes a recursive structural equation model (SEM) using AMOS 5 (Arbuckle & Wothke, 1999).[10] SEMs entail, according to Byrne (1998), two implications. First, that the causal processes under study are represented by a series of structural (i.e., regression) equations. Second, the structural relations can be presented graphically. The hypothesized model can be tested statistically in a simultaneous analysis of the entire system of variables to determine the extent to which it is consistent with the data.

RESULTS

The study focuses on two issues: (1) How BJW affects willingness to participate in social action and (2) how personality factors, political orientation, and social characteristics influence both BJW and willingness to participate in social action. To address these issues, a theoretical model was created and empirically examined. According to the model (see Fig. 1), social context characteristics influence both personality factors and political orientation, which influence individuals' BJW, which, in turn, influences willingness to participate in social action.

BJW and Willingness to Act

BJW is negatively correlated with willingness to act, therefore, the stronger the BJW, the weaker the willingness to act, as Hypothesis 1 predicted (see Table 1).

Table 1. Correlation Matrix.

		1	2	3	4	5	6	7	8	9	10	11
1	**Willingness to act**	1	−.098**	−.168*	.086**	−.143*	.098**	.092**	.160*	.170*	.202*	−.048
2	**BJW**		1	.057	.262*	-.388*	−.218*	.014	.208*	.092**	−.136*	−.178*
3	**Powerlessness**			1	−.033	−.049	.006	.018	.045	.113*	−.084	.010
4	**Self-esteem**				1	−.187*	−.098**	.020	.085	.032	.017	.024
5	**Authoritarianism**					1	.507*	.059	−.342*	−.094**	.353*	.299*
6	**Patriotism**						1	.183*	−.240*	−.047	.446*	.226*
7	**National identity (Ranked 1 = 1)**							1	−.038	.077	.234*	.099*
8	**Education**								1	.188*	−.148*	−.350*
9	**Income**									1	−.091*	−.010
10	**Religiosity**										1	.322*
11	**Ethnicity (Asian origin = 1; else = 0)**											1

This finding supports earlier conclusions according to which, if inequality exists, it is often seen as just, because it is considered the result of differences in individual abilities and efforts. These suggestions may have significant social implications, as strong BJW may undermine peoples' willingness to act to increase social justice: It is easier to assume that forces beyond their control are responsible for injustice, and its correction.

Moreover, when the other variables in the model are controlled, the relationship between BJW and willingness to act strengthens (from $r = -.098$, $p = .05$ to $r = -.14$, $p = .00$) (see Table 1), so that those who have strong BJW are even less willing to participate in social action. This indicates that the other variables in the model strengthen the influence of BJW on willingness to act (among them: patriotism, which has a significant negative influence on BJW and a significant positive influence on willingness to act; authoritarianism, which has a significant indirect positive effect on willingness to act that counterbalances its negative direct effect, and so forth.[11]

Effects of Personality Factors, Political Orientation, and Social Characteristics on BJW and Willingness to Act

According to the bivariate correlations in Table 1, most of the personality factors, political orientation, and social characteristics influence both BJW and willingness to act. Highly educated, well-off, secular individuals, and/or those of European descent believe that the world is more just than less educated, poor, religious, and individuals of Asian-African descent. It is easy to understand why the rich and well-educated see the world as more just, but why do the secular see it as more just than religious individuals? Justification of BJW for religious and seculars may be based on different philosophies. Jewish religion, like Christianity and Islam, proclaims that in most cases good deeds are rewarded and evil ones are punished, and that reversal of this principal is rare and temporary (For example: "Trust in the Lord, and do good, ... and thou shalt be fed with its riches" (Psalms, 37, p. 3). "For evildoers shall be cut off: but they that wait upon the Lord, they shall inherit the land" (Psalms, 37, p. 9). The fact that religious individuals have weaker BJW indicates, perhaps, that "being religious" refers to behaviors according to religious decrees (i.e. prayer, covering hair), not necessarily according to religious beliefs (other influences were analyzed only for willingness to act).

Examining who are the most willing to donate funds, to participate in political demonstrations, and/or to volunteer, Table 1 shows that religious individuals, those who are well-off, and individuals with higher education are more willing to act than poor, less educated, and/or secular individuals. Table 2 also examines the basic relationships between willingness to act and personality and political orientation measures in the model and shows that they are indeed related to all the models variables and measures (except political attitudes): Powerlessness is negatively correlated (i.e., the stronger the powerlessness, the weaker the willingness to act); self-esteem is positively correlated (i.e., the higher the self-esteem, the stronger the willingness to act); authoritarianism is negatively correlated (i.e., the stronger the authoritarianism the weaker the willingness to act); and national identity is positively correlated (i.e., the stronger the identity, the stronger the willingness to act)and patriotism is positively correlated (i.e., the stronger the patriotism, the stronger the willingness to act).

To examine the direct and indirect influences of all the variables and measures on willingness to act, a recursive SEM was used. The analysis shows that when all the factors are included, some of their influences on willingness to act (presented in Table 1) become stronger than they were while other influences weaken (see Table 2).

The empirical examination of the model reveals that most expected relationships are indeed confirmed (see Fig. 2). Even after controlling for other effects, BJW significantly influences willingness to act. Thus, willingness to act is directly influenced by BJW, powerlessness, self-esteem, authoritarianism and patriotism. It is indirectly influenced by national identities (through its influence on patriotism), by income and education (through their influence on authoritarianism and powerlessness), and by religiosity and ethnicity (through their influence on authoritarianism and patriotism).

In addition, a stronger tendency to believe in a just world is associated with stronger self-esteem and weaker authoritarianism, as the review of these factors suggests, but it is not related to weaker patriotism, higher status, or higher education.

Analysis of the model also shows that the *higher* the self-esteem, the *stronger* the BJW, indicating that when individuals have a positive attitude toward life, value their accomplishments, and believe in their abilities, they are not only more willing to participate in social action, but also more able to see their world as just and fair.

Also as the review anticipated, *higher* levels of authoritarianism are associated with a *stronger* the BJW, indicating that authoritarians seem to

Table 2. Recursive Structural Equation ($N = 510$) Scalar Estimates (Default Model).

		Unstandardized Estimates	Standard Error	Critical Ratio[a]	Standardized Estimates
Education	<–Religiosity	–.260	.299	–.869	–.038
Education	<–Ethnicity	–2.440	.320	–7.635	–.337*
Income	<–Ethnicity	.061	.123	.492	.023
Income	<–Education	.081	.017	4.742	.225*
Identity	<–Religiosity	.215	.040	5.437	.234*
Authoritarian	<–Religiosity	1.789	.276	6.473	.280*
Authoritarian	<–Ethnicity	.749	.304	2.466	.110*
Authoritarian	<–Education	–.250	.040	–6.211	–.265*
Authoritarian	<–Identity	–.178	.285	–.625	–.026
Patriotism	<–Religiosity	2.658	.391	6.803	.281*
Patriotism	<–Ethnicity	.145	.398	.364	.014
Patriotism	<–Identity	.987	.387	2.547	.096*
Patriotism	<–Authoritarian	.591	.059	9.956	.399*
Self-esteem	<–Ethnicity	.362	.276	1.310	.062
Self-esteem	<–Education	.090	.039	2.284	.111**
Self-esteem	<–Income	–.042	.103	–.404	–.019
Powerless	<–Education	–.001	.007	–.168	–.008
Powerless	<–Income	–.049	.018	–2.721	–.125*
Powerless	<–Authoritarian	.011	.008	1.296	.070
Powerless	<–Patriotism	–.004	.005	–.779	–.040
Powerless	<–Self-esteem	.007	.008	.952	.042
BJW	<–Ethnicity	–.173	.106	–1.630	–.073
BJW	<–Education	.017	.015	1.129	.053
BJW	<–Income	.001	.039	.013	.001
BJW	<–Authoritarian	–.102	.018	–5.763	–.295*
BJW	<–Patriotism	–.002	.011	–.204	–.010
BJW	<–Self-esteem	.080	.017	4.777	.198*
BJW	<–Powerless	–.108	.096	–1.129	–.047
Willingness	<–Authoritarian	–.045	.016	–2.833	–.154*
Willingness	<–Patriotism	.047	.010	4.590	.237*
Willingness	<–Self-esteem	.045	.015	2.933	.132*
Willingness	<–Powerless	–.170	.086	–1.991	–.088**
Willingness	<–BJW	–.119	.041	–2.916	–.141*

Notes: Chi-square = 59.704; degrees of freedom = 22; probability level = .000; RMSEA = .05.
*$p \leq .001$.
**$p \leq .05$.
[a]Critical ratio is the parameter estimate divided by its standard error. The estimate is significantly different from zero at the .05 level.

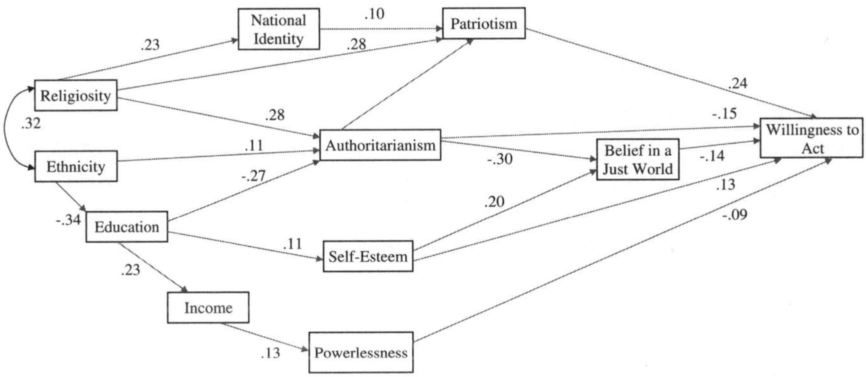

Fig. 2. Empirical Model.

accept the existing social order as the just order of things. Moreover, the fact that higher authoritarianism is *not* associated with lower powerlessness supports this interpretation: If the authoritarians expect the world to be just, they have no cause to feel powerless in it.

Examination of the groups more likely to be authoritarian shows that, in accord with previous findings, right-wing, religious and Jews of Asian origin, are more authoritarian than left-wing, secular and European ones, and highly educated individuals are less authoritarian than less educated ones. This study cannot determine whether authoritarianism influences political attitudes or vice versa, but the emerging pattern is clear – Jews of Asian origin tend to be more religious and more among them consider themselves right-wingers. Their education is also lower and they tend to be more authoritarian than that of European Jews. As authoritarianism reduces the willingness to participate in social action, it is clear that religious Jews of Asian origin will be less willing to act (even though religiosity itself is positively related with willingness to act (see Table 1).

DISCUSSION

Willingness to act is indeed influenced by many of the diverse factors included in the model. Willingness to participate in social action is related – directly or indirectly – to such concepts as BJW, self-esteem, authoritarianism, powerlessness, patriotism, national identities, education, income, ethnicity, and religiosity. These factors represent individual (personal) characteristics, political orientation, and the social context. Although much of the variance remains unexplained, these factors proved significant for the prediction of willingness to act.

The main questions this study aimed to examine were: Does the BJW *reduce* willingness to participate in social action? And what are the main social, political and personality factors that influence both BJW and willingness to participate in social action?

The analyses clearly show that BJW is significantly – and negatively – correlated with willingness to act, even when other factors are included in the analysis. This finding indicates that in Israel, much like in other Western societies, people who believe that the world is just are *less* willing to act in order to change it. As was expected, support for BJW is stronger among the advantaged groups (the rich, secular, and/or people of European origin). The disadvantaged group both see the world as more unjust and place a higher priority on social responsibility, but they are also more powerless to change the situation. Thus, BJW seem to represent the value system of the socially advantaged groups.

It is interesting to note that while political orientation (i.e., patriotism, political attitudes, and national identity) does not influence BJW, it does influence the willingness to act. In fact, the impact of patriotism on willingness to act is stronger than all other influences (so that the more patriotic are more willing to participate in social action). As patriotism is directly influenced by political attitudes, national identity, and religiosity, one may conclude that in Israeli society, religious individuals, with a salient national identity, who are right-wingers, consider themselves more patriotic than secular, left-wingers with less salient national identities, and will be more willing to act for their society. It seems that Israel's recent history and the vehement demonstrations against evacuations of Jews from Gaza and the parts of the West Bank show that this is true, at least in the political sphere.

The importance of the socio-demographic characteristics is clear. Religiosity, ethnicity, education, and income influence – directly or indirectly – both BJW and the willingness to act. Religiosity, ethnicity, income, and education are correlated and many of their influences interact (especially those of religion and ethnicity) so that poor, religious Jews of Eastern origin are a distinct group tend to see the world as unjust, they are the most powerless, and the most relatively deprived group. They are also more authoritarian than other groups, the most patriotic, and a greater proportion among them are right-wingers. Their education is also lower than that of all other groups.

Further research is necessary to ascertain whether these findings reflect a major change in Israeli society. When created almost 60 years ago, Israel was a collectivistic society in which economic inequality was among the smallest in the world (Ben David, 1963). The basically underdeveloped, agricultural society that existed before Israel's independence went through a process of modernization and rapid development of its industry, followed by a tremendous growth in its service sector. These changes were accompanied by a shift from a predominant socialist and collectivistic ideology to a more materialistic and individualistic value system, which is more typical of highly industrialized societies. It is impossible to determine on the basis of the present study what the ideological trend in Israel is, and whether it is turning away from individualism as other Western societies seem to be doing. Only a longitudinal study may shed some light on this issue. It may be interesting to see whether societies that were until recently under communist regimes undergo the same process of individualization, and whether the same forces influence the process.

Also, further research is necessary in order to examine additional individual-personal characteristics on the one hand and the social-political context on the other hand. Although the current research elaborates our knowledge of how willingness to participate in social action is formed and the examined factors were found relevant and significant, their contribution to the explaining of willingness to act is not high. Other factors that were not examined in this study may, perhaps, further contribute to the explaining of willingness to participate in social action.

NOTES

1. In Israel, for example, the levels of involvement are particularly high in both the political and the social spheres: In most elections, 85–88% of the adult population turn out to vote; 2–5% of the entire population may be seen in a demonstration organized by either peace activists or by anti-concessionists (which, in American proportions, would mean 6–15 million individuals).

2. Not all possible recursive relations were examined. Some were not examined because they are irrelevant, others – because it seemed less important to examine them in the present context (e.g., does patriotism influence political attitudes or vice versa).

3. The reverse was also examined in a nonrecursive AMOS model and was found to be similarly effective, but less theoretically viable.

4. Diverse definitions of authoritarianism were offered: It was defined as a personality trait by Adorno, Frenkel- Brunswik, Levinson, and Sanford (1950),

as the result of socialization processes by Lederer (1993), as a learning process by Altemeyer (1981), and as a behavioral directive by Ray (1991).

5. However, studies of authoritarianism also show that when combined with domination (as measured by Social Dominance Orientation scale), the worst elements in both characteristics become apparent and the tendency of social dominators to be power hungry, unsupportive of equality and amoral, strengthens ethnocentric and dogmatic right-wing authoritarianism (Altemeyer, 2004).

6. The data set includes other measures (like political attitudes) as well. The measures that were chosen for the analysis are not necessarily those with highest correlations, but they more relate to the theoretical issues.

7. The Jewish–Arab distinction is an additional and highly significant categorization, but is irrelevant in the present study which deals with Jews only.

8. Not all possible recursive relations were examined. Some were not examined because they are irrelevant, others – because it seemed less important to examine them in the present context (e.g., does patriotism influence political attitudes or vice versa).

9. Some items that are not relevant or do not apply to Israeli society – like "Capital punishment should be abolished" – were removed.

10. AMOS was preferred because it avoids both list-wise deletion of cases and the biases associated with some of the other methods (see also Fox, 1980).

11. Influence matrices available from the author.

ACKNOWLEDGMENTS

I wish to thank Daniel Bar-Tal, Susan Clayton, Dan Jacobson, and the editors – Karen Hegtvedt and Jody Clay-Warner – for their very constructive comments and suggestions, the Research Authority of the College of Management-Academic Studies for financing the research, and Mina Tzemach, Head of Dahaf Research Institute, for her assistance in constructing the questionnaire and collecting the data.

REFERENCES

Abrams, D., & Emler, N. (1992). Self-denial as a paradox of political and regional social identity: Findings from a study of 16- and 18-year olds. *European Journal of Social Psychology*, *22*, 279–295.

Adorno, T. W., Frenkel-Brunswik, E., Levinson, D. J., & Sanford, R. N. (1950). *The authoritarian personality*. New York: Harper.

Altemeyer, B. (1981). *Right wing authoritarianism*. Winnipeg: University of Manitoba Press.

Altemeyer, B. (2004). Highly dominating, highly authoritarian personalities. *Journal of Social Psychology*, *144*, 421–447.

Altemeyer, B., & Hunsberger, B. (2005). Fundamentalism and authoritarianism. In: R. F. Paloutzian & C. L. Park (Eds), *Handbook of the psychology of religion and spirituality* (pp. 378–393). New York: Guilford Press.

Altemeyer, R. (1996). *The authoritarian specter*. Boston, MA: Harvard University Press.

Antonucci, T. C. (2001). Social relations: An examination of social networks, social support, and sense of control. In: J. E. Birren & K. Warner Schai (Eds), *Handbook of the psychology of aging* (5th ed., pp. 427–453). San Diego, CA: Academic Press.

Appelbaum, L., Lennon, M. C., & Aber, J. L. (2003). *How belief in a just world influences views of public policy*. Research Report #2. The National Center for Children in Poverty (NCCP). Mailman School of Public Health, Columbia University (www.nccp.org/pub_pat03b.html, downloaded on November 4, 2006).

Arbuckle, J., & Wothke, W. (1999). *AMOS 4.0 user's guide*. Chicago: SPSS.

Arneson, R. (2002). In: Edward N. Zalta (Ed.), *Egalitarianism. The Stanford encyclopedia of philosophy (Fall 2002ed.)*. plato.stanford.edu/archives/fall2002/entries/egalitarianism/

Baron, J., & Miller, J. G. (2000). Limiting the scope of moral obligations to help: A cross-cultural investigation. *Journal of Cross Cultural Psychology*, *31*, 703–725.

Bar-Tal, D., & Ben-Amos, A. (2004). Patriotism as a social psychological phenomenon: Introduction to the analysis of the Israeli case. In: A. Ben-Amos & D. Bar-Tal (Eds), *Patriotism: Homeland love* (pp. 13–28). Tel Aviv: Hakibbutz Hameuhad (Hebrew).

Battle, J. (1990). *Self-esteem: The new revolution*. Edmonton, Alberta, Canada: James Battle & Associates.

Begue, L. (2002). Beliefs in justice and faith in people: Just world, religiosity, and interpersonal trust. *Personality and Individual Differences*, *32*, 375–382.

Begue, L. (2005). Self esteem regulation in threatening social comparison: The roles of belief in a just world and self efficacy. *Social Behavior and Personality*, *33*, 69–76.

Bell, W. (1998). Making people responsible: The possible, the probable, and the preferable. *American Behavioral Scientist*, *42*, 323–339.

Ben David, J. (1963). Professions in the class system of present-day societies. *Current Sociology*, *12*, 247–298.

Bierhoff, H. W. (2002). Just world, social responsibility, and helping behavior. In: M. Ross & D. T. Miller (Eds), *The justice motive in everyday life* (pp. 189–203). New York: Cambridge University Press.

Blank, T. (2003). Determinants of national identity in East and West Germany: An empirical comparison of theories on the significance of authoritarianism, anomie, and general self-esteem. *Political Psychology*, *24*, 259–288.

Blascovich, J., & Tomaka, J. (1991). Measures of self-esteem. In: J. Robinson, P. R. Shaver & L. S. Wrightsman (Eds), *Measure of personality and social psychological attitudes* (pp. 115–121). New York: Academic Press.

Bulman, R. J., & Wortman, C. B. (1977). Attributions of blame and coping in the "real world": Severe accident victims react to their lot. *Journal of Personality and Social Psychology*, *35*, 351–363.

Byrne, B. M. (1998). *Structural equation modeling with LISREL, PRELIS, and SIMPLIS: Basic concepts, applications, and programming*. Mahwah, NJ: Lawrence Erlbaum.

Cass, B. (1994). Integrating private and social responsibilities: Better partnerships between families, governments and communities. *Family Matters*, *37*, 20–27.

Clayton, S., & Opotow, S. (2003). Justice and identity: Changing perspectives on what is fair. *Personality-and Social-Psychology-Review*, *7*, 298–310.

Cohn, E. S., & Modecki, K. L. (2007). Gender differences in predicting delinquent behavior: Do individual differences matter? *Social Behavior and Personality*, *35*, 359–374.

Cole, M., Clay, J., & Hill, D. (1990). The citizen as "individual" and "nationalist" or "social" and internationalist? What is the role of education? *Critical Social Policy*, *3*, 68–87.

Crosby, F., & Ropp, S. (2002). Awakening to discrimination. In: M. Ross & D. T. Miller (Eds), *The justice motive in everyday life* (pp. 382–396). New York: Cambridge University Press.

Dalbert, C. (1999). The world is more just for me than generally: About the personal belief in a just world scale's validity. *Social Justice Research*, *12*, 79–98.

Dalbert, C. (2002). Beliefs in a just world as a buffer against anger. *Social Justice Research*, *15*, 123–145.

Dzuka, J., & Dalbert, C. (2002). Mental health and personality: The impact of belief in a just world. *Journal of Applied Social Psychology*, *32*, 732–757.

Ellemers, N., & Bos, A. E. R. (1998). Social identity, relative deprivation, and coping with the threat of position loss: A field study among native shopkeepers in Amsterdam. *Journal of Applied Social Psychology*, *28*, 1987–2006.

Fabick, S. D. (2004). Us & them: Reducing the risk of terrorism. In: C. E. Stout (Ed.), *Psychology of terrorism: Coping with the continuing threat, condensed edition* (pp. 95–115). Westport, CT: Praeger Publishers/Greenwood Publishing Group.

Faunce, W. (1989). An occupational *status*-assignment systems: The effect of status on self esteem. *The American Journal of Sociology*, *95*, 378–400.

Feather, N. T. (1993). Authoritarianism and attitudes toward high achievers. *Journal of Personality and Social Psychology*, *65*, 152–164.

Feldman, S., & Stenner, K. (1997). Perceived threat and authoritarianism. *Political Psychology*, *18*, 741–770.

Ferge, Z. (1997). The perils of the welfare state's withdrawal. *Social Research*, *64*, 1381–1402.

Flanagan, C. A., Gallay, L. S., Gill, S., Gallay, E., & Nti, N. (2005). What does democracy mean? Correlates of adolescents' views. *Journal of Adolescent Research*, *20*, 193–218.

Fox, J. (1980). Effect analysis in structural equations models. *Sociological Methods and Research*, *9*, 3–28.

France, A. (1998). 'Why should we care?': Young people, citizenship and questions of social responsibility. *Journal of Youth Studies*, *1*, 97–111.

Furnham, A. (1991). Just world beliefs in twelve societies. *The Journal of Social Psychology*, *133*, 317–329.

Geis, K. J., & Ross, C. E. (1998). A new look at urban alienation: The effect of neighborhood disorder on perceived powerlessness. *Social Psychology Quarterly*, *61*, 232–246.

Gecas, V. (2000). Value identities, self-motives, and social movements. In: S. Stryker, T. J. Owens & R. W. White (Eds), *Self, identity, and social movements* (pp. 93–109). Boston: Allyn and Bacon.

Green, A. (2003). Celebrating diversity: Building self esteem in today's multicultural classroom. *International Journal for the Advancement of Counseling*, *25*, 193–195.

Hafer, C. L. (2002). Why we reject innocent victims. In: M. Ross & D. T. Miller (Eds), *The justice motive in everyday life* (pp. 109–126). New York: Cambridge University Press.

Hegtvedt, K. A. (2004). Legitimizing legitimacy: Shaping a new frontier of research. *Social Justice Research*, *17*, 93–109.

Hegtvedt, K. A. (2005). Doing justice to the group: Examining the roles of the group in justice research. *Annual Review of Sociology*, *31*, 25–45.

Hinkle, S., Fox Cardamone, L., Haseleu, J. A., Brown, R., & Irwin, L. M. (1996). Grassroots political action as an intergroup phenomenon. *Journal of Social Issues*, *52*, 39–51.

Hogg, M. A. (2003). Social identity. In: M. R. Leary & J. P. Tangney (Eds), *Handbook of self and identity* (pp. 401–421). New York: Guilford Press.

Horowitz, D., & Lissak, M. (1989). *Troubles in utopia*. Albany, NY: SUNY Press.

Hunt, M. O. (2000). Status, religion, and the "belief in a just world": Comparing African Americans, Latinos, and Whites. *Social Science Quarterly*, *81*, 325–343.

Israeli Bureau of Statistics. (2005). *The statistical yearbook*, Jerusalem, Israel.

Jasso, G. (2005). Culture and the sense of justice: A comprehensive framework for analysis. *Journal of Cross Cultural Psychology*, *36*, 14–47.

Jost, J. T., & Sidanius, J. (Eds). (2004). *Key readings in social psychology*. New York: Psychology Press.

Kalkhoff, W., & Barnum, C. (2000). The effects of status organizing and social identity processes on patterns of social influence. *Social Psychology Quarterly*, *63*, 95–115.

Karuza, J., Jr.., & Carey, T. O. (1984). Relative preference and adaptiveness of behavioral blame for observers of rape victims. *Journal of Personality*, *52*, 249–260.

Keyes, C. L. (2002). Social civility in the United States. *Sociological Inquiry*, *72*, 393–408.

Kimmerling, B., & Moore, D. (1997). Collective identity as agency and structuration of society (the Israeli case). *International Review of Sociology*, *7*, 25–49.

Lambert, A. J., Burroughs, T., & Chasteen, A. L. (1998). Belief in a just world and right-wing authoritarianism as moderators of perceived risk. In: M. J. Lerner & L. Montada (Eds), *Responses to victimizations and belief in a just world* (pp. 107–125). New York: Plenum.

Lambert, A. J., Burroughs, T., & Nguyen, T. (1999). Perceptions of risk and the buffering hypothesis: The role of just world beliefs and right-wing authoritarianism. *Personality and Social Psychology Bulletin*, *25*, 643–656.

Lederer, G. (1993). Authoritarianism in German adolescents: Trends and cross cultural comparisons. In: W. F. Stone, G. Lederer & R. Christie (Eds), *Strength and weakness: The authoritarian personality today* (pp. 182–198). New York: Springer.

Lefcourt, H. M. (1981). *Locus of control: Current trends in theory and research*. Hillsdale, NJ: Erlbaum.

Lerner, M. J. (1980). *The belief in a just world: A fundamental delusion*. New York: Plenum.

Lerner, M. J., & Simmons, C. H. (1966). Observer's reaction to the "innocent victim": Compassion or rejection? *Journal of Personality and Social Psychology*, *4*, 203–210.

Lerner, M. J., & Somers, D. G. (1992). Employees' reactions to an anticipated plant closure: The influence of positive illusions. In: L. Montada, F. Sigrun-Heide & M. J. Lerner (Eds), *Life crises and experiences of loss adulthood* (pp. 229–253). Hillsdale, NJ: Lawrence Erlbaum Associates.

Levi, M. J (2005). The authoritarian personality, 50 years later: What questions are there for political psychology? *Political Psychology*, *22*, 1–26.

Lewis, S. K., Ross, C. E., & Mirowsky, J. (1999). Establishing a sense of personal control in the transition to adulthood. *Social Forces*, *77*, 1573–1599.

Libow, J., & Doty, D. (1979). An exploratory approach to self-blame and self-derogation by rape victims. *American Journal of Orthopsychiatry*, *49*, 670–679.

Linney, J. A. (2004). The making of a community psychologist: Naive idealism, supportive contexts and good fortune. *Journal of Prevention and Intervention in the Community*, *28*, 81–102.

Lipkus, I. M., & Siegler, I. C. (1993). The belief in a just world and perceptions of discrimination. *The Journal of Psychology*, *127*, 465–474.

Markus, H. R., Ryff, C. D., Conner, A. L., Pudberry, E. K., & Barnett, K. L. (2001). Themes and variations in American understandings of responsibility. In: A. S. Rossi (Ed.), *Caring and doing for other: Social responsibility in the domains of family, work, and community* (pp. 349–399). Chicago, IL: University of Chicago Press.

McDonough, P., Barnes, S. H., & Pina, A. L. (1988). Social identity and mass politics in Spain. *Comparative Political Studies*, *21*, 200–230.

Mikula, G. (1990). What people regard as unjust. *European Journal of Social Psychology*, *20*, 133–149.

Mirowsky, J., Ross, C. E., & van Willigen, M. (1996). Instrumentalism in the land of opportunity. *Social Psychology Quarterly*, *59*, 322–337.

Montada, L., Schmitt, M., & Dalbert, C. (1986). Thinking about justice and dealing with one's own privileges: A study of existential guilt. In: H. W. Bierhoff, R. L. Cohen & J. Greenberg (Eds), *Justice in social relations* (pp. 125–143). New York: Plenum Press.

Moore, D. (2000a). Intolerance of 'others' among Palestinian and Jewish students in Israel. *Sociological Inquiry*, *70*, 280–312.

Moore, D. (2000b). Gender identity, nationalism, and social action among Jewish and Arab women in Israel: Redefining the social order? *Gender Issues*, *18*, 3–28.

Moore, D., & Aweiss, S. (2004). *Bridges over troubled water: Political, economic and social attitudes (cross-cultural comparisons of Palestinians and Israelis)*. Englewood Cliffs, CA: Greenwood Publishing Group.

Moore, D., & Aweiss, S. (2007). Strategies of constructing social identities in conflict-ridden areas: The case of young Jews, Arabs, and Palestinians. *Studies in Ethnicity and Nationalism*, *7*, 2–27.

Mudrack, P. E. (2005). An outcomes based approach to just world beliefs. *Personality and Individual Differences*, *38*, 817–830.

Mummendey, A., Kessler, T., Klink, A., & Mielke, R. (1999). Strategies to cope with negative social identity: Predictions by social identity theory and relative deprivation theory. *Journal of Personality and Social Psychology*, *76*, 229–245.

Myers, D. G. (2000). *The American paradox: Spiritual hunger in an age of plenty*. New Haven, CT: Yale University Press.

Nicolaides, P. (1997). The role of the state in the single European market: How to reconcile social responsibility with competition. *Journal of Business and Society*, *10*, 35–56.

Oliner, S. P., & Krause, J. D. (2001). Racial and ethnic attitudes in rural America: Humboldt. *Journal of Social Relations*, *26*, 11–55.

O'Neill, P., Duffy, C., Enman, M., Blackmer, E., & Campbell, R. E. (1988). Cognition and citizen participation in social action. *Journal of Applied Social Psychology*, *18*, 1067–1083.

Paulhus, D. L. (1983). Sphere-specific measures of perceived control. *Journal of Personality and Social Psychology*, *44*, 1253–1265.

Pentony, J. F., Petersen, K. S. E., Philips, O., Leong, C., Harper, P., Bakowski, A., Steward, S., & Gonzales, R. (2000). A comparison of authoritarianism in the United States, England, and Hungary with selected nonrandom samples. *European Psychologist*, *5*, 259–268.

Peterson, B. E. (2003). Authoritarianism and methodological innovation. *Analyses of Social Issues and Public Policy*, *3*, 185–187.

Prenda, K. M., & Lachman, M. E. (2001). Planning for the future: A life management strategy for increasing control and life satisfaction. *Psychology and Aging*, *16*, 206–216.

Ray, J. J. (1991). Attitude toward authority scale. In: J. P. Robinson, P. R. Shaver & L. S. Wrightsman (Eds), *Measures of personality and social psychological attitudes* (pp. 547–550). New York: Academic Press.

Realo, A., & Allik, J. (1999). A cross-cultural study of collectivism: A comparison of American' Estonian, and Russian Students. *The Journal of Social Psychology*, *139*, 133–145.

Reynolds, K. J., Turner, J. C., Haslam, S. A., & Ryan, M. K. (2001). The role of personality and group factors in explaining prejudice. *Journal of Experimental Social Psychology*, *37*, 427–434.

Rosenberg, M. (1965). *Society and the adolescent self-image*. Princeton, NJ: Princeton University Press.

Rossi, A. S. (2001). Domains and dimensions of social responsibility: A sociodemographic profile. In: A. S. Rossi (Ed.), *Caring and doing for other: Social responsibility in the domains of family, work, and community* (pp. 97–134). Chicago: University of Chicago Press.

Rotter, J. B., Chance, J. E., & Phares, E. J. (1972). *Applications of a social learning theory of personality*. New York: Holt, Rinehart and Winston.

Rubin, Z., & Peplau, L. A. (1975). Who believes in a just world. *Journal of Social Issues*, *31*, 65–89.

Rubinstein, G. (1995). Authoritarianism in Israeli society. *Journal of Social Psychology*, *135*, 237–249.

Staub, E. (1997). Blind versus constructive patriotism: Moving from embeddedness in the group to critical loyalty and action. In: D. Bar-Tal & E. Staub (Eds), *Patriotism in the lives of individuals and nations* (pp. 213–228). Chicago: Nelson-Hall.

Steffenhagen, R. A., & Burns, J. (1987). *Social dynamics of self-esteem*. New York: Praeger.

Stryker, S., & Serpe, R. T. (1994). Identity salience and psychological centrality: Equivalent, overlapping or complementary concepts? *Social Psychology Quarterly*, *57*, 16–35.

Sutton, M. S., & Carlson, H. M. (1977). Attitude and personality differences among men and women studying police science. *Journal of Social Psychology*, *102*, 161–162.

Sutton, R. M., & Douglas, K. M. (2005). Justice for all, or just for me? More evidence of the importance of the self other distinction in just world beliefs. *Personality and Individual Differences*, *39*, 637–645.

Tajfel, H., & Turner, J. C. (1986). The social identity theory of intergroup behavior. In: S. Worchel & W. G. Austin (Eds), *Psychology of intergroup relations* (pp. 7–24). Chicago: Nelson-Hall.

Tyler, T. R., & Blader, S. L. (2003). The group engagement model: Procedural justice, social identity, and cooperative behavior. *Personality and Social Psychology Review*, *7*, 349–361.

Unger, R. K., & Safir, M. (1994). Sex, religiosity, and political tolerance. Paper presented at the Second International Congress on Prejudice, Discrimination, and Conflict, Jerusalem, Israel, July 7.

Walker, I. (1999). Effects of personal and group relative deprivation on personal and collective self-esteem. *Group Processes and Intergroup Relations*, *2*, 365–380.

Warren, N. D. (2002). The idea of responsibility. *Society*, *5*, 17–21.

Wenzel, M. (2001). A social categorization approach to distributive justice: Social identity as the link between relevance of inputs and need for justice. *British Journal of Social Psychology*, *40*, 315–335.

ATTENDING TO IDENTITIES: IDEOLOGY, GROUP MEMBERSHIPS, AND PERCEPTIONS OF JUSTICE

Susan Clayton

ABSTRACT

Identities reside not just in objective realities but also in the perceptions of actors and observers, reflecting actual group memberships as well as ideologies about their relevance and significance. Salient group identities can influence perceptions of the justice of social events and policies as well as perpetuating intergroup conflicts. This chapter reviews the relationship between psychological perspectives on identity and beliefs about justice, including new data illustrating the relevance of identity to support for animal rights. Experiences that emphasize shared identities between groups may reduce the deindividuation of outgroup members and promote the resolution of intergroup conflicts.

Assessments of justice are widespread, if not universal, processes. People respond to many events by evaluating whether or not they are fair; that is, whether those involved have been treated fairly and received the outcomes that they deserve (cf. Finkel, 2001; Lerner, 1980). These evaluations in turn

Justice
Advances in Group Processes, Volume 25, 241–266

ISSN: 0882-6145/doi:10.1016/S0882-6145(08)25011-3

affect behavior and emotions. Although they often appear absolute and objective, judgments about what is fair in real social settings are affected by myriad factors including the cultural context, the nature of the resource being allocated, and the relationships among the participants. One of the most important determinants of whether a particular state of affairs is construed as just or unjust is identity: the attributes, roles, and affiliations of those involved, particularly as they define the relationships among participants (Clayton & Opotow, 2003). Group identities, the particular focus of this chapter, reflect a sense of belonging to or involvement with a group-based on shared values, goals, or characteristics; they arise from ascribed characteristics such as race or gender as well as from experiences of similarity. In response to social and political events, group identities influence evaluations of how just a situation is as well as judgments about what would be a just resolution or outcome.

Why do identities have this impact? For one thing, identities serve to direct attention, with events that are seen as self-relevant attracting more attention than those that are not. Shared identities make even remote events personally involving, leading to emotional reactions that make a situation more vivid and noteworthy to a perceiver and direct attention toward relevant actors and events. Identities also suggest preferences. People want to maintain a positive sense of themselves as group members, so they may be predisposed to perceive outcomes that advance their groups' interests as fair, and to justify actions and values ascribed to those groups.

Because we have multiple identities, the way that identities are constructed in a specific situation is both flexible and manipulable. Particular identities – how we are seen by others as well as how we see ourselves – are highlighted by the immediate situation and by the surrounding culture. Of the many possible ways of describing the actors in the situation, only some will become important in framing our understanding of the situation. The identity that is salient is not just a description of the person or people involved, but a judgment about what attributes are important.

The ways in which we respond to a situation depend not only on which identities are salient, but also on the significance of group identities as compared to individual identities. Ideologies provide a framework that can encourage conceptualizing people as individuals or as interchangeable members of groups, and can specify the appropriate relationships among groups. This has corresponding but not always obvious effects on judgments about justice, which can vary depending on whether the focus is on the individual or the collective, and on whether the goal is equality or differentiation. Once a situation has been interpreted in terms of group identities and intergroup relations, beliefs about the appropriate relationship between groups become important. One perspective is that some groups are better than others, even more human; from a different perspective, all are equally deserving.

This chapter will examine the ways in which ideologies about identity suggest and promote different perspectives on justice in public and/or political contexts through a message about the importance of group identities and the relationships among different groups. I first review research on levels of identity, concentrating on what it means to define people as group members rather than as individuals. I also identify factors that influence the tendency to focus on group rather than individual identities. One such factor is ideology, or the belief systems associated with certain types of group. Political ideology and personal disposition have both been tied to beliefs about the significance of group identities. Next, I note some basic processes concerning the way in which identities affect perceptions of justice, and analyze the correspondence between levels of identities and those of justice perceptions. Several social issues are then presented to demonstrate the way ideologies about identity are reflected in political positions. I further illustrate this point by presenting the results of a study about attitudes toward animal rights in order to show the impact of beliefs about the similarities between groups and the degree of hierarchy between groups on attitudes about what is fair. Finally, I consider the ways in which group identities are implicated in intergroup conflict and resolution.

INDIVIDUAL AND GROUP IDENTITIES

Levels of Identity: Individuals as Group Members

People can be defined both by their individual attributes and relationships and by their category memberships. For example, I could be described as impatient, a mother, a psychologist, or an American, among other labels. Along with being multiple and layered, identities are fluid. The meaning and salience of different identities vary according to past experience and present context, including the sociopolitical context. My identity as an American is not something I am usually very conscious of, but it is highlighted when I am identified as an American while traveling in another country. Similarly, the connotations of being American are different when American achievements are being praised than when American policies draw international criticism. My identification as an individual or a group member affects both my own self-perception and the ways in which I am perceived by others: when I am defined as a group member, I am subject to the stereotypes associated with that group.

In addition to suggesting that certain characteristics can be attributed to an individual, group memberships also affect the extent to which someone is perceived as an individual. People from a different group are often subject to the outgroup homogeneity effect (e.g., Judd & Park, 1988); that is, they are less individuated than ingroup members. To members of different groups, my similarity to my fellow group members will be enhanced and my differences will be minimized. Meanwhile, differences between my own group and other groups will be exaggerated. In cases of intergroup conflict, outgroup members may even seem less human compared to the ingroup (Opotow, 1990, 1994).

This deindividuation and dehumanization of an outgroup has advantages for the ingroup. If outgroup members are less than human, they do not deserve the same rights and moral consideration as the ingroup. When societal resources are inequitably distributed, derogating the group that receives fewer resources serves to justify the existing system and allows the privileged group to feel comfortable with their advantages rather than guilty. It is striking that media coverage of the aftermath to Hurricane Katrina disproportionately emphasized the criminal and violent activity of the local population and particularly the Black citizens, allowing the rest of the country to "blame the victim" and feel comfortable that perhaps the local residents did not deserve the same standard of living enjoyed by the majority of Americans (Sommers, Apfelbaum, Dukes, Toosi, & Wang, 2006).

If outgroup members have committed aggression, then deindividuating and dehumanizing them may serve as a way to explain the violence. There is a psychic and perhaps even a moral cost to a perspective which considers terrorists, or Nazis, as merely human, just like the rest of us. If the perpetrators of atrocities are similar to us, can they really be responsible for their actions? And would we behave similarly in their position? Several authors (cf. Miller, 2004) have noted that considering harmdoers to be normal people in unusual circumstances runs the risk of sliding from understanding to forgiveness. Certainly, emphasizing the difference between themselves and the perpetrators of violence helps people to maintain a positive sense of their own identity, which would be threatened by an acknowledgment of similarity.

Deindividuating the outgroup also can facilitate a retributive response to an aggressive act by the outgroup. In conflicts between groups, aggression by a member or members of one group toward a member or members of the other group is often initiated on the basis of group rather than individual identities. As a consequence, acts of retribution may also be based on group rather than individual identities. Targets of retribution may be outgroup members who were not involved in the original attack. Indeed, sometimes it is not possible to seek retribution against the actual aggressor, so substituting another member of the group is necessary to satisfy the retributive urge. Whether an aggressive act is considered to be part of an intergroup conflict depends on a number of things in addition to the act itself. Lickel, Miller, Stenstorm, Denson, and Schmader (2006) have discussed various factors that contribute to the interpretation of an act in terms of intergroup relations, including the context of the act, the nature of the act, the identity of the attacker, and the identity of the victim. Once the act has been categorized as intergroup aggression, however, vicarious retribution may be seen as justified.

In addition to deindividuating outgroup members, there are circumstances in which people may deindividuate members of their own groups, seeing them primarily as fellow group members rather than as separate individuals. Even self-perceptions can be affected, so that people feel more anonymous, defined by their group identity more than by their individual attributes. Emphasizing similarities among group members (e.g., in experiences or values), following group norms, or expressing attitudes that are considered typical of the ingroup are all means of demonstrating a strong group identity. For individuals, this may function to confirm their status as valued group members. It may also serve to enhance the group's interests, by motivating the group to pursue its stated goals or by forcing others to recognize the entitativity or "groupness" of the group (Klein, Spears, & Reicher, 2007). Klein et al. have argued that individuals may act in a way that reflects group norms in order to affirm their own status within the group or the group's status within an intergroup system, or in order to achieve group objectives. The sense of the group as a collective whole rather than as a collection of individuals may encourage a focus on group goals, values, and outcomes.

The solidarity of group identification enhances the sense of shared identity among group members and thus encourages a focus on collective well-being rather than on individual entitlement. Patriotism, for example, is a force that encourages both a feeling of collective national identity and a willingness to act on behalf of the nation (Bar-Tal, 2007). This type of identification may also lead individuals to commit hostile or aggressive acts on behalf of the group because they have been freed from the self-restraints associated with their individual identities. A tendency to focus on group rather than individual identities can thus be seen to serve a strategic purpose in advancing ingroup goals and in legitimating aggression against the outgroup.

Attending to Group Identities: Influences on Individuation

Variability in the extent to which group identities are highlighted is produced by differences in the situational context as well as by fundamental group ideologies. Cultures vary in the extent to which they stress the individual or the group. Those that are more individualistic emphasize the self as independent and prioritize personal goals, while those that are more collectivist focus on group goals and on the interdependence of self with others (Murphy-Berman & Berman, 2002). As Moore (this volume) points out, the salience of an individual or collective identity may also be affected by the "central debates" in a society. When nation-building is ongoing and national goals are salient, patriotism is high and people may be more likely to see things in terms of their collective national identity as compared to more personal and individual identities. Perceived ingroup homogeneity often increases when there is a threat to a valued group identity (Doosje, Spears, Ellemers, & Koomen, 1999).

More specific contextual factors also affect the salience of group identity. As Lickel et al. (2006) discuss, some acts may prime a particular ingroup–outgroup distinction. Burning a cross on the lawn of an African American will probably be interpreted in terms of hostility between ethnic groups. Other factors that increase the likelihood that an act will be interpreted on the basis of group relations rather than individual ones include the identity of the attacker and the victim: Are they seen as representatives of their group? Are they known for their hostility toward the outgroup? What is the entitativity of the groups to which they belong? An insult against a gay man from Oregon is more likely to be interpreted as anti-gay than as anti-Oregon, in the absence of other information, because gay men are seen as having more common goals, more shared interaction, and a higher degree of group identification than are Oregonians.

It is not always clear whether an act is individual-based or group-based. An act that is prompted by hostility toward an individual may nonetheless be read to imply group-based hostility, and vice versa. Despite the ambiguity, interpreting an act as group-focused or as individual-focused can have powerful consequences. In the fall of 2006, U.S. Senator George Allen got wide media attention when he referred to a dark-skinned spectator who was filming him at a political event with the word "macaca." Although Allen insisted that it was merely a nonsense word, it was interpreted as a racist slur; Senator Allen's derogatory comment thus carried the implication that he was criticizing an entire group rather than an individual. This incident is seen as having contributed to Allen's loss in the November election.

The interpretation of a situation as based on group rather than individual identities can be related to underlying beliefs and dispositions as well as to situational factors. In the case of Senator Allen, the Republican candidate defined the incident as taking place between individuals, while his Democratic opponents were attentive to its significance for intergroup relations. Political ideologies have implications for whether situations are interpreted in terms of individual or group identities. Jost (2006) has described the core dimensions underlying ideologies as well as the personality characteristics that are associated with liberal or conservative ideologies. One key factor that distinguishes liberals from conservatives is attitudes toward inequality; conservatives accept greater inequality within a society and liberals prefer greater equality. In order to achieve equality, it is necessary to evaluate the outcomes and the treatment different groups receive and perhaps take action to promote equality. Democratic policies are more likely to attend to possibae disparities among groups than are Republican policies.

Jost (2006), among others (e.g., Pratto & Cathey, 2002) notes that conservatives are also more likely to endorse prejudiced attitudes toward members of disadvantaged groups. Conservatives are more likely than liberals to perceive threats and to fear crime and terrorism. In the U.S., conservatives are more likely to display a U.S. flag, while liberals are more likely to have maps of countries other than the U.S. In all these ways, liberals appear to be more likely to see some fundamental similarities among all people, while conservatives are more likely to make distinctions and to perceive a potentially hostile or competitive relationship between ingroup and outgroup. Political ideology includes beliefs about the appropriate organization of social relationships, including beliefs about how much group identities matter, and consequently beliefs about justice.

IDENTITY AND JUSTICE

Perceptions of Justice: The Impact of Group Identities

Identity has significant implications for perceptions of justice, and vice versa (Clayton & Opotow, 2003). Group identities provide a defining context for the evaluation of justice and injustice, affecting the cognitive representation of sociopolitical events, and thus the evaluation of how fair the situation is as well as what is perceived as a just resolution. Both cognitive and motivational processes contribute to this effect of position on interpretation.

First, identities direct attention to certain phenomena. For example, procedural misdeeds by outgroup members receive more attention than similar behavior by members of the ingroup, with the consequence that outgroup members may be seen to have violated procedural justice and to deserve less in a just allocation of resources. Hastorf and Cantril (1954) provided a classic example of this in their 1954 analysis of an intercollegiate football game: when Princeton students and Dartmouth students watched films of the same game, Princeton students identified twice as many illegal plays by Dartmouth players as the Dartmouth students did. A more recent example found differences in the way Blacks and Whites perceived the aftermath of Hurricane Katrina (Adams, O'Brien, & Nelson, 2006). Blacks more often than Whites perceived the negative outcomes that were disproportionately experienced by Black residents of New Orleans to be evidence of racism – a clear case of unjust behavior by the predominantly White government, equivalent to the illegal plays of the footballers in the Hastorf and Cantril study.

Second, identities have consequences for attributional processes. Perceivers tend to generate more situational attributions for themselves and for people whose perspectives they are able to take, while making dispositional attributions for the behavior of dissimilar others (Storms, 1973). Self-serving biases also come into play: People tend to give themselves and their groups credit for positive outcomes while blaming negative ones on circumstances. However, if an outgroup member is responsible for a negative outcome, it is seen as evidence of incompetence or malign intent, while a positive outcome is attributed to luck. Attributions are made to support our stereotypes (Pettigrew, 1979), with clear implications for perceived justice. For example, whereas African Americans make the dispositional attribution that the inadequate response to Hurricane Katrina by the White authorities was due to racism, Whites may attribute it to the overwhelming nature of the event.

In addition to underlying cognitive processes, outcomes that threaten our group identities are likely to be perceived as unjust and to evoke a corresponding emotional reaction. For example, Conejero and Elxebarria (2007) found that Spaniards responded to the March 2004 bombing in Madrid with more powerful emotions when they had a higher self-identification with Spain. Mullen and Skitka (2006a) suggest that when an issue or outcome violates core moral values, anger at the outcome leads to the conclusion that both distributive and procedural justice have been violated. If group membership is a core component of a person's identity, outcomes that disadvantage a group with which a person strongly identifies may give rise to this type of anger. Such a reaction could be seen following the trial over the Rodney King case, in which White police officers in Los Angeles were accused and acquitted by an all-white jury of beating a Black motorist. An analysis of letters to the editor by Mullen and Skitka (2006b) showed that people expressed more concern about the unjustness of the procedure, and made more accusations of racism, after the verdict was announced. In other words, emotional responses to the outcome, which were tied to the group identities of those involved, had clear implications for the perceived justice of the trial.

Along with post hoc evaluations of the justice of outcomes, people tend to be more motivated to achieve justice for those with whom they share an identity. In laboratory research, Huo (2002) asked university students to read scenarios about groups that were either similar to or different from the ingroup. Participants rated the more similar group as more deserving of economic resources as well as of procedurally fair treatment than the dissimilar group. Wenzel (2000) has argued that judgments of what a target deserves are based on his or her social category. In general, people are likely to show biases in favor of fellow group members when it comes to evaluating their work or allocating resources.

Perhaps because identity matters so much to justice, the reverse is also true. A perception that someone has been treated fairly or unfairly affects the view of that person's identity, and even that person's sense of his or her own status within a group (Tyler & Blader, 2000). Fair treatment connotes some sort of inclusion in the human community. Well-known instances in which serious wrongdoers have been granted due process rights, such as the Nuremberg trials, affirmed a shared humanity and the need to provide basic rights to all people. In contrast, the decision that certain legal rights do not pertain to prisoners being held at the Guantanamo Bay prison depicts a world that is divided between those who merit fair treatment and those devalued outsiders whose status does not qualify them for ethical consideration.

This example illustrates the impact of identity, in that categorizing people as ingroup or outgroup members determines the treatment they are judged to deserve. The criminals in each case are seen either as members of a common group, deserving the standard of justice allotted to all humans, or as members of a different group, who can be treated according to different standards. But there are also underlying beliefs related to a focus on sameness or difference. Republican politicians in the U.S. are more likely to argue that the treatment of the Guantanamo prisoners was deserved, while U.S. opponents of this treatment are more likely to be Democrats. In part, this may be due to shared political identity: people's desire to position themselves in support of a president from the same party or in opposition to a president from the opposing party. It may also reflect a fundamental difference in the beliefs about justice associated with right and left-wing ideologies, with right-wingers more likely to stress differences between ingroup and outgroup members than are those on the political left.

Levels of Justice: The Role of Identity

The distinction between a focus on the individual and a focus on the collective is reflected in different conceptions of justice. Brickman, Folger Goode, and Schul (1981) described an important distinction among different levels of justice, which they called "microjustice" and "macrojustice." Microjustice is concerned with the fairness of rewards to individuals, whereas macrojustice describes the overall fairness of a reward distribution. Justice principles that define a person's outcome in terms of their individual characteristics, such as merit or meeting a required precondition, are microjustice principles. Those that specify characteristics of the distribution, such as a guaranteed minimum outcome, or equality for everyone, are macrojustice principles.

Microjustice and macrojustice are tied to a focus on individuals or on the collective. To apply a microjustice principle, it is necessary to consider people as individuals and to make evaluations of their individual attributes. This does not preclude the influence of group identities, since group membership may be considered a relevant individual characteristic. A woman may be considered more or less qualified for a job, and given more or fewer "points" in a job interview, without any attempt to consider the distribution of jobs to women as a whole. Thus an individual or an ideology may consider group membership to be a very important variable, while still stressing microjustice principles of reward allocation. Macrojustice, however, discourages attention to individual qualifications. As Brickman et al. (1981) state, "Principles of macrojustice are deindividuating" (p. 177). A judgment about macrojustice requires some conception of a collective whole, within which the distribution of outcomes can be assessed.

Emphasizing a particular level of identification affects a focus on micro- or macrojustice. If people are attentive to individual identities, they are likely to make comparisons between themselves and others, perhaps particularly ingroup others. A feeling of solidarity with a group, however, makes people more likely to focus on collective outcomes. Brickman et al. (1981) describe a high degree of group awareness as the cause of a macrojustice orientation. As Wenzel puts it, "Identification with the superordinate category commits people to the justice of the outcome distribution" (2004, p. 74). In general, increased identification with a group has been shown to increase concerns with macrojustice (e.g., DeCremer & Van Vugt, 1999). When a group identity is strong, people are more likely to support macrojustice principles such as equality. Murphy-Berman and Berman (2002) found that people from individualistic cultures were more likely to endorse merit as a distributive principle than were people from collectivist cultures; the latter were more likely to endorse need. (Although need, because it assesses individual characteristics, is ostensibly also a principle of microjustice, Brickman et al. have described it as a "stalking horse" for macrojustice, because it has the intent of ensuring that no one falls below a minimum level.)

Work on relative deprivation has shown that identification with a collective can lead to the recognition of group-level injustices. Women who are more self-identified with women as a whole are more likely to perceive sex discrimination (Crosby, 1982, 1984; Clayton & Crosby, 1992). One's sense of oneself as an individual, or a woman, or an American, can affect the choice of standard against which justice is assessed. A self-identified woman is more likely to consider whether she is making the same salary, or has the same working conditions, as a man, whereas a woman who is less identified with women in general may not think to make such a comparison. Smith, Spears, and Oyen (1994) were able to show that an experimental manipulation of level of identification affected the perceived fairness of an outcome distribution. Individuals primed to think of themselves as group members were more likely to report noticing that the group was disadvantaged than were those who were primed to think of themselves as individuals, and group-primed individuals who were relatively deprived rated the experiment as less fair than did people who were relatively advantaged or individual-primed participants.

Wenzel (2004) clearly describes the way in which self-definition and sense of identification with a collective can affect not only the outcome of a justice judgment but the very type of justice that is salient. In a large Australian sample, Wenzel found that identification with the nation as a whole or with a subgroup determined the impact of perceived justice on tax compliance. Those who identified with the Australian nation but not with a subgroup were more likely to comply with tax laws if they perceived the overall distribution of taxes to be fair – a macrojustice assessment. Those who identified with a smaller group were more likely to comply if they perceived their own individual tax burden to be fair – a microjustice judgment.

A conservative political ideology, with its focus on individualism, should place more emphasis on principles of microjustice. A liberal ideology, however, should privilege macrojustice. The liberal preference for equality is itself an endorsement of a macrojustice principle. In fact, in laboratory research, Brickman et al. (1981) found that Democrats, compared to Republicans, were more likely to endorse macrojustice principles across a variety of policy domains. Survey research suggests that conservatives are more affected than liberals by individual deservingness in determining outcomes, and McClosky and Zaller (1984) define conservatism as in part associated with a preference for differential economic rewards. In a review, Skitka and Mullen (2002) report that conservatives, compared to liberals, are more sensitive to the reason why people contract AIDS or suffer organ failure when deciding whether to support policies to help them. In general, people with a macrojustice orientation are less concerned about attributions of responsibility (Brickman et al., 1981).

Related work is found in research on social dominance orientation (SDO; Pratto, Sidanius, Stallworth, & Malle, 1994). SDO reflects a preference for unequal relations between groups (Pratto & Cathey, 2002). Thus, once people have been acknowledged to have different group identities, SDO will be positively associated with treating people differently on the basis of that group membership. SDO is considered to be a personality variable that may predispose individuals toward an ideological position; politically, SDO is associated with a conservative ideology. The preference, held by those high in SDO, for group-based inequality is compatible with the conservative tendency to attend to group identities.

In addition to predicting attitudes, SDO is expected to influence behavior such that people high in SDO are more likely to take on roles that serve to enhance inequality between groups. SDO is also related to attitudes of hostility toward outgroups, such as racism, sexism, and nationalism (Pratto et al., 1994). Pratto, Tatar, and Conway-Lanz (1999) demonstrated that people high in SDO were likely to favor a merit-based distribution, whereas those low in SDO considered a need-based distribution to be fairer. A consideration of need tends to smooth out the differences in outcomes, whereas a consideration of merit treats people differently based on their personal qualifications. Thus we can see that a preference for different types of relationships among groups is not only associated with preference for outcome distributions that either enhance or minimize group differences, but with acting in a way that tends to bring about those outcomes.

IDEOLOGY, IDENTITY, AND SOCIAL JUSTICE

The link between ideology and level of identity, with consequences for views about justice, can be seen in a variety of social issues. Below I first discuss these processes with regard to two political examples: affirmative action and retributive punishment. I then use a study on animal rights to illustrate the implications of identity for this political issue. Although the political connotations of each example differ, each demonstrates how policy positions are differentially associated with a focus on individual or group identity, and consequently with different conceptions of justice.

Political Examples

Affirmative action is a social issue whose justice is frequently and vehemently debated. Affirmative action entails proactive efforts to avoid discrimination against members of protected groups, in employment and education, by active recognition of group membership. These efforts can include things such as targeted recruiting, special mentoring or training programs, or preference for job or college applicants. Attitudes toward affirmative action reflect the influence of group identities in several ways. First, group-based self-interest is apparent. Members of beneficiary groups, i.e. women and ethnic minorities, are more supportive than non-members, supporting the idea that views about the justice of social policies can protect the interests of the groups to which one belongs. Beyond this, opposition to affirmative action also serves to preserve the identity of those in the majority (Whites and males), not only by protecting their interests, but also by supporting the system within which they occupy a privileged position. A perceived threat from the outgroup, either a real threat-like economic competition or a symbolic threat-like conflicting values, is associated with opposition to affirmative action (Beaton & Tougas, 2001). Position on affirmative action serves to affirm the identities of the groups that are prototypically associated as proponents or opponents.

Second, attitudes toward affirmative action reflect ideologies about the importance of individual or group identity. Liberals are more likely to support affirmative action than are conservatives. One of the objections raised by those who consider it unjust is that it treats individuals as group members. Thus we can conclude not only that group identities are associated with a determination that affirmative action is, or is not, a just procedure but also that attitudes toward affirmative action are associated with attitudes toward treating individuals as group members. As Brickman et al. state, "The debate over affirmative action is largely a debate between micro- and macroprinciples of justice" (1981, p. 196). Those who believe in meritocracy – that individuals are rewarded according to their own qualifications and regardless of their group memberships – find affirmative action to be an unjust system.

Third, affirmative action attitudes reflect attitudes about the appropriate relationships among groups. SDO has been found to be negatively correlated with support for affirmative action (e.g., Pratto et al., 1994), suggesting that affirmative action is perceived to ignore distinctions among members of different groups and treat everyone as equally deserving. This apparently conflicting set of findings, that affirmative action is criticized for focusing on group identity and yet disliked by those who favor group-based distinctions, illustrates the complex role of group identities. Identities can be attended to in order to ensure equality between groups and the well-being of the larger collective, or they can be legitimized as valid markers of distinctions in group deservingness.

A second political example, retributive punishment, refers to the consequences of a crime for the criminal. Such consequences can include extreme violence, such as torture, or death, through capital punishment. Retribution can reflect different motives, including a focus on the offender and what he or she deserves or a focus on the community that has been threatened and damaged by the offence.

Punishing an offender can be undertaken in order to reflect and acknowledge the identity of the offender, which has been determined to be of less value following the crime, by allocating the negative consequences that the individual offender deserves (Wenzel & Thielmann, 2006). It can also be done in order to make a statement about the identity of the community whose rules have been violated, by affirming the values of that identity and restoring social ties within the community. A punishment orientation, then, should be associated with an individualizing tendency – a focus on the criminal and/or the victim and what they deserve. Value restoration, alternatively, should be associated with a collectivist focus on the well-being of the entire community.

Examining qualitatively different responses to criminal acts, Wenzel and Thielmann (2006) hypothesized that a sense of community identity would be positively associated with support for a value restoration approach following a "victimless" crime. Looking at responses to tax evasion and social security fraud among a sample of Australian citizens, they found that community identity was correlated with support for alternative punishments. Those with a stronger sense of Australian identity were more supportive of an alternative punishment, which in turn was correlated with support for value restoration. Similarly, Hamilton and Sanders (1988) found that respondents from a collectivist culture (Japan) were likely to endorse restitutive responses to a norm violation, such as apologies or counseling, whereas those from an individualist culture (the U.S.) supported retributive responses such as firing or loss of privileges.

Reflecting this focus on individual rather than group identity, political conservatives are, in general, more punitive toward offenders than are liberals. SDO also is positively correlated with support for severe criminal sanctions such as capital punishment and torture (Sidanius, Mitchell, Haley, & Navarrete, 2006). It is not surprising that those high in SDO are motivated to distinguish between criminals and non-criminals in allocating outcomes. Assigning them to a group status, that of convicted criminals, which is less valuable or worthy justifies the hostile attitude and retributive punishment.

Animal Rights

Animals as an outgroup are not typically the focus of hostile attitudes. Because there is no real history of conflict between humans and other animals, the decision to support or oppose granting moral consideration to animals rather than leaving them merely subject to human preferences should reflect attitudes about the relationship between the two groups as cognitive categories rather than the human desire to maintain a competitive advantage over animals. In some ways the question of animal rights is a particularly clear case of moral inclusion or exclusion (Opotow, 1990). People who perceive animals to be similar to humans (i.e., a shared identity of sorts) think that animals should be within the scope of justice. However, those who consider animals to be fundamentally different from humans are likely to exclude them from the scope of justice and to oppose animal rights.

In a recent study (Martens, Kosloff, Greenberg, Landau, & Schmader, 2007), people who were relatively high in perceived similarity to bugs were more reluctant to kill bugs unless they had first been induced to kill one or more bugs. If they had first killed five bugs, they actually went on to kill more bugs than those low in perceived similarity, apparently in response to the threat to their self-image evoked by the initial killing.

Recognition of similarity between human and non-human animals, or a sense of shared identity, should lead to the attitude that animals deserve some of the same rights as humans (Allen et al., 2002; Opotow, 1990, 1994; Plous, 1993). The Environmental Identity (EID) scale was developed to measure a sense of shared identity between self and nature (Clayton, 2003). It has been shown to predict pro-environmental behavior and to relate to environmental attitudes as well as to the perception that the natural environment has certain rights. A high level of EID should also be associated with a perception of relatedness between oneself and animals, and with an acknowledgment that the way in which one treats these animals is an ethical issue.

Support for animal rights, however, may also reflect basic beliefs about the importance of group identities. Whereas some people may support animal rights because of a sense of shared identity with animals, others may feel that animals are very different from humans but nevertheless feel that these different identities are of equal value.

To test this hypothesis, a study was conducted to measure EID and SDO as well as support for animal rights. Both SDO and EID were expected to correlate with support for animal rights; SDO negatively and EID positively. EID was expected to show a negative relationship with SDO because an EID is more egalitarian than hierarchical. By focusing on what is shared by both human and non-human animals, as opposed to the distinctions between them, EID, like environmental attitudes, should be more compatible with egalitarian rather than hierarchical beliefs. Research has shown EID to be positively correlated to collectivism and negatively correlated with individualism (Clayton, 2003). Of interest was whether EID would serve to mediate the relationship between SDO and support for animal rights or whether SDO would contribute unique predictive ability. If perceived similarity is the principal predictor of support for animals, then SDO should have no impact when EID is controlled. If, however, animal rights are also predicted by beliefs about non-hierarchical relations between animals and humans, then SDO should contribute independent variance.

Method

Sixty undergraduate students (27 male, 29 female, and 4 whose sex was not specified) completed the EID scale (Clayton, 2003), SDO scale (Pratto et al.,

1994), and a six-item scale measuring support for animal rights (full scale available from the author). They also read about four issues involving questions about the ethical treatment of animals. The order in which materials were presented to participants was randomized.

A sample of a question from the EID scale is: "I think of myself as a part of nature, not separate from it." Respondents indicated on a 7-point scale whether the statement was "Not at all true of me" (1) to "Completely true of me" (7). The SDO includes items such as "All humans should be treated equally." The anchors for the 7-point scales ranged from feeling "Very negative" (1) to feeling "Very positive" (7) about the statement. Finally, the animal rights scale consists of items like "Justice is not only for humans; animals also deserve justice." Respondents noted their agreement with each item, ranging from "Strongly disagree" (1) to "Strongly agree" (7).

Scenarios addressed the four questions:

- Should the slaughter of wild horses be allowed, or should the populations be controlled by alternative, more expensive means such as sterilization or relocation?
- Should the Iditarod sled race be banned because of the potential for suffering of the dogs that pull the sleds?
- Should alternate procedures, which do not cause pain or stress to animals, be undertaken to test new pet food formulas?
- Should veterinarians have ethical standards that prohibit painful and unnecessary cosmetic procedures?

Participants were asked to give their opinion about how the issue should be resolved, on a scale of 1–5, where 1 indicated little support for animal rights and 5 indicated a high level of support. They were also asked to rate their degree of concern about the issue on a 1–7 scale, with a higher score reflecting greater concern.

Results

All scales were reliable: EID had a Cronbach's alpha of .89, SDO had an alpha of .89, and the animal rights scale had an alpha of .81. When the responses to the scenarios were combined to form a single scale, the alpha was .78.

As expected, all variables were significantly correlated (Table 1).

The strongest predictor of responses to the scenarios was support for animal rights, followed by EID and SDO. Regression analyses (Table 2) explored the extent to which EID and SDO contributed separate variance to

Table 1. Correlations among Social Dominance Orientation (SDO), Environmental Identity (EID), Support for Animal Rights, and Animal-Oriented Responses to Scenarios.

	EID	SDO	Animal Rights
SDO	−.28*		
Animal rights	.53***	−.50***	
Response to scenarios	.34**	−.28*	.55***

*$p < .05$. **$p < .01$. ***$p < .001$.

Table 2. Standardized Regression Coefficients for the Effects of SDO, EID, and Animal Rights on Responses to Scenarios.

	Scenario Responses	Animal Rights
SDO	−.04	−.38***
EID	.08	.42***
Support for animal rights	.49***	–
df	(3,55)	(2,57)
F for model	8.01***	20.04***
R^2	.30	.41

***$p \leq .001$.

predicting responses to the scenarios and support for animal rights. In a first analysis, response to the scenarios was regressed on EID, SDO, and support for animal rights.

The relationships between EID and response to these specific scenarios, and between belief in social dominance and response to the scenarios, were completely mediated by support for animal rights (cf. Baron & Kenny, 1986). A second regression analysis was conducted with support for animal rights as the criterion. Both EID and SDO contributed significant independent variance.

The negative relationship between EID and SDO is consistent with previous research suggesting that support for the environment is associated with egalitarian beliefs (Clayton, 1998; Pratto et al., 1994). As expected, EID and SDO are both associated with support for animal rights. However, EID did not mediate the relationship between SDO and animal rights. This supports a conclusion that endorsing animal rights is associated with a preference for egalitarian relations between groups, as well as with other factors associated with an environmental identity.

Discussion: Study Results and Political Examples

The results of the animal rights study along with the political examples illustrate the relevance of group identity to political attitudes. First, the groups to which a person belongs will affect their perception of what is fair. As demonstrated by the role of EID in support for animal rights, of national identity in the study by Wenzel and Thielmann (2006), and of ethnic background in support for affirmative action, a sense of shared identity is important. Second, the prioritization of group membership or of individual characteristics also affects attitudes, as shown most clearly in discussions about affirmative action but also in the difference between a punitive and a value-restoration approach to retribution. Finally, as illustrated by the influence of political ideology and SDO, an emphasis on differentiating groups by allocating different treatment or consequences is also influential in determining political attitudes.

JUSTICE IN THE SERVICE OF GROUP IDENTITY: CONFLICT AND RESOLUTION

Implicit in the discussion of group identities and of the relationship among groups is the possibility of conflict. One of the objections to focusing on group identities, for example in affirmative action programs, is that it can increase the perceived competition, and thus conflict, between groups. Awareness of group identities is fundamental to understanding real-world conflicts, where identities may both encourage and be strengthened by conflict in a self-perpetuating feedback loop. Identities may, perhaps, also be deliberately utilized in order to resolve intergroup conflict.

Although interactions between groups have traditionally been interpreted in terms of group-based self-interest, with each group seeking to have more power or resources for itself, more recent discussions of intergroup behavior have included an examination of social identity processes. As described by Social Identity Theory, group behavior is in part devoted to maintaining and enhancing a positive social identity (Tajfel & Turner, 1986). Conflict may highlight and enhance group identity by making group values more salient through comparison. A positive group identity can be attained by a downward comparison to other groups, in which the other group's characteristics or values are derogated with the effect of enhancing the relative status of the ingroup. Even animals can serve this function. For some people, the maintenance of a positive identity associated with being human appears to be enhanced by negative attitudes toward animals. Thus visitors to zoos can sometimes be heard to derogate the animals, possibly to enhance their own self-image by comparison (Clayton, 2006).

Shared perceptions of justice provide one set of values that can be used to create or strengthen group identity, with social groups defined in part by their standards for justice. Huo (2002), for example, makes the compelling argument that support for relational justice – that is, treating people equally, with respect and dignity – is part of the American ideology. Thus, justice judgments are not merely a consequence of self-interest associated with group identities; they serve to reinforce and legitimize those identities, and follow from the ideologies associated with those groups. A consequence is that violations of justice norms can threaten the very identity of a group. Group members may perceive an obligation to restore justice, and retribution is designed at least in part to do so.

Identification with a group increases the perception of the group's legitimacy (Hegtvedt & Johnson, 2000). Even in an aggressive intergroup conflict, the actions of one's own side are likely to be perceived as legitimate and just (Lickel et al., 2006). By emphasizing group identities, conflict tends to deindividuate actors. This is most striking when retributive aggression is directed at people who were not responsible for the initial aggressive act but merely belong to the same group. A microjustice assessment of whether civilians in a shop, or at a bus stop, deserve to be blown up based on their individual characteristics would almost certainly lead to the conclusion that they do not. However, if the focus is on the macrolevel relations between two groups, then those individuals are guilty by virtue of their membership in the opposing group and their fate is just.

Group identities may not only justify conflict but also be strengthened by it. Conflict tends to increase ingroup cohesiveness (Fisher, 2006). Affirming the values and norms, including justice norms, associated with a particular group serves to preserve the identity of the group and one's own membership in that group. System justification, the tendency to defend existing social arrangements as fair and legitimate, may serve to protect one's identification with a political system. System justification is particularly likely when a threat to the system is perceived. For example, Napier, Mandisodza, Andersen, and Jost (2006) describe the fact that presidential approval ratings in the U.S. went up after the events of 9/11, and also when the terror alert level was raised. In Israel, people exposed to system threat showed greater stereotyping of both high-status (Ashkenazi Jews) and lower-status (Sephardic Jews) groups (Jost, Kivetz, Guermandi,

Rubini, & Mosso, 2005). Whether or not it is deliberate, increasing the perceived threat to a system serves to enhance support for the respective groups and government, and to increase reliance on stereotypes that justify the status quo.

Conflicts may also be maintained because they provide a source of identity for the groups involved, which are defined by their opposition. Opotow and McClelland (2007) discuss the ways in which historical events can contribute to group identities that are based on hostility toward other groups, referring to "the building of community based on righteous victimhood" (p. 79). When group identity is predicated on continued conflict, resolutions to the conflict are unlikely to be seen as just. The conflict between Israelis and Palestinians represents a classic confrontation over identity. According to Kelman (2007), each party "has incorporated negation of the other's identity in its own national narrative" (p. 289), creating a situation in which "acknowledging the other's identity has been seen as tantamount to jeopardizing its own identity and existence" (p. 288). It is difficult for the two sides to negotiate when each sees the other as denying its existence. Conflicts in which a threat is perceived not only to oneself and one's fellow group members but to the fundamental group identity are sometimes described as intractable (Kelman, 2007).

The more group-like or homogeneous a group is perceived to be, the more these identity-focused motives for conflict hinder a search for resolution. Deindividuating outgroup members, for example, leads to resistance to attempts to resolve a conflict (Fisher, 2006). Social psychologists like Herbert Kelman have worked to promote conflict resolution by encouraging individual interactions between people from opposing sides in order to differentiate the enemy image and highlight the identity elements that are shared (Kelman, 1999).

Conflicts between groups may be intractable as long as people retain a high level of identification with those groups. If identifications can be shifted, e.g. to a superordinate group, not only will the salience of the conflict decrease, the conceptions of a just resolution will also change (Sherif, Harvey, White, Hood, & Sherif, 1961). Increased individuation of outgroup members may increase awareness of a shared group membership, at least in the sense of shared humanity. In a laboratory setting, Haslam and Bain (2007) showed that although people tended to dehumanize an abstract "average" student, relative to themselves, they did not show this tendency when they compared themselves to a student who was individuated by information about age, gender, and initials. Although data are sparse, it appears that a similar process may be the case in considering animal rights.

There is some indication that observing animals, which may help to individuate them, leads to greater sympathy to their needs and may foster a heightened sense of commonality between humans and other animals. (Clayton, Fraser, & Saunders, 2008; Hayward & Rothenberg, 2004).

Dovidio et al. (2004) report research with college students in which taking the perspective of an individual outgroup member reduced prejudice toward that outgroup, by encouraging "self-other merging" (p. 1538). They suggest that perspective taking can increase the salience of superordinate categories that include both self and other. Inducing a common identity through experiencing a common threat had a similar effect to that of perspective taking. In a very different context, Kanganyara, Rime, Phillippot, and Yzerbyt (2007) found that participation in a collective justice ritual by both survivors and perpetrators of genocidal actions in Rwanda was able to reduce the negative stereotypes of the outgroup and the perceived homogeneity of the outgroup among both parties. The authors speculate that the shared discussion, with its "reciprocal stimulation of emotion" (p. 389), fostered a state of emotional communion which served to humanize the outgroup.

CONCLUSION

It is not novel to argue that policy opinions, and beliefs about what is just, are linked to group membership. Concern about group interests and the desire for a positive group identity can lead to biased interpretations of relevant inputs and outcomes. Less obvious, perhaps, is the impact of group identity in conflict situations, where a focus on collective rather than individual identities has implications for attitudes and behavior directed toward both the ingroup and the outgroup.

This chapter attempts to illustrate the role of underlying beliefs about identity, and in particular about the significance of group identities, on perceptions of justice. Situations that are fair when evaluated in terms of outcomes to individuals may seem less fair when considering the distribution of outcomes as a whole, and vice versa. There is no solution to this disagreement; both microjustice and macrojustice claims have merit. There are important differences among individuals that may be appropriate to consider when determining a just outcome distribution. However, there are also important ways in which individuals share an identity, and these, too, merit consideration.

The impact of a focus on individual or group identities can be seen in the policies associated with political orientation. Political ideologies differentially focus on individuals or groups; the conservative emphasis on individual differences, and the liberal emphasis on collective well-being, are reflected in the different policy prescriptions associated with the political right and left. This difference may be rooted in personality characteristics such as SDO, and even more fundamental characteristics, such as openness to experience (Jost, 2006), that have been identified by personality psychologists as core dimensions defining individual personalities. Understanding the basis for the difference may enable the two sides to have a more productive debate over the issues.

Perspectives on identities are not only due to underlying personality differences. The salience of individual or collective identities can be strategically manipulated to: promote support for a person or a cause; stimulate conflict; or encourage a resolution. In conflicts between groups, people may be encouraged to deindividuate members of the opposing group, and sometimes even members of their own group. This enables hostile attitudes and aggressive acts toward outgroup individuals that they do not, in a microjustice sense, "deserve." It also affirms ingroup identity in the face of threats to its existence and goals. However, conflict can then become entwined in identities, perceived as an essential and definitional aspect of the groups.

Interventions that encourage individuation of outgroup members and/or promote the salience of a superordinate identity may serve to disentangle the group identities from the conflict. A shift in focus from the characteristics that distinguish people to the characteristics they share may be useful and even necessary to resolve intergroup conflicts in a way that is perceived as just by members of all parties.

ACKNOWLEDGMENTS

Thanks to Jody Clay-Warner, Karen Hegtvedt, and Dahlia Moore for their insightful comments on an earlier draft. The data reported here were presented at the meeting of the International Society for Justice Research in Berlin, Germany, August 2006.

REFERENCES

Adams, G., O'Brien, L., & Nelson, J. (2006). Perceptions of racism in Hurricane Katrina. *Analyses of Social Issues and Public Policy*, *6*, 215–235.

Allen, M., Hunstone, M., Waerstad, J., Foy, E., Hobbins, T., Wikner, B., & Wirrel, J. (2002). Human-to-animal similarity and participant mood influence punishment recommendations for animal abusers. *Society and Animals*, *10*, 267–284.

Baron, R. M., & Kenny, D. A. (1986). The moderator–mediator variable distinction in social psychology research: Conceptual, strategic, and statistic considerations. *Journal of Personality and Social Psychology*, *51*, 1173–1182.

Bar-Tal, D. (2007). Socio-psychological foundations of intractable conflicts. *American Behavioral Scientist*, *50*, 1430–1453.

Beaton, A., & Tougas, F. (2001). Reactions to affirmative action: Group membership and social justice. *Social Justice Research*, *14*, 61–78.

Brickman, P., Folger, R., Goode, E., & Schul, Y. (1981). Microjustice and macrojustice. In: M. J. Lerner & S. C. Lerner (Eds), *The justice motive in social behavior* (pp. 173–202). New York: Plenum Press.

Clayton, S. (1998). Preference for macrojustice versus microjustice in environmental decisions. *Environment and Behavior*, *30*, 162–183.

Clayton, S. (2003). Environmental identity: A conceptual and an operational definition. In: S. Clayton & S. Opotow (Eds), *Identity and the natural environment* (pp. 45–65). Cambridge, MA: MIT Press.

Clayton, S. (2006). Why and how people care for nature. Invited presentation, American Psychological Association, New Orleans.

Clayton, S., & Crosby, F. (1992). *Justice, gender, and affirmative action*. Ann Arbor: University of Michigan Press.

Clayton, S., Fraser, J., & Saunders, C. (2008). Zoo experiences: Conversations, connections, and concern for animals. *Zoo Biology*, *27*, in press.

Clayton, S., & Opotow, S. (2003). Justice and identity: Changing perspectives on what is fair. *Personality and Social Psychology Review*, *7*, 298–310.

Conejero, S., & Elxebarria, I. (2007). The impact of the Madrid bombing on personal emotions, emotional atmosphere and the emotional climate. *Journal of Social Issues*, *63*, 273–287.

Crosby, F. (1982). *Relative deprivation and working women*. New York: Oxford University Press.

Crosby, F. (1984). Relative deprivation in organizational settings. *Research in Organizational Behavior*, *6*, 51–93.

DeCremer, D., & Van Vugt, M. (1999). Social identification effects in social dilemmas: A transformation of motives. *European Journal of Social Psychology*, *29*, 871–893.

Doosje, B., Spears, R., Ellemers, N., & Koomen, W. (1999). Perceived group variability in intergroup relations: The distinctive role of social identities. In: W. Stroebe & M. Hewstone (Eds), *European review of social psychology* (Vol. 10, pp. 41–74). Chichester: Wiley.

Dovidio, J., ten Vergent, M., Stewart, T., Gaertner, S., Johnson, J., Esses, V., Riek, B., & Pearson, A. (2004). Perspective and prejudice: Antecedents and mediating mechanisms. *Personality and Social Psychology Bulletin*, *30*, 1537–1549.

Finkel, N. (2001). *Not fair! The typology of commonsense unfairness*. Washington, DC: American Psychological Association.

Fisher, R. (2006). Intergroup conflict. In: M. Deutsch, P. Coleman & E. Marcus (Eds), *The handbook of conflict resolution, 2/e* (pp. 176–196). San Francisco: Jossey-Bass.

Hamilton, V., & Sanders, J. (1988). Punishment and the individual in the United States and Japan. *Law and Society Review*, *22*, 301–328.

Haslam, N., & Bain, P. (2007). Humanizing the self: Moderators of the attribution of lesser humanness to others. *Personality and Social Psychology Bulletin, 33*, 57–68.
Hastorf, A., & Cantril, H. (1954). They saw a game: A case study. *Journal of Abnormal and Social Psychology, 49*, 129–134.
Hayward, J., & Rothenberg, M. (2004). Measuring success in the *Congo Gorilla Forest* Conservation Exhibition. *Curator, 47*, 261–282.
Hegtvedt, K., & Johnson, C. (2000). Justice beyond the individual: A future with legitimation. *Social Psychology Quarterly, 63*, 298–311.
Huo, Y. (2002). Justice and the regulation of social relations: When and why do group members deny claims to social goods? *British Journal of Social Psychology, 41*, 535–562.
Jost, J. (2006). The end of the end of ideology. *American Psychologist, 61*, 651–670.
Jost, J., Guermandi, G., Rubini, M., & Mosso, C. (2005). System-justifying functions of complementary status stereotypes. *Social Justice Research, 18*, 305–333.
Judd, C., & Park, B. (1988). Out-group homogeneity: Judgments of variability at the individual and group levels. *Journal of Personality and Social Psychology, 54*, 778–788.
Kanganyara, P., Rime, B., Phillippot, P., & Yzerbyt, V. (2007). Collective rituals, emotional climate, and intergroup perception. *Social Justice Research, 63*, 387–403.
Kelman, H. (1999). The interdependence of Israeli and Palestinian national identities: The role of the other in existential conflicts. *Journal of Social Issues, 55*, 581–600.
Kelman, H. (2007). The Israeli-Palestinian peace process and its vicissitudes. *American Psychologist, 62*, 287–303.
Klein, O., Spears, R., & Reicher, S. (2007). Social identity performance: Extending the strategic side of SIDE. *Personality and Social Psychology Review, 11*, 28–45.
Lerner, M. J. (1980). *The belief in a just world.* New York: Plenum Press.
Lickel, B., Miller, N., Stenstorm, D., Denson, T., & Schmader, T. (2006). Vicarious retribution: The role of collective blame in intergroup aggression. *Personality and Social Psychology Review, 10*, 372–390.
Martens, A., Kosloff, S., Greenberg, J., Landau, M., & Schmader, T. (2007). Killing begets killing: Evidence from a bug-killing paradigm that initial killing fuels subsequent killing. *Personality and Social Psychology Bulletin, 33*, 1251–1264.
McClosky, H., & Zaller, J. (1984). *The American ethos: Public attitudes toward capitalism and democracy*. Cambridge, MA: Harvard University Press.
Miller, A. (2004). What can the Milgram obedience experiments tell us about the Holocaust? In: A. Miller (Ed.), *The social psychology of good and evil* (pp. 193–239). New York: Guilford.
Mullen, E., & Skitka, L. (2006a). Exploring the psychological underpinnings of the moral mandate effect: Motivated reasoning, group differentiation, or anger? *Journal of Personality and Social Psychology, 90*, 629–643.
Mullen, E., & Skitka, L. (2006b). When outcomes prompt criticism of procedures: An analysis of the Rodney King case. *Analyses of Social Issues and Public Policy, 6*, 1–14.
Murphy-Berman, V., & Berman, J. J. (2002). Cross-cultural differences in perceptions of distributive justice. *Journal of Cross-Cultural Psychology, 33*, 157–170.
Napier, J., Mandisodza, A., Andersen, S., & Jost, J. (2006). System justification in responding to the poor and displaced in the aftermath of Hurricane Katrina. *Analyses of Social Issues and Public Policy, 6*, 57–73.
Opotow, S. (Ed.). (1990). Moral exclusion and injustice. *Journal of Social Issues, 46*(1).
Opotow, S. (1994). Predicting protection: Scope of justice and the natural world. *Journal of Social Issues, 50*(3), 49–63.

Opotow, S., & McClelland, S. (2007). The intensification of hating: A theory. *Social Justice Research, 20*, 68–97.

Pettigrew, T. (1979). The ultimate attribution error. *Personality and Social Psychology Bulletin, 5*, 461–476.

Plous, S. (1993). Psychological mechanisms in the human use of animals. *Journal of Social Issues, 49*, 11–52.

Pratto, F., & Cathey, C. (2002). The role of social ideologies in legitimizing political attitudes and public policy. In: V. Ottati, R. S. Tindale, J. Edwards, F. Bryant, L. Heath, D. O'Connell, Y. Suarez-Balcazar & E. Posavac (Eds), *The social psychology of politics* (pp. 135–155). New York: Kluwer.

Pratto, F., Sidanius, J., Stallworth, L. M., & Malle, B. F. (1994). Social dominance orientation: A personality variable predicting social and political attitudes. *Journal of Personality and Social Psychology, 67*, 741–763.

Pratto, F., Tatar, D., & Conway-Lanz, S. (1999). Who gets what and why: Determinants of social allocations. *Political Psychology, 20*, 127–150.

Sherif, M., Harvey, O., White, B., Hood, W., & Sherif, C. (1961). *Intergroup conflict and cooperation: The Robbers Cave experiment.* Norman, OK: University of Oklahoma Institute of Intergroup Relations.

Sidanius, J., Mitchell, M., Haley, H., & Navarrete, C. (2006). Support for harsh criminal sanctions and criminal justice beliefs: A social dominance perspective. *Social Justice Research, 19*, 433–449.

Skitka, L., & Mullen, E. (2002). Psychological determinants of public opinion. In: V. Ottati, R. S. Tindale, J. Edwards, F. Bryant, L. Heath, D. O'Connell, Y. Suarez-Balcazar & E. Posavac (Eds), *The social psychology of politics* (pp. 107–134). New York: Kluwer.

Smith, H., Spears, R., & Oyen, M. (1994). "People like us:" The influence of personal deprivation and group member salience on justice evaluations. *Journal of Experimental Social Psychology, 30*, 277–299.

Sommers, S., Apfelbaum, E., Dukes, K., Toosi, N., & Wang, E. (2006). Race and media coverage of Hurricane Katrina. *Analyses of Social Issues and Public Policy, 6*, 39–55.

Storms, M. (1973). Videotape and the attribution process. *Journal of Personality and Social Psychology, 27*, 165–175.

Tajfel, H., & Turner, J. (1986). The social identity theory of intergroup behavior. In: S. Worchel & W. Austin (Eds), *Psychology of intergroup relations* (pp. 7–24). Chicago: Nelson-Hall.

Tyler, T., & Blader, S. (2000). *Cooperation in groups: Procedural justice, social identity, and behavioral engagement*. Philadelphia: Psychology Press.

Wenzel, M. (2000). Justice and identity: The significance of inclusion for perception of entitlement and the justice motive. *Personality and Social Psychology Bulletin, 26*, 157–176.

Wenzel, M. (2004). Social identification as a determinant of concerns about individual-, group-, and inclusive-level justice. *Social Psychology Quarterly, 67*, 70–87.

Wenzel, M., & Thielmann, I. (2006). Why we punish in the name of justice. *Social Justice Research, 19*, 450–470.

IS PROCEDURAL JUSTICE ENOUGH? AFFECT, ATTRIBUTION, AND CONFLICT IN ALTERNATIVE DISPUTE RESOLUTION

Jessica L. Collett

ABSTRACT

Since its inception in the 1970s, procedural justice has taken center stage in research on the outcomes of alternative dispute resolution. Such perceptions of procedural fairness, while important, are fairly transient whereas relationships between disputants endure. In the following chapter I argue that more research should explore the relational outcomes of dispute resolution, highlighting relevant insight from social exchange and organizational behavior on affect, attribution, and conflict. In discussing how each can add to the study of alternative dispute resolution, a paradox emerges – arbitration may be better for ongoing relationships than mediation, although the latter is considered more procedurally just.

Trends in corporations, communities, and couples suggest that, in the United States especially, alternatives to traditional litigation are growing in popularity and are often quite successful at settling disputes (Burgess & Burgess, 1997; Morrill, 2006). The broad term for these innovative

Justice
Advances in Group Processes, Volume 25, 267–289

ISSN: 0882-6145/doi:10.1016/S0882-6145(08)25003-4

resolution strategies and processes is alternative dispute resolution, or ADR. Although such alternatives to court-based adjudication date back hundreds of years, a relatively recent movement has brought these types of conflict resolution into new realms, including the family, the workplace, and government agencies.

Increasing interest in the practice of ADR has subsequently amplified attention in research as well, especially concerns over the procedural fairness of various conflict resolution processes (e.g. Tyler, 2002). While perceptions of procedural justice (Leventhal, Karuza, & Fry, 1980; Lind & Tyler, 1988; Thibaut & Walker, 1975, 1978) – the perceived fairness of the procedures – are important, given that most conflict resolution occurs between individuals with ongoing relationships (Brockner, 2002), it is time to turn our attention more pointedly to the disputants (McEwen, 1999; Pillutia & Murnighan, 2003; Sacks, Reichart, & Proffitt, 1999).[1]

To date it has been largely assumed that mediation is better for continuing relationships than processes with higher levels of third party intervention (e.g. arbitration) because perceptions of fairness of the process should lead to a variety of positive outcomes, including preserving the relationship between disputants (Tyler, Boeckmann, Smith, & Huo, 1997; Tyler, Degoey, & Smith, 1996; Tyler & Lind, 1992). In the following chapter I reveal a paradox of arbitration. Drawing on theories in both social exchange and organizational behavior, I provide a rationale for why increased levels of third party intervention in arbitration might actually be better for ongoing relationships than the procedural fairness of mediation. In doing so I argue that research should move beyond the almost exclusive focus on procedural justice when studying alternative dispute resolution and instead center on the "relational outcomes" of these conflict resolution processes. Disputants' perceptions of one another (fairness, general positive regard) and their relationship have lasting effects, including implications for the tone of future interactions, long after the processes are over.

BACKGROUND

Alternative Dispute Resolution

The term alternative dispute resolution includes any resolution strategy that serves as an alternative to litigation. In practice, negotiation – where two parties negotiate the terms of a settlement themselves – is the most prevalent type of alternative dispute resolution (e.g. Bazerman, Curhan, Moore, & Valley, 2000; Jacob, 1992). However, I focus my attention here on the two processes that involve a third party and that are most common in research on conflict resolution – mediation and arbitration.

Although mediation takes many forms, it represents a situation where an intermediary is involved in the resolution process by relaying requests, offers, and information between parties so that the disputants are not required to interact one-on-one (Rebach, 2001). Mediators' roles vary immensely – some counsel, others address points of compromise, and still others just act as the go-between and keep conflicting parties from having to deal with one another directly. The key attribute of mediation is that in this type of conflict resolution, the disputing parties ultimately decide the outcome themselves (Wall, Stark, & Standifer, 2001). It is also important to note that mediation is often non binding, meaning that the parties can choose whether or not to comply with the final agreement.

Arbitration, however, is generally binding and parties are obligated to fulfill their end of agreements. Like mediation, arbitration comes in many forms. However, in most arbitration processes the two parties state their cases and, after considering the range of the evidence, the arbitrator makes a ruling. This is the key attribute of arbitration: it is the arbitrator, not the conflicting parties, who ultimately decides the outcome. A new form of arbitration, "final-offer," emerged recently in response to the often unreasonable demands of disputants in arbitration. Unlike in traditional arbitration, arbitrators in final-offer arbitration are restricted to selecting one of the two parties' proposed terms of settlement. This arguably makes disputants' proposals more reasonable to enhance their attractiveness to the arbitrator (Chelius & Dworkin, 1980; Marburger, 1994). This, in turn, helps to limit the differences between the proposed offers and to lessen the competitive nature of arbitration.

The key differences between mediation and arbitration, regardless of the specific type in question, are the processes involved in reaching an agreement and who ultimately decides on that outcome. In mediation, the two disputants, with the help of a mediator, work with one another to come to an agreement and the disputants have the final say on the outcome. Because the two disputants are so involved in the process and the outcome, the third party's role is relatively minor. This represents a low level of intervention. In arbitration, however, each disputant interacts with the arbitrator, not one another, during the process and the arbitrator determines the final decision, not the disputants. In other words, there are high levels of third party intervention in arbitration.

As more courts, organizations, and individuals turn to these alternatives, it is imperative that research keep pace and ask new questions about the benefits and drawbacks of these processes. Specifically, I suggest we should weigh the potential benefits of procedural justice that come with low levels of third party intervention against the potential drawbacks of increased task interdependence.

Procedural Justice

Procedural justice, in instrumental terms, is the amount of perceived control a procedure affords a disputant or the efficacy one feels in shaping the process and determining the outcome (Thibaut & Walker, 1975, 1978). The more control a disputant has, the more just the procedure. In conflict resolution, this type of control is a zero-sum game – the more process and decision control a third party wields, the less disputants have, and vice versa. As a result, procedural justice ratings in types of conflict resolution are negatively related to third party intervention (Karambayya & Brett, 1989), and mediation is considered fairer than arbitration, which, in turn, is fairer than adjudication.

Other important components of procedural justice emerged after Thibaut and Walker's (1975, 1978) innovative research program. Leventhal et al. (1980) outlined criteria for fair procedures including: suppression of bias, consistency, representation of all parties' interests, accuracy of information, ethicality, and correctability. Greenberg (Greenberg & Folger, 1983) highlighted the importance of voice for disputants' perceptions of procedural justice. Finally, Lind and Tyler (1988, 1992) introduced the group-value model and the relational model. The group-value model argues that procedures are fair if they promote within-group relationships and provide participants with information about their own place in the group, while the relational model (1992) highlights standing, neutrality, and trust as important antecedents for perceptions of procedural justice. Research supports each of these conceptualizations (see Tyler, 1988, 2002 for examples), and these theories serve as an important rationale for promoting meditation over heavier-handed approaches like arbitration and adjudication (e.g. Applebey, 2002; Porter & Taplin, 1987; Tyler, 2002).[2]

Research indicates that there are a number of benefits of procedural fairness. Perceptions of procedural justice enhance perceptions that outcomes are also fair, create more positive attitudes toward authorities, and produce a variety of positive behavioral reactions (Tyler et al., 1996,

1997; Tyler & Lind, 1992). In other words, this research suggests that if individuals think the *process* – the way that the agreement was reached – is fair, then they will likely think of the final decision as fair and the third party (if there's one present) as fair as well. Further, research suggests that judgments about procedural fairness are similar across gender (Lind, Huo, & Tyler, 1994), cultural groups (Lind, Tyler, & Huo, 1997), and countries (Cohn, White, & Sanders, 2000). However, while many have assumed, few have tested, whether the procedural justice offered by mediation positively impacts the relationship between disputants.

Addressing Assumptions about Mediation

According to MacDougall (1984), there are four criteria for assessing conflict resolution processes: their effectiveness in ending the dispute, the cost of the process, the justice of the process and outcome, and the promotion of social goals. While there is substantial – although often contradictory – research on the first three criteria in mediation, the last one has been largely ignored by scholars and practitioners. The assumption that mediation promotes social goals in the sense of enhancing the future relationship of disputing parties is just that – a widely accepted, and largely unchallenged, assumption (Ogus, Jones-Lee, Cole, & McCarthy, 1990; Walker, 2002).

For instance, while Applebey (2002) alludes to the importance of the ongoing relationships of disputants in a chapter on alternative dispute resolution and justice, he *assumes* that mediation is the preferred method of conflict resolution for individuals with continuing contact. Without citing any research he asserts that when a relationship is to continue, a solution brought about, or agreed upon, by both parties is *thought to be* more acceptable than one imposed by a court of law (Applebey, 2002). He supports this statement with the "*perception* among many that litigation [exacerbates] the hostility between the parties to divorce and that this [has] a particularly harmful effect on the children involved" (Applebey, 2002, p. 36, italics added). However, there is research that suggests that mediation does not improve the post-dispute climate between parties. Further, this is true in a range of types of disputes, including community disputes, divorces, and international conflicts (Kressel & Pruitt, 1989; Pearson & Thoennes, 1989; Toews & McKenry, 2001; Walker, 2002; Wall & Lynn, 1993).

In a publicly funded study of post-divorce outcomes in the United Kingdom, Walker found that mediation "did not necessarily resolve the dispute and as one issue was settled, others seemed to emerge. At the end of [the] study, many couples were still in disagreement about a range of issues" (2002, p. 38). Mediation is also not as successful in improving the communication between conflicting parents or increasing the well-being of disputants as some might assume (Burgess & Burgess, 1997). Research in the United States by Toews and McKenry (2001) finds similar results. Involvement in divorce mediation versus traditional court proceedings was actually a predictor for greater post-divorce conflict among parents (Toews & McKenry, 2001). Because of these pitfalls and others, Block (1991) recommends arbitration as an alternative to divorce mediation.

To reconcile the assumptions about mediation and the above research, those concerned with justice and conflict resolution must follow Block (1991) and others (e.g. MacCoun, 2005; Pillutia & Murnighan, 2003; Sacks et al., 1999) and consider the implications mediation might have beyond perceptions of procedural fairness. Theories in social psychology and organizational behavior that have been often overlooked in research on conflict resolution and procedural justice offer considerable insight in this important line of inquiry.

INTEGRATING "NEW" THEORETICAL APPROACHES

Theories of affect (Lawler, 2001), attribution (Heider, 1958; Jones & Davis, 1965; Kelley, 1972), and conflict (Hegtvedt & Killian, 1999; Molm, Collett, & Schaefer, 2006; Thompson & Loewenstein, 1992), while hardly new in social psychology, are remarkably absent in research on mediation and alternative dispute resolution. In this section I formulate a theoretical model (Fig. 1) that describes the mediating effects of task interdependence, affect, attributions, and conflict, in the relationship between level of third party intervention and relationships outcomes.[3], [4] I then discuss avenues for further research.

Level of Intervention and Task Interdependence

Task interdependence, or jointness of task, stems from structural interdependencies (Lawler, 2001; Lawler & Thye, 1999). Any mediation process is, by definition, high on task interdependence as mediation implies mutual consensus (Porter & Taplin, 1987). In mediation, the two parties

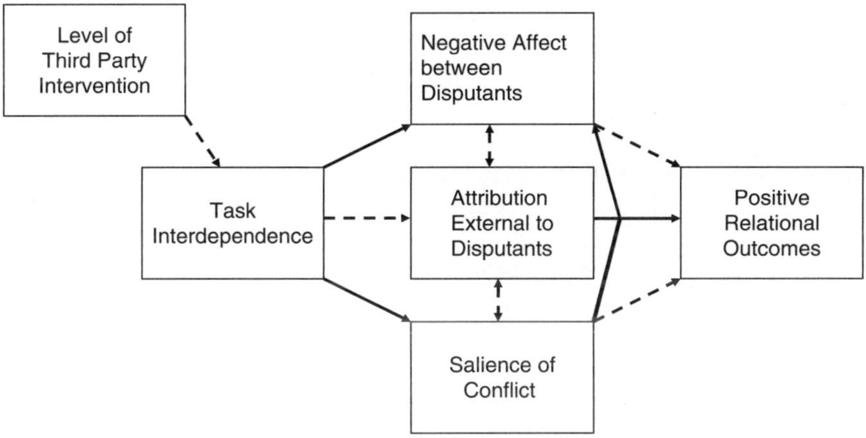

Fig. 1. Third Party Intervention, Task Interdependence, Cognitive and Affective Processes, and Relational Outcomes. *Note:* Solid Lines Represent Positive Relationships, Dashed Lines Negative Ones.

work together, with third party intervention of varying degrees, to reach a decision. The dialogue of offers and counter-offers can continue back and forth for quite some time. The decision is ultimately made by the disputing parties and mutually agreed upon before it is finalized. The mediator has no control over the settlement or enforcing it. With the non-binding nature of most mediation, it is up to the two disputants to uphold their commitments to any agreement.

Arbitration, however, entails very little task interdependence. The two parties make a request to the arbitrator – a proposed dispute settlement – and it is up to the arbitrator to determine the final outcome. Not only is interdependence lessened, but the direction of interaction shifts as well. The parties are not relying on one another to come to an agreement. They interact with the arbitrator before, during, and after the settlement decision; they do not interact with one another. Arbitration is a one-shot deal, without the back and forth of negotiations in mediation, and decisions are binding.

In other words, as illustrated in Fig. 1, level of third party intervention is negatively related to the degree of task interdependence. It is this task interdependence that is most important for the level of affect, the type and target of attributions, and the salience of conflict in a dispute resolution processes and these, in turn, affect relational outcomes.

The Role of Affect

Social psychologists have become increasingly interested in both affective and cognitive responses to exchange. Affective responses in this research are typically general evaluations of exchange partners or the group (Lawler & Yoon, 1993, 1996, 1998; Lawler, Yoon, & Thye, 2000; Molm, Collett, & Schaefer, 2007), while common cognitive concerns are attributions of blame and perceptions of distributive, procedural, and interactional justice (Hegtvedt & Killian, 1999; Molm et al., 2006; Molm, Quist, & Wiseley, 1994; Molm, Takahashi, & Peterson, 2000, 2003).[5] Most of this research is in the social exchange tradition (Blau, 1964; Emerson, 1972; Homans, 1961), which examines how individuals (e.g. exchange partners, disputants) obtain and contribute benefits in social interaction (Molm & Cook, 1995). While early research in this tradition focused on power and inequality in exchange relations and networks (Molm & Cook, 1995, p. 209), recent attention has shifted to other outcomes of exchange, including perceptions of justice, conflict, affect, and attributions (Hegtvedt & Killian, 1999; Lawler & Yoon, 1993, 1996, 1998; Lawler et al., 2000; Molm et al., 1994; Molm et al., 2000; Molm et al., 2003; Molm et al., 2006; Schaefer, Molm, & Collett, 2004; Takahashi, 2000).

Corresponding with this growth in research on exchange outcomes, Lawler (2001) formalizes an *affect theory of social exchange*. The theory offers six theoretical propositions, but essentially argues (1) that exchange outcomes, whether rewards or punishments, have emotional effects, and (2) the degree of jointness of task or interdependence that exchange partners share influences the salience of the relation as the target of these emotions or cognitions (Lawler, 2001, p. 322). For example, Lawler's own findings (e.g. Lawler et al., 2000; Lawler & Yoon, 1993, 1996, 1998) suggest that *positive* outcomes (specifically reaching agreements) produce *positive* emotions, which are then attributed to the group to the degree that there was task interdependence. The more people work together to exchange successfully, the more they attribute the positive emotions generated by completed exchanges to the group and their social relations. These attributions, in turn, enhance commitment to the group.

Although Lawler has focused on positive emotion (e.g. Lawler et al., 2000; Lawler & Yoon, 1993, 1996, 1998), his theory (2001) argues that a negative outcome – like failing to make an agreement, accepting an unfair agreement, or receiving less than one expects or feels they deserve – should produce negative emotion (anger toward the other or shame toward the self). In addition, the greater the jointness of task or shared responsibility in a disappointing outcome, the more likely the resulting negative emotion is attributed to the relation or social unit, or directly at the other person (Lawler, 2001). In other words, rather than enhancing commitment, such attributions could exacerbate conflict between disputants.

Unfortunately, in alternative dispute resolution, such negative emotions are common (Tyler, 2002). The main cause of this is the conflict of interests, or the non-correspondent nature of the dispute (Thibaut & Walker, 1975, 1978), where the benefit of one comes at the expense of another. Further, most individuals engaged in alternative dispute resolution do not fare as well as they hoped and perceive the outcome as unfair (Melli, 1991; Tyler, 2002).[6] Therefore, under conditions of high conflict of interest – where negative emotions are likely, and the other party or the relation are assumed to be the source of this affect – increased task interdependence should be positively related to negative affect between disputants. Fig. 1 illustrates this relationship.

Tyler (2002) uses divorce as an example when he asserts that in many dispute settlements, people are dissatisfied with the outcome:

> In divorce cases, for example, both parties often begin without any real awareness of the extent to which their life-style will be affected by the division of marital assets. Both parties imagine themselves unrealistically well-off after the settlement. In such a situation both are likely to end up receiving less than they expect and feel that they deserve in the settlement. (p. 20)

Although Tyler uses this example to support the importance of procedural justice in such disputes, it might be interpreted differently. Imagine the different perceptions an individual would have leaving a mediator's office, where the decision was made, in part, by the person they are divorcing. Compare that to the experiences and perceptions of someone leaving a courtroom where the judge or arbitrator is the one who made the final, and disappointing, decision. In either case, the affect would be negative, but the target and level of the harmful emotion would vary with interdependence. Mediation's higher levels of interdependence would create higher levels of negative affect as well, and the negative affect would be directed toward the other disputant.

In an extension of social exchange to situations involving a third party, I suggest that according to the affect theory of social exchange, arbitration – where there is very little jointness of task – should produce much less affect (which, in this case, would be negative) than mediation. Therefore, arbitration should lessen animosity toward the other disputant and enhance relational outcomes. In other words, despite arbitration's lower level of procedural fairness, the process might be better for relational outcomes than mediation. Because there is less jointness of task in arbitration than mediation and because arbitration's decision maker is someone external to the relationship, the other disputant and the relationship between disputants are less likely to be the target of the negative affect produced by a disappointing outcome. Of course, central to this process is the connection between affect and attribution.

The Role of Attributions

Throughout our daily lives we observe events and behavior, and the effects of those, and we ask ourselves why it is that things happen or why people do what they do. When we make inferences about the causes of such events and actions, we are making causal attributions. Attribution theory (Heider, 1958; Jones & Davis, 1965; Kelley, 1972) is the second social psychological theory under-represented in work on conflict resolution. For Lawler (2001), attributions are important because the emotion felt during exchange is more likely to be attributed to the relation if the exchange has high task interdependence. Individuals recognize their emotional state, search for a source of that emotion, and, with the salience of the relation in a mutual task, attribute the cause of the emotion to the relation (Lawler, 2001). Although significant, attribution is an important concern in conflict resolution for other reasons as well. The two key attributions are those regarding *blame for the outcome* (Is it my fault, the other disputant's fault, or the third party's fault that things turned out this way?) and *the causes of behavior* (Is it the process or the other disputant's personality that is leading her to act this way?). Both can significantly impact reactions individuals have to perceived injustice (Cohen, 1982; Homans, 1961; Shepelak, 1987; Utne & Kidd, 1980).

While recent research in social exchange has incorporated attributions in considerations of justice (Hegtvedt & Killian, 1999; Molm et al., 2006), the majority of new research and theoretical development is in the area of organizational behavior. Organizational behavior, or OB, a dimension of organizational studies, draws heavily from social psychology as it explores individual and group dynamics in organizational life. Organizational behavior's interest in attributions includes both the sources and effects of attributions on employee, employer, and customer reactions to negative events and perceptions of organizational justice (e.g. Beugré, 2005; Conlon & Murray, 1996; Kim, Dirks, Cooper, & Ferrin, 2006; Shaw, Wild, &

Colquitt, 2003) – including distributive, procedural, and interactional justice (Cropanzano, Prehar, & Chen, 2002; Greenberg, 1990; Roch & Shanock, 2006).

In organizations, and in other areas of social life, attributions can be situational (i.e. external, attributed to aspects of the situation or surroundings) or dispositional (i.e. internal, stemming from personality or stable characteristics of self or other). These work in a hydraulic fashion – as situational factors increase in salience, dispositional attributions for outcomes or behavior decrease (Kelley, 1972). Although there is a strong tendency to make dispositional attributions about another's actions (Ross, 1977), it is reasonable to assume that attributing another disputant's actions or a disappointing outcome to external, or situational, influences would help mitigate his or her blame (Kim et al., 2006). These forces external to the disputants and their relationship are particularly important in the case of negative events because such events elicit more consideration of causal information than positive or neutral events (Folger, 1986; Kim & Smith, 2005; Wong & Weiner, 1981).

Research on justice and attributions suggests that in a situation where an individual fares less well than they think they deserve, as in most non-correspondent disputes, they will seek out a reason as to why this happened (Cohen, 1982; Hegtvedt & Johnson, 2000; Kidd & Utne, 1978). This is particularly true when they could have imagined a different scenario (Folger, 1986), as many disputants do who engage in alternative dispute resolution. To preserve a positive view of self, they will try to blame someone or something else for the disappointing outcome (Brockner, 2002; Shepelak, 1987). This could be the disposition of another or it could be something about the situation. Because searching for situational information is a cognitively strenuous activity, such attributions are most likely when external forces are a salient aspect of the event (Hassebrauck, 1987; Ployhart & Harold, 2004).

Attributions people make for the cause of their treatment and outcomes significantly impact their reactions to such events (Ployhart & Harold, 2004). While dispositional attributions lead to aggressive cognitions, situational attributions of blame flatten aggression (Beugré, 2005). Recent research in organizations suggests that situational explanations have other positive benefits as well. External explanations for transgressions increase trust and cooperation, decrease retaliation and withdrawal, and can improve justice judgments (e.g. Kim et al., 2006; Kim & Smith, 2005; Shaw et al., 2003). Also, when mitigating circumstances are clear *before* a wrongdoing there is less physiological arousal and negative affect than when they are brought to light after the event (Beugré, 2005; Johnson & Rule, 1986).

While the recent organizational behavior research focuses on individuals' accounts of situational circumstances (i.e. excuses, explanations, justifications), the same rationale could be applied to a salient external force like third party intervention in a conflict resolution process. The more third party intervention and the less task interdependence, the more accessible a source of attribution or blame that is external from the two conflicting parties becomes to the participants. Blaming this factor that is external to the other disputant (the resolution process or the disposition of a different target, the third party) for the other disputant's behavior will lessen the likelihood that one would make negative dispositional attributions.

Attributions of blame for the outcome should shift as well. When a third party is responsible for determining a negative outcome, the disappointed individual will attribute responsibility to the third party or the process. The blame is taken off the other individual (Blount, 1995), and the third party or the dispute resolution process should shoulder the negative affective responses. Deflecting blame to a third party or the process should improve relational outcomes, lessen the post-dispute conflict, and enhance future interactions (Utne & Kidd, 1980).

In other words, task interdependence is negatively related to attributions of blame for behavior or the outcome that are external to the other disputant. For instance, in mediation, the divorcing couple will be responsible for the final outcome. This increases the likelihood that blame for behavior or events will be attributed internally, to the other disputants' disposition or the relationship between the disputants, which may have negative consequences if the outcome is disappointing. In arbitration, however, where the arbitrator makes the final decision, a divorcing husband might decide that his wife's request for a substantial amount of the settlement is a natural product of the arbitration process or that the fact she was actually awarded that amount as a result of the arbitrator's own bias.

Because of the self-serving bias, individuals take credit for good things that happen and place blame for bad things that occur (Miller & Ross, 1975). As a result, the husband in the above example would be unlikely to take responsibility for a disappointing outcome. Thus, if the husband were directly involved in the settlement process, as he would be in mediation, he might attribute both his wife's behavior and the unfair settlement to her personality or her contemptuous views of him. In arbitration, a self-serving attribution that does not include a disparaging view of the other disputant is possible because task interdependence is low.

Therefore, as illustrated in Fig. 1, arbitration, with lower task interdependence and with salient factors external to the disputants, should generate more external attributions for both the other disputant's behavior and the final outcome. This lessens the likelihood that the other disputant will shoulder blame for negative events and should result in more positive relational outcomes. Further, attributing the other disputants' behavior, or the outcome, to external forces like the arbitration process or the arbitrator will also lessen negative affect and the salience of conflict between disputants.

The Role of (Salience of) Conflict

It is important to consider the salience of conflict inherent in even the most procedurally just of resolution processes. Task interdependence likely increases salience of conflict. The more salient the conflict is in a situation – that is the more aware two disputants are of their opposed interests – the more likely that each disputant will view the process in a self-interested manner (Hegtvedt & Killian, 1999; Molm et al., 2003, 2006). In such situations fairness judgments become more egocentric, and individuals are more concerned with the comparison of their outcome to others' than with the absolute value of their own outcome (Thompson & Loewenstein, 1992). This leads to greater levels of dissatisfaction, with the outcome and with the other party. Further, the more salient the conflict, the more intent attributed to the other disputant (Hegtvedt & Killian, 1999). While situational attributions for outcomes or behavior should reduce the blame attributed to the offending party – lessening disapproval of, and anger toward, that individual – and decrease the level of conflict between the parties (Sitkin & Bies, 1993), recent research in social exchange suggests that third party intervention might reduce conflict in other ways.

Although social exchange research has yet to incorporate third parties (see Collett, 2006 for an exception), I argue that current theoretical developments in the area of conflict (Molm et al., 2006) are relevant to alternative dispute resolution. The more conflictual a relation seems, and the more competitive one considers an exchange partner, the more salient the conflict. Molm et al. (2003, 2006) document the salience of conflict in negotiated exchange, which is viewed as a procedurally fair and cooperative process (Lawler, 2001; Lawler & Yoon, 1993, 1996, 1998; Molm, Peterson, & Takahashi, 1999). This research suggests that the same attributes that make negotiation a structurally cooperative process – the back and forth nature of requests and offers, concessions necessary for agreements, and joint decision making – also work to heighten the salience of conflict between exchange partners (Molm et al., 2006). The salience of conflict, in turn, leads to higher levels of negative affect (toward outcomes and exchange partners) in negotiated versus other forms of exchange (Molm et al., 1999, 2003, 2006; Schaefer et al., 2004).

Mediation shares many of negotiation's conflictual qualities, particularly mediation processes with minimal third party involvement. While mediation is designed to lessen the intensity of conflict in bargaining by eliminating direct negotiations between disputants, many of the conflict-heightening features of negotiation remain intact. In mediation, like negotiation, the two parties exchange offers and counter-offers in a back and forth process. Each counter-offer suggests a failed attempt at reaching an agreement, heightening the salience of conflict between disputants. The nature of agreements increases the salience of conflict as well, with the benefit to one so clearly coming at the concession of another (Hegtvedt & Killian, 1999; Molm et al., 2003). In mediation, like negotiation, there is a clear relationship between one disputant's gain and another's loss (Molm et al., 2006). Finally, in mediation, like in negotiation, actors' outcomes are easily compared, and unequal outcomes are perceived as an intentional consequence of an exchange partner's behavior – acts of commission (Molm et al., 2003, 2006).

Arbitration processes should reduce this conflict substantially, particularly because they are lacking in the cooperative, interdependent features discussed earlier with regard to the affect theory of social exchange (Lawler, 2001). First, disputants in arbitration interact with the arbitrator, not the other disputant. This limits any conflict-inducing interaction between them. Second, disputants are only allowed to make one proposal to the arbitrator, which he or she grants or does not, eliminating the back and forth process of mediation. There are no failed attempts at agreement in arbitration, only outcomes that might be perceived as just or unjust. Third, benefits for one come from the arbitrator's decisions, not the concessions of the other. Finally, in arbitration the disputants' positions seem opposed to the arbitrator, not one another. This should increase the focus on how the arbitrators' settlement benefited them, and lessen thoughts of how their share compared with the other disputants'.

In sum, the conflict disputants are addressing during alternative dispute resolution is not only what they brought with them but also the conflict brought about by the dispute resolution process. Task interdependence greatly increases the salience of this latter conflict, which has the potential of being higher in mediation than arbitration. The salience of this conflict can also influence perceptions of fairness (distributive and interactional) directly and affect relational outcomes (Molm et al., 2006). In other words, in a process with lower task interdependence, like arbitration, the salience of conflict should be reduced, which, because conflict is negatively related to relational outcomes, should result in more positive relational outcomes than in mediation.

To summarize the theoretical model illustrated in Fig. 1, level of third party intervention in alternative dispute resolution should be positively related to relational outcomes. This is expected because third party intervention decreases task interdependence which, in turn, decreases negative affect, increases the likelihood of external attributions for the other disputant's behavior and the disappointing outcome, and reduces the salience of conflict. Each of these should increase perceptions of fairness of, and general positive regard toward, the other disputant, as well as ease future conflict and interactions between the conflicting parties.

CONCLUSION

The idea that arbitration, ostensibly a less procedurally fair process, could be more beneficial for disputing parties than mediation is the ultimate sociological irony (Anderson & Sharrock, 1983). However, it is a consideration that deserves further thought. Procedural justice took center stage in social psychological research on conflict resolution in the 1970s and has remained there because of its positive impact on perceptions of outcome fairness and on attitudes toward the third party. With the majority of disputes settled with alternative dispute resolution occurring between individuals who have continued contact after leaving the mediator's office or agreeing to contract terms, though, it is important for researchers and practitioners to turn their attention toward how procedural justice and third party intervention affects perceptions disputants have of one another.

Such relational outcomes are the focus of recent research in both organizational behavior and social exchange theory. Organizational behavior has experienced a significant growth of research on interactional justice, or fair treatment (Bies, 2002; Bies & Moag, 1986), and its positive effects for future interactions between individuals. There is a burgeoning attention to perceptions of interactional fairness in social exchange theory as well (Molm et al., 2006). In addition to these perceptions of fairness of exchange partners, exchange research is also exploring general positive regard and emotional responses between exchange partners (Lawler &

Yoon, 1993, 1996, 1998; Lawler et al., 2000; Molm et al., 2000, 2003, 2007), as well as their optimism about positive future interactions (Collett, 2006).

This chapter presents three social psychological theories that have potential in expanding research on the "relational effects" of third party intervention in conflict resolution – the affect theory of social exchange (Lawler, 2001), attribution theory (Heider, 1958; Jones & Davis, 1965; Kelley, 1972), and recent work on conflict in social exchange (Hegtvedt & Killian, 1999; Molm et al., 2006). However, there is further work to be done in social psychology to test the applicability of these to conflict situations both in the laboratory and beyond.

First, while Lawler and Yoon's work (1993, 1996, 1998; Lawler, 2001) calls attention to the potential benefits of affect and attribution, this line of inquiry should be further pursued in both social exchange and alternative dispute resolution to address negative affect and its implications for attributions and relationships as well. Mediation is not guaranteed to end in an agreement or to result in individuals following through with terms. Future research in this area should look at the effect of *perceived* fairness of agreements (as those who fare best may perceive their outcomes as less fair (Collett, 2006; Melli, 1991)) and failed agreements on affect and attributions. In addition, work should be done to include neutral third parties in the exchange processes explored in work on social exchange more broadly, but also in work on affect and social exchange.

Second, there is much more work to be done with regard to the effect of third party intervention on attributions. While a great deal of recent work in organizational behavior explores the potential benefits of external attributions, these attributions are explicitly articulated by one person to another (e.g. Kim et al., 2006; Kim & Smith, 2005; Ployhart & Harold, 2004; Shaw et al., 2003). In this chapter I assert that such external forces could be inferred by the salience of the third party intervention in the resolution process (Collett, 2006), but further research should test this directly. In addition, research must explore how third party presence affects the potential targets of attributions, particularly self-serving attributions, and the effects of internal and external attributions on emotion, conflict, and ongoing relations.

Finally, following the lead of social exchange research (Molm et al., 2006), there must be renewed attention to the importance of conflict in alternative dispute resolution. Mediation flourishes because people assume that it is less conflictual than arbitration or litigation. I argue that this is not necessarily true and that the mediation process has the potential to make conflict more salient between disputants than arbitration. It is important to note that the mediation I refer to throughout this chapter is an abstract form and the ideas set forth here are not applicable to all mediation processes. There are mediation processes with the explicit aim to teach parties to deal with conflict and to establish the foundation for a harmonious post-dispute relationship. However, it should not be assumed that all mediation fits this bill or achieves these goals. Practitioners and researchers alike must recognize that conflict exists, not only between parties who seek to resolve disputes, but also in the process of dispute resolution, itself. Only when this conflict is recognized can it be effectively addressed.

To this end, future research must move beyond exploring how conflict going into the dispute affects the resolution process and also look to how the resolution process affects the salience of conflict between parties. Does a neutral third party exacerbate or ameliorate conflict between disputants, and how does increased intervention affect the salience of conflict? Research must also explore the effects of this conflict on perceptions disputants have of one another, the outcome, the process, and the third party, and how each of these impacts the ongoing relationship between the disputants.

In conclusion, this chapter opens up an interesting and important line of inquiry, the effect of third party intervention on relational outcomes. It also cautions against the proliferation of mediation without research into the benefits and drawbacks of such an approach, particularly for the individuals involved. Recent social psychological research and theory in affect, attribution, and conflict offers insight to this end, and should be extended to include situations with a neutral third party. In addition to this expanded focus in social psychology, it is time for research in alternative dispute resolution to move beyond perceptions of procedural justice and the positive effects of such perceptions and to explore perceptions disputants have of one another and the powerful effects that those perceptions have on life after the dispute.

NOTES

1. This chapter does not address distributive justice – the perceptions of fairness of outcomes (Adams, 1965; Homans, 1961; Jasso, 1980) – primarily because distributive justice's role in research on alternative dispute resolution has been dwarfed by an overwhelming focus on procedural justice. This is not to say that distributive justice is unimportant, as clearly it is (e.g. Barrett-Howard & Tyler, 1986). This chapter's main goal is not to argue that procedural justice is the only type of justice that matters in conflict resolution, but to move future work in conflict resolution toward new social psychological frameworks and concerns.

2. It is important to note that even Thibaut and Walker (1978) suggest that in instances of high conflict of interests, as in the vast majority of disputes resolved with ADR, arbitration would be a more beneficial process to all the parties involved than negotiation (i.e. bargaining) or mediation. They cite the distribution of process and decision control as key. Arbitration affords the disputants control over the process but assigns decision control to the third party, which is vital when the disputants are unlikely to be able to reach an agreement on their own.

3. This model is taken, in part, from Collett (2006). I thank Jody Clay-Warner and Karen Hegtvedt for suggestions on this reformulation.

4. The theoretical model is only applicable in situations where there is a conflict of interests and there is no outcome that would mutually benefit the disputants. Instead, the benefit of one party only comes at the expense of the other.

5. Interactional justice (Bies, 2002; Bies & Moag, 1986) is specifically concerned with the quality and fairness of interaction between individuals (Cropanzano et al., 2002).

6. Melli (1991) and Collett (2006) actually found that the parties with the best settlements (measured in percentage of assets earned) were among the least satisfied with the settlement outcome.

ACKNOWLEDGMENTS

These ideas emerged during the writing of my dissertation, and I thank my committee members – Linda Molm, Henry Walker, Mark Chaves, and Kieran Healy – for their guidance during that process. I also benefited from comments of Omar Lizardo, Jody Clay-Warner, and Karen Hegtvedt provided on earlier drafts and the research assistance of Ellen Childs.

REFERENCES

Adams, J. S. (1965). Inequity in social exchange. *Advances in Experimental Social Psychology*, *2*, 267–299.

Anderson, D. C., & Sharrock, W. W. (1983). Irony as a methodological theory: A sketch of four sociological variations. *Poetics Today*, *4*, 565–579.

Applebey, G. (2002). Alternative dispute resolution and the civil justice system. In: K. J. Mackie (Ed.), *A handbook of dispute resolution: ADR in action* (pp. 26–42). New York: Routledge.

Barrett-Howard, E., & Tyler, T. R. (1986). Procedural justice as a criterion in allocation decisions. *Journal of Personality and Social Psychology*, *50*, 296–304.

Bazerman, M. H., Curhan, J. R., Moore, D. A., & Valley, K. L. (2000). Negotiation. *Annual Review of Psychology*, *51*, 279–314.

Beugré, C. D. (2005). Understanding injustice-related aggression in organizations: A cognitive model. *International Journal of Human Resource Management*, *16*, 1120–1136.

Bies, R. S. (2002). Interactional (in)justice: The sacred and the profane. In: J. Greenberg & R. Cropanzano (Eds), *Advances in organizational justice* (pp. 89–118). Stanford, CA: Stanford University Press.

Bies, R. S., & Moag, J. S. (1986). Interactional justice: Communication criteria of fairness. In: R. J. Lewicki, B. H. Sheppard & M. H. Brazerman (Eds), *Research on negotiations in organizations* (Vol. 1, pp. 43–55). Greenwich, CT: JAI Press.

Blau, P. M. (1964). *Exchange and power in social life*. New York, NY: Wiley.

Block, R. R. (1991). Divorce arbitration: An alternative to mediation. In: R. L. Brown (Ed.), *Encyclopedia of matrimonial practice* (pp. 521–529). Englewood Cliffs, NJ: Prentice Hall.

Blount, S. (1995). When social outcomes aren't fair: The effect of causal attributions on preferences. *Organizational Behavior & Human Decision Processes*, *63*, 131–144.

Brockner, J. (2002). Making sense of procedural fairness: How high procedural fairness can reduce or heighten the influence of outcome favorability. *The Academy of Management Review*, *27*, 58–76.

Burgess, H., & Burgess, G. M. (1997). *Encyclopedia of conflict resolution*. Santa Barbara, CA: ABC-CLIO.

Chelius, J. R., & Dworkin, J. B. (1980). An economic analysis of final-offer arbitration as a conflict resolution device. *Journal of Conflict Resolution*, *24*, 293–310.

Cohen, R. L. (1982). Perceiving justice: An attributional perspective. In: J. Greenberg & R. L. Cohen (Eds), *Equity and justice in social behavior* (pp. 119–160). New York: Academic Press.

Cohn, E. S., White, S. O., & Sanders, J. (2000). Distributive and procedural justice in seven nations. *Law and Human Behavior*, *24*, 553–579.

Collett, J. L. (2006). *Third-party intervention and relationship outcomes: Extending social exchange theory through the incorporation of intermediaries*. Unpublished dissertation. University of Arizona.

Conlon, D. E., & Murray, N. M. (1996). Customer perceptions of corporate responses to product complaints: The role of explanations. *Academy of Management Journal*, *39*, 1040–1056.

Cropanzano, R., Prehar, C. A., & Chen, P. Y. (2002). Using social exchange theory to distinguish procedural from interactional justice. *Group Organization Management*, *27*, 324–351.

Emerson, R. (1972). Exchange theory, Part I: A psychological basis for social exchange and exchange theory, Part II: Exchange relations and networks. In: J. Berger, M. Zelditch Jr. & B. Anderson (Eds), *Sociological theories in progress* (pp. 38–87). Boston, MA: Houghton Mifflin.

Folger, R. (1986). Rethinking equity theory: A referent cognitions model. In: H. M. Bierhoff, R. L. Cohen & J. Greenberg (Eds), *Justice in social relations* (pp. 145–162). New York: Plenum Press.

Greenberg, J. (1990). Organizational justice: Yesterday, today, and tomorrow. *Journal of Management*, *16*, 399–432.

Greenberg, J., & Folger, R. (1983). Procedural justice, participation, and the fair process effect in groups and organizations. In: P. B. Paulus (Ed.), *Basic group processes* (pp. 235–256). New York: Springer.

Hassebrauck, M. (1987). The influence of misattributions on reactions to inequity: Towards a further understanding of inequity. *European Journal of Social Psychology*, *17*, 295–304.

Hegtvedt, K., & Killian, C. (1999). Fairness and emotions: Reactions to process and outcomes of negotiations. *Social Forces*, *78*, 269–302.

Hegtvedt, K., & Johnson, C. (2000). Justice beyond the individual: A future with legitimation. *Social Psychology Quarterly*, *63*, 298–311.

Heider, F. (1958). *The psychology of interpersonal relations*. New York: Wiley.

Homans, G. C. (1961). *Social behavior: Its elementary forms*. New York: Harcourt, Brace and World.

Jacob, H. (1992). The elusive shadow of the law. *Law and Society Review*, *26*, 565–590.

Jasso, G. (1980). A new theory of distributive justice. *American Sociological Review*, *45*, 3–32.

Johnson, T. E., & Rule, B. G. (1986). Mitigating circumstance information, censure, and aggression. *Journal of Personality and Social Psychology*, *50*, 537–542.

Jones, E. E., & Davis, K. E. (1965). From acts to dispositions: The attribution process in social psychology. In: L. Berkowitz (Ed.), *Advances in experimental social psychology* (Vol. 2, pp. 219–266). New York: Academic Press.

Karambayya, R., & Brett, J. (1989). Managers handling disputes: Third party roles and perceptions of fairness. *Academy of Management Journal*, *32*, 687–704.

Kelley, H. H. (1972). Attribution in social interaction. In: E. E. Jones, D. E. Kanouse, H. H. Kelley, R. E. Nisbett, S. Valins & B. Weiner (Eds), *Attribution: Perceiving the causes of behavior* (pp. 1–26). Morristown, NJ: General Learning Press.

Kidd, R. F., & Utne, M. K. (1978). Reactions in inequity: A prospective on the role of attributions. *Law and Human Behavior*, *2*, 301–312.

Kim, P. H., Dirks, K. T., Cooper, C. D., & Ferrin, D. L. (2006). When more blame is better than less: The implications of internal vs. external attributions for the repair of trust after a competence – vs. integrity – based trust violation. *Organizational Behavior and Human Decision Processes*, *99*, 49–65.

Kim, Y. K., & Smith, A. K. (2005). Crime and punishment: Examining customers' responses to service organizations' penalties. *Journal of Service Research*, *8*, 162–180.

Kressel, K., & Pruitt, D. G. (1989). Conclusion: A research perspective on the mediation of social conflict. In: K. Kressel & D. Pruitt (Eds), *Mediation research* (pp. 394–436). San Francisco, CA: Jossey-Bass.

Lawler, E. J. (2001). An affect theory of social exchange. *American Journal of Sociology*, *107*, 321–352.

Lawler, E. J., & Thye, S. R. (1999). Bringing emotions into social exchange theory. *Annual Review of Sociology*, *25*, 217–244.

Lawler, E. J., & Yoon, J. (1993). Network structure and emotion in exchange relations. *American Sociological Review*, *63*, 871–894.

Lawler, E. J., & Yoon, J. (1996). Commitment in exchange relations: Test of a theory of relational cohesion. *American Sociological Review*, *61*, 89–108.

Lawler, E. J., & Yoon, J. (1998). Network structure and emotion in exchange relations. *American Sociological Review*, *63*, 871–894.

Lawler, E. J., Yoon, J., & Thye, S. R. (2000). Emotion and group cohesion in productive exchange. *American Journal of Sociology*, *106*, 616–657.

Leventhal, G. S., Karuza, J., Jr., & Fry, W. R. (1980). Beyond fairness: A theory of allocation preferences. In: G. Mikula (Ed.), *Justice and social interaction*. New York: Springer.

Lind, E. A., Huo, Y. J., & Tyler, T. R. (1994). And justice for all: Ethnicity, gender, and preferences for dispute resolution procedures. *Law and Human Behavior*, *18*, 269–290.

Lind, E. A., & Tyler, T. (1988). *The social psychology of procedural justice*. New York: Plenum Press.

Lind, E. A., Tyler, T., & Huo, Y. J. (1997). Procedural context and culture: Variations in the antecedents of procedural justice judgments. *Journal of Personality and Social Psychology*, *73*, 767–780.

MacCoun, R. J. (2005). Voice, control, and belonging: The double-edged sword of procedural fairness. *Annual Review of Law and Social Science*, *1*, 171–201.

MacDougall, D. J. (1984). Negotiated settlement of family disputes. In: J. Eekelaar & S. N. Katz (Eds), *The resolution of family conflict: Comparative legal perspectives*. Toronto, ON: Butterworths.

Marburger, D. R. (1994). Bargaining power and the structure of salaries in major league baseball. *Managerial and Decision Economics*, *15*, 433–441.

McEwen, C. A. (1999). Toward a program-based ADR research agenda. *Negotiation Journal*, *15*, 325–338.

Melli, M. S. (1991). Bargaining under no fault divorce. In: R. L. Brown (Ed.), *Encyclopedia of matrimonial practice* (pp. 286–291). Englewood Cliffs, NJ: Prentice Hall.

Miller, D. T., & Ross, M. (1975). Self-serving biases in the attribution of causality: Fact or fiction? *Psychological Bulletin*, *82*, 213–225.

Molm, L. D., Collett, J. L., & Schaefer, D. R. (2006). Conflict and fairness in social exchange. *Social Forces*, *84*, 2325–2346.

Molm, L. D., Collett, J. L., & Schaefer, D. R. (2007). Building solidarity through generalized exchange: A theory of reciprocity. *American Journal of Sociology*, *113*, 205–242.

Molm, L. D., & Cook, K. S. (1995). Social exchange and exchange networks. In: K. S. Cook, G. A. Fine & J. S. House (Eds), *Sociological perspectives on social psychology* (pp. 209–235). Boston, MA: Allyn and Bacon.

Molm, L. D., Peterson, G., & Takahashi, N. (1999). Power in negotiated and reciprocal exchange. *American Sociological Review*, *105*, 1396–1427.

Molm, L. D., Quist, T. M., & Wiseley, P. A. (1994). Imbalanced structures, unfair strategies: Power and justice in social exchange. *American Sociological Review*, *59*, 98–121.

Molm, L. D., Takahashi, N., & Peterson, G. (2000). Risk and trust in social exchange: An experimental test of a classical proposition. *American Journal of Sociology*, *105*, 1396–1427.

Molm, L. D., Takahashi, N., & Peterson, G. (2003). In the eye of the beholder: Procedural justice in social exchange. *American Sociological Review*, *68*, 128–153.

Morrill, C. (2006). *Institutional change through interstitial emergence: The growth of alternative dispute resolution in American law, 1965–1995*. Unpublished manuscript. University of California, Irvine.

Ogus, A., Jones-Lee, M., Cole, W., & McCarthy, P. (1990). Evaluating alternative dispute resolution: Measuring the impact of family conciliation on costs. *The Modern Law Review*, *53*, 57–74.

Pearson, J., & Thoennes, N. (1989). Divorce mediation: Reflections on a decade of research. In: K. Kressel & D. Pruitt (Eds), *Mediation research* (pp. 9–30). San Francisco, CA: Jossey-Bass.

Pillutia, M. M., & Murnighan, J. K. (2003). Fairness in bargaining. *Social Justice Research*, *16*, 241–262.

Ployhart, R. E., & Harold, C. M. (2004). The applicant attribution-reaction theory (AART): An integrative theory of applicant attributional processing. *International Journal of Selection & Assessment*, *12*, 84–98.

Porter, J., & Taplin, R. (1987). *Conflict and conflict resolution: A sociological introduction*. New York: University Press.

Rebach, H. (2001). Mediation and alternative dispute resolution. In: H. M. Rebach & J. G. Bruhn (Eds), *Handbook of clinical sociology* (Vol. 2, pp. 197–224). New York: Kluwer Academic Press.

Roch, S. G., & Shanock, L. R. (2006). Organizational justice in an exchange framework: Clarifying organizational justice distinctions. *Journal of Management*, *32*, 299–322.

Ross, L. (1977). The intuitive psychologist and his shortcomings: Distortions in the attribution process. In: L. Berkowitz (Ed.), *Advances in experimental social psychology* (Vol. 10, pp. 173–220). New York: Academic Press.

Sacks, M. A., Reichart, K. S., & Proffitt, W. T., Jr.. (1999). Broadening the evaluation of dispute resolution: Context and relationships over time. *Negotiation Journal*, *15*, 339–345.

Schaefer, D. R., Molm, L. D., & Collett, J. L. (2004). Risk, trust and solidarity: Explaining effects of the form of exchange. Presented at the American Sociological Association annual meeting, San Francisco, CA.

Shaw, J. C., Wild, W., & Colquitt, J. A. (2003). To justify or excuse? A meta-analytic review of the effects of explanations. *Journal of Applied Psychology*, *88*, 444–458.

Shepelak, N. J. (1987). The role of self-explanations and self-evaluations in legitimating inequality. *American Sociological Review*, *52*, 495–503.

Sitkin, S. B., & Bies, R. J. (1993). Social accounts in conflict situations: Using explanations to manage conflict. *Human* Relations, *46*, 349–371.

Takahashi, N. (2000). The emergence of generalized exchange. *American Journal of Sociology*, *105*, 1105–1134.

Thibaut, J. W., & Walker, L. (1975). *Procedural justice: A psychological analysis*. New York: Wiley.

Thibaut, J. W., & Walker, L. (1978). A theory of procedure. *California Law Review*, *66*, 541–566.

Thompson, L. L., & Loewenstein, J. (1992). Egocentric interpretations of fairness and interpersonal conflict. *Organizational Behavior & Human Decision Processes*, *51*, 176–197.

Toews, M., & McKenry, P. (2001). Court-related predictors of parent cooperation and conflict after divorce. *Journal of Divorce and Remarriage*, *35*, 57–73.

Tyler, T. (1988). What is procedural justice?: Criteria used by citizens to assess the fairness of legal procedures. *Law and Society Review*, *22*, 103–135.

Tyler, T. (2002). Procedure or result: What do disputants want from legal authorities? In: K. J. Mackie (Ed.), *A handbook of dispute resolution: ADR in action* (pp. 19–25). New York: Routledge.

Tyler, T., Degoey, P., & Smith, H. (1996). Understanding why the justice of group procedures matters: A test of the psychological dynamics of the group-value model. *Journal of Personality & Social Psychology*, *70*, 913–930.

Tyler, T., & Lind, E. A. (1992). Relational model of authority in groups. In: M. P. Zanna (Ed.), *Advances in experimental social psychology* (Vol. 25, pp. 115–191). San Diego: Academic Press.

Tyler, T. R., Boeckmann, R. J., Smith, H. J., & Huo, Y. J. (1997). *Social justice in a diverse society*. Boulder, CO: Westview.

Utne, M. K., & Kidd, R. F. (1980). Equity and attribution. In: G. Mikula (Ed.), *Justice and social interaction* (pp. 63–93). New York: Springer.

Walker, J. (2002). Family conciliation: From research to practice. In: K. J. Mackie (Ed.), *A handbook of dispute resolution: ADR in action* (pp. 134–145). New York: Routledge.

Wall, J. A., Jr., & Lynn, A. (1993). Mediation: A current review. *Journal of Conflict Resolution, 37*, 160–194.

Wall, J. A., Jr., Stark, J. B., & Standifer, R. L. (2001). Mediation: A current review and theory development. *Journal of Conflict Resolution, 45*, 370–391.

Wong, P. T.. P., & Weiner, B. (1981). When people ask 'why' questions, and the heuristics of attributional search. *Journal of Personality and Social Psychology, 40*, 650–663.

THE SYMBOLIC MEANING OF TRANSGRESSIONS: TOWARDS A UNIFYING FRAMEWORK OF JUSTICE RESTORATION

Tyler G. Okimoto and Michael Wenzel

ABSTRACT

This chapter proposes and provides evidence for a conceptual framework for understanding the restoration of justice. Specifically, there is a fundamental distinction between two primary symbolic concerns that follow from transgressions: concern over the status/power relations between the involved parties, and over the violation of the values those parties expect to share. Recognizing these concerns is paramount to understanding the psychological needs of injustice victims, how they conceptualize the restoration of justice, and the processes by which various interventions instill feelings of justice. This framework also elucidates when alternative avenues towards justice might be more effective than traditional retributive responses.

Much of the research in the field of justice has focused on understanding why and under what conditions people care about fairness, as well as attempting to recognize the individual, group, and societal-level outcomes

Justice
Advances in Group Processes, Volume 25, 291–326

ISSN: 0882-6145/doi:10.1016/S0882-6145(08)25004-6

associated with fairness. Such an understanding is imperative to effectively manage those outcomes by *promoting* fairness and *preventing* injustice. However, injustice (and conflict more generally) is unavoidable, and surprisingly little research has been done focusing on *restoring* justice. This is highlighted by the fact that, despite significant advances in our understanding of justice processes, there continues to be widespread victim dissatisfaction and disillusionment with current judicial policy. What exactly *do* people want done in response to an injustice, and why?

In this chapter, we propose a theoretical framework that aids our understanding of responses to injustice. Specifically, we suggest that there is a fundamental distinction that can be identified in the literature between two types of concerns that follow from the experience of injustice – concerns that stem from two primary *symbolic implications* of transgressions. First, transgressions can upset the status and power balance between offenders, victims, and society as a whole. When victims interpret an injustice as a disruption of this status and power equilibrium, their status/power becomes a principal concern, relative to the offender and within the group in which the injustice occurred. Second, transgressions can violate values that victims expect to share with the offender due to their personal relationship or common membership in a group or society. When victims interpret an injustice as a threat to these shared values, the validity of those values becomes a principal concern. We argue that concerns over these two symbolic implications affect victim attitudes and behaviors following a transgression, and any injustice response *must* address a victim's salient concerns about status/power, values, or both, in order to be considered satisfactory and restore their sense of justice (Wenzel, Okimoto, Feather, & Platow, in press).

While any justice violation has the potential to elicit both concerns to varying degrees, the relative importance of each is dependent on a number of contextual and/or dispositional variables. Herein lies the difficulty that may underlie widespread victim dissatisfaction with legal policies – institutionalized guidelines (based on offence type) dictate the injustice response rather than victim concerns. Any transgression may be subjectively construed as either undermining the victim's status/power or shared values, making the match between offence type and resolution extremely variable in its acceptability. Given this difficulty, we propose that distinguishing between and recognizing these two fundamental injustice concerns can assist in a greater understanding of what people want done in response to injustice and how to go about addressing those concerns.

This chapter serves as an exploration of these two psychological concerns. We first examine these concerns as they are discussed in the injustice literature and suggest key contextual factors that, based on theory and empirical research, determine when each concern is most salient. Second, we will examine injustice reparations commonly used in public, organizational, and legal policy, and briefly discuss the relevant research literature in order to identify how these responses might address the two concerns. Finally, we will suggest that these two fundamental concerns are indicative of a broader understanding of how to achieve justice. Specifically, we outline a framework for conceptualizing *two distinct lay-philosophical notions of justice* (Okimoto, Wenzel, & Feather, in press; Wenzel et al., in press; Wenzel & Thielmann, 2006) – a *retributive notion* where justice is dependent on the unilateral imposition of punishments, versus a *restorative notion* where justice is dependent on bilateral dialogue and consensus between the involved parties.

VICTIM CONCERNS UNDERLYING TRANSGRESSIONS

When a transgression has occurred, a number of different concerns may drive a victim's need to see something done about the offence.[1] As research in the injustice literature has shown, transgressions are breaches of distributive (e.g., Lerner, 1991; Wenzel, 2004) and/or procedural (e.g., Sunshine & Heuer, 2002; Tyler & Lind, 1992) rules and norms that determine the entitlements of their victims. Violations of distributive fairness undermine entitlements to outcomes, whereas violations of procedural fairness undermine entitlements to unbiased and consistent decision-making procedures and interpersonal treatment (for review see Tyler, Boeckmann, Smith, & Huo, 1997). As such, victims may firstly be concerned with the violation of their distributive and procedural entitlements.

When such entitlements have been violated, victims often demand some type of compensatory response. Actions must be taken that re-establish distributive and procedural fairness – outcomes must be fairly re-distributed and the procedures that gave rise to feelings of injustice must be rectified before the injustice response will be seen as satisfactory. This notion of restoring the situation to an earlier state of affairs or undoing the harm done by the offence through restitution, reparations, or policy changes, underlies what researchers have termed *compensatory justice* (Darley & Pittman, 2003).[2]

Such compensatory actions must undo all aspects of the harm to the victim, not just material losses. For example, if a victim is robbed of something that carries emotional value (e.g., a family heirloom), fair compensation would reimburse those emotional losses as well as the material ones. And if the harm of the offence cannot be undone, compensation of equivalent value must be provided (but see also Fiske & Tetlock, 1997).

While the restoration of distributive and procedural fairness may be necessary for a satisfactory injustice response, such compensatory justice alone is often not sufficient. As Darley and Pittman (2003) suggest, particularly when an offence is seen as intentional, equitable compensation is not enough. Even in negligent acts, if the offender is assigned responsibility for the victim's losses, restitution is insufficient (Okimoto & Tyler, 2007). Punishments assigned to an offender are often more severe than equity standards dictate (Darley & Pittman, 2003; Horai, 1977), suggesting that something must be done about the transgression *beyond* undoing of the harm. Why is compensatory justice insufficient? What motivates these demands for some additional response to rule-breaking?

One possible motive underlying the need for an additional sanctioning response is the desire for behavior control – to deter the offender (and other observers) from repeating similar offences. Such concerns over the prevention of future violations may be addressed by increasing the expected penalty for future transgressions and communicating to all parties that "crime does not pay." However, despite widespread use of behavior control as a justification of severe criminal penalties (Nagin, 1998), there is inconsistent evidence regarding the effectiveness of punitive forms of behavior control (such as monetary penalties or incarceration) for motivating future adherence to societal rules (e.g., MacCoun, 1993; Ross, 1981; Tyler, 2006). Furthermore, psychological research has suggested that demands for additional punishments beyond compensatory justice are *not* due to deterrence motives but rather to the *restoration of justice* (Carlsmith, Darley, & Robinson, 2002; Darley, Carlsmith, & Robinson, 2000).

The remainder of this chapter focuses on this need to restore justice. Based on recent theory regarding the distinction between retributive and restorative notions of justice (Wenzel et al., in press), we suggest that beyond issues of behavior control and compensatory justice, transgressions have *two primary symbolic implications* that underlie desires for justice. Specifically, transgressions elicit demands for justice because they upset the status/power relations between the involved parties, as well as violate values that those parties are expected to share. As such, when these concerns are salient, justice demands their restoration.

Status/Power Concerns

Through their transgression, offenders symbolically (and in many cases actually) remove power from their victims (Heider, 1958). By intentionally violating shared rules or norms, the offender steals a victim's control, and the victim's status relative to the offender is demeaned. Hence, injustice victims feel disempowered and humiliated as a result of a transgression. As asserted by Murphy and Hampton (1988), "Intentional wrongdoing insults us and attempts (sometimes successfully) to degrade us" (p. 25). Many injustice theorists have suggested that this status and power implication of transgressions is at the core of injustice reactions (e.g., Heider, 1958, Miller, 2001; Murphy & Hampton, 1988), and that it is our concern with the offender's usurping of undeserved status/power that elicits strong injustice responses. While status and power are separate concepts, they are closely linked (Thye, Willer, & Markovsky, 2006) and both define the victim–offender relationship as competitive (the two parties struggle over relative hierarchy, control, or resources). As such, they are treated as a single type of concern in our current analysis.

For example, imagine that an academic finds out that a colleague had unfairly disparaged her work to others behind her back. This transgression may be interpreted primarily as an attempt by the offender to diminish the victim's status, perhaps with the goal of making the offender look good at the victim's expense. Such a diminishing of status (and perhaps usurping of control over one's own reputation) may elicit desires not only to rectify the misperceptions of others resulting from the offence (i.e., restoration of fair outcomes), but also to restore feelings of justice.

Notably, these status and power concerns can be relevant in all types of conflicts, not just interpersonal conflicts as discussed above. In *intragroup* contexts, in addition to diminished status relative to the offender, injustice victims may also question their *membership status* in the relevant group (Okimoto, in press a, in press b). As relational models of justice suggest (Tyler & Lind, 1992; Tyler & Blader, 2003), fairness judgments affect the extent to which individual group members evaluate their standing within the group, particularly if the offender's beliefs are seen as representative of the entire group, such as when the offender is an authority figure or a prototypical group member (Tyler, Degoey, & Smith, 1996). Status and power concerns may also be elicited at the *intergroup* (between-group) level, where offenders (and/or the group they represent) undermine the status/power of the victims' group. The offender's contempt for the victims' group and what it stands for diminishes their status/power and social identity

(Tajfel & Turner, 1979). Status/power concerns may also be particularly salient in intergroup situations where the offender is an outgroup member, as outgroups are often assumed to be negatively interdependent with the ingroup – the increased status/power of competing outgroups is tied to the diminished ingroup status/power (Sherif, 1966). Indeed, a recent study by Okimoto and Wenzel (2007a) investigating reactions to terrorism suggests that transgressions which attempt to diminish the victimized group's status/power threaten a group's social identity more when committed by an outgroup compared to an ingroup offender, particularly when respondents strongly identify with the victimized group.

Value Concerns

Transgressions also have the potential to upset the social fabric by undermining the values on which group rules and norms are based. When an offender deliberately acts counter to shared expectations of appropriate behavior, that act implies that the offender disagrees with the values dictating such expectations (Durkheim, 1964). The deliberate violation of group values challenges the perception that other group members agree with them, questioning the extent to which there is a shared consensus about those values and potentially undermining their validity (Tyler & Boeckmann, 1997; Vidmar, 2000). As Vidmar (2000) succinctly noted, "An offence is a threat to community consensus about the correctness – that is the moral nature – of a rule and hence the values that bind social groups together" (p. 42).

The importance of group value consensus has been alluded to in past research documenting strong reactions to ingroup deviance. Norm violations elicit stronger injustice responses when committed by ingroup members versus outgroup members (Marques, 1990), particularly those who are prototypical of the group (Kerr, Hymes, Anderson, & Weathers, 1995), suggesting concern over discrepant beliefs and attitudes within the group. Value consensus is important because it helps define relationships, stipulating shared attitudes and beliefs that a particular group abides by. Sharing an identity implies a set of shared values that define that relationship (Haslam, McGarty, & Turner, 1996; Turner, 1987a), and blatant disregard for those shared expectations has the potential to cause group members to question their social identity. Therefore, an undermining of group values can elicit strong injustice reactions, particularly in intragroup contexts when victim and offender are perceived to share a common identity (Okimoto & Wenzel, 2007a; Okimoto et al., in press; Wenzel, Okimoto, Feather, & Platow, 2008). Further, the value implications of an offence should be important to the extent that one identifies with the group in which the injustice occurred (Okimoto & Wenzel, 2007a; Wenzel & Thielmann, 2006).

As an example, imagine the case where a researcher intentionally plagiarizes the work of another academic in their discipline. The offender and victim both share a common identity (i.e., as researchers in the same field) and the violation undermines a value that is expected to be shared (i.e., academic integrity). As such, the flagrant violation may give rise to uncertainty over the shared nature of the values violated by the act, eliciting concern that one's academic colleagues do not value ethical practices as much as initially thought. And to the extent that academic work is defined by integrity and adherence to ethical practices, acts of plagiarism threaten the identity of that field of research.

Although we have generally discussed concern over the values violated by a transgression as a group-level concern, value concerns may also be relevant at the interpersonal level. Interpersonal violations may be important because, if relationship-defining values are broken, the violation questions the extent to which both parties agree, thus threatening how the two parties define their relationship. At the other extreme, the value meaning of an offence may also be a human-level concern if common humanity is salient as a superordinate identity and the transgression is perceived to undermine basic human rights or universally held morals.

Interrelations and Differentiations between Justice Concerns

While our discussion of these justice concerns suggests a clear conceptual distinction between status/power and value issues, as well as from issues of behavior control, these constructs are not necessarily independent. Concerns over personal status/power and group values following a transgression are not completely removed from concerns over deterrence. The loss of control implied by disempowerment and the loss of consistent expectations implied by a questioning of values both may elicit concern over future behavior. These interrelations, however, do not diminish the contribution of the current conceptual distinction. Even if concerns for these two symbolic implications are based in fear of future victimization, such fears can still be viewed as concerns over personal status/power versus the values and identity of the group. And recognizing such a distinction still contributes to a more complete understanding of how to satisfactorily address such fears.

Further complicating the distinction, a group may have value-based expectations *about* status and power – shared expectations grounded in an established group hierarchy or in behavioral directives relating to interpersonal respect and trust. For example, many groups have shared expectations about appropriate levels of intragroup (within-group) respect. Individuals may expect other ingroup members to exhibit a certain level of respect, and perceived disrespect may not only threaten the status/power balance between victim and offender, but also may lead to questioning respect as a shared group value. Do others in my group really value respect? Is my group really the respectful group I thought it was? However, for a transgression here to be perceived as primarily a value issue, status and power-related values such as interpersonal respect, respect for authorities, and egalitarianism must be salient identity-defining values. In such cases, while the transgression undermines the victim's status/power, it is likely to be primarily seen as threatening the identity of the group as a whole.

Generally, most transgressions have the potential to elicit distress over *both* status/power and value issues, and in many cases may indeed raise both psychological concerns. Importantly, however, the relative magnitude of each concern should vary depending on characteristics of the context. While a complete overview of these characteristics is beyond the scope of this chapter, it is important to highlight the identity of the involved parties as a key contextual variable that is likely to affect the symbolic interpretation of a transgression. Specifically, a lack of shared identity between victim and offender may predispose victims to interpret a transgression as more of a threat to their status/power. The struggle over status and power between the involved parties implies a categorical differentiation between self and other that facilitates a competitive orientation and a perception that the two parties are at odds over resources and dominance – the diminished status/power of one individual is related to increased status/power of another (Turner, 1981). Similarly, *intergroup* conflicts are likely to speak to the status/power of the ingroup as it compares with a competitive outgroup (Tajfel & Turner, 1979). In contrast, sharing a common identity may elicit stronger concerns over group values. To the extent that victims see themselves and the offender as both members of a common group, their self-concept is depersonalized and their sense of self is inclusive of the offender (Turner, 1987a). In such cases, victims may be less likely to perceive a transgression in terms of status/power, and more as a violation of shared values. According to self-categorization theory, members of a common ingroup are expected to share identity-defining beliefs and values (Haslam et al., 1996), and to the extent that the transgression violates such value expectations, the transgression questions the validity of those values for the group (Turner, 1987b).

Therefore, when victims perceive themselves to be separate from the offender, not sharing a common identity, they will be more likely to interpret, and/or respond to, a transgression as a usurping of status/power. Alternately, when victims perceive themselves as sharing a common identity, they will be more likely to interpret, and/or respond to, a transgression as a violation of shared values. This framework essentially views an emphasis between status/power versus values as determined by the relative salience of a shared identity. Recent research has begun to validate these assertions. In two correlational studies, Wenzel and Thielmann (2006) assessed citizens' reactions to tax evasion and social welfare fraud as a function of national identity. Concerns over the disproportionality of the situation (i.e., just deserts motives, which is theoretically related to status/power) were associated with stronger injustice reactions, particularly for respondents whose national identification was weak. Conversely, concerns over value restoration were associated with stronger injustice reactions, particularly for respondents whose national identification was strong. Another study by Okimoto and Wenzel (2007a) examined reactions to a terrorist attack against Australia (the relevant ingroup), manipulating the ingroup/outgroup membership of the offenders, and the offenders' self-confessed motives for the transgression in terms of status/power or values. Injustice reactions were most severe when the attack was committed by outgroup members (i.e. foreigners) attempting to demean the status/power of Australia, and when the attack was committed by ingroup members (i.e. Australians) attempting to undermine Australia's national values.

Interestingly, this discussion suggests that the interpretation of a transgression in terms of values is partly dictated by the respondent's identification with the group in which the injustice occurred (Okimoto & Wenzel, 2007a; Wenzel & Thielmann, 2006), as well as their shared identification with the offender (Okimoto & Wenzel, 2007a; Wenzel et al., 2008). This suggests that even if the offender and victim are from different social groups, if the respondent's *superordinate identity* is salient, transgressions should be more likely to be interpreted as an intragroup (within-group) conflict if the values of the more inclusive, superordinate group are threatened. Making a superordinate identity salient makes shared goals and beliefs salient (Sherif, 1966; Turner, Hogg, Oakes, Reicher, & Wetherell, 1987), decreasing the competitive nature of interactions (Gaertner, Mann,

Murrell, & Dovidio, 1989). Adopting such a superordinate perspective, according to the current framework, should elicit empathetic responses towards injustice victims while also leading victims to interpret the transgression more in terms of shared values that need to be consensualized in order to restore justice. This heightened emphasis on shared values, while it may not reduce the feelings of injustice spawned through intergroup conflict, may have interesting implications for the effectiveness of more constructive conflict resolution interventions.

Various personality traits may also determine whether people interpret a transgression primarily in terms of status/power or values. For example, victims with dispositional need for power (McClelland, 1987), higher right-wing authoritarianism (Altemeyer, 1988), and a social dominance orientation (Pratto, Sidanius, Stallworth, & Malle, 1994), may be particularly likely to interpret a transgression as a loss of status/power, as such individuals are characterized as having particular focus on status/power concerns (e.g., Feather, 1996; Gollwitzer, 2004). Likewise, individuals with a narcissistic personality (Raskin & Terry, 1988), who have high self-perceptions of superiority and inflated self-esteem, might be more likely to interpret a transgression against them as a personal insult and threat to their sense of self (Bushman & Baumeister, 1998). Conversely, following from our previous discussion on identity, victims who have a high interdependent self-construal (Singelis, 1994), value benevolence and harmony (Feather, 1996, 1999), or cultural values such as collectivism (Triandis, 1995) may interpret a transgression in terms of values, as such individuals are more likely to see offenders as *us* rather than *them*.

THE INJUSTICE RESPONSE

The current approach suggests that in order for justice to be restored in the eyes of the victim, the relevant motives underlying feelings of injustice must be addressed. To the extent that an injustice victim interprets a transgression in terms of its status/power implications, that victim's *status and power relative to the offender must be restored.* Consequently, justice demands disempowerment and degradation of the offender and/or empowerment and elevation of the victim.

The offender must be cut down to size or humiliated in order to take away his or her status and reassert the status/power of the victim and community (Bies & Tripp, 1996; Miller, 2001). This is the process that underlies *just deserts*; transgressions disturb the moral balance, but this balance can be leveled by inflicting harm upon the offender, restoring *moral proportionality* to the situation and thus restoring justice (Carlsmith et al., 2002). Similarly, when the injustice raises questions in the victim about his/her status position in the group as a whole, sufficient justice restoration must reaffirm the importance of that victim's membership in the group (Okimoto, in press a, in press b).

However, to the extent that an injustice victim interprets a transgression in terms of its value implications for the group, the *perceived consensus regarding the validity of those values must be restored.* In this case, justice demands reinforcement and revalidation of the values violated by the offence. And if a victim is upset by the transgression because of *both* status/power and value concerns, the transgression response must repair relative status/power while also re-establishing consensus regarding shared values. Responses that adequately address the salient concerns of victims will be deemed as more satisfactory, and in some cases more fair, just, and appropriate. In the following discussion, we note the defining characteristics of common injustice responses, state how these interventions have the potential to speak to *both* status/power and value issues, and then propose that each intervention primarily addresses one or the other motive, speaking to their relative contribution.

Punishments

Punishment is a dominant and common response to injustice (see Ellsworth & Gross, 1994), and the prevailing procedure by which most Western systems of criminal justice attempt to address transgressions. Punishments are, in practice, often *unilateral* in nature – a punishment is assigned to the offender by the injustice victim or an objective third-party, and the offender must accept that outcome irrespective of their opinions regarding its appropriateness. Criminal justice systems do not typically view offender agreement as a necessary component of punishment; offender agreement is more often viewed as inconsequential to the justice process.

Status/Power Concerns

The unilateral imposition of negative outcomes for the offender gives punishment a status/power reduction meaning. Punishments symbolically (and in many cases actually) take power away from the offender and demean his/her status (Miller, 2001). The majority of the psychological research on punishment has focused on this status perspective

(Bies & Tripp, 1996; Heider, 1958; Vidmar, 2000). Because of the offender degradation it implies, we suggest that punishments primarily address a victim's status/power concerns (Wenzel et al., in press). Therefore, to the extent that a victim is upset by the transgression because of the offender's usurping of his or her status/power, that victim is more likely to demand punishment in order to rebalance the scales of justice. A victim's perceived status loss as a result of the transgression does indeed lead to stronger punitive tendencies (Bies & Tripp, 1996). Another recent investigation examining victim responses to theft scenarios provides further evidence that punishments serve to address status and power concerns (Wenzel et al., 2008). Calls for punishments were shown to be related to concrete desires to humiliate, disrespect, penalize, and impose a decision on the offender, while also giving the victim voice, removing the offender's opportunity for voice, and holding the offender accountable for his/her actions. Furthermore, calls for punishment were predicted by concerns over status/power and the anger and outrage such concerns elicited.

Consistent with the assertion that punishments serve a status/power restoring function, punishments are often directly associated with just deserts motives (Darley, 2002; Feather, 1999; Vidmar, 2000) – offenders deserve to receive a punishment in order to return moral proportionality to the situation (Carlsmith, et al., 2002). The punishment itself restores justice, and the offender humiliation and suffering that it implies. In this way, offender agreement with a punishment may actually be perceived as *counter* to the reestablishment of justice, as such agreement might imply a lack of suffering. If the offender made the victim feel powerless and demeaned by the transgression, so should too the offender be disempowered and demeaned by punishment.

Value Concerns

Although status and power concerns appear to be the primary purpose of punishment, some theoretical work, albeit few empirical studies, has suggested a direct link between demands for punishment and group values (Feather, 1996, 1999; Tyler et al., 1997; Vidmar, 2000). A recent paper by Okimoto and Wenzel (in press) proposed that punishments can re-consensualize group values in two ways. First, by symbolically labeling the offence as wrong, punishments communicate to others that the group does not and should not condone the violation of the group values. Punishment provides a "social account" (Tedeschi & Reiss, 1981) for the group, distancing the offender's actions from the group's beliefs and labeling the transgression as counter-normative (Bies, 1987). This process is similar to the "black sheep effect" (Marques, 1990), which suggests that devaluing the offender protects the group from the identity implications of value violations (Marques & Paez, 1994; Marques, Abrams, & Serôdio, 2001). Indeed, *subtyping* a deviant group member as part of an immoral minority may allow others in the group to maintain their positive social identity (Richards & Hewstone, 2001). Consistent with this symbolic labeling argument, Okimoto and Wenzel (in press) showed that public punishments were perceived to reinforce values towards the group more than private punishments, and that public punishments were evaluated as more appropriate when value concerns were salient.

Second, punishments can help consensualize values if they encourage the offender to revise his/her values to be consistent with those of the group, speaking directly to the source of the value breach. Okimoto and Wenzel (in press) showed that inclusively framed punishments (i.e., framed as a vehicle by which the offender could rejoin the group) were perceived to reinforce values towards the offender more than punishments framed as excluding the offender from the group, and were evaluated as more appropriate particularly when value concerns were salient. These findings suggest that values can be consensualized at two levels: reinforcing values towards other group members and/or towards the offender. Notably, however, this second route to value consensus (via the offender) is dependent on the offender's acceptance of the punishment as appropriate, an assumption that is not inherent to most legal processes employing punishment. Other injustice responses may be more suitable for achieving offender value consensus, such as those offered by restorative conferencing (to be discussed later). The suggestion that punishments can speak to value concerns through consensualization *with* an offender contrasts with the prevailing understanding about how punishments restore justice, as such consensus implies offender (bilateral) agreement with the punishment decision. Taking responsibility through *self-punishment* may indeed communicate an offender's agreement with group values.

There is also preliminary evidence supporting the notion that, when given the opportunity, people do indeed use punishment for both status/power and value restoration purposes. Across two scenario studies investigating reactions to transgressions, Wenzel et al. (2008) found that demands for punishments were significantly related to both concerns over group values and concerns over victim status/power following instances of theft. Similarly, Okimoto and Wenzel (2007a) showed that punitive reactions to terrorism were affected by terrorist attempts to undermine both national values and national status/power.

Revenge and Retaliation

Revenge/retaliation is an action taken in direct response to a perceived wrongdoing that is intended to damage, injure, or punish the responsible party (Allred, 1999; Bies & Tripp, 1996). Such retaliation can take the form of theft (Greenberg, 1990), antisocial behavior (Robinson & O'Leary-Kelly, 1998), aggression (Folger & Skarlicki, 1998), and in extreme cases, violence (Folger & Baron, 1996). Revenge is most often used as a way for the *victims themselves* to restore justice, when group authorities have failed to address their concerns (Skarlicki & Folger, 1997).

Status/Power Concerns

Acts of revenge are similar to punishments in that they attempt to respond to perceived injustice through the unilateral imposition of harm against the offender; it is the victim him/herself, however, that takes punitive action. As discussed earlier, the imposition of harm disempowers and demeans its recipient (Miller, 2001), serving a status/power restoring function for the victim/revenge-taker. Indeed, revenge is often conceptualized as an attempt by injustice victims to reaffirm their damaged personal identity (Felson, 1992; Tedeschi & Felson, 1994). Consistent with these assertions, research has shown that theft from the offending party has the potential to address feelings of diminished personal respect and status (Greenberg, 1997). Desires to exact revenge have also been shown to be higher following transgressions where the offender was of lower relative status than the victim in both field (Aquino, Tripp, & Bies, 2006) and laboratory settings (Kim, Smith, & Brigham, 1998). Such effects may be partly explained by the ability to take revenge, as a victim of higher relative status may be able to use his or her power against the offender (Aquino et al., 2006). However, in light of the current perspective, this finding also supports the notion that revenge serves as a way for victims to reassert that status/power, addressing concerns that are heightened when an offender's actions violate the victim's deserved respect afforded by their higher status.

Value Concern

While revenge and retaliation have primarily been discussed in terms of status and power, like punishments, revenge may also have symbolic implications for group values. Bies and Tripp (1996) propose that revenge is a response to both personal identity threats (i.e., status/power) as well as to a damaged sense of "civic order." They argue that violations of agreed-upon rules and expected codes of conduct also motivate the need for revenge.

Revenge may carry these important value-restoring effects because, again parallel with our earlier punishment argument, it may communicate to both the offender and other group members that the offender's act was wrong and worthy of censure, thereby attempting to elicit consensus regarding the value meaning of the transgression. Some empirical evidence has also suggested a potential link between value violations and revenge. Victims have been shown to be more vengeful following both feelings of diminished status and perceived rule violations (Aquino et al., 2006). Similarly, there is evidence that the link between perceived injustices (i.e., group-level procedural violations) and retaliation is mediated by identity concerns – concerns over both the identity of the group in general as well as with the victim's status within that group (Blader, Chang, & Tyler, 2001).

Compensation

Material compensation as a response to injustice is most often conceptualized in terms of compensatory justice – undoing the harm done by the offence through restitution (returning monetary losses to the victim) or reparations (compensation beyond material losses). Compensation in the legal system is *not* often explicitly used as a way to send a symbolic message but rather to restore the material losses of the victim (actual or anticipated as a result of the offence). That being said, this does not negate the possibility that victims are *satisfied* with or *desire* compensation for reasons other than material gain – compensation can also carry important symbolic implications that go beyond the material value of the monetary award. Even if court systems only assign compensation for equity-restoration purposes, victims may *seek* compensation as a way to punish the offender, as monetary penalties may carry symbolic implications similar to punishments. Indeed, compensatory payments are more satisfying to victims when framed as a punishment (van Prooijen, 2004). Importantly, similar to punishments, compensation may speak to multiple injustice concerns. On the one hand, compensation may be viewed as restoring justice because it makes the offender suffer, taking on a status/power reduction meaning. On the other, the imposition of compensation can also send a symbolic message that the values violated by the offence are indeed important and should be adhered to.

These symbolic messages can also be identified in legal exchange. In court systems, the value meaning of compensation is sometimes explicitly communicated through the assignment of *nominal damages*, which are small monetary awards meant to acknowledge a wrongdoing when there is no proof of actual harm to the victim. Particularly egregious transgressions may also be met with *punitive* or *exemplary damages* – monetary awards that are over and above what may be considered equitable to the victim's losses, instituted only in egregious transgressions to send a symbolic message to the offender and other observers. This symbolic meaning is also evident in the use of *monetary fines* (e.g., traffic violations) paid to a common pool of societal resources, ostensibly compensating the entire group. Such monetary penalties are meant to censor the transgression, communicating that the offender is not above the law (i.e., status/power) and that the transgression goes against important rules (i.e., values).

Material compensation is also interesting because, different from punishments, it may be offered on behalf of the entire *group* in which the injustice occurred (e.g., victims of crime compensation schemes in legal systems). To the extent that the group is deemed responsible for the injustice (perhaps through negligence of being unable to control the behavior of its members), victims may view institutional compensation in the same way that they view offender compensation – as a form of punishment. However, if the group is not accountable, compensation may have symbolic meaning for the injustice victim's membership status in the group. Specifically, unwarranted compensation communicates the extent of a group's concern following an injustice. A series of studies by Okimoto (in press a) showed that voluntary compensation from the group results in favorable reactions, not because of materialistic desires, but rather because it makes the victim feel like a valued and respected group member. Such compensation, while it may not speak directly to a victim's status/power concerns, can reaffirm the victim's status within the larger group context. It may also suggest that the group as a whole does not agree with the offender's actions, providing a social account for the group (Tedeschi & Reiss, 1981) and revalidating the group values violated by the offence.

Unfortunately, with the exception of theoretical work discussing the symbolic meaning of money (e.g., Furnham & Argyle, 1998; Opsahl & Dunnette, 1966), little research has been conducted investigating these potential implications, which is surprising given the prevalence of compensation as an injustice response in organizational, consumer, and legal contexts. Empirical research is needed that disentangles exactly what motivates victim desires for compensation: value concerns, status/power concerns, materialistic desires, or (more likely) a combination of all three.

Restorative Justice Practices

Some legal systems have begun to utilize a relatively new type of injustice response, interventions classified under the umbrella of "*restorative justice*" (Bazemore, 1998; Braithwaite, 1999).[3] Generally, these practices treat transgressions as conflicts that should be given back to their rightful owners to resolve – victims, offenders, and affected communities (Christie, 1977). They typically involve the affected parties (including the offender) dealing with the injustice through interaction and mutual understanding. The parties present their perspective on the issue, voice their opinions, and attempt to come to some sort of agreement about the nature of the wrong, the damage it has caused, the offender's responsibility, and what actions should be taken to resolve the matter and restore justice (Marshall, 1998). Following voluntary expressions of remorse and apology by the offender, victims are also encouraged to offer their forgiveness (Roche, 2003; Strang, 2002). Importantly, these processes often do not view punishment as important for their own sake, but rather as a way to repair the harm (Bazemore, 1998). In sum, these processes emphasize healing of the victim and his/her suffering, healing the offender and his/her moral self, and healing the group as a whole and its relationships (Braithwaite, 2002). Notably, in practice victims tend to prefer these types of procedures over traditional court procedures, although willingness to participate, satisfaction with the resolution, and resulting recidivism tends to vary widely depending on the context (Braithwaite, 2002; Latimer, Dowden, & Muise, 2005; Strang, 2002).

Status/Power Concerns

Restorative practices have been argued to entail some degree of empowerment (Braithwaite, 2003; Zehr, 1985), although empowerment that applies to victims, offenders, and members of the community as a whole. Such practices may often involve "reintegrative shaming" (Braithwaite, 1989) of the offender in order to facilitate value reform, shaming that may also carry relative status/power implications for the victim. Apologies received as part of the restorative procedure may also be empowering for the victim (which we discuss in the next section). While there appears to be potential for addressing status/power concerns through restorative practices, to date little empirical work has been conducted exploring this issue. Moreover, we believe in restorative practices, status/power issues take a secondary position behind value concerns (Wenzel et al., in press). The institution of punishment and/or reintegrative shaming as part of restorative processes is often directed towards achieving consensus about the harm done by the offence, not the meting out of just deserts or imposition of offender suffering.

Value Concerns

Wenzel et al. (in press) have recently suggested that the important thread underlying restorative procedures is a reliance on *bilateral* discussion and decision-making, with the goal of arriving at some type of mutual agreement about the offence and how to repair it (see also Okimoto et al., in press). Central to this bilateral agreement is the goal of *consensus between all parties* – through these procedures, the affected parties attempt to establish consensus about the implications of the offence and what should be done to restore justice. Such a focus on mutual understanding and consensus highlights the potential group value-restoring properties of restorative practices. They allow for consensus seeking regarding the meaning of the offence and a reassertion that the values that have been violated are important. Therefore, if a transgression is seen primarily as a threat to group values, victims should be more likely to desire restorative processes (Wenzel et al., in press). Recent empirical investigations in laboratory contexts support this consensus-building argument. Heightened concerns over group values, while in some cases also leading to more punitive reactions, elicit a preference for restorative interventions (Wenzel et al., 2008).

To provide a more concrete example, we conducted a study investigating reactions to a failed terrorist attack in Australia (Okimoto & Wenzel, 2007b). In this study 110 Australian students were presented with a fake newspaper article about a terrorist attack against Australia (see also Okimoto & Wenzel, 2007a). Participants were asked the extent to which they: (1) felt like Australia's status/power and group values were affected by the attack (items adapted from Wenzel et al., 2008); (2) felt like the injustice response should restore status/power, communicate values to the group, and communicate values to the offender (items adapted from Okimoto & Wenzel, in press); and (3) desired punitive versus restorative action. As anticipated, concerns over Australia's status/power predicted desires to diminish the status/power of the offenders, which predicted demands for punishment. However, concerns over Australia's values predicted desires to communicate values to both the group and the offender, which predicted demands for punishments and restorative practices, respectively (Fig. 1). This pattern supports our earlier argument regarding the status/power and value restoring effects of punishment. These findings also

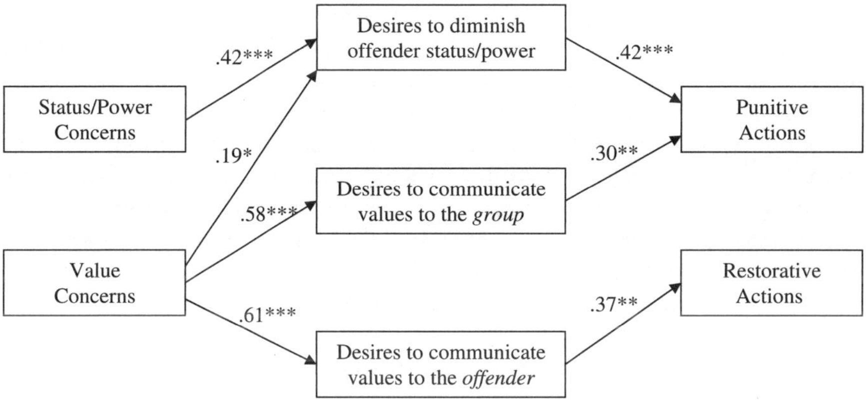

Fig. 1. Direct and Indirect Effects of Status/Power Concerns and Value Concerns on Punitive and Restorative Actions. *Notes*: Punitive measure: 7 items, $\alpha = .85$; e.g., "I would like to be on the jury that sentences the offenders to life in prison." Restorative measure: 7 items, $\alpha = .81$; e.g., "I would like to make the offenders understand that theirs is not the right way." Structural equation modeling in AMOS was used for the analysis. Non-significant relationships and error variance correlations are not shown in the figure. The model was fully identified, so fit statistics are not included; further, the interpretation of fit is not appropriate given the sample size. Manipulations were included, but did not affect the nature of the results discussed; therefore these variables were removed from the analysis to increase statistical power for the analysis. Partial mediation is also apparent when examining the relationships between salient concerns and desired actions. Contact the authors for full results of the analysis. $^{*}p<.05$, $^{**}p<.005$, $^{***}p<.001$. *Source:* Drawn from unpublished research by Okimoto and Wenzel (2007b).

highlight the fact that using punishment to consensualize group values ignores offender reform as a route to consensus; particular concern over value consensus with the offender predicted preferences for restorative practices, not punishment.

The fact that restorative practices commonly include a number of specific procedural features raises two important questions. First, what happens when restorative practices are unsuccessful in reaching an agreement about the harm and how to repair it? Unfortunately, objective assessments of these practices are often hampered by self-selection issues, as actual restorative programs require the voluntary participation of both victim and offender (Latimer et al., 2005). The existing experimental evidence suggests that unsuccessful restorative practices do not reduce a victim's feelings of injustice (Gromet & Darley, 2006). Second, do different aspects of restorative practices (e.g., apologies or forgiveness) have independent effects, or is there something about this constellation of processes that elicit some type of synergistic effect? Scheff (1998) suggests that symbolic reparations following an offence demand an apology by the offender *as well as* forgiveness and reacceptance from the injustice victim and the affected community; empirical research, however, is needed to verify their synergistic properties. Apologies and forgiveness may be part of a three-step dialogical exchange where the victim demands an apology, the offender apologizes, and the victim expresses forgiveness (Abel, 1998; Tavuchis, 1991). Notably, however, both apologies and forgiveness have independently been associated with the reduction of injustice concerns and moral outrage.

Apologies

Apologies are a statement of remorse from an offender, one where the offender does not attempt to deny responsibility for the transgression. The psychological literature on apologies is very broad, and a review of this literature is beyond the scope of this chapter. However, the importance of apologies in achieving justice are denoted by a wealth of evidence showing that apologies and other expressions of remorse reduce victim outrage (e.g., Baron, 1990; Ohbuchi, Agarie, & Kameda, 1989) and the severity of punishments assigned to the offender (e.g., Darby & Schlenker, 1989; Felson & Ribner, 1981; Robbennolt, 2003; Rumsey, 1976).

Status/Power Concerns

Apologies have been conceptualized as an equity-restoring response (see Wood & Mitchell, 1981), equalizing the deserved status balance between victim and offender. In this sense, expressions of offender remorse represent a type of self-castigation or self-censure (Scher & Darley, 1997), indicating an admitted "moral inferiority" (Abel, 1998). Moreover, through the apology, the offender empowers the victim, allowing that victim the decision to accept the apology as equalizing the relative balance of status/power (Karp, 1998), or reject the apology and maintain that position of higher moral superiority (Abel, 1998). As such, apologies may serve as a justice-restoring response when the transgression is perceived in terms of a threat to personal status/power.

Value Concerns

Importantly, however, many researchers take an alternative (or additional) perspective on why apologies are effective in reducing punishment severity. They suggest that apologies affect punishment deservingness because they function as a social account for the offender (Gonzales, Haugen, & Manning, 1994; Tedeschi & Reiss, 1981). In the same way that excuses and justifications attempt to reduce blameworthiness, apologies separate the offender from the offence, implying that the transgression is not representative of the offender's true values and beliefs (Bobocel & Zdaniuk, 2005; Shaver, 1985). In Goffman's view (1971), apologies are particularly useful when other social accounting strategies are insufficient in convincing victims that the offence was acceptable. Goffman (1971) states that, "an apology is a gesture through which the individual splits himself in two parts, the part that is guilty of an offense and the part that dissociates itself from the deceit and affirms a belief in the offended rule" (p. 113). Such a perspective suggests a value consensus purpose of apologies – expressions of remorse attempt to communicate agreement and acknowledge that the offence was wrong (see also Abel, 1998; Tavuchis, 1991). Through a sincere expression of apology, offenders acknowledge their role in the offence and reaffirm the values underlying the rules that have been violated (Darby & Schlenker, 1989). As such, not only might apologies reduce perceived offender blameworthiness, but they may also function as a way to restore justice following a transgression that is seen primarily in terms of its value violation.

Forgiveness

Similar to apologies, forgiveness is also associated with a reduction of hostile emotions towards the offender and diminished punishment severity (e.g., McCullough, Worthington, & Rachal, 1997; Worthington, 2006). However, the reason for this association seems to be less straightforward. The definition of forgiveness, as it has been most often conceptualized in the psychological literature, seems to contradict our exploration of forgiveness as a justice-restoring intervention. Most forgiveness researchers define forgiveness as a *letting go* of the negative feelings about one's victimization (e.g., McCullough et al., 1997), suggesting a surrendering or loosening of justice (Exline & Baumeister, 2000; Reed & Aquino, 2003) rather than the restoration of it. Such a definition insinuates that forgiveness is antithetical to justice. Other researchers have suggested that justice may be a *predictor* of the decision to forgive (Tripp, Bies, & Aquino, 2007), indicating that the victim's injustice concerns have been addressed and their negative feelings have been reduced (Exline, Worthington, Hill, & McCullough, 2003; Worthington, 2006). Recently, however, Wenzel and Okimoto (2007) have alternatively conceptualized forgiveness as part of the *justice restoration process*, rather than an ends signaling the abandonment or finality of justice. From this perspective, forgiveness may be instrumental for victims as a way to address their injustice concerns.

Status/Power Concerns

First, a victim's forgiveness of the offender may foster feelings of increased victim status and empowerment. As with apologies, forgiveness can be conceptualized in terms of equity. Forgiveness as an undeserved gift to the offender may increase the perceived debt that the offender owes to the victim, placing the victim in an even higher position of control (Kelln & Ellard, 1999). By forgiving, the victim takes mercy on the offender and offers an unmerited pardon, thereby retaining a degree of power and superiority over the offender (Bies & Tripp, 1996). Forgiveness can also indicate the victim's higher moral status and superiority as the victim refuses to be brought down to the low moral level of the offender (Heider, 1958). Indeed, recent empirical work has shown that expressions of forgiveness by the victim lead to increased feelings of status and power, feelings that contribute to an overall sense of justice (Wenzel & Okimoto, 2007). While the status and power messages communicated by forgiveness may be subtle when compared to revenge or unilateral punishment, the ability of such a response to restore justice is important as it has the potential to diffuse the conflict and cultivate future cooperative interactions without condoning the wrongdoing (Aquino, Grover, Goldman, & Folger, 2003).

Value Concerns

Expressions of forgiveness may also serve to revalidate consensus regarding the values violated by the offence, particularly when part of a larger dialogical process including an apology (Scheff, 1998). A victim's offer of forgiveness can express the perception, assumption, or hope that the offender endorses and shares the values that the transgression violated (Eaton, Struthers, & Santelli, 2006). Indeed, recent research has shown that by conveying an expression of forgiveness, an injustice victim perceives greater potential for value consensus with the offender, and through that reaffirmation, forgiveness restores a sense of justice in the victim (Wenzel & Okimoto, 2007). However, the prevalence of such value-restoring effects of forgiveness in absence of a more complete dialogical process including an apology remains unanswered. Further investigation is necessary to better appreciate the boundaries of these effects, the relative contribution of forgiveness in restoring victim status/power and offender value consensus, and the importance of forgiveness as a step in the dialogical process towards consensus.

RETRIBUTIVE VERSUS RESTORATIVE NOTIONS OF JUSTICE

From the preceding discussion, it would seem as if we have further complicated the task of adequately responding to injustice by suggesting that most interventions have the ability to speak to both status/power and value concerns. On the contrary, we present this discussion because it suggests a more parsimonious framework for understanding injustice responses. Specifically, this literature review illustrates that the status/power versus values dichotomy is fundamental to both the *experience* of injustice and the *restoration* of justice, integrating these literatures and providing a framework for understanding a wide variety of injustice interventions and why those interventions restore justice. Furthermore, we argue that the victim's need to address these two fundamental concerns is not only evocative of the mechanisms by which justice is restored (i.e., through status/power versus value restoration) but is also related to the very notion of justice that people adopt. Specifically, we suggest that there are *two lay-philosophical notions of justice* following a transgression (Okimoto et al., in press; Wenzel et al., in press; Wenzel & Thielmann, 2006), which are defined by different processes and outcomes required for a sense of justice.

Retributive Notion of Justice

The dominant notion of "justice," as it is most often discussed in the literature (and indeed in Western criminal justice systems) is retributive in nature (Darley, 2002; Feather, 1999; Tyler et al., 1997; Vidmar, 2000). A *retributive notion of justice* seeks to restore justice through assertion against the offender (Okimoto et al., in press; Wenzel et al., in press; Wenzel & Thielmann, 2006). Specifically, retributive justice entails a process of assertion and imposition, with the offender's deprivation, suffering, degradation, and/or humiliation as principal outcomes. Thus, unilaterally imposed punishments, forced compensation, and revenge might be particularly satisfying from the perspective of a retributive justice notion. Because of the implied disempowerment and degradation of the offender in a retributive process, this notion should be particularly salient when a victim perceives a transgression predominantly in terms of status and power.

Implied in this retributive notion is the concept of "just desert" (Carlsmith et al., 2002; Darley et al., 2000; Tyler & Webber, 1983) – offenders deserve to be punished in an attempt to restore proportionality to the situation. As such, a victim's desire to seek retributive justice is determined by the key variables such as severity of the offence (Walster, Walster, & Berscheid, 1978) and offender blameworthiness or intent (Darley & Pittman, 2003; Miller & McCann, 1979). Notably, under a retributive notion of justice, punishment is seen as *sufficient and necessary* to achieve justice. A punitive response is deserved and should be meted out regardless of the offender's remorse or agreement that the response is fair. Therefore, if one assumes that justice is achieved through retributive means, punishment is central to the justice process, while consensus-building interventions such as forgiveness are antithetical to justice (see Wenzel & Okimoto, 2007). Importantly, while punishment and revenge may have implications for a group's values, we suggest that victims whose primary concerns are over values will be less inclined to such punitive responses as they are more likely to adopt a *restorative* notion of justice.

Restorative Notion of Justice

An alternative philosophical conception of justice has recently been proposed, rising out of disillusionment with the criminal justice system and its lack of recognition of victims' needs (see Braithwaite, 2002; Christie, 1977; Walgrave, 1995). Termed after the class of recently introduced restorative practices (discussed earlier), this alternative *restorative notion of justice* seeks to achieve justice through bilateral consensus with the offender (Okimoto et al., in press; Wenzel et al., in press). Specifically, restorative justice entails a process of dialogue between the affected parties with the principal outcome of achieving an agreement about the wrongdoing, the harm done, and the response required to repair that harm. Thus, under a restorative notion of justice, apologies, bilateral compensation, forgiveness, or a combination of these as part of restorative conferencing, might be particularly satisfying.

The primary concern under a restorative notion of justice is gaining a shared understanding of the values violated by the offence and the harm such a violation has caused. As such, a victim's desire to seek restorative justice is determined by the extent to which the transgression violates shared identity-defining values and is regarded as egregious primarily because it questions those values (Wenzel et al., 2008). In such cases, reaffirming the validity of those values through shared agreement about the harm, perhaps through an exchange of apology and forgiveness, is central to the justice process. Under such a restorative notion of justice, non-constructive retributive interventions that marginalize the offender without regard for his/her views may in some cases be construed as antithetical to justice. And again, while apologies and forgiveness may carry implications relevant to the victim's status/power, we suggest that victims whose primary concerns are over status/power will be less inclined to such consensus-oriented responses as they are more likely to adopt a retributive notion of justice.

Preliminary Empirical Evidence

A recent scenario study by Okimoto et al. (in press) manipulated retributive and restorative justice aspects of an injustice response, conceptualized in terms of punishment and bilateral consensus, respectively. They found that retributive and restorative interventions had independent effects on perceived resolution fairness, suggesting that they indeed tapped into two additive aspects of justice. Moreover, consistent with theoretical expectations, retributive justice was moderated by transgression severity and offender intent, while restorative justice was moderated by perceived shared identity with the offender.

Another recent investigation by Wenzel et al. (2008) developed a measure assessing retributive and restorative notions of justice (see the appendix). They provided evidence of discriminant validity, showing that a retributive notion of justice was positively related to penalizing the offender, humiliating the offender, and unilateral punishment, but was negatively related to offender voice, willingness to forgive, respect for the offender, and bilateral decisions on punishment. Conversely, a restorative notion of justice was positively related to apology seeking, offender voice, willingness to forgive, respect for the offender, and bilateral decisions on punishment, but was negatively related to humiliation of the offender and unrelated to penalizing the offender. Using this same measure, Okimoto, Wenzel, and Feather (2008) showed that these retributive and restorative notions were also distinctly related to different aspects of personality, traits associated with heightened concerns over status/power versus shared values. Only a restorative notion was positively related to interdependent self-construal (Singelis, 1994) and the conventionalism facet of right-wing authoritarianism (Altemeyer, 1988; Feather, 1996). However, only a retributive notion was positively related to narcissistic entitlement (Raskin & Terry, 1988) and authoritarian aggression (Altemeyer, 1988; Feather, 1996).

To provide a more concrete example of these relationships, we conducted a correlational study examining status/power versus value concerns (measures drawn from Wenzel et al., 2008), and their relationship to retributive versus restorative notions of justice (Wenzel et al., 2007). Participants in the study were asked to imagine that a thief had broken into their house and robbed them. Results of the study show that the concern over the status/power implications of the offence predicted endorsement of a retributive notion of justice, $\beta = .56$, $p < .001$, but value concerns did not, $\beta = .04$, ns. Conversely, concern over the value implications of the offence predicted endorsement of a restorative notion of justice, $\beta = .42$, $p < .001$, but status/power concerns did not, $\beta = .19$, ns (Fig. 2).

These empirical findings are consistent with our assertion that concerns over status/power versus values lead to endorsement of different notions of what it means to restore justice. As such, when given the option to select their intervention of choice, the salience of these concerns determines victim preferences for retributive versus restorative responses. This is a potentially important contribution, as legal practitioners have yet to identify a viable

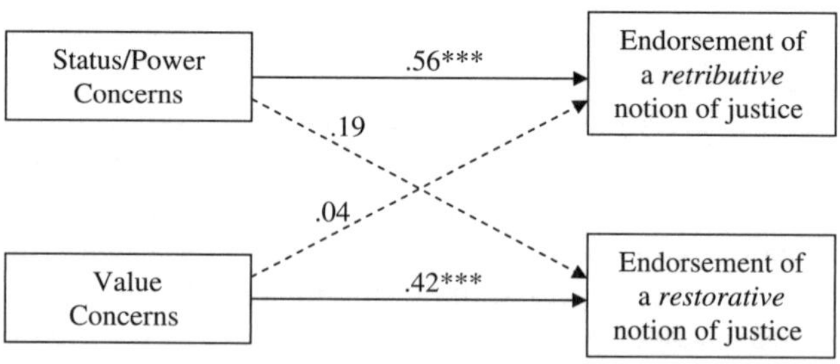

Fig. 2. Effects of Status/Power Concerns and Value Concerns on Retributive and Restorative Justice. *Notes:* A series of regressions were used in the analysis, regressing each notion of justice onto status/power and value concerns in order to judge their relative contribution. Contact the authors for full results of the analysis. $^{***}p < .001$. *Source:* Drawn from unpublished research by Wenzel, Okimoto, and Feather (2007).

framework for understanding when restorative justice practices will be preferred over traditional retributive practices, or when these restorative practices might be more successful in addressing victim concerns (Strang et al., 2006). Further research is needed in field settings in order to fully realize the predictive validity of this approach for understanding victim reactions to administrative responses to injustice.

CONCLUSIONS

In conclusion, we suggest that the distinction between status/power and value-based injustice concerns is useful because it provides a parsimonious and viable framework for understanding injustice victim concerns and appropriately responding to those concerns. First, we believe that this framework reflects fundamental distinctions that consistently appear in the injustice literature. Concerns over group values and over status/power have both been discussed as underlying the experience of injustice, and in various explanations as to *why* different interventions are effective. However, the current perspective presents the first attempt to integrate these literatures into a coherent framework, speaking to the effectiveness of numerous different types of injustice interventions rather than suggesting independent explanations for each type of response.

Second, this distinction is vital to recognizing the relevant needs of injustice victims. Is it concern over personal status/power that motivates the desire for justice, or is it concern over their shared relationship with the offender and what that relationship represents? Such insight is necessary to identify the important characteristics of any injustice response. Even if direct assessment of a victim's concerns is not feasible, taking an identity framework assists in determining *when* injustice victims might be primarily concerned with the status/power versus value implications of the transgression. Further, this distinction helps researchers and practitioners understand how a victim is likely to conceptualize the pursuit of justice. Do victims understand justice as reaching a shared understanding and consensus with the offender (i.e., restorative notion), or as the imposition of punishment and suffering on the offender (i.e., retributive notion)?

Third, while commonly utilized *retributive* interventions may be somewhat effective in speaking to all types of victim concerns, understanding a victim's underlying needs and the available avenues towards justice restoration allows us to recognize when alternative interventions might be effective – *restorative* interventions that skirt the normative drawbacks of retributive interventions as they are used in legal processes (see Tyler, 1997, 2003). Retributive interventions can be very costly to society, have not been shown to consistently influence future behavior (Tyler, 2006), and can lead to further escalation of conflict between the offender and victim (Andersson & Pearson, 1999) and within the group as a whole (Halleck, 1980; Robinson & O'Leary-Kelly, 1998). Moreover, utilizing retributive interventions as a way to address value concerns, while it may psychologically distance offenders, is an incomplete approach to group value consensus as such interventions provide no expectation or evidence of offender reform and value readoption.

Fourth, this approach provides an alternative to prescribing injustice reparations based on the type of justice violation (i.e., distributive or procedural). While there has been some theoretical work attempting to link justice types to injustice reparations (e.g., Reb, Goldman, & Cropanzano, 2006), there is consistent evidence that distributive and procedural justice evaluations are highly correlated (Cohen-Charash & Spector, 2001) and often elicit *multiple* underlying concerns (see Cropanzano & Ambrose, 2001). While differentiating between different types of justice may be important to understand how to *prevent* injustice, as well as why and when different forms of injustice are deemed egregious, a focus on the theoretical conditions under which *all types* of injustice are likely to elicit status/power versus value concerns may serve as a more appropriate perspective from which to understand what constitutes a suitable *response* to injustice, and why.

Lastly, the current framework presents a novel (and useful) approach to justice restoration, conceptualizing a victim's desire to see justice done as an effort towards *identity-maintenance*. Victims seek justice as a way to protect their own status and power (relative to the offender and within the relevant group), as well as the social identity of the group as a whole, in an attempt to manage their personal and social identities. Responses to injustice can therefore be conceptualized as routes to *protecting*, *enhancing*, and *restoring* a victim's identity. Such an approach integrates the study of injustice into the wider literature on group processes, suggesting numerous avenues for continued research investigating what constitutes effective injustice reparations.

NOTES

1. The extension of our analysis to the observer perspective is beyond the scope of this chapter; however we believe that such a perspective would operate similarly, albeit with a greater emphasis on group-level concerns.

2. Some researchers have used the term "restorative justice" to mean compensatory justice, as we have defined it – restoring the situation to the state prior to the transgression (Schroeder, Steel, Woodell, & Bembenek, 2003; van Prooijen, 2004).

3. Restorative practices represent one type of *Alternative Dispute Resolution* (ADR) procedure. ADR procedures, however, also include practices such as arbitration or victim–offender mediation. ADR practices may share important justice-restoring characteristics, but are not discussed in this chapter (see Collett, 2008, in this volume).

REFERENCES

Abel, R. (1998). *Speaking respect, respecting speech.* Chicago, IL: University of Chicago Press.

Allred, K. G. (1999). Anger driven retaliation: Toward an understanding of impassioned conflict in organizations. In: R. J. Bies, R. J. Lewicki & B. H. Sheppard (Eds), *Research on negotiations in organizations* (Vol. 7, pp. 27–58). Greenwich, CT: JAI Press.

Altemeyer, B. (1988). *Enemies or freedom: Understanding right-wing authoritarianism.* San Francisco, CA: Jossey-Bass.

Andersson, L. M., & Pearson, C. M. (1999). Tit for tat? The spiraling effect of incivility in the workplace. *Academy of Management Review, 24*, 452–471.

Aquino, K., Grover, S. L., Goldman, B., & Folger, R. (2003). When push doesn't come to shove: Interpersonal forgiveness in workplace relationships. *Journal of Management Inquiry, 12*, 209–216.

Aquino, K., Tripp, T. M., & Bies, R. J. (2006). Getting even or moving on? Power, procedural justice, and types of offense as predictors of revenge, forgiveness, reconciliation, and avoidance in organizations. *Journal of Applied Psychology, 91*, 653–668.

Baron, R. A. (1990). Countering the effects of destructive criticism: The relative efficacy of four interventions. *Journal of Applied Psychology, 75*, 235–245.

Bazemore, G. (1998). Restorative justice and earned redemption: Communities, victims, and offender reintegration. *American Behavioral Scientist, 41*, 768–813.

Bies, R. J. (1987). The predicament of injustice: The management of moral outrage. In: L. L. Cummings & B. M. Staw (Eds), *Research in organizational behavior* (Vol. 9, pp. 289–319). Greenwich, CT: JAI Press.

Bies, R. J., & Tripp, T. M. (1996). Beyond distrust: "Getting even" and the need for revenge. In: R. M. Kramer & T. R. Tyler (Eds), *Trust in organizations: Frontiers of theory and research* (pp. 246–260). Thousand Oaks, CA: Sage.

Blader, S. L., Chang, C., & Tyler, T. R. (2001). Procedural justice and retaliation in organizations: Comparing cross-nationally the importance of fair group processes. *The International Journal of Conflict Management, 12*, 295–311.

Bobocel, D. R., & Zdaniuk, A. (2005). Do explanations influence perceived fairness in the workplace? In: J. Greenberg & J. Colquitt (Eds), *The handbook of organizational justice* (pp. 469–498). Mahwah, NJ: Lawrence Erlbaum Associates.

Braithwaite, J. (1989). *Crime, shame, and reintegration.* Cambridge: Cambridge University Press.

Braithwaite, J. (1999). Restorative justice: Assessing optimistic and pessimistic accounts. In: M. Tonry (Ed.), *Crime and justice: A review of research* (Vol. 25, pp. 1–127). Chicago: University of Chicago Press.

Braithwaite, J. (2002). *Restorative justice and responsive regulation*. New York: Oxford University Press.

Braithwaite, J. (2003). Principles of restorative justice. In: A. von Hirsch, J. V. Roberts, A. Bottoms, K. Roach & M. Schiff (Eds), *Restorative justice and criminal justice: Competing or reconcilable paradigms?* (pp. 1–20). Oxford: Hart.

Bushman, B. J., & Baumeister, R. F. (1998). Threatened egotism, narcissism, self-esteem, and direct and displaced aggression: Does self-love or self-hate lead to violence? *Journal of Personality and Social Psychology*, *75*, 219–229.

Carlsmith, K. M., Darley, J. M., & Robinson, P. H. (2002). Why do we punish? Deterrence and just deserts as motives for punishment. *Journal of Personality and Social Psychology*, *83*, 284–299.

Christie, N. (1977). Conflicts as property. *British Journal of Criminology*, *17*, 1–15.

Cohen-Charash, Y., & Spector, P. E. (2001). The role of justice in organizations: A meta-analysis. *Organizational Behavior and Human Decision Processes*, *86*, 278–321.

Collett, J. (2008). Is procedural justice enough? Reconsidering 'justice' in alternative dispute resolution. In: K.A. Hegtvedt & J. Clay-Warner, (Eds), *Advances in group processes: Justice* (Vol. 25, pp. 267–289). Elsevier, Oxford.

Cropanzano, R., & Ambrose, M. L. (2001). Procedural and distributive justice are more similar than you think: A monistic perspective and a research agenda. In: J. Greenberg & R. Cropanzano (Eds), *Advances in organizational justice* (pp. 119–151). Stanford, CA: Stanford University Press.

Darby, B. W., & Schlenker, B. R. (1989). Children's reactions to transgressions: Effects of the actor's apology, reputation and remorse. *British Journal of Social Psychology*, *28*, 353–364.

Darley, J. (2002). Just punishments: Research on retributional justice. In: M. Ross & D. T. Miller (Eds), *The justice motive in everyday life* (pp. 314–333). Cambridge: Cambridge University Press.

Darley, J. M., Carlsmith, K. M., & Robinson, P. H. (2000). Incapacitation and just deserts as motives for punishment. *Law and Human Behavior*, *24*, 659–683.

Darley, J. M., & Pittman, T. S. (2003). The psychology of compensatory and retributive justice. *Personality and Social Psychology Review*, *7*, 324–336.

Durkheim, E., (1964). *The division of labor in society* (G. Simpson, Trans.). Glencoe, IL: The Free Press (Original work published 1902).

Eaton, J., Struthers, C., & Santelli, A. G. (2006). The mediating role of perceptual validation in the repentance-forgiveness process. *Personality and Social Psychology Bulletin*, *32*, 1389–1401.

Ellsworth, P., & Gross, S. R. (1994). Hardening of the attitudes: American's views on the death penalty. *Journal of Social Issues*, *50*, 19–52.

Exline, J. J., & Baumeister, R. F. (2000). Expressing forgiveness and repentance: Benefits and barriers. In: M. E. McCullough, K. I. Pargament & C. E. Thoresen (Eds), *Forgiveness: Theory, research, and practice* (pp. 133–155). New York: Guilford.

Exline, J. J., Worthington, E. L., Jr., Hill, P., & McCullough, M. E. (2003). Forgiveness and justice: A research agenda for social and personality psychology. *Personality and Social Psychology Review*, *7*, 337–348.

Feather, N. T. (1996). Reactions to penalties for an offense in relation to authoritarianism, values, perceived responsibility, perceived seriousness, and deservingness. *Journal of Personality and Social Psychology*, *71*, 571–587.

Feather, N. T. (1999). *Values, achievement, and justice: Studies in the psychology of deservingness*. New York: Kluwer/Plenum Press.

Felson, R. (1992). "Kick'em when they're down": Explanations of the relationship between stress and interpersonal aggression and violence. *Sociological Quarterly*, *33*, 1–16.

Felson, R. B., & Ribner, S. A. (1981). An attributional approach to accounts and sanctions for criminal violence. *Social Psychology Quarterly*, *44*, 137–142.

Fiske, A. P., & Tetlock, P. E. (1997). Taboo trade-offs: Reactions to transactions that transgress the spheres of justice. *Political Psychology*, *18*, 255–297.

Folger, R., & Baron, R. A. (1996). Violence and hostility at work: A model of reactions to perceived injustice. In: G. R. Vandenbos & E. Q. Bulato (Eds), *Workplace violence* (pp. 51–85). Washington, DC: American Psychological Association.

Folger, R., & Skarlicki, D. P. (1998). A popcorn metaphor for employee aggression. In: R. W. Griffin, A. O'Leary-Kelly & J. Collins (Eds), *Monographs in organizational behavior and industrial relations: Vol. 23* (pp. 43–81). Greenwich, CT: JAI Press.

Furnham, A., & Argyle, M. (1998). *The psychology of money*. Florence, KY: Taylor & Frances/ Routledge.

Gaertner, S., Mann, J., Murrell, A., & Dovidio, J. (1989). Reducing intergroup bias: The benefits of re-categorization. *Journal of Personality and Social Psychology*, *57*, 239–249.

Goffman, E. (1971). *Relations in public*. New York: Basic Books.

Gollwitzer, M. (2004). Do normative transgressions affect punitive judgments? An empirical test of the psychoanalytic scapegoat hypothesis. *Personality and Social Psychology Bulletin*, *30*, 1650–1660.

Gonzales, M. H., Haugen, J. A., & Manning, D. J. (1994). Victims as 'narrative critics': factors influencing rejoinders and evaluative responses to offenders' accounts. *Personality and Social Psychology Bulletin*, *20*, 691–704.

Greenberg, J. (1990). Employee theft as a reaction to underpayment inequity: The hidden cost of pay cuts. *Journal of Applied Psychology*, *75*, 561–568.

Greenberg, J. (1997). The STEAL motive: Managing the social determinants of employee theft. In: R. A. Giacalone & J. Greenberg (Eds), *Antisocial behavior in organizations* (pp. 85–108). Thousand Oaks, CA: Sage.

Gromet, D. M., & Darley, J. (2006). Restoration and retribution: How including retributive components affects the acceptability of restorative justice processes. *Social Justice Research*, *19*, 395–432.

Halleck, S. L. (1980). Vengeance and victimization. *Victimology*, *5*, 99–109.

Haslam, S. A., McGarty, C., & Turner, J. C. (1996). Salient group memberships and persuasion: The role of social identity in the validation of beliefs. In: J. L. Nye & A. M. Brower (Eds), *What's social about social cognition? Research on socially shared cognition in small groups* (pp. 29–56). Thousand Oaks, CA: Sage.

Heider, F. (1958). *The psychology of interpersonal relations*. New York: Wiley.

Horai, J. (1977). Attributional conflict. *Journal of Social Issues*, *33*, 88–100.

Karp, D. R. (1998). The judicial and judicious use of shame penalties. *Crime and Delinquency*, *44*, 277–294.

Kelln, B. R. C., & Ellard, J. H. (1999). An equity theory analysis of the impact of forgiveness and retribution on transgressor compliance. *Personality and Social Psychology Bulletin*, *25*, 864–872.

Kerr, N. L., Hymes, R. W., Anderson, A. B., & Weathers, J. E. (1995). Defendant-juror similarity and mock juror judgments. *Law & Human Behavior*, *19*, 545–567.

Kim, S. H., Smith, R. H., & Brigham, N. L. (1998). Effects of power imbalance and the presence of third parties on reactions to harm: Upward and downward revenge. *Personality and Social Psychology Bulletin*, *24*, 353–361.

Latimer, J., Dowden, C., & Muise, D. (2005). The effectiveness of restorative justice practices: A meta-analysis. *Prison Journal*, *85*, 127–144.

Lerner, M. J. (1991). Integrating societal and psychological rules of entitlement. In: R. Vermunt & H. Steensma (Eds), *Social justice in human relations* (Vol. 1, pp. 13–32). New York: Plenum Press.

MacCoun, R. J. (1993). Drugs and the law: A psychological analysis of drug prohibition. *Psychological Bulletin*, *113*, 497–512.

Marques, J. M. (1990). The black sheep-effect: Out-group homogeneity in social comparison settings. In: D. Abrams & M. A. Hogg (Eds), *Social identity theory: Constructive and critical advances* (pp. 131–151). New York: Springer.

Marques, J. M., Abrams, D., & Serôdio, R. G. (2001). Being better by being right: Subjective group dynamics and derogation of in-group deviants when generic norms are undermined. *Journal of Personality and Social Psychology*, *81*, 436–447.

Marques, J. M., & Paez, D. (1994). The 'black sheep effect': Social categorization, rejection of ingroup deviates, and perception of group variability. In: W. Stroebe & M. Hewstone (Eds), *European review of social psychology* (Vol. 5, pp. 37–68). Chichester: Wiley.

Marshall, T. F. (1998). *Restorative justice: An overview*. A report by the Home Office Research Development and Statistics Directorate. Home Office, London.

McClelland, D. C. (1987). *Human motivation*. New York: Cambridge University Press.

McCullough, M. E., Worthington, E. L., Jr., & Rachal, K. C. (1997). Interpersonal forgiving in close relationships. *Journal of Personality and Social Psychology*, *73*, 321–336.

Miller, D. T. (2001). Disrespect and the experience of injustice. *Annual Review of Psychology*, *52*, 527–553.

Miller, D. T., & McCann, C. D. (1979). Children's reactions to the perpetrators and victims of injustices. *Child Development*, *50*(3), 861–868.

Murphy, J. G., & Hampton, J. (1988). *Forgiveness and mercy*. Cambridge: Cambridge University Press.

Nagin, D. S. (1998). Criminal deterrence at the onset of the 21s[t] century. *Crime and Justice*, *23*, 1–42.

Ohbuchi, K., Kameda, M., & Agarie, N. (1989). Apology as aggression control: Its role in mediating appraisal of and response to harm. *Journal of Personality and Social Psychology*, *56*, 219–227.

Okimoto, T. G. (in press a). Outcomes as affirmation of membership value: Material compensation as an administrative response to procedural injustice. *Journal of Experimental Social Psychology*. doi:10.1016/j.jesp.2008.04.009.

Okimoto, T. G. (in press b). The moderating and mediating role of group identification in observers' reactions to intragroup disrespect. *European Journal of Social Psychology*. doi:10.1002/ejsp.474.

Okimoto, T. G., & Tyler, T. R. (2007). Is compensation enough? Relational concerns in responding to unintended harm. *Group Processes and Intergroup Relations*, *10*, 399–420.

Okimoto, T. G., & Wenzel, M. (2007a). *National identity and retributive responses to terrorism: Symbolic identity implications in inter and intra-group conflict*. Manuscript submitted for publication.
Okimoto, T. G., & Wenzel, M. (in press). *Punishment as restoration of group and offender values following a transgression: Value consensus through symbolic labelling and offender reform. European Journal of Social Psychology*, doi:10.1002/ejsp.537.
Okimoto, T. G., & Wenzel, M. (2007b). *Concerns underlying terrorism and preferences for retributive and restorative justice*. Unpublished raw data.
Okimoto, T. G., Wenzel, M., & Feather, N. T. (in press). *Beyond retribution: Conceptualizing restorative justice and exploring its determinants. Social Justice Research.*
Okimoto, T.G., Wenzel, M., & Feather, N.T. (2008). *Conceptualizing retributive, and restorative notions of justice: Personality, values, and preferences for judicial interventions*. Manuscript submitted for publication.
Opsahl, R. L., & Dunnette, M. D. (1966). Role of financial compensation in industrial motivation. *Psychological Bulletin, 66*, 94–118.
Pratto, F., Sidanius, J., Stallworth, L. M., & Malle, B. F. (1994). Social dominance orientation: A personality variable predicting social and political attitudes. *Journal of Personality and Social Psychology, 67*, 741–763.
Raskin, R., & Terry, H. (1988). A principal-components analysis of the narcissistic personality inventory and further evidence of its construct validity. *Journal of Personality and Social Psychology, 54*, 890–902.
Reb, J., Goldman, B. M., & Cropanzano, R. (2006). Different wrongs, different remedies? Reactions to organizational remedies after procedural and interactional injustice. *Personnel Psychology, 59*, 31–64.
Reed, A. I., & Aquino, K. F. (2003). Moral identity and the expanding circle of moral regard toward out-groups. *Journal of Personality and Social Psychology, 84*, 1270–1286.
Richards, Z., & Hewstone, M. (2001). Subtyping and subgrouping: Processes for the prevention and promotion of stereotype change. *Personality and Social Psychology Review, 5*, 52–73.
Robbennolt, J. K. (2003). Apologies and legal settlement: An empirical examination. *Michigan Law Review, 102*, 460–516.
Robinson, S. L., & O'Leary-Kelly, A. (1998). Monkey see, monkey do: The influence of work groups on the antisocial behavior of employees. *Academy of Management Journal, 41*, 658–672.
Roche, D. (2003). *Accountability in restorative justice*. Oxford: Oxford University Press.
Ross, H. L. (1981). *Deterring the drunk driver*. Lexington, MA: Lexington Books.
Rumsey, M. G. (1976). Effects of defendant background and remorse on sentencing judgments. *Journal of Applied Social Psychology, 6*, 64–68.
Scheff, T. J. (1998). Therapeutic jurisprudence forum: Community conferences: Shame and anger in therapeutic jurisprudence. *Revista Juridica Universidad de Puerto Rico, 67*, 97–119.
Scher, S. J., & Darley, J. M. (1997). How effective are the things people say to apologize? Effects of the realization of the apology speech act. *Journal of Psycholinguistic Research, 26*, 127–140.
Schroeder, D. A., Steel, J. A., Woodell, A. J., & Bembenek, A. F. (2003). Justice within social dilemmas. *Personality and Social Psychology Review, 7*, 374–387.
Shaver, K. G. (1985). *The attribution of blame: Causality, responsibility, and blameworthiness*. New York: Springer.

Sherif, M. (1966). *Group conflict and cooperation: Their social psychology*. London: Routledge and Kegan Paul.

Singelis, T. M. (1994). The measurement of independent and interdependent self-construals. *Personality and Social Psychology Bulletin*, *20*, 580–591.

Skarlicki, D. P., & Folger, R. (1997). Retaliation in the workplace: The roles of distributive, procedural, and interactional justice. *Journal of Applied Psychology*, *82*, 434–443.

Strang, H. (2002). *Repair or revenge: Victims and restorative justice*. London: Oxford University Press.

Strang, H., Sherman, L., Angel, C. M., Woods, D. J., Bennett, S., Newbury-Birch, D., & Inkpen, N. (2006). Victim evaluations of face-to-face restorative justice experiences: A quasi-experimental analysis. *Journal of Social Issues*, *62*, 281–306.

Sunshine, J., & Heuer, L. (2002). Deservingness and perceptions of procedural justice in citizen encounters with the police. In: M. Ross & D. T. Miller (Eds), *The justice motive in everyday life* (pp. 397–415). Cambridge: Cambridge University Press.

Tajfel, H., & Turner, J. C. (1979). The social identity theory of intergroup behaviour. In: S. Worchel & W. Austin (Eds), *Psychology of intergroup behaviour*. Chicago: Nelson Hall.

Tavuchis, N. (1991). *Mea culpa: A sociology of apology and reconciliation*. Stanford, CA: Stanford University Press.

Tedeschi, J., & Felson, R. (1994). *Violence, aggression, and coercive action*. Washington, DC: American Psychological Association.

Tedeschi, J. T., & Reiss, M. (1981). Predicaments and verbal tactics of impression management. In: C. Antaki (Ed.), *The psychology of ordinary language explanations of social behavior*. San Diego, CA: Academic Press.

Thye, S. R., Willer, D., & Markovsky, B. (2006). From status to power: New models at the intersection of two theories. *Social Forces*, *84*, 1471–1495.

Triandis, H. C. (1995). *Individualism and collectivism*. Boulder, CO: Westview Press.

Tripp, T. M., Bies, R. J., & Aquino, K. (2007). A vigilante model of justice: Revenge, reconciliation, forgiveness, and avoidance. *Social Justice Research*, *20*, 10–34.

Turner, J. C. (1981). The experimental social psychology of intergroup behaviour. In: J. C. Turner & H. Giles (Eds), *Intergroup behaviour* (pp. 66–101). Oxford: Basil Blackwell.

Turner, J. C. (1987a). A self-categorization theory. In: J. C. Turner, M. A. Hogg, P. J. Oakes, S. D. Reicher & M. S. Wetherell (Eds), *Rediscovering the social group: A self-categorization theory* (pp. 42–67). Oxford: Blackwell.

Turner, J. C. (1987b). The analysis of social influence. In: J. C. Turner, M. A. Hogg, P. J. Oakes, S. D. Reicher & M. S. Wetherell (Eds), *Rediscovering the social group: A self-categorization theory* (pp. 68–88). Oxford: Blackwell.

Turner, J. C., Hogg, M. A., Oakes, P. J., Reicher, S. D., & Wetherell, M. S. (1987). *Rediscovering the social group: A self-categorization theory*. New York: Basil Blackwell.

Tyler, T. R. (1997). Citizen discontent with legal procedures. *American Journal of Comparative Law*, *45*, 869–902.

Tyler, T. R. (2003). Procedural justice, legitimacy, and the effectiveness of law. *Crime and Justice*, *30*, 431–505.

Tyler, T. R. (2006). *Why people obey the law*. Princeton, NJ: Princeton University Press.

Tyler, T. R., & Blader, S. L. (2003). The group engagement model: Procedural justice, social identity, and cooperative behavior. *Personality and Social Psychology Review*, *7*, 349–361.

Tyler, T. R., & Boeckmann, R. J. (1997). Three strikes and you are out, but why? The psychology of public support for punishing rule breakers. *Law and Society Review*, *31*, 237–265.

Tyler, T. R., Boeckmann, R. J., Smith, H. J., & Huo, Y. J. (1997). *Social justice in a diverse society*. Boulder, CO: Westview Press.

Tyler, T. R., Degoey, P., & Smith, H. J. (1996). Understanding why the justice of group procedures matters: A test of the psychological dynamics of the group-value model. *Journal of Personality and Social Psychology*, *70*, 913–930.

Tyler, T. R., & Lind, E. A. (1992). A relational model of authority in groups. In: M. Zanna (Ed.), *Advances in experimental social psychology* (Vol. 25, pp. 115–191). New York: Academic Press.

Tyler, T. R., & Webber, R. (1983). Support for the death penalty. *Law and Society Review*, *17*, 201–224.

van Prooijen, J.-W. (2004). Retributive versus restorative justice: Is punishing offenders more important than compensating victims. Paper presented at the 10th biennial meeting of the International Society for Justice Research, Regina, Canada.

Vidmar, N. (2000). Retribution and revenge. In: J. Sanders & V. L. Hamilton (Eds), *Handbook of justice research in law* (pp. 31–63). New York: Kluwer/Plenum Press.

Walgrave, L. (1995). Restorative justice for juveniles: Just a technique or a fully fledged alternative? *The Howard Journal of Criminal Justice*, *34*, 228–249.

Walster, E., Walster, G. W., & Berscheid, E. (1978). *Equity: Theory and research*. Boston: Allyn and Bacon.

Wenzel, M. (2004). A social categorisation approach to distributive justice. In: W. Stroebe & M. Hewstone (Eds), *European review of social psychology* (Vol. 15, pp. 219–257). Hove: Psychology Press.

Wenzel, M., & Okimoto, T. G. (2007). *How acts of forgiveness restore a sense of justice: Addressing status/power and value concerns raised by transgressions*. Manuscript submitted for publication.

Wenzel, M., Okimoto, T. G., & Feather, N. T. (2007). *Retributive and restorative notions of justice, emotions, and the symbolic implications of a transgression*. Unpublished raw data.

Wenzel, M., Okimoto, T. G., Feather, N. T., & Platow, M. J. (in press). Retributive and restorative justice. *Law and Human Behavior*, doi:10.1007/S10979-007-9116-6.

Wenzel, M., Okimoto, T. G., Feather, N. T., & Platow, M. J. (2008). *Justice through consensus: Shared identity and the preference for a restorative notion of justice*. Manuscript submitted for publication.

Wenzel, M., & Thielmann, I. (2006). Why we punish in the name of justice: Just desert versus value restoration and the role of social identity. *Social Justice Research*, *19*, 450–470.

Wood, R. E., & Mitchell, T. R. (1981). Manager behavior in a social context: The impact of impression management on attributions and disciplinary actions. *Organizational Behavior and Human Performance*, *28*, 356–378.

Worthington, E. L. (2006). *Forgiveness and reconciliation: Theory and application*. New York: Routledge.

Zehr, H. (1985). *Retributive justice, restorative justice*. New Perspectives on Crime and Justice, Vol. 4: Occasional papers of the MCC Canada Victim Offender Ministries Program and the MCC, U.S. Office of Criminal Justice. Elkhart, Ind.: Mennonite Central Committee; Kitchener, Ontario: Canada Victim Offender Ministries Program.

APPENDIX. RETRIBUTIVE/RESTORATIVE LAY-PHILOSOPHICAL NOTIONS OF JUSTICE

Retributive notion: (average coefficient $\alpha = .87$)

1. As a matter of fairness, the offender should be penalized.
2. The only way to restore justice is to punish the offender.
3. Justice is served at the moment that the offender is punished.
4. Only a punishment restores the justice disrupted by the incident.
5. For the sake of justice, some degree of suffering has to be inflicted on the offender.
6. The offender deserves to be penalized.

Restorative notion: (average coefficient $\alpha = .78$)

1. For justice to be reinstated, the affected parties need to achieve agreement about the values violated by the incident.
2. To restore justice, the offender and I need to reaffirm consensus on the values and rules we share.
3. Without the offender's sincere acknowledgement of having acted inappropriately, the injustice is not completely restored.
4. A sense of justice requires that the offender and I develop a shared understanding of the harm done by the incident.
5. Justice is restored as soon as the offender has learnt to endorse the values violated by the incident.
6. For a sense of justice, we all, including the offender and I, need to reaffirm our belief in shared workplace values.

Notes: Drawn from research by Wenzel et al. (2008). In all studies, this distinction was verified through factor analyses. Scales are formed by averaging across items. All items are measured on 7-point scales, with higher numbers indicating agreement.

SHALL WE KILL OR ENSLAVE CAESAR? ANALYZING THE CAESAR MODEL

Guillermina Jasso

ABSTRACT

When a society overthrows a ruler – call the ruler Caesar – what determines whether Caesar is killed or enslaved? This chapter presents a model of killing versus enslaving Caesar, based on a new theory which unifies justice, status, and power. The model pertains to societies which value ordinal goods like bravery, yielding predictions for three of the five types of societies – justice-nonmaterialistic, status, and power-nonmaterialistic. Results cover members' gains, effects of own rank and group size, and relative gains from killing or enslaving Caesar. Further results suggest that Caesar will be killed only in a justice-nonmaterialistic society, and from the noblest of motives – to achieve equal gains for members.

Uneasy lies the head that wears a crown.

– William Shakespeare, Henry IV, Part II

One of the most efficacious remedies that a prince can have against conspiracies is not to be hated and despised by the people, for he who conspires against a prince always expects to please them by his removal; but when the conspirator can only look forward

Justice
Advances in Group Processes, Volume 25, 327–343

ISSN: 0882-6145/doi:10.1016/S0882-6145(08)25009-5

to offending them, he will not have the courage to take such a course, for the difficulties that confront a conspirator are infinite.

– Nicolò Machiavelli, The Prince

1. INTRODUCTION

We have grown up with images of kings killed and emperors assassinated. From the stabbing of Caesar to the guillotining of Louis XVI to the shooting of Czar Nicholas, we have asked *why*. Why not send them into exile? Or imprison them? Or place them under house arrest? *Why kill them?* There are two important pertinent scholarly traditions, one historical, the other philosophical. The historical tradition provides a positive account of the long series of killings of tyrants. And the philosophical tradition offers a normative discussion of the conditions under which tyrannicide is permissible, or even obligatory (and of who should or should not participate and the means by which it should be carried out). Yet the behavioral question remains. *Why kill Caesar?*[1]

Meanwhile, as scientific understanding of human behavior grows, new theories yield new insights. One of the grand insights of twentieth century social science – inherited from the Greeks – was the centrality of justice processes (Homans, 1974; Berger, Zelditch, Anderson, & Cohen, 1972; Jasso, 1980). The long reach of justice can be discerned in virtually all of human behavior, from love to crime, from gifts to revolution, from religious institutions to disasters.

In this chapter, we use the lens of justice analysis to explore the old question, why kill Caesar? We use the axiomatization developed by Jasso in a long series of papers (starting in 1978 and 1980 and recently summarized in 2005, 2006b, and 2007 (and more briefly in 2006a)). This axiomatization distinguishes between societies which value *cardinal* things (like wealth and land) – called *materialistic societies* – and societies which value *ordinal* things (like beauty and intelligence) – called *nonmaterialistic societies*. But the engine is the same for both, namely, the justice force.

The justice axiomatization begins with the four central questions in the study of justice, as compiled by Jasso and Wegener (1997):

1. What do individuals and societies think is just, and why?
2. How do ideas of justice shape determination of actual situations?
3. What is the magnitude of the perceived injustice associated with departures from perfect justice?
4. What are the behavioral and social consequences of perceived injustice?

The work reported in this chapter falls under the fourth central question but uses the building-blocks developed to address the other questions, notably the justice evaluation function, which addresses the third question and in theoretical justice analysis operates as first postulate.

There is a large literature on the fourth central question, often referred to as the literature on reactions to injustice (Hegtvedt, 2006). Examples include Adams (1965), Cohen-Charash and Spector (2001), and Tyler, Boeckmann, Smith, and Huo (1997), as well as Jasso's theoretical work on justice and comparison processes, some of which is referenced in this chapter. For more general overviews of justice analysis, see Hegtvedt (2006) and Jasso (2006a). Besides the literature on reactions to injustice, there is another large literature on ideas about what is just (addressing the first central question). Hegtvedt (2006, p. 47) and Jasso (2007, pp. 339, 343–344) show how the justice evaluation function serves as a bridge that connects the two literatures.

For a long time, perhaps all of the twentieth century, it was known that not all persons or societies fall under the aegis of justice. Like the tone-deaf or color-blind, some persons seem justice-oblivious, as do the societies they form.

And, similarly, for a long time it was unclear how justice is related to other basic processes, such as status and power. Indeed, some authors used the terms interchangeably, while for others one or the other had primacy. Certainly everyone agreed that all three candidates for basic forces – *status*, *justice*, *power* – are responsive to the same human characteristics. Wealth, for example, increases status, and it pushes toward unjust overreward, and it increases power. So do beauty, intelligence, and skills of all kinds (athletic, musical, artistic). There is a status hierarchy, and a power hierarchy, and a justice hierarchy (though sometimes "continuum" is used instead of "hierarchy").

Status and power, like justice, are also addressed by large literatures. For brief introduction to status theory, see Berger and Webster (2006), Jasso (2001b), and Ridgeway (2006). Jasso and Kotz (2007) describe how the mathematical foundation for studying status was laid by Berger, Cohen, and Zelditch (1966), Berger, Fisek, Norman, and Zelditch (1977), Goode (1978), and Sørensen (1979). Jasso (2004) proposes a list of four central questions in the study of status. The work reported in this chapter addresses the fourth question, which, paralleling the list in justice analysis, is: "What are the behavioral and social consequences of according and receiving status and of discrepancies between expected and received status?"

The literatures on power are voluminous. For example, one literature can be traced to the classic paper by Emerson (1962) and brief introduction to more than 40 years of elaboration and extension is provided by Cook, Cheshire, and Gerbasi (2006).

The early twenty-first century has brought a possible solution to the puzzle of the exact relations among the three candidate forces – justice, status, and power. This possible solution rests on the suggestion that they each have *distinctive rates of change* (Jasso, 2007, 2008). Although all three are increasing functions of the same things (such as wealth or beauty), they each increase at a distinctive rate. Jasso's axiomatization of justice includes a proof that the justice evaluation increases as the logarithm of the ratio of the actual reward to the just reward, thus implying that justice increases at a decreasing rate with the valued good (Jasso, 1990). The axiomatization of status based on the Goode–Sørensen formulation proposes that status increases at an increasing rate with the valued good (Jasso, 2001b). Thus, if power is truly a distinct force – and not merely another name for status, or for justice – it must increase at a constant rate.[2] To visualize the distinctive rates of change, Fig. 1 depicts the three sociobehavioral forces in a 12-person group which values an ordinal good.

This proposed solution led to a *new unified theory* with its own new axiomatization and a new view of the three sociobehavioral forces as not

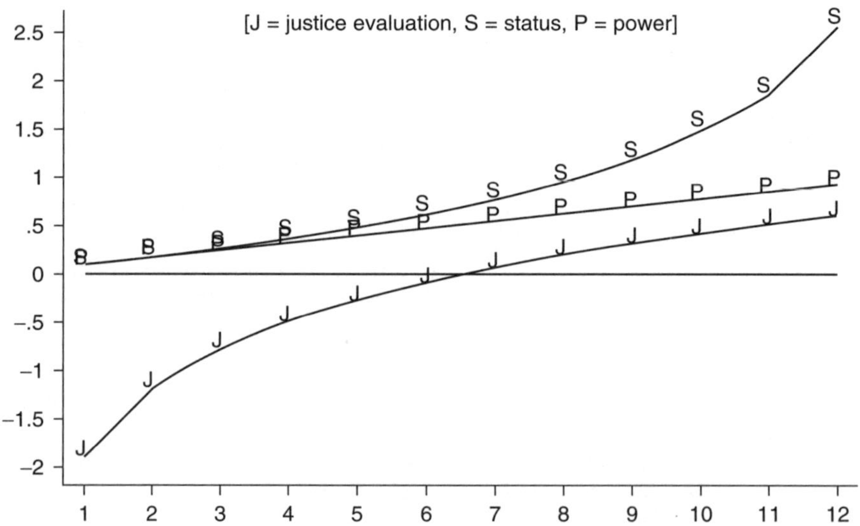

Fig. 1. Justice, Status, and Power in a 12-Person Group.

only fundamental but also, and importantly, in competition with each other for the hearts and minds of persons and the societies they form. The justice-oblivious may be votaries of status or acolytes of power.

As well, the new unified theory suggests that each of the three sociobehavioral forces generates, during the time it is active, identity and happiness.

Accordingly, it follows that correct understanding of the sense of justice is not possible without understanding its rivals, for to understand justice is to understand its boundaries and limitations. In this chapter, we thus explore the question, Why kill Caesar? using not only the justice lens but also the status and power lenses. As will be seen, this approach enables a strong conclusion about the part played by justice processes in "killing Caesar."

As noted, in justice theory, people and societies can be materialistic or nonmaterialistic. So, too, in power societies; people can care about wealth or about beauty, the first treated as a cardinal good and the second as an ordinal good. Not so in the world of status. The Goode–Sørensen formulation asserts that status notices only relative ranks; the status votary may care about wealth but only in the form of wealth rank, not in the form of wealth amount. Thus, in the new unified theory of sociobehavioral forces, there are five main types of societies: justice-materialistic, justice-nonmaterialistic, status, power-materialistic, and power-nonmaterialistic.

The killing-Caesar model we develop notices only ranks. Thus, we explore three possible kinds of societies: justice-nonmaterialistic, status, and power-nonmaterialistic. It is possible, of course, to examine killing Caesar in a materialistic regime, but we think it less natural and leave it to a future exercise.

Further, we must consider an alternative to killing Caesar. The alternative we choose is enslaving Caesar. Empirically, enslaving can take the form of house arrest, imprisonment, or actual enslavement. The important feature of enslavement is that Caesar topples from top rank to bottom rank.

Finally, our results are general and can be applied to many different kinds of real-world situations. For example, the focal group can be a set of conspirators or an entire society. Similarly, the setting can be a country, an association, or a club. In some contexts, the killing-Caesar option is equivalent to permanent exile. We leave to future work a further analysis to distinguish between killing and exiling Caesar, while noting that in some contexts, such as clubs, throwing someone out of the club is the operational equivalent of killing Caesar.

2. THEORETICAL SETUP

2.1. Elements of the Setup Common to All Three Kinds of Societies

Consider a group with N members. The members all value the same good – such as wealth, land, cattle, military prowess, bravery, or horsemanship. If the good is cardinal (such as wealth, land, or head of cattle), the members value its ordinal manifestation. Accordingly, the N members are ranked, with the rank i going from 1 for the lowest-ranked to N for the highest-ranked. The sociobehavioral force generates a score for each person – such as a magnitude of status or of the justice evaluation – and also generates an identity and a magnitude of happiness (Jasso, 2007, 2008).

In the situation we explore, the highest-ranked person – Caesar – is overthrown. Empirically, this can be the work of all the other members, or of a subset of conspirators, or even of an outsider. The group remains intact (except for Caesar's unseating); no outsider becomes a member.

The top-ranked person may, but need not, be a ruler; if a ruler, the top-ranked person may be tyrannical or beneficent. Obviously, the case of the tyrant is the classic case discussed by Plato, Aristotle, Augustine, John of Salisbury, Aquinas, and others in their analyses of sedition as a response to injustice. "Without justice, what are kingdoms but great robberies," asks Augustine (*City of God*, Book IV, Ch. 4). And Thomas Aquinas (*Summa Theologica* II-II, Q. 42, Art. 2), analyzing the morality of tyrannicide, notes, "It is the tyrant rather that is guilty of sedition."

Again, the model is applicable to any group or society with a hierarchy based on a valued ordinal characteristic. Caesar is the top-ranked person in the group's hierarchy.

Killing Caesar – what happens to group size and own rank? It is obvious that in the killing scenario, group size diminishes by one. Formally, group size at Time 1 is N; at Time 2 it is N–1. Given that the top person is killed, own rank stays the same for all other group members. Formally, own rank is i at both Time 1 and Time 2.

Enslaving Caesar – what happens to group size and own rank? In this scenario it is obvious that group size stays the same. Formally, group size is N at both Time 1 and Time 2. Own rank, however, increases by 1 for all group members, given that Caesar is now the lowest-ranked person. Formally, own rank is i at Time 1 and increases to $i+1$ at Time 2.

To analyze the effects on each group member, we use the technique of theoretical derivation known as the *micromodel* strategy. The basic idea is that an event – in this case, killing or enslaving Caesar – produces a *change* in each group member's well-being by altering the justice, status, or power score. The change may be positive or negative; that is, individuals may become better-off or worse-off as a result of the focal event. This technique has been used to analyze effects of gifts, theft, disasters, and so on.[3]

2.2. Caesar Model in a Justice-Nonmaterialistic Society

The justice-nonmaterialistic version of the Caesar model begins with the first postulate of justice theory, the justice evaluation function, expressed for ordinal goods:

$$J = \ln\left(\frac{r_{\mathrm{A}}}{r_{\mathrm{C}}}\right), \tag{1}$$

where J denotes the justice evaluation, r the individual's relative rank, and the subscripts A and C the *actual* and *just* elements, respectively. The relative rank is approximated by $i/(N+1)$, where, as before, i is the absolute rank and N the group size, leading to:[4]

$$J = \ln\left\{\frac{[i/(N+1)]_{\mathrm{A}}}{[i/(N+1)]_{\mathrm{C}}}\right\}. \tag{2}$$

The change in the justice evaluation from Time 1 to Time 2 is denoted CJ and written:

$$CJ = \ln\left\{\frac{[i/(N+1)]_{\mathrm{A}}}{[i/(N+1)]_{\mathrm{C}}}\right\}_2 - \ln\left\{\frac{[i/(N+1)]_{\mathrm{A}}}{[i/(N+1)]_{\mathrm{C}}}\right\}_1, \tag{3}$$

where the subscripts "1" and "2" denote Time 1 and Time 2, respectively.

Assuming that the just reward remains the same from Time 1 to Time 2, we obtain:

$$CJ = \ln\left\{\frac{[i/(N+1)]_{\mathrm{A2}}}{[i/(N+1)]_{\mathrm{A1}}}\right\}, \tag{4}$$

and thence:

$$CJ = \ln\left[\frac{i_2(N_1+1)}{i_1(N_2+1)}\right]. \tag{5}$$

Applying to formula (5) the rules in Section 2.1 for the changes in own rank i and group size N in the killing and enslaving scenarios yields the final expressions for CJ in the two scenarios:

$$CJ = \begin{cases} \ln\left(\frac{N+1}{N}\right), & \text{kill Caesar} \\ \ln\left(\frac{i+1}{i}\right), & \text{enslave Caesar.} \end{cases} \tag{6}$$

2.3. Caesar Model in a Status Society

The status version of the Caesar model begins with the first postulate of status theory, the status function (also known as the S1 function):

$$S = \ln\left(\frac{1}{1-r}\right), \tag{7}$$

where S denotes status and r the relative rank.[5] Replacing r by its approximation $i/(N+1)$ yields:

$$S = \ln\left(\frac{N+1}{N+1-i}\right), \tag{8}$$

where, as before, i and N denote own rank and group size, respectively.

The change in status from Time 1 to Time 2 is denoted CS and written:

$$CS = \ln\left(\frac{N+1}{N+1-i}\right)_2 - \ln\left(\frac{N+1}{N+1-i}\right)_1, \tag{9}$$

where, as before, the subscripts "1" and "2" denote Time 1 and Time 2, respectively. Formula (9) reduces to:

$$CS = \ln\left[\frac{(N_2+1)(N_1+1-i_1)}{(N_1+1)(N_2+1-i_2)}\right]. \tag{10}$$

Applying to formula (10) the rules in Section 2.1 for the changes in own rank i and group size N in the killing and enslaving scenarios yields the final expressions for CS in the two scenarios:

$$CS = \begin{cases} \ln\left[\dfrac{N(N+1-i)}{(N+1)(N-i)}\right], & \text{kill Caesar} \\ \ln\left(\dfrac{N+1-i}{N-i}\right), & \text{enslave Caesar.} \end{cases} \tag{11}$$

2.4. Caesar Model in a Power Society

The power version of the Caesar model begins with the first postulate of the fledgling power theory. Here power increases at a constant rate with the valued good. For ordinal goods, power increases at a constant rate with relative rank:

$$P = r \tag{12}$$

where P denotes power and, as before, r the relative rank. Replacing r by its approximation $i/(N+1)$ yields:

$$P = \frac{i}{N+1} \tag{13}$$

The change in power from Time 1 to Time 2 is denoted CP and written:

$$CP = \left(\frac{i}{N+1}\right)_2 - \left(\frac{i}{N+1}\right)_1. \tag{14}$$

Applying to formula (14) the rules in Section 2.1 for the changes in own rank i and group size N in the killing and enslaving scenarios yields the final expressions for CP in the two scenarios:

$$CP = \begin{cases} \dfrac{i}{N^2+N}, & \text{kill Caesar} \\ \dfrac{1}{N+1}, & \text{enslave Caesar.} \end{cases} \tag{15}$$

2.5. Analyzing CJ, CS, and CP

To assess the effects of killing versus enslaving Caesar, we pose the following questions:

1. For each group member, is the change in well-being (*CJ*, *CS*, or *CP*) positive or negative?
2. What is the ceteris paribus effect of own rank *i* on *CJ*, *CS*, and *CP*?
3. What is the ceteris paribus effect of group size *N* on *CJ*, *CS*, and *CP*?
4. Under which scenario – killing or enslaving Caesar – are group members better-off?

To answer the first question, we evaluate the sign of formulas (6), (11), and (15) for *CJ*, *CS*, and *CP* in the two scenarios. To answer the second and third questions, we obtain the first partial derivatives of the six formulas in (6), (11), and (15) with respect to own rank and group size. Finally, to answer the fourth question, we set up and solve the inequality formed by the formulas for the two scenarios in each of the three force-regimes.

3. THEORETICAL RESULTS

3.1. Do Group Members Become Better-off When Caesar Is Killed or Enslaved?

Evaluating the sign of the six change formulas (Panel A of Table 1) indicates that all six are positive. Lingering over the results for the justice-nonmaterialistic regime, it is easy to see that *CJ* is positive because in both the killing and the enslaving cases, *CJ* is the logarithm of a ratio and the numerator of the ratio is larger than the denominator. The same is true in the two status cases. The formulas in the two power cases are obviously positive. Thus, when Caesar is killed or enslaved, under all three force-regimes, every group member becomes better-off.

Expressed formally, we have the first theoretical result:

Result 1 (Universal Gain from Overthrowing Caesar). In a justice-nonmaterialistic society, a status society, or a power-nonmaterialistic society, everyone gains from overthrowing Caesar, regardless of whether Caesar is killed or enslaved.

3.2. Does Own Rank Affect the Gain from Killing or Enslaving Caesar?

Inspecting the change formulas in Table 1, it is evident that own rank has no effect on *CJ* in the killing case and on *CP* in the enslaving case, as it does not appear in the formulas. In the other four cases we take the first partial derivatives of the change formulas with respect to *i* and find that the effect is

Table 1. Gains from Removing Caesar, by Sociobehavioral Regime and Killing or Enslaving Scenario.

Sociobehavioral Regime					
Justice-Nonmaterialistic		Status		Power-Nonmaterialistic	
Killing Caesar	Enslaving Caesar	Killing Caesar	Enslaving Caesar	Killing Caesar	Enslaving Caesar
A. Formulas for change in justice, status, and power from killing or enslaving Caesar – all are positive					
$\ln\left(\frac{N+1}{N}\right)$	$\ln\left(\frac{i+1}{i}\right)$	$\ln\left(\frac{N(N+1-i)}{(N+1)(N-i)}\right)$	$\ln\left(\frac{N+1-i}{N-i}\right)$	$\frac{i}{N^2+N}$	$\frac{1}{N+1}$
B. Effect of own rank i on gain from killing or enslaving Caesar					
Zero	Negative	Positive	Positive	Positive	Zero
C. Effect of group size N on gain from killing or enslaving Caesar					
Negative	Zero	Negative	Negative	Negative	Negative
D. Is the gain larger in the killing or enslaving scenario?					
Enslaving Caesar		Enslaving Caesar		Enslaving Caesar	

negative in the justice-enslaving case and positive in both status cases and the power-killing case. Thus, holding constant group size, the gains are equal in two cases and unequal in the other four. Moreover, in the unequal cases, we find both a case where lower-ranked members reap greater gains than higher-ranked members and three cases where the opposite occurs. These results are collected in Panel B of Table 1.

Expressed formally, we have the second theoretical result which we report as a set of results and which, because it is based on partial derivatives, pertains to the case where group size is held constant (including, of course, application to a single society):

Result 2 (Equal and Unequal Gains from Overthrowing Caesar, Holding Group Size Constant). The gains from overthrowing Caesar are equal in two of the six cases considered and unequal in the other four.

Result 2.1 (Equal and Unequal Gains from Overthrowing Caesar, by Type of Regime). In a justice-nonmaterialistic society, the gains from overthrowing Caesar are equal if Caesar is killed and unequal if Caesar is enslaved. In a status society, the gains from overthrowing Caesar are always unequal. In a power-nonmaterialistic society, the gains from overthrowing Caesar are equal if Caesar is enslaved and unequal if Caesar is killed.

Result 2.2 (Equal and Unequal Gains from Overthrowing Caesar, by Killing or Enslaving). If Caesar is killed, the gains are equal in a justice-nonmaterialistic society and unequal in a status society or a power-nonmaterialistic society. If Caesar is enslaved, the gains are equal in a power-nonmaterialistic society and unequal in a justice-nonmaterialistic society or a status society.

Result 2.3 (Unequal Gains from Overthrowing Caesar, by Rank). In the four cases of unequal gains from overthrowing Caesar, the gain is a decreasing function of rank in the justice-nonmaterialistic/enslaving-Caesar case and an increasing function of rank in a status society and in the power-nonmaterialistic/killing-Caesar case.

If persons with greater gains are more likely to lead the mutiny or insurrection, then the higher-ranking always lead the revolution in a status society and sometimes in a power-nonmaterialistic society, but never in a justice-nonmaterialistic society. In a justice-nonmaterialistic society, the leaders of the rebellion will come from the bottom or randomly from across all ranks.

3.3. Does Group Size Affect the Gain from Killing or Enslaving Caesar?

Inspection of the change formulas shows that group size has no effect on *CJ* in the enslaving case, as it does not appear in the formula. In the other five cases we take the first partial derivatives of the change formulas with respect to N and find that the effect is negative in all five. These results are summarized in Panel C of Table 1.

Expressed formally:

Result 3 (Equal and Unequal Gains from Overthrowing Caesar, Holding Own Rank Constant). The gains from overthrowing Caesar are equal in one of the six cases considered and unequal in the other five.

Result 3.1 (Equal and Unequal Gains from Overthrowing Caesar, by Type of Regime). In a justice-nonmaterialistic society, the gains from overthrowing Caesar are impervious to group size if Caesar is enslaved and vary with group size if Caesar is killed. In a status society or a power-nonmaterialistic society, the gains from overthrowing Caesar always vary by group size.

Result 3.2 (Equal and Unequal Gains from Overthrowing Caesar, by Killing or Enslaving). If Caesar is killed, group size always affects the gains. If Caesar is enslaved, group size affects the gains in a status society or a power-nonmaterialistic society but has no effect in a justice-nonmaterialistic society.

Result 3.3 (Unequal Gains from Overthrowing Caesar, by Group Size). In the five cases where group size affects the gains, the effect is negative, so that the larger the group, the smaller the gain from overthrowing Caesar.

Thus, these results indicate that, with the exception of the justice-enslaving case (the case where group size has no effect), the gains are larger in small societies, suggesting that toppling Caesar is a phenomenon of relatively small groups.

3.4. Is the Gain Larger from Killing or Enslaving Caesar?

Solving the inequality within each force-regime, we find that the gains are always larger under the enslaving option. For example, in the justice-nonmaterialistic case, contrasting the gain from killing Caesar – $\ln[(N+1)/N]$ – with that from enslaving Caesar – $\ln[(i+1)/i]$ – indicates that the killing gain is always smaller than the enslaving gain. Mathematically, this is due to the logarithmic operation, whereby $1/N$ is always smaller than $1/i$; for example, in a group of size 100, 1/100 is a smaller quantity than 1/2 or 1/3 or 1/4, etc. These results are collected in Panel D of Table 1.

Expressed formally, we have the fourth result:

Result 4 (Greater Gain from Enslaving Caesar Than From Killing Caesar). In the three types of societies considered – justice-nonmaterialistic, status, and power-nonmaterialistic – the gain from enslaving Caesar always exceeds the gain from killing Caesar.

3.5. If the Gain Is Always Greater under the Enslaving Option, Why Kill Caesar?

These results suggest that a plausible answer involves the desire for equality, the desire, that is, to achieve equal gains. As we have seen, equal gains are only possible in a justice society. So we may speculate that killing Caesar only occurs in a justice society and that the reason it occurs is to ensure that all group members reap equal gains.

4. DISCUSSION

Shakespeare was right. The ruler – or any top-ranked person – is vulnerable on many fronts and especially vulnerable to removal. Moreover, our results suggest that the people's gain from unseating the ruler is always positive. Thus, Machiavelli's prescription to gain the esteem of the people as a buffer against conspirators requires measures from beyond the ordinary world of sociobehavioral forces – measures to substantially offset the gain from unseating Caesar.

Our analysis indicates that although everyone gains, the gains are not necessarily equal for all group members. In one scenario – enslaving Caesar in a justice-nonmaterialistic regime – the lower-ranked reap greater gains, while in three scenarios – killing Caesar in a power-nonmaterialistic regime and always in a status regime – the opposite occurs, namely, the higher-ranked reap greater gains. There are two scenarios, however, in which all gains are equals – enslaving Caesar in a power-nonmaterialistic regime and killing Caesar in a justice-nonmaterialistic regime.

Group size also matters, according to our results. In five of the six scenarios, the gains from overthrowing Caesar are greater in small groups than in large groups. In the sixth scenario, the gains do not vary by group size. Thus, toppling Caesar would seem to be a phenomenon of small groups – not only small societies but also small sets of conspirators.

Finally, we asked the question that has fired the universal imagination, Why kill Caesar? We established that in all three societies examined – justice-nonmaterialistic, status, and power-nonmaterialistic – group members reap greater gains from enslaving than from killing Caesar. Thus, it would seem that no insightful conspirator, no rebel who has studied the historical record, would kill Caesar. Rather, Caesar would be imprisoned or exiled, like Napoleon, or even re-educated, like the last emperor of China.

Alas, justice theory suggests a reason for killing rather than enslaving Caesar. In a justice-nonmaterialistic world, the gains from removing Caesar are equal if and only if Caesar is killed. In a power-nonmaterialistic world, remember, the gains from removing Caesar are equal if and only if Caesar is enslaved. Thus, there are in general two paths to achieve equal gains. But in a world already under the aegis of justice, only a single path to equal gains remains – killing Caesar. Thus we speculate that Caesar is killed only in a justice-nonmaterialistic regime and with the otherwise noble purpose of achieving equality.

These are all theoretical predictions, of course, and subject to empirical test. Moreover, it is important to obtain parallel results for the two other kinds of societies, the materialistic justice and power societies. If it turns out that among all five basic types of societies, only the two justice societies yield equal gains from killing Caesar, then these results provide the beginnings of a fresh interpretation of the historical record. In that long line of slain tyrants, the societies valued justice, and equality was the killers' motive. If only the justice-nonmaterialistic society yields equal gains from killing Caesar, then there is additional information about the dominance of ordinal valued goods. Further, it is important as well to obtain results for societies which combine elements of the five ideal types, as such results would place further necessary and sufficient conditions on the links between tyrannicide and the three sociobehavioral forces.[6] Thus, the work reported in this chapter serves to highlight new directions of inquiry and to underscore yet again the long reach of the three sociobehavioral forces and the possible primacy of justice.

These results also lead to a further speculation. If everyone gains from removing Caesar, then perhaps no second-in-command or third-in-command will participate in removing Caesar, for they would themselves immediately become vulnerable to removal. The best defense against removal may well be the knowledge that mortal threat comes with the top rank, and whoever holds top rank is thereby vulnerable.

NOTES

1. The historical and philosophical literatures on tyrannicide are voluminous. See, for example, the classic *Policraticus* by John of Salisbury ([1159] 1909) and the extensive commentaries in the 849 years since its publication.

2. Power is widely thought to increase with personal quantitative characteristics – such as wealth – but the research record is sparse with respect to the form of the function (Webster, 2006). Thus, the power force is compatible with a constant rate of change.

3. For comprehensive exposition of the micromodel and an extended example, see Jasso (2001a); for two additional extended examples, see Jasso (2004, 2006b).

4. The relative ranks have several appealing properties. First, their arithmetic mean is exactly one-half. Second, the first and Nth relative ranks are equidistant from 0 and 1, respectively, and also from the mean. Third, the elements of each subrange pair (e.g., 2 and N–1) are equidistant from 0 and 1, respectively, and also from the mean.

5. The unsubscripted relative rank is equivalent to the "actual" relative rank in the justice evaluation. While status is generated by the actual rank alone, the justice evaluation is generated by comparison of the actual relative rank to the "just" relative rank.

6. Jasso (2008) suggests that persons can be characterized by the configuration of quantitative characteristics, qualitative characteristics, and sociobehavioral forces in their identities, and societies by the configuration of elements in their members' identities. The individual's configuration is termed *personality*, and the society's configuration is termed *culture*. Jasso (2008) goes on to suggest that one of the ensuing empirical challenges is to correctly describe real-world societies in terms of these configurations of personal quantitative characteristics, personal qualitative characteristics, and sociobehavioral forces. For further discussion of the general empirical challenges that arise in testing the predictions of deductive theories, see Jasso (2004, 2006b).

ACKNOWLEDGMENTS

I am grateful to Joseph Berger, Bernard P. Cohen, Thomas Fararo, Samuel Kotz, Jui-Chung Allen Li, Stefan Liebig, Eva M. Meyersson Milgrom, Kjell Törnblom, Murray Webster, Bernd Wegener, and Morris Zelditch for many valuable discussions and to Jody Clay-Warner and Karen Hegtvedt for a close reading of the chapter and many valuable comments and suggestions. I also gratefully acknowledge the intellectual and financial support provided by New York University.

REFERENCES

Adams, J. S. (1965). Inequity in social exchange. *Advances in Experimental Social Psychology*, *2*, 267–299.

Augustine, St. ([413–426] 1952). *The city of God.* (M. Dods, trans.). Chicago: Britannica.

Berger, J., Cohen, B. P., & Zelditch, M., Jr. (1966). Status characteristics and expectation states. In: J. Berger, M. Zelditch, Jr. & B. Anderson (Eds), *Sociological theories in progress* (Vol. 1, pp. 29–46). Boston: Houghton Mifflin.

Berger, J., Fisek, M. H., Norman, R. Z., & Zelditch, M., Jr. (1977). *Status characteristics and social interaction*. New York: Elsevier.

Berger, J., & Webster, M., Jr. (2006). Expectations, status, and behavior. In: P. J. Burke (Ed.), *Contemporary social psychological theories* (pp. 268–300). Stanford, CA: Stanford University Press.

Berger, J., Zelditch, M., Jr., Anderson, B., & Cohen, B. P. (1972). Structural aspects of distributive justice: A status-value formulation. In: J. Berger, M. Zelditch & B. Anderson (Eds), *Sociological theories in progress* (Vol. 2, pp. 119–246). Boston: Houghton Mifflin.

Cohen-Charash, Y., & Spector, P. E. (2001). The role of justice in organizations: A meta analysis. *Organizational Behavior and Human Decision Processes*, *86*, 278–321.

Cook, K. S., Cheshire, C., & Gerbasi, A. (2006). Power, dependence, and social exchange. In: P. J. Burke (Ed.), *Contemporary social psychological theories* (pp. 194–216). Stanford, CA: Stanford University Press.

Emerson, R. M. (1962). Power-dependence relations. *American Sociological Review*, *27*, 31–41.

Goode, W. J. (1978). *The celebration of heroes: prestige as a control system*. Berkeley, CA: University of California Press.

Hegtvedt, K. A. (2006). Justice frameworks. In: P. J. Burke (Ed.), *Contemporary social psychological theories* (pp. 46–69). Stanford, CA: Stanford University Press.

Homans, G. C., (1974). *Social behavior: Its elementary forms* (rev. ed.) New York: Harcourt, Brace, Jovanovich.

Jasso, G. (1978). On the justice of earnings: A new specification of the justice evaluation function. *American Journal of Sociology*, *83*, 1398–1419.

Jasso, G. (1980). A new theory of distributive justice. *American Sociological Review*, *45*, 3–32.

Jasso, G. (1990). Methods for the theoretical and empirical analysis of comparison processes. *Sociological Methodology*, *20*, 369–419.

Jasso, G. (2001a). Rule-finding about rule-making: Comparison processes and the making of norms. In: M. Hechter & K.-D. Opp (Eds), *Social norms* (pp. 348–393). New York: Russell Sage.

Jasso, G. (2001b). Studying status: An integrated framework. *American Sociological Review*, *66*, 96–124.

Jasso, G. (2004). The tripartite structure of social science analysis. *Sociological Theory*, *22*, 401–431.

Jasso, G. (2005). Culture and the sense of justice: A comprehensive framework for analysis. *Journal of Cross Cultural Psychology*, *13*, 14–47.

Jasso, G. (2006a). Distributive justice. In: G. Ritzer (Ed.), *The Blackwell encyclopedia of sociology* (Vol. III, pp. 1189–1195). Malden, MA: Blackwell Publishing.

Jasso, G. (2006b). The theory of comparison processes. In: P. J. Burke (Ed.), *Contemporary social psychological theories* (pp. 165–193). Stanford, CA: Stanford University Press.

Jasso, G. (2007). Theoretical unification in justice and beyond. *Social Justice Research*, *20*, 336–371. Manuscript available as IZA Discussion Paper No. 2641 at www.iza.org

Jasso, G. (2008). A new unified theory of sociobehavioral forces. *European Sociological Review*, *24*.

Jasso, G., & Kotz, S. (2007). A new continuous distribution and two new families of distributions based on the exponential. *Statistica Neerlandica*, *61*, 305–328. Manuscript available as IZA Discussion Paper No. 2598 at www.iza.org

Jasso, G., & Wegener, B. (1997). Methods for empirical justice analysis: Part I. Framework models, and quantities. *Social Justice Research*, *10*, 393–430.

John of Salisbury. ([1159] 1909). *Policraticus* (C. C. J. Webb, Ed.). Oxford: Clarendon Press.

Ridgeway, C. (2006). Status construction theory. In: P. J. Burke (Ed.), *Contemporary social psychological theories* (pp. 301–323). Stanford, CA: Stanford University Press.

Sørensen, A. B. (1979). A model and a metric for the analysis of the intragenerational status attainment process. *American Journal of Sociology*, *85*, 361–384.

Thomas Aquinas, St. ([1267–1273] 1952). *Summa theologica*. Two volumes. Translated by the Fathers of the English Dominican Province. Revised by D. J. Sullivan. Chicago: Britannica.

Tyler, T. R., Boeckmann, R. J., Smith, H. J., & Huo, Y. J. (1997). *Social justice in a diverse society*. Boulder, CO: Westview Press.

Webster, M., Jr. (2006). Status research since 2000. Paper presented at the annual Group Processes Conference, Montreal, Canada, August 2006.

MODULARIZING AND INTEGRATING THEORIES OF JUSTICE

Barry Markovsky, Lisa M. Dilks, Pamela Koch, Shannon McDonough, Jennifer Triplett and Leia Velasquez

ABSTRACT

Theories in the justice area have proliferated with little regard either to their interconnections or to the general scientific criterion of parsimony. Recently, there have been several attempts to integrate justice theories. However, there has been practically no discussion of theoretical method, that is, precisely what it means to integrate two or more theories and what must be done to accomplish it. This chapter advocates building integrated theories by developing smaller modularized theories that can be formulated and assembled for multiple purposes. To illustrate the process, we construct five modules addressing different areas connected to justice issues and show how they may be combined into a single integrated structure.

Writing for a recent special issue of *Social Justice Research*, David Wagner (2007) asserted that while the notion of a general theory of society is

Justice
Advances in Group Processes, Volume 25, 345–371

ISSN: 0882-6145/doi:10.1016/S0882-6145(08)25008-3

chimerical, integration at more modest scales, such as two or more theories within the justice area, is both possible and desirable. If one believes that we should strive for theories of ever-increasing breadth, depth and parsimony, then it would be hard to disagree with Wagner's assessment. Integration is an important tool for achieving scientific progress. Despite over two decades of calls for integration in the justice area (Colquitt, Greenberg, & Zapata-Phelan, 2005), there remains a clear need for justice theories to develop in integrative ways (Markovsky & Younts, 2001). For proper integrations to transpire, however, the theories to be integrated must be constructed according to rigorous standards. We will lay out our general strategy before illustrating it with justice theories.

Key to our approach to integration is the idea of *theory modules* – discrete explanatory devices that may be used individually, or else readily combined into larger modular theories. We will advocate the development of theory modules that may be integrated as needed to help solve intellectual or practical problems. Following this, we will attempt to illustrate the potential benefits of modular integration by suggesting directions for integrating several different theoretical strands in the justice area.

MODULARIZING AND INTEGRATING THEORIES

The justice area reflects typical theory construction practices in the social sciences. Throughout the history of justice theory and research there has not been a great deal of interest in the prospect of integrating theories. Especially of late, most of the activity seems to be of an opposite sort: proliferating theories rather than integrating them. There are some exceptions, however. Recent collections on organizational justice (Greenberg & Colquitt, 2005; Greenberg & Cropanzano, 2001) have several contributions focusing on the integration of different theoretical areas two at a time. Also, the special issue of *Social Justice Research* mentioned earlier was devoted entirely to integration. We will begin by clarifying what we mean by "integration."

The Meaning of Integration and Modularization

For Wagner (2007), the culmination of the process of theoretical integration is a transformation of two or more theories into one integrating theory.[1] Our approach to integrated theories differs from Wagner's in that the process of integration merely connects existing theories without replacing them. The original theories are treated as modules, pulled off the shelf and plugged into one another as needed, and still available in their un-integrated form for use in other integrations. This is deeply analogous to the *integrated circuit* in electronics. Progress in integrated circuitry has meant taking large, discrete electronic elements and devices, making them smaller and more efficient, and bringing them into ever-closer physical proximity. Prior to computer chips, separate sets of electronic components were required to receive, amplify, filter, process, store, or output electrical signals and information. Less than a half-century ago these functions were handled by large vacuum tubes linked with mazes of wires.

With the advent of semiconductors in the 1960s and microprocessors in the 1970s, basic components – transistors, diodes, resistors and capacitors could be packed onto silicon wafers, permitting devices of increasing sophistication and functionality. Such progress was only made possible by simplifying, standardizing and reducing the size of the basic components and, in turn, the subsystems built from these components. Today's integrated circuits still carry out the same old functions handled by vacuum tubes and, later, transistors, diodes, etc., and are still arranged into subsystems that serve the same old device functions of processing, storage, etc. However, evolution in the integration of components and subsystems has led to steady decreases in the size and cost of integrated circuits, along with steady improvements in their operation.

Modularization and integration processes evolve hand-in-hand. *Modularization* is the process that has fueled the electronics revolution. An object is modularized to the extent that it is designed for efficient assembly and functionality with other objects in a system. A *module* is most useful when, without modification, it is usable in a wide range of specific applications. For example, owners of any brand of PC who seek increased long-term storage capacity may purchase additional hard drives from a variety of manufacturers. Modularization also benefits a wide variety of other construction processes from computers and software to furniture and houses. Their benefits in the manufacturing realm are undeniable, and market forces make progress all but inevitable. Modular construction is the de facto approach to designing and building virtually any multi-component system.

Modularizing Theories

Theories are logical devices made of discrete elements that work in concert to create explanations. Well-built theories are efficient packages of tightly integrated components. At a higher level of aggregation, science is a tapestry of integrated theories covering an incredible array of phenomena. Theories within the "fabric of science" are intertwined via threads that link intellectually adjacent theories. At a practical level, this means that theories must be able to plug into one another so that in concert they are able to provide better explanations than they could individually. This is how a field such as evolutionary biology can benefit from other fields as diverse as geology and microbiology. The threads holding together the fabric of knowledge are the channels through which theories share critical elements and information.

These connecting threads link theoretical elements, of which there are several kinds.[2] *Terms* are words or symbols that express the theorist's ideas. *Definitions* assign meanings to terms. *Propositions* are statements that assert connections of various types between terms, as when something designated by one term is asserted to cause something else to occur. *Arguments* employ logical or mathematical rules to arrive at "derivations" from sets of propositions. Finally, *scope conditions* assert the domain to which the given theory is intended to apply.

For two theories to integrate, they must share one or more terms. Imagine that Theory A identifies factors that produce variation in phenomenon X, and that Theory B identifies factors that produce variation in phenomenon Y. For these theories to be integrated there must be at least one term that appears in both theories. Perhaps X, which does not otherwise appear within Theory B, can be used as a factor to explain variations in Y. In essence, Theory A has been plugged into Theory B for purposes of better understanding phenomenon Y.[3]

Modularizing and Integrating Justice Theories

Building theories with an eye toward modularization can only improve the prospects for integration within and across disciplines. The issue is especially pertinent in the justice area where most of our theories are written in very informal prose. There are some exceptions, particularly among distributive justice theories with a tradition of mathematical formalization spanning four decades (e.g., Adams, 1965; Berger, Zelditch, Anderson, & Cohen, 1972; Jasso, 2001). Although each of these theories employs a formal *logic*, they do not always employ formal *languages* in the sense of clearly defining key terms. This impedes empirical testing and applications by creating uncertainty as to appropriate operationalizations of those terms.

Theories on a variety of justice-related issues have proliferated over the past decade. In a field once dominated by work on distributive justice we now find interest in a variety of kinds of justice including retributive, procedural, interactional, restorative and others. Each represents a different object of evaluation, for example, allocations, punishments, procedures, interpersonal treatment or the degree of "wholeness" rendered by a criminal to his victim in compensation for a crime. Each area also represents a different array of potential terms, propositions, arguments and applications for justice theories. A reasonable question for anyone interested in theoretical integration is whether a distinct theory is needed for each kind of justice.

We believe that the justice area is ripe for modularization and integration. Earlier we wrote that progress in electronic integration was made possible by "simplifying, standardizing and reducing the size of the basic components." The same is true for progress in theoretical integration. Formalization is the best way we know to simplify theories – to minimize the numbers of terms and propositions while striving to maximize their explanatory power. Simplified theories are much easier to integrate than complex theories, the latter typically being large, informal, discursive theories whose meanings and logic are not readily apparent. In what follows we illustrate a strategy for integrating modularized justice theories that are designed to plug into a single core theory, thereby extending its functionality by leaps and bounds.

A MODULARIZED AND INTEGRATED JUSTICE THEORY

Modularizing theories is an evolving, never-ending process. Our purpose here is to illustrate the potential for modularization and integration in the justice area, not to produce an integrated theory that is ready for application. We will explicate each module in the sub-sections to follow, ultimately building to an integrated five-module structure.[4]

The proliferation of theories for different kinds of justice and injustice may be unnecessary or, worse, a hindrance to progress. In physics, rather than creating theories for every kind of object that may be set into motion, one theory covers all objects. Analogously, rather than devising theories for everything about which one may formulate a justice evaluation, to have one theory for *any* kind of justice evaluation would be a preferable state of affairs – one consistent with the criterion of parsimony and with the goals of theory integration. This was accomplished in the physical sciences by conceptualizing the phenomenon *abstractly, generally* and *precisely*. It is also conceivable that properties common across all forms of justice evaluation may be captured via a small set of integrated modules that manifest those same three properties.

Abstractness allows a variety of concrete phenomena to be accommodated as instances of the same theoretical concept. Abstraction entails divorcing an idea from specific objects and events in the world, focusing instead on its key properties. An abstract conceptualization of "justice" may impel us to consider the commonalities across different kinds of justice evaluations and allow us to discover ways to span a wider variety of contexts using fewer terms, propositions and theories than is presently the case.

Generality has two dimensions: breadth and veracity. That is, a theory cannot be general without having both extensive applicability and strong empirical support. Abstractness helps to promote generality in the first sense, but it would hardly make sense to deem a theory "general" unless the lion's share of available evidence also suggests that it is also true.

Precision as a criterion for theory building helps to ensure that derived hypotheses are true in more than a trivial sense. A theory which claims nothing more than that "Sometimes people feel they are treated unfairly" is true, but trivial. A theory that correctly predicts the experience of injustice 98 times out of 100, and also correctly predicts the absence of an injustice experience 98 times out of 100 is preferable to one that succeeds only 90% of the time; and a theory that accurately predicts magnitudes of injustice experience measured on a ratio scale is preferable to one that allows only categorical predictions.

The "modules" that follow are designed to fit together to address different justice-related issues. Module 1 formulates a "fundamental justice process." Module 2 addresses how people choose referents in making comparative judgments. Module 3 addresses the choice of a justice criterion. Module 4 considers the impact of uncertainty in justice evaluations. Module 5 looks at emotional responses to injustice.

We should make several disclaimers at this point. First, many readers will recognize that each module is a selective condensation of a much larger literature. This is the case for any good theory, especially if the individual theories are informal and the larger body of literature does not speak in a unified voice. A single theory clearly stated is preferable to a hundred ambivalent formulations. Second, none of the modules strays far from justice issues. In practice, modules may come from a much wider variety of areas, even areas not previously connected to justice, or areas formulated at a more micro or a more macro level of analysis. A theorist may integrate a microbiological module if interested in the physiological consequences of long-term experiences of injustice. Jasso's (1980) speculations about group-level consequences of the distribution of injustice evaluations suggest the potential for integrating on the macro side. Third, although we are advocating the integration of modules as needed to address theoretical or practical issues, we have not assembled our modules for any unitary explanatory purpose other than to demonstrate that we *can* integrate a variety of modules.

Module 1: Fundamental Justice Process

To borrow a page from Berger, Eyre, and Zelditch's (1989) notion of *interactor theories,* we conceive of situational conditions as giving rise to justice processes. That is, certain theoretically specified conditions must exist in order for a justice (or other social) process to become activated within a given situation. The process remains active so long as these conditions hold and subsides when conditions change in a way that they no longer support the process. This implies that there are three phases through which the justice process moves: *activation, procession* and *deactivation.* We will refer to this as the *fundamental justice process* and incorporate it into Module 1. Notably, it is conceivable that this module could itself be decomposed into several modules, perhaps capturing theoretical insights from the psychologies of sensation, perception and judgment. For our purposes, however, a unitary Module 1 will suffice.

Activation

When a theory specifies activation conditions, it asserts when a phenomenon will go from not happening to happening, and telling us all we need to know about when that transition occurs. Logically, this can be handled by a combination of scope conditions and propositions. To illustrate, scope conditions in the status value theory of distributive justice (Berger et al., 1972) require a *referential structure* that captures beliefs about connections between the rewards and characteristics of generalized others, and that explicitly connects people and rewards in the local setting to elements of the referential structure. Although they do not refer to "activation" per se, the scope conditions tell us that *things start to happen* when actors in the local setting recognize certain kinds of incongruence between local and referential elements. For instance, a justice process will ensue if a new attorney believes that "$90,000" is the salary associated with "new attorneys," but her own salary is "$75,000." Another kind of incongruence may occur in the procedural domain. For example, assume that the prevailing norm at a power plant is to assign more senior employees their preferred shifts. A new manager then takes over and assigns employees to shifts based on his personal relationships with them rather than on their seniority. Whether or not outcomes (actual shift assignments) are fair, the new procedure may be viewed as incongruent vis-à-vis the procedural referent standard.

The following illustrates a reasonable activation proposition that covers either type of situation. Here, *p* indicates a focal actor whose perceptions and responses are at issue and key terms in this module are italicized as they are introduced.

> **Proposition 1.1.** If *p's comparison* function yields an incongruence between an actual or imagined *event* and a *reference condition*, then *p*'s *justice interests* are activated.

The event can be virtually any phenomenon toward which *p* has a non-neutral value stance, that is, something that *p* desires or disdains, however strongly or weakly. This could be a particular level of pay, a given punishment, or an observed procedure. The reference condition could be a norm or precedent for the allocation or procedure under scrutiny. The comparison function indicates the criterion that *p* applies in comparing an actual event to a standard or reference condition. Examples from the literature include equity ratios, equality rules and other fairness criteria. For judging procedures, a binary matching/non-matching criterion may apply. For purposes of specifying a fundamental justice process, however, it is reasonable to include the comparison function as a "black box" to be illuminated by other modules, as we will show later. In this way, Module 1 serves as a junction box for other kinds of justice-relevant factors and outcomes to be captured in subsequent modules.

Procession

Justice and injustice perceptions occur in real time and remain salient as long as they continue to be fueled by psychological and situational factors. Here we offer a very general multi-part proposition, later to be linked to a more refined proposition. In this proposition, an incongruence is *valid* if *p* believes that the information it contains is accurate and reliable.

> **Proposition 1.2.1.** If *p*'s justice interests are activated, then he or she *seeks information* to determine the validity of the incongruence.

> **Proposition 1.2.2a.** If an incongruence is valid, then *p experiences injustice*.

Proposition 1.2.2b. If an incongruence is invalid, then *p experiences justice*.

Proposition 1.2.3a. If *p* recalls, imagines or is reminded of a valid incongruence, then he or she experiences injustice.

Proposition 1.2.3b. If *p* recalls, imagines or is reminded of an invalid incongruence, then he or she experiences justice.

At this point we could add a strand of theorizing to address actors' responses to injustice. Depending on available courses of action, actors may modify their own contributions, attempt to induce others to do so, attempt to have their own or others' rewards adjusted, or reevaluate the situation in ways that diminish the sense of injustice. For illustrative purposes, however, the propositions listed above will suffice.

Deactivation

When factors that make incongruences salient no longer occur, or when perceived injustices have been resolved, the process comes to a close. The following connects to Propositions 1.2.2b and 1.2.3b above.

Proposition 1.3. If *p* experiences justice, then his or her justice interests are deactivated.

Taken together, the set of propositions in Module 1 (i.e., Propositions 1.*x*.*y*) formulates a simple state transition mechanism that conditionalizes the activation, procession and deactivation of any justice-related process. The key terms appearing in this module are shown in Fig. 1, Module 1. Other modules appearing in the figure are introduced later. To reiterate an earlier point, it is not essential to have a "central module" in a modularized theory. However, Module 1 does effectively become a central module in this particular illustration.

Module 2: Referent Choice

Proposition 1.1 suggests that, in order to make a justice evaluation, an evaluator must have in mind a "reference condition," such as a pay standard, to which he or she may compare an "actual event" such as his or her pay. Depending on the particular formulation, distributive justice theories assume that an actor compares the rewards and investments of

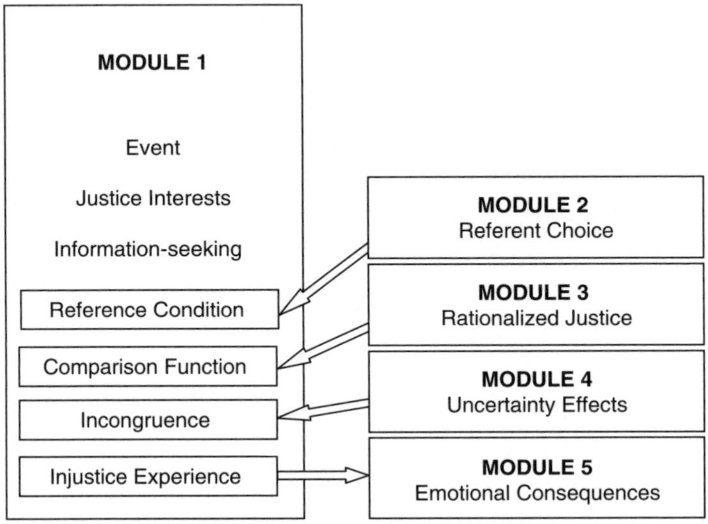

Fig. 1. Integrating Modules.

him/herself, another, his or her group or another's group, to rewards and investments of either another in the immediate situation, a reference individual or group or a generalized other or group in a referential structure (Berger et al., 1972; Berger, Fisek, Norman, & Wagner, 1985; Jasso, 1980; Markovsky, 1985). Reward expectations also can come from other sources such as prior experiences (van den Bos et al., 2005), imagined alternatives (Turner, 2007) or status characteristics (Berger et al., 1985). Numerous factors have been identified as affecting referent choices in one way or another. Below we examine several that we find particularly interesting or that are relatively prominent in the literature.

Salience

The same outcome that appears unjust vis-à-vis one referent may appear just with an alternative referent. Because the particular choice for a referent profoundly affects the justice evaluation, it is important to consider factors that may affect the salience of a referent in the justice evaluation process. We begin with the following:

Proposition 2.1. The more salient a referent is for *p*, the more likely *p* will choose the referent for a justice evaluation.

We explore this further by focusing on social and contextual factors that affect the choice of motivated cognitions and, consequently, the salience of a given referent.

Motivated Cognitions

Motivated cognitions (Kunda, 1990) operate as frames through which situations are assessed, thereby affecting which referents are called upon in making justice evaluations. Gamliel and Peer (2006) show that both positive and negative framing effects influence justice evaluations. If the allocation is presented in a positive way, that is, the delivery of rewards or withholding of punishments, then the actor is more likely to judge the allocation as fair relative to when the allocation is presented in a negative light. It seems reasonable to assume that framing effects occur relative to the motivated cognitions of the actor as well. Motivated cognitions may help to maintain the status quo, sustain a certain affective state or simply make life easier for one's self when there are no conceivable attractive alternatives. For example, Murray (1999) showed that individuals portray their romantic partners in ways which sustain the idea that they have positive attributes and that their relationship is strong. This idea is especially significant when considering research that addresses females' assessments of their romantic partners. Suls (1999) indicates that in these situations individuals choose a motivated social comparison. Therefore, it is likely that individuals will make justice evaluations that construe their romantic partners as fair so as to convey another positive attribute for that individual and to strengthen the perception that the relationship will endure.

Incorporating Kunda's concept of motivated cognition may help to explain why some individuals choose certain referents over others for justice evaluations. Following this logic:

Proposition 2.2. The greater the relevance and the importance of a referent to a motivated cognition, the more salient the referent for *p*.

There are many factors that may affect the importance of justice-relevant motivated cognitions. Below we discuss several that seem especially pertinent.

Social Value Orientations

As the term is generally used in psychology, *social value orientation* refers to stable, trans-situational preferences for the distribution of outcomes between one's self and others (Messick & McClintock, 1968; Van Lange, 1999). Much research has focused on the categories of individualist and prosocial orientations (Simpson, 2004). The former prefer to maximize their own outcomes regardless of the inequality of distributions, whereas the latter tend to maximize their outcomes while minimizing inequality. In a justice evaluation, it is reasonable to assume that these orientations will affect motivated cognitions, including choices of decision rules and referents. For example, after a justice evaluation is activated, a prosocial should more likely be group-oriented, and so more likely to use a legitimated group referent.

Proposition 2.3. The greater *p*'s prosocial orientation, the greater the salience of group referents compared to individual referents.

Some prior research on justice has used a more "situated" distinction between self- and group-oriented justice evaluations (Cook & Hegtvedt, 1983; Hegtvedt, 2006; Hegtvedt & Johnson, 2000; Mueller & Landsman, 2004). That is, either individual or group orientations may be activated, depending on elements of the situation at hand. Determining factors may include interdependence within the group and identification with the group. Greater interdependence and identification each is likely to heighten a prosocial value orientation, and thus the selection of a group referent (Markovsky, 1985; Roberson, 2006):

Proposition 2.4.1. The greater the degree of interdependence in a group, the greater the prosocial orientation.

Proposition 2.4.2. The greater the degree of identification with a group, the greater the prosocial orientation.

Affect

Although emotions frequently occur as outcomes of justice evaluations, they also may affect those evaluations via their influence on referent choices. For instance, research has demonstrated that information that is salient to an individual's immediate mood is more easily recalled (Isen, 1987; Blaney, 1986). Thus, individuals experiencing a negative affective state prior to making a justice evaluation may unwittingly select a social comparison that sustains that state. Conversely, experiencing positive affect is associated with positivity across various domains in people's lives (Isen & Shalker, 1982; Isen, Shalker, Clark, & Karp, 1978; Isen, 1987; Fiske & Taylor, 1991). Consequently, those who are happy would be more likely to select a reference point that reflects a more positive justice evaluation.

Proposition 2.5. *p* will choose a referent that maintains the valence of his or her affective state.

Information Availability

Kulik and Ambrose (1992) identify *availability* of information about a referent as a factor affecting referent choice. At the extreme, having no information on a referent eliminates the possibility of its use. We may conceive of information availability as setting limits on the potential for a referent to be selected:

Proposition 2.6. The less information available on a referent, the less its potential relevance to motivated cognitions.

Many other factors could be identified as potentially affecting referent choices, but the foregoing suffice to illustrate the role that such a module could play. In Fig. 1, Module 2 (the set of propositions on referent choice) links to Module 1 through its impact on "reference condition" appearing in Proposition 1.1.

Module 3: Specifying a Comparison Function

A variety of comparison functions have been suggested for justice evaluations, none of which has gained general acceptance through systematic analysis. In this module we offer a promising alternative function based on ideas from a rational choice framework. Rationality enters the justice process via propositions about evaluators' preferences in justice situations. The underlying assumption is that justice evaluations are based on the pursuit of fairness through the enactment of situation-specific decision rules.

Rational choice theory is not actually a theory but a theoretical framework used in the construction of models of human behavior and decision making. Under this framework, decision makers seek to optimize well-defined objective functions, given a number of constraints. In other words, decision makers generate decisions that are consistent with their own goals and preferences, but at the same time incorporate information they possess about their environments. By assuming a set of preferences and sufficient information for actors to achieve these preferences, a rational choice framework can generate rigorously testable hypotheses about the behavior of individuals and groups (Macy, 2006).

Rational actors behave *as if* they are utility maximizers. An actor's *utility* is defined in terms of his or her preference function. A *preference function* is an ordering of an actor's preferences for particular outcomes or objects in a given situation. In addition to the preference function, actors also have a constraint function. This function includes all the exogenous factors that affect an actor's attempt to maximize his or her utility. The specific preference to be activated is determined by situational factors.

The concept of rationality can take a variety of forms within the rational choice framework. In social psychology this concept is quite different from that traditionally used in economics. When studying human decision making it is best to think of rationality as adaptive rather than calculating (Macy, 2006). *Adaptive rationality* implies behavior that is shaped by experience (i.e., trial and error) and influenced by others (Lave & March, 1975; Macy, 2006). This type of rationality involves recurrent decision scenarios where little cognitive sophistication or information is involved. Adaptive rationality applies to behavior that is based on rules rather than choices (Vanberg, 1994). *Rules* are behavioral routines that provide solutions to recurrent choice problems. Rules that maximize utility continue to be used, while those that minimize utility are discarded or improved upon and then enacted again.

Rationality and Justice

Most research on justice assumes that maximum rewards and maximum fairness do not generally coincide. Although justice evaluations are non-rational judgments in this limited sense, rationality propositions still may be incorporated in a theory of the justice evaluation process. Furthermore, rational choice propositions can simplify what we know about evaluators in a variety of justice conditions, and the idea of an adaptively rational evaluator fits well into the flow of the justice evaluation process.

One of the key propositions in justice research is that individuals strive to make sense of their social experiences (Fiske & Taylor, 1991; van den Bos, Lind, & Wilke, 2001). As a result they may assess justice in many aspects of their lives: outcomes, procedures, interpersonal treatment from others, etc. (Hegtvedt, 2006). Making sense of the social world is a recurring phenomenon with justice evaluations of various kinds arising multiple times daily.

Preference for Fairness

In a rational choice setting, an actor must have a goal in mind and work toward maximizing that goal. To reiterate, adaptively rational actors behave as if they are utility maximizers, where their utility is a function of their preferences in a given situation. We begin with the initial condition that actors in the situation seek justice as a goal of interaction. This serves as the antecedent condition for this module's first proposition:

> **Proposition 3.1.** If *p* possesses a goal of justice, then *p* engages in a fundamental justice process.

Experiences of injustice produce feelings of distress and tension among at least some parties in the situation (Adams, 1965; Walster, Walster, & Berscheid, 1978). In contrast, situations of fairness create feelings of satisfaction and in some cases, happiness. From other areas of research, we know that states of imbalance or inconsistency are disagreeable and individuals seek to avoid them at all cost (Festinger, 1957; Heider, 1958; Smith-Lovin & Heise, 1988). Furthermore, justice researchers find that when injustice is experienced, actors work to restore justice, thereby restoring balance to their emotional and cognitive states (Adams, 1965; van den Bos et al., 2001). Finally, because the foundation of most justice research is in the area of social exchange, many theories assume that individuals are instrumentally motivated, meaning they wish to maximize their positive outcomes (Hegtvedt, 2006).

Now that we have assumed individuals work to maximize justice and avoid injustice, the question is how maximization is accomplished. The fairness goal can be pursued through a variety of decision-making rules or heuristics (informational shortcuts) and other individual or situational constraints. These rules, in conjunction with their constraints, are discussed next.

Constraints on Fairness

Recall that adaptive rationality is based on *rules*. Rules are behavioral routines that provide solutions to recurrent choice problems. They operate just like heuristics or rules-of-thumb. The justice literature is replete with discussions of how individuals use distribution rules, allocation rules, procedural rules, etc. to assess justice and injustice. Thus, the next proposition:

> **Proposition 3.2.** *p* chooses the decision rule that minimizes his or her experience of injustice.

Although we assume a rational evaluator, recall that our definition is based on adaptive rationality – a definition that allows social and contextual factors to influence the process of optimizing an evaluator's utility. Moreover, factors exogenous to an evaluator also may influence which decision rule is enacted and situated constraints may affect how the rule is enacted. To demonstrate the constraints placed on the choice of decision rule, Deutsch (1985) identified the following factors that affect rule choice, specifically in cases of distributive justice.

1. In cooperative relations in which economic productivity is a primary goal, equity rather than equality or need will be the dominant principle.
2. In cooperative relations in which the fostering or maintenance of enjoyable social relations is the common goal, equality will be the dominant principle.
3. In cooperative relations in which the fostering of personal development and personal welfare is the common goal, need will be the dominant principle.

Although this is but one example of the influence of exogenous factors on the choice of decision rules (Leventhal, Karuza, & Fry, 1980; Jasso, 1983 discuss others), it is reasonable to assume that each type of justice situation imposes its own constraints on utility maximization. Therefore, it is likely that the constraint function includes parameters representing the effect of each specific kind of justice situation on the optimization process. Evaluations in distributive justice situations may differ subtly from those made in procedural or other justice situations.

Fig. 1 shows this module connecting to Module 1 via the comparison function. Although untested for these purposes, rational choice models offer a plausible direction for improving our understanding of justice evaluation processes. They have proven to be versatile across a broad range of applications, and the concept of an adaptively rational actor provides a judgment model to a justice field that has not paid much serious attention to such fundamental issues.

Module 4: Uncertainty Effects

For most, uncertainty is an undesirable state. Not only does it imply uncomfortable doubt about oneself and one's surroundings, but it is also a very common condition in the realm of human experience. People can be uncertain about themselves, others around them, the structures organizing their social worlds and many other things. This uncertainty can cause discomfort, prompting individuals to seek out ways to reduce it. In the present section, we consider uncertainty as it pertains to social psychological theories of justice. As in other areas of social psychology, uncertainty in the justice literature is conceptualized as a lack of full knowledge regarding one's environment or place within it. Actors can be uncertain about almost any aspect of the justice process: outcome evaluations, procedural evaluations, enforcement of justice standards, etc.

Uncertainty research spans a number of areas in social psychology and organizational studies (e.g., Cook & Emerson, 1978; Downey & Slocum, 1975; Ellemers & Rink, 2005; Galbraith, 1973; Hogg, 2005; Kollock, 1994; Lawler, Thye, & Yoon, 2000). Its importance to relationship development, group identification, environmental perceptions, role commitment and commitment in small groups has been made evident. However, uncertainty is not limited to the phenomena described above. Uncertainty can exist in almost any other situation and may be particularly endemic and critical to situations of justice.

Uncertainty has been shown to be a disagreeable state in justice settings and in other types of social contexts (e.g., Lind & van den Bos, 2002; van den Bos, 2000). As such, actors in these settings may utilize a variety of coping mechanisms to reduce uncertainty. When elements of the justice process are uncertain, actors may unwittingly compensate by over-relying on irrelevant or unreliable information as they are prone to do in other kinds of judgment contexts. For instance, heuristics such as *anchors* may be used in attempts to fill the crucial gaps left by missing information (Lind & van den Bos, 2002; van den Bos, 2000, 2001; van den Bos & Lind, 2002; van den Bos & Miedema, 2000; Markovsky, 1988). Processes such as these can have a strong impact on important decisions such as legal judgments, promotion decisions or school admissions. As a starting point we offer two basic propositions:

Proposition 4.1. Uncertainty is an undesirable state for individuals and groups.

Proposition 4.2. Under conditions of uncertainty, individuals and groups seek to reduce or eliminate uncertainty.

Often, uncertainty in justice situations stems from a lack of information – a condition that has not been addressed in the justice literature. Justice theories generally assume that evaluators have full and accurate information with which to assess justice situations (Eriksson & Markovsky, 2005). However, it is more likely that having full information is the exception rather than the rule. In many situations, the information individuals hold is incomplete or utterly inaccurate. As noted by van den Bos (2001, p. 868), "[P]eople typically tend to be somewhat uncertain as to how to rate the fairness of the outcome they have received and how to rate their feelings of affect after having received the outcome."

Again, this uncertainty is not limited to evaluating the outcomes of justice situations. It may apply to any aspect of justice situations, including procedural and interactional processes, and it can be far-reaching in its impact. In recognition of this, anchoring and heuristic research has illustrated some of the ways that individuals cope with uncertainty. These lines of research suggest that the use of coping mechanisms can have both positive and negative consequences.

Fairness heuristic theory suggests that individuals use a particular kind of judgment heuristic to cope with uncertainty in exchange situations (Lind & van den Bos, 2002; van den Bos, 2001; van den Bos & Lind, 2002; van den Bos & Miedema, 2000). Individuals draw on these heuristics as a reference point to guide them through subsequent justice situations. It must be noted, however, that either the individual's assessment of previous justice situations used to develop the heuristic, or the choice of the fairness heuristic in general, may be biased. According to Lind (2001, p. 81), "[T]he general thrust of the theory is that a perceiver 'grabs' any justice-relevant information that is handy, forms a quick general fairness judgment, and then gets out of the business of processing fairness experiences." As a result, the first bits of relevant information exert undue influence on subsequent justice evaluations.

As noted above, anchors also have been shown to serve as judgment heuristics under conditions of uncertainty in justice contexts (Markovsky, 1988; Eriksson & Markovsky, 2005). Salient anchors may influence judgments about any element of the justice setting, that is, actual rewards, referent rewards, degree of incongruence or even the choice of comparison function. Prior research shows the effects of anchors sometimes to be extremely large. Research in progress by the first author tests the hypothesis that the magnitude of the anchor effect is positively related to the magnitude of uncertainty.

The above justice research suggests that individuals have an array of coping mechanisms to choose from in uncertain justice situations. When actors are missing information important to making justice decisions, they can make inferences using alternative sources of information, however flawed. This leads to a third proposition:

Proposition 4.3. If a justice evaluation has uncertain elements and alternative salient information exists, that information is used to infer missing elements.

Fig. 1 shows where propositions in Module 4 plug into Module 1. The uncertainty module essentially preconditions incongruence evaluations according to the kinds of factors described above. It provides a fuller model of incongruence evaluations by taking into account contextual information that is overlooked in most justice theory and research.

Module 5: Emotional Consequences

Modules 2–4 in Fig. 1 all serve as inputs to the fundamental justice process in Module 1. In contrast, Module 5 serves as an outcome module, extending and refining the *injustice experience* by illustrating the relevance of emotional consequences. Sociological approaches to emotions tend to emphasize extra-individual processes, that is, how situational factors color the experience of emotions and ensuing responses (Rosenberg, 1990; see reviews by Smith-Lovin, 1995; Turner & Stets, 2005, 2006). The role of emotions in the social justice processes gradually is receiving increased attention as well (e.g., Folger, Cropanzano, & Goldman, 2005; Hegtvedt, 2006). It is possible that emotions play a role throughout the fundamental justice evaluation process and serve as both reactions to, and stimuli for cognitive processes (Markovsky, 1985; Scher & Heise, 1993; Turner & Stets, 2005). For illustrative purposes, here we consider just a few basic emotional outcomes and how they may condition subsequent responses.

Writing on distributive injustice, Homans (1974) argued that particular emotional outcomes are conditioned on the direction of the justice evaluation vis-à-vis expected rewards. Specifically, he associated over-reward with *guilt*, under-reward with *anger* and just reward with *pleasure*. Although Homans' theory has been refined since it first appeared, it still serves to illustrate the utility of this module.

Proposition 5.1.1. If injustice is experienced then *p* experiences negative emotions.

Proposition 5.1.2. If justice is experienced, then *p* experiences positive emotions.

Proposition 5.1.3. All else equal, negative emotions due to injustice are more intense and of greater duration than positive emotions due to justice.

Ultimately, individuals strive for positive emotions in social settings (Turner & Stets, 2005). Negative emotions thus provide motivation for altering unjust situations. The idea that injustice motivates change is ancient, but the notion that distributive injustices might induce particular *kinds* of emotions that each motivates a different *kind* of social response is not so well theorized. Next we offer a few possibilities for the realm of distributive injustice.

Negative Injustice

Although Homans suggested that anger results from negative injustices, it would be reasonable to assume that other kinds of negative emotional responses also could occur depending upon how the situation is interpreted. For instance, we might speculate the following based on *p*'s attribution of responsibility for an injustice:

Proposition 5.2.1. If *p* is uncertain about the cause of a negative injustice, then *p* experiences anger.

Proposition 5.2.2. If *p* is certain that a specific other is the cause of a negative injustice, then *p* experiences resentment.

Proposition 5.2.3. If *p* is certain that he or she is the cause of another's negative injustice, then *p* experiences feelings of unworthiness.

In the first case, the evaluator's emotional response is relatively diffuse in the sense that there is no clear cause and nobody or nothing clearly to hold accountable. The second case stipulates that someone or something (e.g., a person or a procedure) was responsible for the injustice and so provides a target for *p's* negative emotions. When *p* blames him/herself for the unexpectedly bad outcome, his or her bad feelings are self-directed.

Positive Injustice

Unjust overrewards may be called positive injustices. Contrary to a narrow interpretation of rational choice theory, the emotional consequences of overreward may produce negative emotions that differ from those of underreward. Homans (1974) conjectured that guilt is the relevant outcome when the overreward is perceived to be at the expense of another, but others may occur. The following consider *p*'s reactions to benefiting from positive injustices under different conditions:

Proposition 5.3.1. If *p* is uncertain about the cause of the positive injustice, then *p* experiences pleasure.

Proposition 5.3.2. If *p* is certain that a specific other is the cause of a positive injustice, then *p* experiences embarrassment.

Proposition 5.3.3. If *p* is certain that he or she is the cause of a positive injustice, then *p* experiences guilt.

Again, which path is taken to the emotional outcome is likely to determine subsequent cognitions and behaviors.

Just Outcomes

Although we proposed earlier that the justice evaluation process deactivates when justice is experienced, if positive emotions have occurred then other kinds of social processes may ensue. Just as the specific negative emotion that follows from a negative injustice is likely to hinge on more specific aspects of the nature of that injustice, what ensues from positive justice-related emotions also may be a function of the social setting. We conjecture:

Proposition 5.4.1. If *p* is uncertain about the cause of a just outcome, then *p* experiences contentment.

Proposition 5.4.2. If *p* is certain that a specific other is the cause of a just outcome, then *p* experiences gratitude.

Proposition 5.4.3. If *p* is certain that he or she is the cause of a just outcome, then *p* experiences pride.

Once again, pride, gratitude and contentment are likely to differ in their consequences for subsequent cognitions and behaviors. The potential for more nuanced elaborations of this module should be evident and, we hope, a portent of work to come.

CONCLUSIONS

As shown in our illustration, an integrated justice theory may consist of central modules based on time-tested theorizing in the justice area, along with plug-ins from other fields with relatively tenuous connections to justice such as the sociology of emotions. Not emphasized thus far is the potential utility of individual modules – each a complete theory in its own right, capable of explaining phenomena within its scope. The same criteria that promote the construction of well-formed modules also promote the construction of well-formed theories. The only difference is that module-building encourages the theorist to imagine the theory not as a singular shining achievement, but rather as a potential component of a larger system of theories that may be used to revisit old issues or for purposes yet to be imagined.

Modular development also can be understood from the standpoint of an evolutionary epistemology (Campbell, 1974; Markovsky, 1997; Toulmin, 1967). Theories improve over time as those that are more "fit" for their explanatory purposes survive to be further developed, while those that fare less well fade into oblivion from accumulated falsifications and disuse. Just as biological evolution unfolds at multiple levels (e.g., cells, organs and gross anatomy), so do automobiles, homebuilding techniques, integrated circuits and theories. That is because theories respond to selection pressures from multiple sources. In response to self-criticism and peer review, responsible authors will replace ambivalent terms with clearer ones; ill-specified propositions with better ones; overly narrow scope conditions with broader ones. For a field interested in modularization, there is another selection pressure: Modularized theories that work well with other modules will be used more than those that seem only to work in isolation. It is a case of *survival of the most useful.* Useful modules will tend to persist and, with continued use and adjustments, will evolve in ways that only enhance their integrative potential with time. This is not a process that the theorist needs to shepherd in a conscious way. It simply happens as a consequence of good theory-building practices.

We have argued that theories constructed in a modular fashion encourage integrations in the sense of joining together multiple theories by bridging across certain internal components. There are at least two important uses for the products of this kind of theory building. First, modularization encourages creative solutions to theoretical problems by producing tool kits with multiple attachments serving a variety of purposes. A diversity of abstract and general theoretical modules ensures greater potential for fruitful integrations unbounded by disciplinary lines. There is no telling how justice theories could be used not only in the solution of justice questions, but potentially as central or peripheral modules specifying the conditions for, or the consequences of, a variety of other kinds of phenomena in fields well removed from the social sciences. As but one brief example, it is not hard to imagine justice processes affecting climate change policy and ultimately, via a series of causal threads, geophysical phenomena on a global scale. Second, for burgeoning disciplines such as social justice theory and research, with its dozens of theories and hundreds upon hundreds of published empirical studies, building theories with an eye toward modularization helps to provide order to an otherwise disheveled and confusing knowledge base. At the same time it helps to instill healthy scientific motives such as precision and parsimony – motives that clearly are not guiding developments in the area today.

NOTES

1. Wagner also discussed the integration of *metatheories*, however in this chapter we are only concerned about integrating theories. See Berger and Zelditch (1993, p. 10) for another view on integration.

2. See Markovsky (2005) for more details on the components of theories, or Cohen (1989) for a very comprehensive discussion.

3. The informality of most social psychological theories makes this type of integration relatively infrequent. However, it can be found in formalized theories such as those of Willer, Lovaglia, and Markovsky (1997) and Barnum and Markovsky (2007).

4. For the sake of brevity, and because this is intended to be an illustration and not a comprehensive theory, we are not explicating scope conditions or definitions for all key terms. However, many of these theoretical elements may be gleaned from previously published work, such as Berger et al. (1972) and Markovsky (1985).

ACKNOWLEDGMENTS

We thank Joe Berger, Nick Berigan, Jan Stets, Kjell Törnblom and Buzz Zelditch for their helpful comments on an earlier draft.

REFERENCES

Adams, J. S. (1965). Inequity in social exchange. In: L. Berkowitz (Ed.), *Advances in experimental social psychology* (Vol. 2, pp. 267–269). New York: Academic Press.

Barnum, C., & Markovsky, B. (2007). Group membership and social influence. *Current Research in Social Psychology, 13*, 22–38.

Berger, J., Eyre, D., & Zelditch, M., Jr. (1989). Theoretical structures and the micro-macro problem. In: J. Berger, M. Zelditch, Jr. & B. Anderson (Eds), *Sociological theories in progress: New formulations* (pp. 11–34). Thousand Oaks, CA: Sage.

Berger, J., Fisek, M. H., Norman, R. Z., & Wagner, D. G. (1985). The formation of reward expectations in status situations. In: J. Berger & M. Zelditch, Jr. (Eds), *Status, rewards and influence* (pp. 215–261). San Francisco: Jossey-Bass.

Berger, J., & Zelditch, M., Jr. (1993). Orienting strategies and theoretical growth. In: J. Berger & M. Zelditch, Jr. (Eds), *Theoretical research programs: studies in the growth of theory* (pp. 3–19). Stanford, CA: Stanford University Press.

Berger, J., Zelditch, M., Jr., Anderson, B., & Cohen, B. P. (1972). Structural aspects of distributive justice: A status value approach. In: J. Berger, M. Zelditch, Jr. & B. Anderson (Eds), *Sociological theories in progress* (Vol. 2, pp. 119–146). Boston: Houghton-Mifflin.

Blaney, P. H. (1986). Affect and memory: A review. *Psychological Bulletin, 99*, 229–246.

Campbell, D. T. (1974). Evolutionary epistemology. In: P. A. Schilpp (Ed.), *The philosophy of Karl Popper, book I* (pp. 413–463). La Salle, IL: Open Court Press.

Cohen, B. P. (1989). *Developing sociological knowledge*. Chicago: Nelson-Hall.

Colquitt, J. A., Greenberg, J., & Zapata-Phelan, C. P. (2005). What is organizational justice? A historical overview. In: J. Greenberg & J. A. Colquitt (Eds), *Handbook of organizational justice* (pp. 3–56). Florence, KY: Lawrence Erlbaum.

Cook, K. S., & Emerson, R. M. (1978). Power, equity, and commitment in exchange network. *American Sociological Review, 43*, 721–739.

Cook, K. S., & Hegtvedt, K. A. (1983). Distributive justice, equity and equality. *Annual Review of Sociology, 9*, 217–241.

Deutsch, M. (1985). *Distributive justice: A social-psychological perspective*. New Haven: Yale University Press.

Downey, H. K., & Slocum, J. W. (1975). Uncertainty: Measures, research, and sources of variation. *The Academy of Management Journal, 18*, 562–578.

Ellemers, N., & Rink, F. (2005). Identity in work groups: The beneficial and detrimental consequences of multiple identities and group norms for collaboration and group performance. In: S. R. Thye & E. J. Lawler (Eds), *Advances in group processes* (Vol. 22, pp. 1–41). New York: Elsevier Press.

Eriksson, K., & Markovsky, B. (2005). Inferring just rewards. Presented at the Annual Meetings of the American Sociological Association, Philadelphia.

Festinger, L. (1957). *A theory of cognitive dissonance*. Evanston, IL: Row, Peterson.

Fiske, S. T., & Taylor, S. E. (1991). *Social cognition*. Columbus, OH: McGraw-Hill.

Folger, R., Cropanzano, R., & Goldman, B. (2005). What is the relationship between justice and morality? In: J. Greenberg & J. A. Colquitt (Eds), *Handbook of organizational justice* (pp. 215–245). Florence, KY: Lawrence Erlbaum.

Galbraith, J. (1973). *Designing complex organizations*. Reading, MA: MIT Press.

Gamliel, E., & Peer, E. (2006). Positive versus negative framing affects in justice judgments. *Social Justice Research, 19*, 307–322.

Greenberg, J., & Colquitt, J. A. (Eds). (2005). *Handbook of organizational justice*. Florence, KY: Lawrence Erlbaum.

Greenberg, J., & Cropanzano, R. (Eds). (2001). *Advances in organizational justice*. Palo Alto, CA: Stanford University Press.

Hegtvedt, K. A. (2006). Justice frameworks. In: P. J. Burke (Ed.), *Contemporary social psychological theories* (pp. 46–49). Palo Alto, CA: Stanford Social Sciences.

Hegtvedt, K. A., & Johnson, C. (2000). Justice beyond the individual: A future with legitimation. *Social Psychology Quarterly, 63*, 298–311.

Heider, F. (1958). *The psychology of interpersonal relationships*. New York: Wiley.

Hogg, M. A. (2005). Uncertainty, social identity, and ideology. In: S. R. Thye & E. J. Lawler (Eds), *Advances in group processes* (Vol. 22, pp. 203–229). New York: Elsevier.

Homans, G. C. (1974). *Social behavior: Its elementary forms*. New York: Harcourt, Brace & World.

Isen, A. M. (1987). Positive affect, cognitive processes and social behavior. In: L. Berkowitz (Ed.), *Advances in experimental social psychology* (Vol. 20, pp. 203–253). New York: Academic Press.

Isen, A. M., & Shalker, T. E. (1982). Do you accentuate the positive, eliminate the negative when you are in a good mood? *Social Psychology Quarterly*, *45*, 58–63.

Isen, A. M., Shalker, T. E., Clark, M. S., & Karp, L. (1978). Affect accessibility of material in memory and behavior: A cognitive loop? *Journal of Personality and Social Psychology*, *36*, 1–12.

Jasso, G. (1980). A new theory of distributive justice. *American Sociological Review*, *45*, 3–32.

Jasso, G. (1983). Fairness of individual rewards and fairness of the reward distribution: Specifying the inconsistency between micro and macro principles of justice. *Social Psychology Quarterly*, *46*, 185–199.

Jasso, G. (2001). Formal theory. In: J. H. Turner (Ed.), *Handbook of Sociological Theory* (pp. 37–68). New York: Kluwer Academic/Plenum Publishers.

Kollock, P. (1994). The emergence of exchange structures: An experimental study of uncertainty, commitment, and trust. *American Journal of Sociology*, *100*, 313–345.

Kulik, C. T., & Ambrose, M. L. (1992). Personal and situational determinants of referent choice. *The Academy of Management Review*, *17*, 212–237.

Kunda, Z. (1990). The case for motivated cognition. *Psychological Bulletin*, *108*, 480–498.

Lawler, E. J., Thye, S. R., & Yoon, J. (2000). Emotion and group cohesion in productive exchange. *American Journal of Sociology*, *106*, 616–657.

Lave, C. A., & March, J. G. (1975). *An introduction to models in the social sciences*. New York: Harper & Row.

Leventhal, G. S., Karuza, J., Jr., & Fry, W. R. (1980). Beyond fairness: A theory of allocation preferences. In: G. Mikula (Ed.), *Justice and social interaction* (pp. 167–218). New York: Springer-Verlag.

Lind, E. A. (2001). Fairness heuristic theory: Justice judgments as pivotal cognitions in organizational relations. In: J. Greenberg & R. Cropanzano (Eds), *Advances in organizational justice* (pp. 56–88). Palo Alto, CA: Stanford University Press.

Lind, E. A., & van den Bos, K. (2002). When fairness works: Towards a general theory of uncertainty management. *Research in Organizational Behavior*, *24*, 181–223.

Macy, M. W. (2006). Rational choice. In: P. J. Burke (Ed.), *Contemporary social psychological theories* (pp. 70–87). Palo Alto, CA: Stanford University Press.

Markovsky, B. (1985). Toward a multilevel distributive justice theory. *American Sociological Review*, *50*, 822–839.

Markovsky, B. (1988). Anchoring justice. *Social Psychology Quarterly*, *51*, 213–224.

Markovsky, B. (1997). Evolution and nebulousness in theories. *Current Research in Social Psychology, 2* <http://www.uiowa.edu/~grpproc>.

Markovsky, B. (2005). Theory construction. In: G. Ritzer (Ed.), *Encyclopedia of social theory*. Thousand Oaks, CA: Sage.

Markovsky, B., & Younts, C. W. (2001). Prospects for distributive justice theory. *Social Justice Research*, *14*, 45–59.

Messick, D. M., & McClintock, C. G. (1968). Motivational bases of choice in experimental games. *Journal of Experimental Social Psychology*, *4*, 1–25.

Mueller, C. W., & Landsman, M. J. (2004). Legitimacy and justice perceptions. *Social Psychology Quarterly*, *67*, 189–202.

Murray, S. L. (1999). The quest for conviction: Motivated cognition in romantic relationships. *Psychological Inquiry*, *10*, 23–34.

Roberson, Q. M. (2006). Justice in teams: The effects of interdependence and identification on referent choice and justice climate strength. *Social Justice Research*, *19*, 323–344.

Rosenberg, M. (1990). Reflexivity and emotions. *Social Psychology Quarterly*, *53*, 3–12.

Scher, S. J., & Heise, D. R. (1993). Affect and the perception of injustice. In: E. J. Lawler, B. Markovsky, K. Heimer & J. O'Brien (Eds), *Advances in group processes* (Vol. 10, pp. 223–252). Greenwich, CT: JAI Press.

Simpson, B. (2004). Social values, subjective transformations, and cooperation in social dilemmas. *Social Psychology Quarterly*, *67*, 385–395.

Smith-Lovin, L. (1995). The sociology of affect and emotion. In: K. S. Cook, G. A. Fine & J. S. House (Eds), *Sociological perspectives on social psychology* (pp. 118–148). Boston: Allyn & Bacon.

Smith-Lovin, L., & Heise, D. R. (1988). *Analyzing social interaction: Research advances in affect control theory*. New York: Gordon & Breach.

Suls, J. (1999). The importance of the question in motivated cognition and social comparison. *Psychological Inquiry*, *10*, 73–75.

Toulmin, S. E. (1967). The evolutionary development of natural science. *American Scientist*, *55*, 456–471.

Turner, J. H. (2007). Justice and emotions. *Social Justice Research*, *20*, 288–311.

Turner, J. H., & Stets, J. E. (2005). *The sociology of emotions*. New York: Cambridge Press.

Turner, J. H., & Stets, J. E. (2006). Sociological theories of human emotions. *Annual Review of Sociology*, *32*, 25–52.

Vanberg, V. (1994). *Rules and choice in economics*. London: Routledge.

van den Bos, K. (2000). Uncertainty management: The influence of uncertainty salience on reactions to perceived procedural fairness. *Journal of Personality and Social Psychology*, *80*, 931–941.

van den Bos, K. (2001). Assimilation and contrast in organizational justice: The role of primed mindsets in the psychology of the fair process effect. *Organizational Behavior and Human Decision Processes*, *89*, 866–880.

van den Bos, K., Burrows, J. W., Umphress, E., Folger, R., Lavelle, J. J., Eaglestone, J., & Gee, J. (2005). Prior experiences as temporal frames of reference in social justice: The influence of previous fairness experiences on reactions to new and old supervisors. *Social Justice Research*, *19*, 99–120.

van den Bos, K., & Lind, E. A. (2002). Uncertainty management by means of fairness judgments. In: M. P. Zanna (Ed.), *Advances in experimental social psychology* (Vol. 34, pp. 1–60). San Diego, CA: Academic Press.

van den Bos, K., Lind, E. A., & Wilke, H. A. M. (2001). The psychology of procedural and distributive justice viewed from the perspective of fairness heuristic theory. In: R. Cropanzano (Ed.), *Justice in the workplace* (pp. 49–66). Mahwah, NJ: Erlbaum.

van den Bos, K., & Miedema, J. (2000). Toward understanding why fairness matters: The influence of mortality salience of reactions to procedural fairness. *Interpersonal Relations and Group Processes*, *79*, 355–366.

Van Lange, P. A. M. (1999). The pursuit of joint outcomes and equality in outcomes: An integrative model of social value orientation. *Journal of Personality and Social Psychology*, *77*, 337–349.

Wagner, D. G. (2007). The limits of theoretical integration. *Social Justice Research*, *20*, 270–287.

Walster, E., Walster, W., & Berscheid, E. (1978). *Equity: Theory and research*. New York: Allyn & Bacon.

Willer, D., Lovaglia, M., & Markovsky, B. (1997). Power and influence: A theoretical bridge. *Social Forces*, *76*, 571–603.